W9-ANR-581

2000 Supplement

Constitutional Law

EDITORIAL ADVISORY BOARD

 ASPEN PUBLISHERS, INC.
Legal Education Division

Richard A. Epstein
James Parker Hall Distinguished Service Professor of Law
University of Chicago

E. Allan Farnsworth
Alfred McCormack Professor of Law
Columbia University

Ronald J. Gilson
Charles J. Meyers Professor of Law and Business
Stanford University
Marc and Eva Stern Professor of Law and Business
Columbia University

Geoffrey C. Hazard, Jr.
Trustee Professor of Law
University of Pennsylvania

James E. Krier
Earl Warren DeLano Professor of Law
University of Michigan

Elizabeth Warren
Leo Gottlieb Professor of Law
Harvard University

Bernard Wolfman
Fessenden Professor of Law
Harvard University

2000 Supplement
Constitutional Law

Third Edition

Geoffrey R. Stone
Harry Kalven, Jr., Distinguished Service Professor of Law
and Provost
University of Chicago

Louis M. Seidman
Professor of Law
Georgetown University Law Center

Cass R. Sunstein
Karl N. Llewellyn Professor of Jurisprudence
University of Chicago Law School and
Department of Political Science

Mark V. Tushnet
Professor of Law
Georgetown University Law Center

ASPEN LAW & BUSINESS
A Division of Aspen Publishers, Inc.
Gaithersburg   New York

Copyright © 2000 by Geoffrey R. Stone, Robert H. Seidman, Trustee, Cass R. Sunstein, and Judith Broder, Trustee

All rights reserved. No part of this publication may be reproduced or transmitted in any form or by any means, electronic or mechanical, including photocopy, recording, or any information storage and retrieval system, without permission in writing from the publisher. Requests for permission to make copies of any part of this publication should be mailed to:

Permissions
Aspen Law & Business
1185 Avenue of the Americas
New York, NY 10036

Printed in the United States of America

Library of Congress Catalog Card No. 95-80563

ISBN 0-7355-1326-0

1 2 3 4 5 6 7 8 9 0

About Aspen Law & Business, Legal Education Division

With a dedication to preserving and strengthening the long-standing tradition of publishing excellence in legal education, Aspen Law & Business continues to provide the highest quality teaching and learning resources for today's law school community. Careful development, meticulous editing, and an unmatched responsiveness to the evolving needs of today's discerning educators combine in the creation of our outstanding casebooks, coursebooks, textbooks, and study aids.

ASPEN LAW & BUSINESS
A Division of Aspen Publishers, Inc.
A Wolters Kluwer Company
www.aspenpublishers.com

Contents

Contents

Table of Cases

Table of Cases

Table of Authorities

Table of Authorities

Table of Authorities

Table of Authorities

Acknowledgments

Bezanson, Randall. Institutional Speech, 80 Iowa L. Rev. 735, 736, 755, 761, 739 (1995). Copyright © 1995 Iowa Law Review. Reprinted with permission.

Balkin, Media Filters, The V-Chip and The Foundations of Broadcast Regulations, 45 Duke L.J. 1131, 1139, 1142, 1148, 1150, 1157, 1165, 1173 (1996). Copyright © 1996 Duke Law Journal. Reprinted with permission.

Brownstein, Rules of Engagement for Culture Wars: Regulating Conduct, Unprotected Speech, and Protected Expression in Anti-Abortion Protests, 29 U.C. Davis L. Rev. 553, 586-588, 628 (1996). Copyright © 1996 Regents of The University of California. Reprinted with permission.

Cross, B. Frank. Realism About Federalism. 74 N.Y.U. L. Rev. 1304 (1999). By permission of New York University Law Review.

Estlund, Freedom of Expression in the Workplace and The Problem of Discriminatory Harassment. Published originally in 75 Texas Law Review 697 (1997). Copyright © by The Texas Law Review Association. Reprinted by permission.

Flaherty, Martin. The Most Dangerous Branch, 105 Yale Law Journal 1925, 1729-1730 (1996). Copyright © 1996 Yale Law Journal. Reprinted with permission.

Fletcher, George. In God's Image: The Religious Imperative of a Quality Under Law. This article originally appeared at 99 Columbia Law Review, 1608 (1999). Reprinted by permission.

Grossman, B. Joel and Yalof, A. David. The Day After: Do We Need A "Twenty-Eighth Amendment?" 17 Const'l. Com. 7 (2000). With permission of Constitutional Commentaries.

Jacobs, G. Leslie. Pledges, Parades, and Mandatory Payments. 52 Rutgers Law Review, 123 (1999). Copyright © 1999 Rutgers, The State University of New Jersey.

Kagan, Private Speech, Public Purpose: The Role of Governmental Motive in First Amendment Doctrine, 63 U. Chi. L. Rev. 415, 467-475 (1996). Copyright © 1996 University of Chicago Law Review. Reprinted with permission.

Kramer, D. Larry. Putting the Politics Back Into the Political Safeguards of Federalism. This article originally appeared at 100 Columbia Law Review, 215 (2000). Reprinted by permission.

Post, Robert. Prejudicial Appearances: The Logic of American Antidiscrimination Law. 88 California Law Review, 1, 17, 31 (2000). By permission of the University of California Press.

Post, Subsidized Speech. Reprinted by permission of The Yale Law Journal and Fred B. Rothman &Company from The Yale Law Journal, Vol. 106, 151-191.

Strauss, Affirmative Action and the Public Interest, 1995 Sup. Ct. Rev. 1, 3-4, 12-13. Copyright © 1996 University of Chicago Press. Reprinted with permission

2000 Supplement

Constitutional Law

1
THE ROLE OF THE SUPREME COURT IN THE CONSTITUTIONAL SCHEME

A. Introduction: Some Notes on the History and Theory of the Constitution

Page 22.   At the end of section 4 of the Note, add the following:

See also Schacter, The Pursuit of "Popular Intent": Interpretive Dilemmas in Direct Democracy, 105 Yale L.J. 107 (1995), for an illuminating discussion.

Page 23.   At the end of subsection 7, add the following:

For an extended discussion of the transformation of the bill of rights introduced by the Civil War Amendments, see Akhil Amar, The Bill of Rights (1999). Amar urges that the original bill, enacted against the backdrop of the American Revolution and British rule, was understood to contain democracy-protecting, republican-style rights, and that provisions that we now understand in highly individualized terms (such as the right to free speech) had a quite different meaning in the founding era. He contends that the Civil War Amendments, enacted against the backdrop of slavery, offered a far more individualistic and less republic conception of rights—and hence that the bill was dramatically transformed by post-Civil War developments.

Page 39.   After the citation to the Brest article, add the following:

For an extended argument against judicial review on democratic grounds, see Mark Tushnet, Taking the Constitution Away From the Courts (1999).

B. The Basic Framework

Page 43.   After the first paragraph of subsection (c) of the Note, add the following:

Consider the following criticisms of "translation" in Klarman, Antifidelity, 70 S. Cal. L. Rev. 381, 395, 402 (1997):

> Translators have selected an arbitrarily low level of generality at which to translate. They adjust the Framers' constitutional commitments to reflect changed circumstances, but fail to ask whether the Framers would have remained committed to the same concepts had they been aware of future circumstances. Most translators criticize Justice Scalia and Judge Bork for selecting an arbitrarily low level of generality at which to describe the Framers' intentions [but] they themselves are subject to precisely the same objection: Perhaps the Framers would not have remained committed to certain concepts had they foreseen relevant changed circumstances. . . .
>
> [Moreover if] we treat all changed circumstances as relevant variables, then we simply will have converted the Framers into us, and asking how they would resolve a problem is no different from asking how we ourselves would resolve it. Yet a decision to treat some changed circumstances as variables and others as constants seems entirely arbitrary.

Is this position consistent with the fundamental idea of constitutionalism? Would it be appropriate to move to an even higher level of generality and claim (a) that the Framers sought to create a government that would achieve the common good, and (b) that today we understand that we could achieve the common good better by rejecting such specific provisions of the Constitution, for example the allocation of two senators to each state? For some discussion, see Tushnet, The Hardest Question in Constitutional Law, 81 Minn. L.Rev. 1 (1996) (qualified yes); Alexander & Schauer, On Extrajudicial Constitutional Interpretation, 110 Harv. L.Rev. 1359 (1997) (qualified no).

C. The Sources of Judicial Decisions: Text, "Representation-Reinforcement," and Natural Law

Page 75.   At the end of the Note, add the following:

For a qualified defense of "decisional minimalism," see Sunstein, Leaving Things Undecided, 110 Harv. L. Rev. 4 (1996):

> Minimalist judges try to keep their judgments as narrow and as incompletely theorized as possible, consistent with their obligation to offer reasons. They are enthusiastic about avoiding constitutional questions; they like to use doctrines of justiciability, and their authority over their docket, to limit the occasions for judicial intervention into politically contentious areas; the ban on advisory opinions organizes much of their work. They try to reduce the burdens of judgment for Supreme Court justices, to minimize the risks of error introduced by broad rules and abstract theories, and to maximize the space for democratic deliberation about basic political and moral issues. The problem can produce minimalism in the form of incompletely specified abstractions and incompletely theorized narrow rulings.

For an elaboration of this argument, with reference to affirmative action, free speech, and new technologies, and discrimination on the basis of sex and sexual orientation, see Cass R. Sunstein, One Case At A Time: Judicial Minimalism on the Supreme Court (1999).

For an enthusiastic defense of theoretical ambition in law, see Dworkin, In Praise of Theory, 29 Ariz. St. L.J. 353 (1997).

For an interesting argument that adjudication has a democratic character insofar as it embodies principles of participation and responsiveness, see Peters, Adjudication as Representation, 97 Colum. L. Rev. 312 (1997).

Page 98.   Before the Note, add the following:

Steel Company v. Citizens for a Better Environment
— S. Ct. — (1998)

JUSTICE SCALIA delivered the opinion of the Court.

This is a private enforcement action under the citizen-suit provision of the Emergency Planning and Community Right-To-Know Act of 1986. The case presents the merits question, answered in the affirmative by the United States Court of Appeals for the Seventh Circuit, whether EPCRA authorizes suits for purely past violations. It also presents the jurisdictional question whether respondent, plaintiff below, has standing to bring this action.

Respondent, an association of individuals interested in environmental protection, sued petitioner, a small manufacturing company in Chicago, for past violations of EPCRA. EPCRA establishes a framework of state, regional and local agencies designed to inform the public about the presence of hazardous and toxic chemicals, and to provide for emergency response in the event of health-threatening release. Central to its operation are reporting requirements compelling users of specified toxic and hazardous chemicals to file annual "emergency and hazardous chemical inventory forms" and "toxic chemical release forms," which contain, inter alia, the name and location of the facility, the name and quantity of the chemical on hand, and, in the case of toxic chemicals, the waste-disposal method employed and the annual quantity released into each environmental medium. The hazardous-chemical inventory forms for any given calendar year are due the following March 1st, and the toxic-chemical release forms the following July 1st.

Enforcement of EPCRA can take place on many fronts. The Environmental Protection Agency (EPA) has the most powerful enforcement arsenal: it may seek criminal, civil, or administrative penalties. State and local governments can also seek civil penalties, as well as injunctive relief. For purposes of this case, however, the crucial enforcement mechanism is the citizen-suit provision, § 11046(a)(1), which likewise authorizes civil penalties and injunctive relief, see § 11046(c). This provides that "any person may commence a civil action on his own behalf against . . . an owner or operator of a facility for failure," among other things, to "complete and submit an inventory form under section 11022(a) of this title . . . [and] section 11023(a) of this title." As a prerequisite to bringing such a suit, the plaintiff must, 60 days prior to filing his complaint, give notice to the Administrator of the EPA, the State in which the alleged violation occurs, and the alleged violator. The citizen suit may not go forward if the Administrator "has commenced and is diligently pursuing an administrative order or civil action to enforce the requirement concerned or to impose a civil penalty."

In 1995 respondent sent a notice to petitioner, the Administrator, and the relevant Illinois authorities, alleging—accurately, as it turns out—that petitioner had failed since 1988, the first year of EPCRA's filing deadlines, to complete and to submit the requisite hazardous-chemical inventory and toxic-chemical release forms under §§ 11022 and 11023. Upon receiving the notice, petitioner filed all of the overdue forms with the relevant agencies. The EPA chose not to bring an action against petitioner, and when the 60-day waiting period expired, respondent filed suit in Federal District Court. Petitioner promptly filed a motion to dismiss under Federal Rule of Civil Procedure 12(b)(1) and

4

(6), contending that, because its filings were up to date when the complaint was filed, the court had no jurisdiction to entertain a suit for a present violation; and that, because EPCRA does not allow suit for a purely historical violation, respondent's allegation of untimeliness in filing was not a claim upon which relief could be granted. . . .

[The Court concluded that it was appropriate to resolve the constitutional issue whether Congress could grant standing in these circumstances.]

We turn now to the particulars of respondent's complaint to see how it measures up to Article II's requirements. This case is on appeal from a Rule 12(b) motion to dismiss on the pleadings, so we must presume that the general allegations in the complaint encompass the specific facts necessary to support those allegations. The complaint contains claims "on behalf of both [respondent] itself and its members."[6] It describes respondent as an organization that seeks, uses, and acquires data reported under EPCRA. It says that respondent "reports to its members and the public about storage and releases of toxic chemicals into the environment,   advocates changes in environmental regulations and statutes, prepares reports for its members and the public, seeks the reduction of toxic chemicals and further seeks to promote the effective enforcement of environmental laws." The complaint asserts that respondent's "right to know about [toxic chemical] releases and its interests in protecting and improving the environment and the health of its members have been, are being, and will be adversely affected by [petitioner's] actions in failing to provide timely and required information under EPCRA." The complaint also alleges that respondent's members, who live in or frequent the area near petitioner's facility, use the EPRCA-reported information "to learn about toxic chemical releases, the use of hazardous substances in their communities, to plan emergency preparedness in the event of accidents, and to attempt to reduce the toxic chemicals in areas in which they live, work and visit." The members' "safety, health, recreational, economic, aesthetic and environmental interests" in the information, it is claimed, "have been, are being, and will be adversely affected by [petitioner's] actions in failing to file timely and required reports under EPCRA."

As appears from the above, respondent asserts petitioner's failure to provide EPCRA information in a timely fashion, and the lingering effects of that failure, as the injury in fact to itself and its members. We have not had occasion to decide whether being deprived of information that is supposed to be disclosed un-

---

[6] EPCRA states that "any person may commence a civil action on his own behalf. . ." 42 U.S.C. § 11046(1) (emphasis added). "Person" includes an association, see § 11049(7), so it is arguable that the statute permits respondent to vindicate only its own interests as an organization, and not the interests of its individual members. Since it makes no difference to our disposition of the case, we assume without deciding that the interests of individual members may be the basis of suit.

der EPCRA — or at least being deprived of it when one has a particular plan for its use — is a concrete injury in fact that satisfies Article III. And we need not reach that question in the present case because, assuming injury in fact, the complaint fails the third test of standing, redressability.

The complaint asks for (1) a declaratory judgment that petitioner violated EPCRA; (2) authorization to inspect periodically petitioner's facility and records (with costs borne by petitioner); (3) an order requiring petitioner to provide respondent copies of all compliance reports submitted to the EPA; (4) an order requiring petitioner to pay civil penalties of $25,000 per day for each violation of §§ 11022 and 11023; (5) an award of all respondent's "costs, in connection with the investigation and prosecution of this matter, including reasonable attorney and expert witness fees, as authorized by Section 326(f) of [EPCRA]"; and (6) any such further relief as the court deems appropriate. None of the specific items of relief sought, and none that we can envision as "appropriate" under the general request, would serve to reimburse respondent for losses caused by the late reporting, or to eliminate any effects of that late reporting upon respondent.

The first item, the request for a declaratory judgment that petitioner violated EPCRA, can be disposed of summarily. There being no controversy over whether petitioner failed to file reports, or over whether such a failure constitutes a violation, the declaratory judgment is not only worthless to respondent, it is seemingly worthless to all the world.

Item (4), the civil penalties authorized by the statute, see § 11045(c), might be viewed as a sort of compensation or redress to respondent if they were payable to respondent. But they are not. These penalties — the only damages authorized by EPCRA — are payable to the United States Treasury. In requesting them, therefore, respondent seeks not remediation of its own injury — reimbursement for the costs it incurred as a result of the late filing — but vindication of the rule of law — the "undifferentiated public interest" in faithful execution of EPCRA.

. . . Item (5), the "investigation and prosecution" costs "as authorized by Section 326(f)," would assuredly benefit respondent as opposed to the citizenry at large. Obviously, however, a plaintiff cannot achieve standing to litigate a substantive issue by bringing suit for the cost of bringing suit. The litigation must give the plaintiff some other benefit besides reimbursement of costs that are a byproduct of the litigation itself.

[Respondent] asserts that the "investigation costs" it seeks were incurred prior to the litigation, in digging up the emissions and storage information that petitioner should have filed, and that respondent needed for its own purposes. The recovery of such expenses unrelated to litigation would assuredly support Article III standing, but the problem is that § 326(f), which is the entitlement to monetary relief that the complaint invokes, covers only the "costs of litigation." Respondent finds itself, in other words, impaled upon the horns of a dilemma:

for the expenses to be reimbursable under the statute, they must be costs of litigation; but reimbursement of the costs of litigation cannot alone support standing.

The remaining relief respondent seeks (item (2), giving respondent authority to inspect petitioner's facility and records, and item (3), compelling petitioner to provide respondent copies of EPA compliance reports) is injunctive in nature. It cannot conceivably remedy any past wrong but is aimed at deterring petitioner from violating EPCRA in the future. The latter objective can of course be "remedial" for Article III purposes, when threatened injury is one of the gravamens of the complaint. If respondent had alleged a continuing violation or the imminence of a future violation, the injunctive relief requested would remedy that alleged harm. But there is no such allegation here — and on the facts of the case, there seems no basis for it. Nothing supports the requested injunctive relief except respondent's generalized interest in deterrence, which is insufficient for purposes of Article III.

The United States, as amicus curiae, argues that the injunctive relief does constitute remediation because "there is a presumption of [future] injury when the defendant has voluntarily ceased its illegal activity in response to litigation," even if that occurs before a complaint is filed. This makes a sword out of a shield. The "presumption" the Government refers to has been applied to refute the assertion of mootness by a defendant who, when sued in a complaint that alleges present or threatened injury, ceases the complained-of activity. It is an immense and unacceptable stretch to call the presumption into service as a substitute for the allegation of present or threatened injury upon which initial standing must be based. . . .

Having found that none of the relief sought by respondent would likely remedy its alleged injury in fact, we must conclude that respondent lacks standing to maintain this suit, and that we and the lower courts lack jurisdiction to entertain it. However desirable prompt resolution of the merits EPCRA question may be, it is not as important as observing the constitutional limits set upon courts in our system of separated powers. EPCRA will have to await another day.

The judgment is vacated and the case remanded with instructions to direct that the complaint be dismissed.

It is so ordered.

[Justices O'Connor and Breyer write brief concurring opinions.]

JUSTICE STEVENS, with whom JUSTICE SOUTER joins as to Parts I, III, and IV, and with whom JUSTICE GINSBURG joins as to Part III, concurring in the judgment.

. . . The Court's conclusion that respondent does not have standing comes from a mechanistic application of the "redressability" aspect of our standing doctrine. "Redressability," of course, does not appear anywhere in the text of the Constitution. Instead, it is a judicial creation of the past 25 years. . . .

In every previous case in which the Court has denied standing because of a lack of redressability, the plaintiff was challenging some governmental action or inaction. None of these cases involved an attempt by one private party to impose a statutory sanction on another private party.

In addition, in every other case in which this Court has held that there is no standing because of a lack of redressability, the injury to the plaintiff by the defendant was indirect (e.g., dependent on the action of a third party). . . .

. . . The Court acknowledges that respondent would have had standing if Congress had authorized some payment to respondent. Yet the Court fails to specify why payment to respondent—even if only a peppercorn—would redress respondent's injuries, while payment to the Treasury does not. Respondent clearly believes that the punishment of the Steel Company, along with future deterrence of the Steel Company and others, redresses its injury, and there is no basis in our previous standing holdings to suggest otherwise.

When one private party is injured by another, the injury can be redressed in at least two ways: by awarding compensatory damages or by imposing a sanction on the wrongdoer that will minimize the risk that the harm-causing conduct will be repeated. Thus, in some cases a tort is redressed by an award of punitive damages; even when such damages are payable to the sovereign, they provide a form of redress for the individual as well.

History supports the proposition that punishment or deterrence can redress an injury. In past centuries in England,[24] in the American colonies, and in the United States,[25] private persons regularly prosecuted criminal cases. The interest

---

[24] "Several scholars have attempted to trace the historical origins of private prosecution in the United States. Without exception, these scholars have determined that the notion of private prosecutions originated in early common law England, where the legal system primarily relied upon the victim or the victim's relatives or friends to bring a criminal to justice. According to these historians, private prosecutions developed in England as a means of facilitating private vengeance." Bessler, The Public Interest and the Unconstitutionality of Private Prosecutors, 47 Ark. L. Rev. 511, 515 (1994) (footnotes omitted).

[25] "American citizens continued to privately prosecute criminal cases in many locales during the nineteenth century. In Philadelphia, for example, all types of cases were privately prosecuted, with assault and battery prosecutions being the most common. However, domestic disputes short of assault also came before the court. Thus, 'parents of young women prosecuted men for seduction; husbands prosecuted their wives' paramours for adultery, wives prosecuted their husbands for desertion.' Although many estate courts continued to sanction the practice of private prosecutions without significant scrutiny during the nineteenth century, a few state courts outlawed the practice." Id., at 581 (footnotes omitted); A. Steinberg, The Transformation of Criminal Justice: Philadelphia,

in punishing the defendant and deterring violations of law by the defendant and others was sufficient to support the "standing" of the private prosecutor even if the only remedy was the sentencing of the defendant to jail or to the gallows. Given this history, the Framers of Article III surely would have considered such proceedings to be "Cases" that would "redress" an injury even though the party bringing suit did not receive any monetary compensation.[26]

   . . . It could be argued that the Court's decision is rooted in another separation of powers concern: that this citizen suit somehow interferes with the Executive's power to "take Care that the Laws be faithfully executed," Art. II, § 3. It is hard to see, however, how EPCRA's citizen-suit provision impinges on the power of the Executive. As an initial matter, this is not a case in which respondent merely possesses the "undifferentiated public interest" in seeing EPCRA enforced. Here, respondent — whose members live near the Steel Company — has alleged a sufficiently particularized injury under our precedents. App. 5 (complaint alleges that respondent's members "reside, own property, engage in recreational activities, breathe the air, and/or use areas near [the Steel Company's] facility").

Moreover, under the Court's own reasoning, respondent would have had standing if Congress had authorized some payment to respondent. This conclusion is unexceptional given that respondent has a more particularized interest than a plaintiff in a qui tam suit, an action that is deeply rooted in our history.

   . . . Yet it is unclear why the separation of powers question should turn on whether the plaintiff receives monetary compensation. In either instance, a private citizen is enforcing the law. If separation of powers does not preclude standing when Congress creates a legal right that authorizes compensation to the plaintiff, it is unclear why separation of powers should dictate a contrary result when Congress has created a legal right but has directed that payment be made to the federal Treasury. . . .

It is thus quite clear that the Court's holding today represents a significant new development in our constitutional jurisprudence. Moreover, it is equally clear that the Court has the power to answer the statutory question first. It is, therefore, not necessary to reject the Court's resolution of the standing issue in

---

1800-1880, p. 5 (1989) ("Private prosecutions and the minor judiciary were firmly rooted in Philadelphia's colonial past. Both were examples of the creative American adaptation of the English common law. By the seventeenth century, private prosecution was a fundamental part of English common law"); see also F. Goodnow, Principles of the Administrative Law of the United States 412-413 (1905).

[26] When such a party obtains a judgment that imposes sanctions on the wrongdoer, it is proper to presume that the wrongdoer will be less likely to repeat the injurious conduct that prompted the litigation. The lessening of the risk of future harm is a concrete benefit.

order to conclude that it would be prudent to answer the question of statutory construction before announcing new constitutional doctrine.

[Justice Stevens concluded that the statute did not authorize relief for past violations.]

JUSTICE GINSBURG, concurring in the judgment.

Congress has authorized citizen suits to enforce the Emergency Planning and Community Right-to-Know Act of 1986, 42 U.S.C., § 11001 et seq. Does that authorization, as Congress designed it, permit citizen suits for wholly past violations? I agree that the answer is "No." I would . . . resist expounding or offering advice on the constitutionality of what Congress might have done, but did not do.

E. "Case or Controversy" Requirements and the Passive Virtues

Page 121. At the end of the Note, add the following:

Consider in this light Friends of the Earth v. Laidlaw Environmental Services, 120 S. Ct. 693 (2000). Members of Friends of the Earth alleged that they lived near Laidlaw's facility; that Laidlaw discharged water pollutants in violation of the Clean Water Act; that they wanted to fish, camp, swim, and picnic in and near the local river, but that they would not do so because of concern about Laidlaw's discharges. They sought injunction relief and civil penalties, which would go to the U.S. Treasury. The Court held that the allegations about "recreational aesthetic, and economic interests" were sufficient for standing. The Court held it irrelevant that the district court found no "demonstrated harm to the environment"; what mattered was the allegation of the plaintiffs, not the existence of demonstrable harm to the environment. At the same time, the Court held that the Friends of the Earth had standing to seek civil penalties, notwithstanding the objection that those penalties, which would go to the U.S. Treasury, would not redress their injury. The Court said that the civil penalties "deter future violations" and that this was enough for redressability, at least for "violations that are ongoing at the time of the complaint and that could continue into the future if undeterred." Justice Scalia, joined by Justice Thomas, dissented.

5. Standing and voting rights. What kind of injury must a plaintiff show to attack a districting scheme? Consider Shaw v. Hunt, 517 U.S. 899 (1996) (infra this supplement), where the Court said simply,

In United States v. Hays, 515 U.S. — (1995), we recognized that a plaintiff who resides in a district which is the subject of a racial-gerrymander claim has standing to challenge the legislation which created that district, but that a plaintiff from outside that district lacks standing absent specific evidence that he personally has been subjected to a racial classification. Two appellants, Ruth Shaw and Melvin Shimm, live in District 12 and thus have standing to challenge that part of Chapter 7 which defines District 12. The remaining appellants do not reside in District 1, however, and they have not provided specific evidence that they personally were assigned to their voting districts on the basis of race. Therefore, we conclude that only Shaw and Shimm have standing and only with respect to District 12.

Justice Stevens disagreed:

The Court's analysis of the standing question in this [reflects] the fact that the so-called Shaw claim [see text page 879, main volume] seeks to employ the federal courts to impose a particular form of electoral process, rather than to redress any racially discriminatory treatment that the electoral process has imposed. [I] begin by noting that this case reveals the Shaw claim to be useful less as a tool for protecting against racial discrimination than as a means by which state residents may second-guess legislative districting in federal court for partisan ends. The plaintiff-intervenors in this case are Republicans. It is apparent from the record that their real grievance is that they are represented in Congress by Democrats when they would prefer to be represented by members of their own party. They do not suggest that the racial identity of their representatives is a matter of concern, but it is obvious that their political identity is critical. [It] is plain that these intervenors are using their allegations of impermissibly race-based districting to achieve the same substantive result that their previous, less emotionally charged partisan gerrymandering challenge failed to secure.

[While] the plaintiffs purport to be challenging an unconstitutional racial gerrymander, they do not claim that they have been shut out of the electoral process on account of race, or that their voting power has been diluted as a consequence of race-based districting. What then is the wrong that these plaintiffs have suffered that entitles them to call upon a federal court for redress? In Shaw I, the majority construed the plaintiffs' claim to be that the Equal Protection Clause forbids race-based districting designed solely to "separate" voters by race, and that North Carolina's districting process violated the prohibition. Even if that were the claim before us, these plaintiffs should not have standing to bring it. The record shows that North Carolina's districting plan served to require these plaintiffs to share a district with voters of a different race. Thus, the injury that these plaintiffs have suffered, to

11

the extent that there has been injury at all, stems from the integrative rather than the segregative effects of the State's redistricting plan.

Perhaps cognizant of this incongruity, counsel for plaintiffs asserted a rather more abstract objection to race-based districting at oral argument. He suggested that the plaintiffs objected to the use of race in the districting process not because of any adverse consequence that these plaintiffs, on account of their race, had suffered more than other persons, but rather because the State's failure to obey a constitutional command to legislate in a color-blind manner conveyed a message to voters across the State that "there are two black districts and ten white districts."

[To] be sure, as some commentators have noted, we have permitted generalized claims of harm resulting from State-sponsored messages to secure standing under the Establishment Clause. Pildes & Niemi, Expressive Harms, "Bizarre Districts," and Voting Rights: Evaluating Election-District Appearances After Shaw v. Reno, 92 Mich. L. Rev. 483, 499-524 (1993). It would be quite strange, however, to confer similarly broad standing under the Equal Protection Clause because that Clause protects against wrongs which by definition burden some persons but not others.

Here, of course, it appears that no individual has been burdened more than any other. The supposedly insidious messages that *Shaw I* contends will follow from extremely irregular race-based districting will presumably be received in equal measure by all State residents. For that reason, the claimed violation of a shared right to a color-blind districting process would not seem to implicate the Equal Protection Clause at all precisely because it rests neither on a challenge to the State's decision to distribute burdens and benefits unequally, nor on a claim that the State's formally equal treatment of its citizens in fact stamps persons of one race with a badge of inferiority in a context that results in no race-based, unequal treatment.

Consider also Justice Souter's dissenting opinion in Bush v. Vera, 517 U.S. 952 (1996) (infra Chapter V Section E, this supplement):

Whereas malapportionment measurably reduces the influence of voters in more populous districts, and vote dilution predestines members of a racial minority to perpetual frustration as political losers, what *Shaw I* spoke of as harm is not confined to any identifiable class singled out for disadvantage. If, indeed, what *Shaw I* calls harm is identifiable at all in a practical sense, it would seem to play no favorites, but to fall on every citizen and every representative alike. The Court in *Shaw I* explained this conception of injury by saying that the forbidden use of race "reinforces the perception that members of the same racial group . . . think alike, share the same political interests, and will prefer the same candidates at the polls," and that it leads elected officials "to believe that their primary obligation is to represent only the members of that group, rather than their constituency as a whole." This injury is probably best understood as an "expressive harm," that is, one that "results from the idea or attitudes expressed through a governmental action, rather than from the more tangible or material consequences the action brings about." Pildes & Niemi, Expressive Harms, "Bizarre Districts," and Voting Rights: Evaluating Election-District Appearances after Shaw v. Reno, 92 Mich. L. Rev. 483, 506-507 (1993); see also id., at 493 ("The theory of voting rights [that *Shaw I*] endorses centers on the perceived legitimacy of structures of political representation, rather than on the distribution of actual political power between racial or political groups"). To the extent that racial considerations do express such notions, their shadows fall on majorities as well as minorities, whites as well as blacks, the politically dominant as well as the politically impotent.

What exactly is the injury involved in these cases? How, if at all, can the answer to that question be separated from an inquiry into the merits?

For discussion of standing in Shaw-type cases, see Ely, Standing to Challenge Pro-Minority Gerrymanders, 111 Harv. L. Rev. 576 (1997) (arguing that standing should be limited to white voters placed within majority-nonwhite districts to top off those districts' populations in compliance with the one person/one vote requirement); Issacharoff and Karlan, Standing and Misunderstanding in Voting Rights Law, 111 Harv. L. Rev. 2276 (1998) (arguing that "without a theory of constitutionally cognizable injury, it is simply impossible to talk intelligently about standing," and that the Court has not provided that theory).

Should state residents have standing to challenge a decision of the Department of Commerce to use statistical sampling for census purposes? The Court gave an affirmative answer in Department of Commerce v. U.S. House of Rep., 119 S. Ct. 765 (1999), contending that the interest in preventing "vote dilution" was a sufficient injury in fact.

Page 121.   At the end of the Note, add the following:

Raines v. Byrd
117 S. Ct. 2312 (1997)

CHIEF JUSTICE REHNQUIST delivered the opinion of the Court.

The District Court for the District of Columbia declared the Line Item Veto Act unconstitutional. On this direct appeal, we hold that appellees lack standing to bring this suit, and therefore direct that the judgment of the District Court be vacated and the complaint dismissed.

I

The appellees are six Members of Congress, four of whom served as Senators and two of whom served as Congressmen in the 104th Congress (1995-1996). On March 27, 1996, the Senate passed a bill entitled the Line Item Veto Act by a vote of 69-31. All four appellee Senators voted "nay." The next day, the House of Representatives passed the identical bill by a vote of 232-177. Both appellee Congressmen voted "nay." On April 4, 1996, the President signed the Line Item Veto Act (Act) into law. Pub. L. 104-130. The Act went into effect on January 1, 1997. The next day, appellees filed a complaint in the District Court for the District of Columbia against the two appellants, the Secretary of the Treasury and the Director of the Office of Management and Budget, alleging that the Act was unconstitutional.

The provisions of the Line Item Veto Act do not use the term "veto." Instead, the President is given the authority to "cancel" certain spending and tax benefit measures after he has signed them into law. Specifically, the Act provides: "[T]he President may, with respect to any bill or joint resolution that has been signed into law pursuant to Article I, section 7, of the Constitution of the United States, cancel in whole-(1) any dollar amount of discretionary budget authority; (2) any item of new direct spending; or (3) any limited tax benefit; if the President—"(A) determines that such cancellation will-(i) reduce the Federal budget deficit; (ii) not impair any essential Government functions; and (iii) not harm the national interest; and "(B) notifies the Congress of such cancellation by transmitting a special message . . . within five calendar days (excluding Sundays) after the enactment of the law [to which the cancellation applies]." § 691(a). The President's "cancellation" under the Act takes effect when the "special message" notifying Congress of the cancellation is received in the House and Senate. With respect to dollar amounts of "discretionary budget authority," a cancellation means "to rescind." § 691e(4)(A). With respect to "new direct spending" items or "limited tax benefit[s]," a cancellation means that the relevant legal provision, legal obligation, or budget authority is "prevent[ed] . . . from having legal force or effect." §§ 691e(4)(B), (C).

The Act establishes expedited procedures in both Houses for the consideration of "disapproval bills," § 691d, bills or joint resolutions which, if enacted into law by the familiar procedures set out in Article I, § 7 of the Constitution, would render the President's cancellation "null and void," § 691b(a). "Disapproval bills" may only be one sentence long and must read as follows after the enacting clause: "That Congress disapproves of cancellations _____ as transmitted by the President in a special message on _____ regarding _____."

§ 691e(6)(C). (The blank spaces correspond to the cancellation reference numbers as set out in the special message, the date of the President's special message, and the public law number to which the special message relates, respectively.)

The Act provides that "[a]ny Member of Congress or any individual adversely affected by [this Act] may bring an action, in the United States District Court for the District of Columbia, for declaratory judgment and injunctive relief on the ground that any provision of this part violates the Constitution." § 692(a)(1). Appellees brought suit under this provision, claiming that "[t]he Act violates Article I" of the Constitution. Specifically, they alleged that the Act "unconstitutionally expands the President's power," and "violates the requirements of bicameral passage and presentment by granting to the President, acting alone, the authority to 'cancel' and thus repeal provisions of federal law." They alleged that the Act injured them "directly and concretely . . . in their official capacities" in three ways: "The Act . . . (a) alter[s] the legal and practical effect of all votes they may cast on bills containing such separately vetoable items, (b) divest[s] the [appellees] of their constitutional role in the repeal of legislation, and (c) alter[s] the constitutional balance of powers between the Legislative and Executive Branches, both with respect to measures containing separately vetoable items and with respect to other matters coming before Congress."

[We] now hold that appellees have no standing to bring this suit, and therefore direct that the judgment of the District Court be vacated and the complaint dismissed.

II

[To] meet the standing requirements of Article III, "[a] plaintiff must allege *personal injury* fairly traceable to the defendant's allegedly unlawful conduct and likely to be redressed by the requested relief." [Allen v. Wright]. For our purposes, the italicized words in this quotation from *Allen* are the key ones. We have consistently stressed that a plaintiff's complaint must establish that he has a "personal stake" in the alleged dispute, and that the alleged injury suffered is particularized as to him. [And] our standing inquiry has been especially rigorous when reaching the merits of the dispute would force us to decide whether an action taken by one of the other two branches of the Federal Government was unconstitutional.

III

[We] have never had occasion to rule on the question of legislative standing presented here. [The] one case in which we have upheld standing for legislators (albeit state legislators) claiming an institutional injury is Coleman v. Miller,

15

307 U.S. 433 (1939). Appellees, relying heavily on this case, claim that they, like the state legislators in *Coleman*, "have a plain, direct and adequate interest in maintaining the effectiveness of their votes," sufficient to establish standing. In *Coleman*, 20 of Kansas' 40 State Senators voted not to ratify the proposed "Child Labor Amendment" to the Federal Constitution. With the vote deadlocked 20-20, the amendment ordinarily would not have been ratified. However, the State's Lieutenant Governor, the presiding officer of the State Senate, cast a deciding vote in favor of the amendment, and it was deemed ratified (after the State House of Representatives voted to ratify it). The 20 State Senators who had voted against the amendment, joined by a 21st State   Senator and three State House Members, filed an action in the Kansas Supreme Court seeking a writ of mandamus that would compel the appropriate state officials to recognize that the legislature had not in fact ratified the amendment. That court held that the members of the legislature had standing to bring their mandamus action, but ruled against them on the merits.

This Court affirmed. By a vote of 5-4, we held that the members of the legislature had standing. In explaining our holding, we repeatedly emphasized that if these legislators (who were suing as a bloc) were correct on the merits, then their votes not to ratify the amendment were deprived of all validity: "Here, the plaintiffs include twenty senators, whose votes against ratification have been overridden and virtually held for naught although if they are right in their contentions their votes would have been sufficient to defeat ratification. We think that these senators have a plain, direct, and adequate interest in maintaining the effectiveness of their votes. [The] twenty senators were not only qualified to vote on the question of ratification but their votes, if the Lieutenant governor were excluded as not being a part of the legislature for that purpose, would have been decisive in defeating the ratifying resolution. [We] find no departure from principle in recognizing in the instant case that at least the twenty senators whose votes, if their contention were sustained, would have been sufficient to defeat the resolution ratifying the proposed constitutional amendment, have an interest in the controversy which, treated by the state court as a basis for entertaining and deciding the federal questions, is sufficient to give the Court jurisdiction to review that decision." It is obvious, then, that our holding in Coleman stands (at most) for the proposition that legislators whose votes would have been sufficient to defeat (or enact) a specific legislative act have standing to sue if that legislative action goes into effect (or does not go into effect), on the ground that their votes have been completely nullified.

It should be equally obvious that appellees' claim does not fall within our holding in *Coleman*, as thus understood. They have not alleged that they voted for a specific bill, that there were sufficient votes to pass the bill, and that the bill was nonetheless deemed defeated. In the vote on the Line Item Veto Act, their votes were given full effect. They simply lost that vote. Nor can they allege

16

that the Act will nullify their votes in the future in the same way that the votes of the *Coleman* legislators had been nullified. In the future, a majority of Senators and Congressman can pass or reject appropriations bills; the Act has no effect on this process. In addition, a majority of Senators and Congressman can vote to repeal the Act, or to exempt a given appropriations bill (or a given provision in an appropriations bill) from the Act; again, the Act has no effect on this process. *Coleman* thus provides little meaningful precedent for appellees' argument.

Nevertheless, appellees rely heavily on our statement in *Coleman* that the Kansas senators had "a plain, direct, and adequate interest in maintaining the effectiveness of their votes." Appellees claim that this statement applies to them because their votes on future appropriations bills (assuming a majority of Congress does not decide to exempt those bills from the Act) will be less "effective" than before, and that the "meaning" and "integrity" of their vote has changed. The argument goes as follows. Before the Act, Members of Congress could be sure that when they voted for, and Congress passed, an appropriations bill that included funds for Project X, one of two things would happen: (i) the bill would become law and all of the projects listed in the bill would go into effect, or (ii) the bill would not become law and none of the projects listed in the bill would go into effect. Either way, a vote for the appropriations bill meant a vote for a package of projects that were inextricably linked. After the Act, however, a vote for an appropriations bill that includes Project X means something different. Now, in addition to the two possibilities listed above, there is a third option: the bill will become law and then the President will "cancel" Project X.

Even taking appellees at their word about the change in the "meaning" and "effectiveness" of their vote for appropriations bills which are subject to the Act, we think their argument pulls *Coleman* too far from its moorings. Appellees' use of the word "effectiveness" to link their argument to *Coleman* stretches the word far beyond the sense in which the *Coleman* opinion used it. There is a vast difference between the level of vote nullification at issue in *Coleman* and the abstract dilution of institutional legislative power that is alleged here. To uphold standing here would require a drastic extension of *Coleman*. We are unwilling to take that step.

Not only do appellees lack support from precedent, but historical practice appears to cut against them as well. It is evident from several episodes in our history that in analogous confrontations between one or both Houses of Congress and the Executive Branch, no suit was brought on the basis of claimed injury to official authority or power. [The Court gave examples.]

There would be nothing irrational about a system which granted standing in these cases; some European constitutional courts operate under one or another variant of such a regime. But it is obviously not the regime that has obtained under our Constitution to date. Our regime contemplates a more restricted role for Article III courts, well expressed by Justice Powell in his concurring opinion

17

in United States v. Richardson, 418 U.S. 166 (1974): "The irreplaceable value of the power articulated by Mr. Chief Justice Marshall [in Marbury v. Madison, 1 Cranch 137 (1803)] lies in the protection it has afforded the constitutional rights and liberties of individual citizens and minority groups against oppressive or discriminatory government action. It is this role, not some amorphous general supervision of the operations of government, that has maintained public esteem for the federal courts and has permitted the peaceful coexistence of the counter-majoritarian implications of judicial review and the democratic principles upon which our Federal Government in the final analysis rests."

IV

In sum, appellees have alleged no injury to themselves as [individuals], the institutional injury they allege is wholly abstract and widely dispersed (contra *Coleman*), and their attempt to litigate this dispute at this time and in this form is contrary to historical experience. We attach some importance to the fact that appellees have not been authorized to represent their respective Houses of Congress in this action, and indeed both Houses actively oppose their suit. We also note that our conclusion neither deprives Members of Congress of an adequate remedy (since they may repeal the Act or exempt appropriations bills from its reach), nor forecloses the Act from constitutional challenge (by someone who suffers judicially cognizable injury as a result of the Act). Whether the case would be different if any of these circumstances were different we need not now decide.

We therefore hold that these individual members of Congress do not have a sufficient "personal stake" in this dispute and have not alleged a sufficiently concrete injury to have established Article III standing. The judgment of the District Court is vacated, and the case is remanded with instructions to dismiss the complaint for lack of jurisdiction.

JUSTICE SOUTER, concurring in the judgment, with whom JUSTICE GINSBURG joins, concurring.

[Under] our precedents, it is fairly debatable whether this injury is sufficiently "personal" and "concrete" to satisfy the requirements of Article III.

There is, first, difficulty in applying the rule that an injury on which standing is predicated be personal, not official. [Thus,] it is at least arguable that the official nature of the harm here does not preclude standing. Nor is appellees' injury so general that, under our case law, they clearly cannot satisfy the requirement of concreteness. [Appellees] allege that the Act deprives them of an element of their legislative power; as a factual matter they have a more direct and tangible interest in the preservation of that power than the general citizenry has. [On] the other hand, the alleged, continuing deprivation of federal legislative power is not as specific or limited as the nullification of the decisive votes of a group of legislators in connection with a specific item of legislative consideration in Coleman, being instead shared by all the members of the official class who could suffer that injury, the Members of Congress.

Because it is fairly debatable whether appellees' injury is sufficiently personal and concrete to give them standing, it behooves us to resolve the question under more general separation-of-powers principles underlying our standing requirements. [We] have cautioned that respect for the separation of powers requires the Judicial Branch to exercise restraint in deciding constitutional issues by resolving those implicating the powers of the three branches of Government as a "last resort." The counsel of restraint in this case begins with the fact that a dispute involving only officials, and the official interests of those, who serve in the branches of the National Government lies far from the model of the traditional common-law cause of action at the conceptual core of the case-or-controversy requirement. Although the contest here is not formally between the political branches (since Congress passed the bill augmenting Presidential power and the President signed it), it is in substance an interbranch controversy about calibrating the legislative and executive powers, as well as an intrabranch dispute between segments of Congress itself. Intervention in such a controversy would risk damaging the public confidence that is vital to the functioning of the Judicial Branch, by embroiling the federal courts in a power contest nearly at the height of its political tension.

While it is true that a suit challenging the constitutionality of this Act brought by a party from outside the Federal Government would also involve the Court in resolving the dispute over the allocation of power between the political branches, it would expose the Judicial Branch to a lesser risk. Deciding a suit to vindicate an interest outside the Government raises no specter of judicial readiness to enlist on one side of a political tug-of-war, since "the propriety of such action by a federal court has been recognized since Marbury v. Madison, 1 Cranch 137 (1803)." [The] virtue of waiting for a private suit is only confirmed by the certainty that another suit can come to us. The parties agree, and I see no reason to question, that if the President "cancels" a conventional spending or tax provision pursuant to the Act, the putative beneficiaries of that provision will likely suffer a cognizable injury and thereby have standing under Article III. . . .

JUSTICE STEVENS, dissenting.

The Line Item Veto Act purports to establish a procedure for the creation of laws that are truncated versions of bills that have been passed by the Congress and presented to the President for signature. If the procedure were valid, it would deny every Senator and every Representative any opportunity to vote for or against the truncated measure that survives the exercise of the President's cancellation authority. Because the opportunity to cast such votes is a right

19

guaranteed by the text of the Constitution, I think it clear that the persons who are deprived of that right by the Act have standing to challenge its constitutionality. Moreover, because the impairment of that constitutional right has an immediate impact on their official powers, in my judgment they need not wait until after the President has exercised his cancellation authority to bring suit. Finally, the same reason that the respondents have standing provides a sufficient basis for concluding that the statute is unconstitutional.

Article I, § 7, of the Constitution provides that every Senator and every Representative has the power to vote on "Every Bill . . . before it become a law" either as a result of its having been signed by the President or as a result of its "Reconsideration" in the light of the President's "Objections." In contrast, the Line Item Veto Act establishes a mechanism by which bills passed by both Houses of Congress will eventually produce laws that have not passed either House of Congress and that have not been voted on by any Senator or Representative.

Assuming for the moment that this procedure is constitutionally permissible, and that the President will from time to time exercise the power to cancel portions of a just-enacted-law, it follows that the statute deprives every Senator and every Representative of the right to vote for or against measures that may become law. The appellees cast their challenge to the constitutionality of the Act in a slightly different way. Their complaint asserted that the Act "alter[s] the legal and practical effect of all votes they may cast on bills containing such separately vetoable items" and "divest[s] the[m] of their constitutional role in the repeal of legislation." These two claimed injuries are at base the same as the injury on which I rest my analysis. [Whether] one looks at the claim from this perspective, or as a simple denial of their right to vote on the precise text that will ultimately become law, the basic nature of the injury caused by the Act is the same.

In my judgment, the deprivation of this right-essential to the legislator's office-constitutes a sufficient injury to provide every Member of Congress with standing to challenge the constitutionality of the statute. [Moreover,] the appellees convincingly explain how the immediate, constant threat of the partial veto power has a palpable effect on their current legislative choices. Because the Act has this immediate and important impact on the powers of Members of Congress, and on the manner in which they undertake their legislative responsibilities, they need not await an exercise of the President's cancellation authority to institute the litigation that the statute itself authorizes. Given the fact that the authority at stake is granted by the plain and unambiguous text of Article I, it is equally clear to me that the statutory attempt to eliminate it is invalid.

JUSTICE BREYER, dissenting.

[The] harm is focused and the accompanying legal issues are both focused and of the sort that this Court is used to deciding. See, e.g., United States v.

Munoz-Flores, 495 U.S. 385, 392-396 (1990). The plaintiffs therefore do not ask the Court "to pass upon" an "abstract, intellectual proble[m]," but to determine "a concrete, living contest between" genuine "adversaries." Coleman v. Miller, 307 U.S. 433, 460 (1939) (Frankfurter, J., dissenting).

Nonetheless, there remains a serious constitutional difficulty due to the fact that this dispute about lawmaking procedures arises between government officials and is brought by legislators. The critical question is whether or not this dispute, for that reason, is so different in form from those "matters that were the traditional concern of the courts at Westminster" that it falls outside the scope of Article III's judicial power. Justice Frankfurter explained this argument in his dissent in *Coleman*, saying that courts traditionally "leave intra-parliamentary controversies to parliaments and outside the scrutiny of law courts. The procedures for voting in legislative assemblies—who are members, how and when they should vote, what is the requisite number of votes for different phases of legislative activity, what votes were cast and how they were counted—surely are matters that not merely concern political action, but are of the very essence of political action, if 'political' has any connotation at all. . . . In no sense are they matters of 'private damage.' They pertain to legislators not as individuals but as political representatives executing the legislative process. To open the law courts to such controversies is to have courts sit in judgment on the manifold disputes engendered by procedures for voting in legislative assemblies." Justice Frankfurter dissented because, in his view, the "political" nature of the case, which involved legislators, placed the dispute outside the scope of Article III's "case" or "controversy" requirement. Nonetheless, the *Coleman* court rejected his argument.

Although the majority today attempts to distinguish *Coleman*, I do not believe that Justice Frankfurter's argument or variations on its theme can carry the day here. First, as previously mentioned, the jurisdictional statute before us eliminates all but constitutional considerations, and the circumstances mentioned above remove all but the "political" or "intragovernmental" aspect of the constitutional issue.

Second, the Constitution does not draw an absolute line between disputes involving a "personal" harm and those involving an "official" harm.

[Third,] Justice Frankfurter's views were dissenting views, and the dispute before us, when compared to *Coleman*, presents a much stronger claim, not a weaker claim, for constitutional justiciability. The lawmakers in *Coleman* complained of a lawmaking procedure that, at worst, improperly counted Kansas as having ratified one proposed constitutional amendment, which had been ratified by only 5 other States, and rejected by 26, making it unlikely that it would ever become law. The lawmakers in this case complain of a lawmaking procedure that threatens the validity of many laws (for example, all appropriations laws) that Congress regularly and frequently enacts. The systematic nature of the harm immediately affects the legislators' ability to do their jobs. The harms here are more serious, more pervasive, and more immediate than the harm at issue in *Coleman*. [In] sum, I do not believe that the Court can find this case nonjusticiable without overruling *Coleman*. Since it does not do so, I need not decide whether the systematic nature, seriousness, and immediacy of the harm would make this dispute constitutionally justiciable even in *Coleman*'s absence. Rather, I can and would find this case justiciable on *Coleman*'s authority. I add that because the majority has decided that this dispute is not now justiciable and has expressed no view on the merits of the appeal, I shall not discuss the merits either, but reserve them for future argument.

Note: Congressional Standing

1. *Congressional power.* The Court asserts that prior examples of presidents failing to sue to challenge statutes arguably diminishing their authority are "analogous" to *Raines*. There were no statutes specifically authorizing suit by the president in those instances. Consider the following argument: A statute specifically authorizing suit expresses a congressional judgment that the line-item veto statute does impair the voting power of members of Congress, and that judgment should receive some weight in the Court's assessment of whether Article III injury exists. (How much weight? Should the congressional determination be conclusive, on the theory that Congress has expertise that the courts lack in determining what impairs members' voting power?)

2. *Seeking judicial resolution of a dispute between president and Congress.* Does the case present an issue inappropriate for judicial resolution because members of Congress who failed to persuade their colleagues that the line-item veto statute improperly delegated authority to the president were simply seeking to re-fight that battle in court? See INS v. Chadha, Casebook p. 431, rejecting the argument that the president's signature "waives" separation-of-powers objections. Note that these members, who lost on the merits, did persuade their colleagues (and the president, who signed the bill) that it would be appropriate to attempt to secure a judicial determination of its constitutionality. Does this raise a question about whether the substantive line-item veto provisions are severable from the provision held unconstitutional in *Raines*?

Federal Election Commission v. Akins
—S. Ct.— (1998)

JUSTICE BREYER delivered the opinion of the Court.

The Federal Election Commission (FEC) has determined that the American Israel Public Affairs Committee (AIPAC) is not a "political committee" as defined by the Federal Election Campaign Act of 1971 (FECA), and, for that reason, the Commission has refused to require AIPAC to make disclosures regarding its membership, contributions, and expenditures that FECA would otherwise require. We hold that respondents, a group of voters, have standing to challenge the Commission's determination in court, and we remand this case for further proceedings.

I

In light of our disposition of this case, we believe it necessary to describe its procedural background in some detail. As commonly understood, the Federal Election Campaign Act seeks to remedy any actual or perceived corruption of the political process in several important ways. The Act imposes limits upon the amounts that individuals, corporations, "political committees" (including political action committees), and political parties can contribute to a candidate for federal political office. The Act also imposes limits on the amount these individuals or entities can spend in coordination with a candidate. (It treats these expenditures as "contributions to" a candidate for purposes of the Act.) As originally written, the Act set limits upon the total amount that a candidate could spend of his own money, and upon the amounts that other individuals, corporations, and "political committees" could spend independent of a candidate — though the Court found that certain of these last-mentioned limitations violated the First Amendment.

This case concerns requirements in the Act that extend beyond these better-known contribution and expenditure limitations. In particular the Act imposes extensive recordkeeping and disclosure requirements upon groups that fall within the Act's definition of a "political committee." Those groups must register with the FEC, appoint a treasurer, keep names and addresses of contributors, track the amount and purpose of disbursements, and file complex FEC reports that include lists of donors giving in excess of $200 per year (often, these donors may be the group's members), contributions, expenditures, and any other disbursements irrespective of their purposes.

The Act's use of the word "political committee" calls to mind the term "political action committee," or "PAC," a term that normally refers to organizations that corporations or trade unions might establish for the purpose of making contributions or expenditures that the Act would otherwise prohibit.

But, in fact, the Act's term "political committee" has a much broader scope. The Act states that a "political committee" includes "any committee, club, association or other group of persons which receives" more than $1,000 in "contributions" or "which makes" more than $1,000 in "expenditures" in any given year.

This broad definition, however, is less universally encompassing than at first it may seem, for later definitional subsections limit its scope. The Act defines the key terms "contribution" and "expenditure" as covering only those contributions and expenditures that are made "for the purpose of influencing any election for Federal office." Moreover, the Act sets forth detailed categories of disbursements, loans, and assistance-in-kind that do not count as a "contribution" or an "expenditure," even when made for election-related purposes. In particular, assistance given to help a particular candidate will not count toward the $1,000 "expenditure" ceiling that qualifies an organization as a "political committee" if it takes the form of a "communication" by an organization "to its members"—as long as the organization at issue is a "membership organization or corporation" and it is not "organized primarily for the purpose of influencing the nomination . . . or election, of any individual."

This case arises out of an effort by respondents, a group of voters with views often opposed to those of AIPAC, to persuade the FEC to treat AIPAC as a "political committee." Respondents filed a complaint with the FEC, stating that AIPAC had made more than $1,000 in qualifying "expenditures" per year, and thereby became a "political committee." They added that AIPAC had violated the FEC provisions requiring "political committees" to register and to make public the information about members, contributions, and expenditures to which we have just referred. Respondents also claimed that AIPAC had violated § 441b of FECA, which prohibits corporate campaign "contributions" and "expenditures." They asked the FEC to find that AIPAC had violated the Act, and, among other things, to order AIPAC to make public the information that FECA demands of a "political committee."

AIPAC asked the FEC to dismiss the complaint. AIPAC described itself as an issue-oriented organization that seeks to maintain friendship and promote goodwill between the United States and Israel. AIPAC conceded that it lobbies elected officials and disseminates information about candidates for public office. But in responding to the § 441b charge, AIPAC denied that it had made the kinds of "expenditures" that matter for FECA purposes (i.e., the kinds of election-related expenditures that corporations cannot make, and which count as the kind of expenditures that, when they exceed $1,000, qualify a group as a "political committee").

To put the matter more specifically: AIPAC focused on certain "expenditures" that respondents had claimed were election-related, such as the costs of meetings with candidates, the introduction of AIPAC members to candidates, and the distribution of candidate position papers. AIPAC said that its spending on such activities, even if election-related, fell within a relevant exception.

They amounted, said AIPAC, to communications by a membership organization with its members, which the Act exempts from its definition of "expenditures." In AIPAC's view, these communications therefore did not violate

§ 441b's corporate expenditure prohibition. (And, if AIPAC was right, those expenditures would not count toward the $1,000 ceiling on "expenditures" that might transform an ordinary issue-related group into a "political committee.")

The FEC's General Counsel concluded that, between 1983 and 1988, AIPAC had indeed funded communications of the sort described. The General Counsel said that those expenditures were campaign related, in that they amounted to advocating the election or defeat of particular candidates. He added that these expenditures were "likely to have crossed the $1,000 threshold." At the same time, the FEC closed the door to AIPAC's invocation of the "communications" exception. The FEC said that, although it was a "close question," these expenditures were not membership communications, because that exception applies to a membership organization's communications with its members, and most of the persons who belonged to AIPAC did not qualify as "members" for purposes of the Act. Still, given the closeness of the issue, the FEC exercised its discretion and decided not to proceed further with respect to the claimed "corporate contribution" violation.

The FEC's determination that many of the persons who belonged to AIPAC were not "members" effectively foreclosed any claim that AIPAC's communications did not count as "expenditures" for purposes of determining whether it was a "political committee." Since AIPAC's activities fell outside the "membership communications" exception, AIPAC could not invoke that exception as a way of escaping the scope of the Act's term "political committee" and the Act's disclosure provisions, which that definition triggers.

The FEC nonetheless held that AIPAC was not subject to the disclosure requirements, but for a different reason. In the FEC's view, the Act's definition of "political committee" includes only those organizations that have as a "major purpose" the nomination or election of   candidates. Cf. Buckley v. Valeo, 424 U.S. at 79. AIPAC, it added, was fundamentally an issue-oriented lobbying organization, not a campaign-related organization, and hence AIPAC fell outside the definition of a "political committee" regardless. The FEC conesquently dismissed respondents' complaint.

Respondents filed a petition in Federal District Court seeking review of the FEC's determination dismissing their complaint. . . .

II

The Solicitor General argues that respondents lack standing to challenge the FEC's decision not to proceed against AIPAC. He claims that they have failed to satisfy the "prudential" standing requirements upon which this Court has insisted. He adds that respondents have not shown that they "suffer injury in fact," that their injury is "fairly traceable" to the FEC's decision, or that a judicial decision in their favor would "redress" the injury. In his view, respondents' District Court petition consequently failed to meet Article III's demand for a "case" or "controversy."

We do not agree with the FEC's "prudential standing" claim. Congress has specifically provided in FECA that "any person who believes a violation of this Act . . . has occurred, may file a complaint with the Commission." It has added that "any party aggrieved by an order of the Commission dismissing a complaint filed by such party . . . may file a petition" in district court seeking review of that dismissal. History associates the word "aggrieved" with a congressional intent to cast the standing net broadly—beyond the common-law interests and substantive statutory rights upon which "prudential" standing traditionally rested.

Moreover, prudential standing is satisfied when the injury asserted by a plaintiff "arguably [falls] within the zone of interests to be protected or regulated by the statute . . . in question." The injury of which respondents complain— their failure to obtain relevant information—is injury of a kind that FECA seeks to address. We have found nothing in the Act that suggests Congress intended to exclude voters from the benefits of these provisions, or otherwise to restrict standing, say, to political parties, candidates, or their committees.

Given the language of the statute and the nature of the injury, we conclude that Congress, intending to protect voters such as respondents from suffering the kind of injury here at issue, intended to authorize this kind of suit. Consequently, respondents satisfy "prudential" standing requirements.

Nor do we agree with the FEC or the dissent that Congress lacks the constitutional power to authorize federal courts to adjudicate this lawsuit. . . . In our view, respondents here have suffered a genuine "injury in fact."

The "injury in fact" that respondents have suffered consists of their inability to obtain information—lists of AIPAC donors (who are, according to AIPAC, its members), and campaign-related contributions and expenditures—that, on respondents' view of the law, the statute requires that AIPAC make public. There is no reason to doubt their claim that the information would help them (and others to whom they would communicate it) to evaluate candidates for public office, especially candidates who received assistance from AIPAC, and to evaluate the role that AIPAC's financial assistance might play in a specific election. Respondents' injury consequently seems concrete and particular. Indeed, this Court has previously held that a plaintiff suffers an "injury in fact" when the plaintiff fails to obtain information which must be publicly disclosed pursuant to a statute. Public Citizen v. Department of Justice, 491 U.S. 440, 449, (1989) (failure to obtain information subject to disclosure under Federal Advisory Committee Act "constitutes a sufficiently distinct injury to provide standing to sue"). See also Havens Realty Corp. v. Coleman, 455 U.S. 363, 373-374, (1982) (deprivation of information about housing availability constitutes "specific injury" permitting standing).

The dissent refers to United States v. Richardson, 418 U.S. 166 (1974), a case in which a plaintiff sought information (details of Central Intelligence Agency expenditures) to which, he said, the Constitution's Accounts Clause, Art. I, § 9, cl. 7, entitled him. The Court held that the plaintiff there lacked Article III standing. The dissent says that Richardson and this case are "indistinguishable." But as the parties' briefs suggest — for they do not mention Richardson — that case does not control the outcome here.

Richardson's plaintiff claimed that a statute permitting the CIA to keep its expenditures nonpublic violated the Accounts Clause, which requires that "a regular Statement and Account of the Receipts and Expenditures of all public Money shall be published from time to time." The Court held that the plaintiff lacked standing because there was "no 'logical nexus' between the [plaintiff's] asserted status of taxpayer and the claimed failure of the Congress to require the Executive to supply a more detailed report of the [CIA's] expenditures."

In this case, however, the "logical nexus" inquiry is not relevant. Here, there is no constitutional provision requiring the demonstration of the "nexus" the Court believed must be shown in Richardson and Flast. Rather, there is a statute which, as we previously pointed out, does seek to protect individuals such as respondents from the kind of harm they say they have suffered, i.e., failing to receive particular information about campaign-related activities.

The fact that the Court in Richardson focused upon taxpayer standing, not voter standing, places that case at still a greater distance from the case before us. We are not suggesting, as the dissent implies, that Richardson would have come out differently if only the plaintiff had asserted his standing to sue as a voter, rather than as a taxpayer. Faced with such an assertion, the Richardson court would simply have had to consider whether "the Framers . . . ever imagined that general directives [of the Constitution] . . . would be subject to enforcement by an individual citizen." But since that answer (like the answer to whether there was taxpayer standing in Richardson) would have rested in significant part upon the Court's view of the Accounts Clause, it still would not control our answer in case. All this is to say that the legal logic which critically determined Richardson's outcome is beside the point here.

The FEC's strongest argument is its contention that this lawsuit involves only a "generalized grievance." The Solicitor General points out that respondents' asserted harm (their failure to obtain information) is one which is "shared in substantially equal measure by all or a large class of citizens." This Court, he adds, has often said that "generalized grievances" are not the kinds of harms that confer standing. [Lujan; Allen v. Wright; Valley Forge.] Whether styled as a constitutional or prudential limit on standing, the Court has sometimes determined that where large numbers of Americans suffer alike, the political process, rather than the judicial process, may provide the more appropriate remedy for a widely shared grievance.

27

The kind of judicial language to which the FEC points, however, invariably appears in cases where the harm at issue is not only widely shared, but is also of an abstract and indefinite nature — for example, harm to the "common concern for obedience to law." The abstract nature of the harm — for example, injury to the interest in seeing that the law is obeyed — deprives the case of the concrete specificity that characterized those controversies which were "the traditional concern of the courts at Westminster," Coleman, 307 U.S. at 460 (Frankfurter, J., dissenting); and which today prevents a plaintiff from obtaining what would, in effect, amount to an advisory opinion.

Often the fact that an interest is abstract and the fact that it is widely shared go hand in hand. But their association is not invariable, and where a harm is concrete, though widely shared, the Court has found "injury in fact." See Public Citizen, 491 U.S. at 449-450 ("The fact that other citizens or groups of citizens might make the same complaint after unsuccessfully demanding disclosure . . . does not lessen [their] asserted injury"). Thus the fact that a political forum may be more readily available where an injury is widely shared (while counseling against, say, interpreting a statute as conferring standing) does not, by itself, automatically disqualify an interest for Article III purposes. Such an interest, where sufficiently concrete, may count as an "injury in fact." This conclusion seems particularly obvious where (to use a hypothetical example) large numbers of individuals suffer the same common-law injury (say, a widespread mass tort), or where large numbers of voters suffer interference with voting rights conferred by law. We conclude that similarly, the informational injury at issue here, directly related to voting, the most basic of political rights, is sufficiently concrete and specific such that the fact that it is widely shared does not deprive Congress of constitutional power to authorize its vindication in the federal courts.

Respondents have also satisfied the remaining two constitutional standing requirements. The harm asserted is "fairly traceable" to the FEC's decision about which respondents complain. Of course, as the FEC points out, it is possible that even had the FEC agreed with respondents' view of the law, it would still have decided in the exercise of its discretion not to require AIPAC to produce the information and "take no further action" on § 441b allegation against AIPAC. But that fact does not destroy Article III "causation," for we cannot know that the FEC would have exercised its prosecutorial discretion in this way. Agencies often have discretion about whether or not to take a particular action. Yet those adversely affected by a discretionary agency decision generally have standing to complain that the agency based its decision upon an improper legal ground. If a reviewing court agrees that the agency misinterpreted the law, it will set aside the agency's action and remand the case — even though the agency (like a new jury after a mistrial) might later, in the exercise of its lawful discretion, reach the same result for a different reason. Thus respondents' "injury in fact" is "fairly traceable" to the FEC's decision not to issue its complaint, even though the FEC might reach the same result exercising its discretionary powers lawfully. For similar reasons, the courts in this case can "redress" respondents' "injury in fact."

Finally, the FEC argues that we should deny respondents standing because this case involves an agency's decision not to undertake an enforcement action —an area generally not subject to judicial review. In Heckler, this Court noted that agency enforcement decisions "have traditionally been 'committed to agency discretion,'" and concluded that Congress did not intend to alter that tradition in enacting the APA. We deal here with a statute that explicitly indicates the contrary.

In sum, respondents, as voters, have satisfied both prudential and constitutional standing requirements. They may bring this petition for a declaration that the FEC's dismissal of their complaint was unlawful. . . .

For these reasons, the decision of the Court of Appeals is vacated, and the case is remanded for further proceedings consistent with this opinion.

It is so ordered.

JUSTICE SCALIA, with whom JUSTICE O'CONNOR and JUSTICE THOMAS join, dissenting.

The provision of law at issue in this case is an extraordinary one, conferring upon a private person the ability to bring an Executive agency into court to compel its enforcement of the law against a third party. Despite its liberality, the Administrative Procedure Act does not allow such suits, since enforcement action is traditionally deemed "committed to agency discretion by law." If provisions such as the present one were commonplace, the role of the Executive Branch in our system of separated and equilibrated powers would be greatly reduced, and that of the Judiciary greatly expanded.

Because this provision is so extraordinary, we should be particularly careful not to expand it beyond its fair meaning. In my view the Court's opinion does that. Indeed, it expands the meaning beyond what the Constitution permits.

I

It is clear that the Federal Election Campaign Act does not intend that all persons filing complaints with the Commission have the right to seek judicial review of the rejection of their complaints. This is evident from the fact that the Act permits a complaint to be filed by "any person who believes a violation of this Act . . . has occurred," but accords a right to judicial relief only to "any party aggrieved by an order of the Commission dismissing a complaint filed by such party." The interpretation that the Court gives the latter provision deprives it of almost all its limiting force. Any voter can sue to compel the agency to require registration of an entity as a political committee, even though the "aggrievement" consists of nothing more than the deprivation of access to information whose public availability would have been one of the consequences of registration.

This seems to me too much of a stretch. It should be borne in mind that the agency action complained of here is not the refusal to make available information in its possession that the Act requires to be disclosed. A person demanding provision of information that the law requires the agency to furnish — one demanding compliance with the Freedom of Information Act or the Advisory Committee Act, for example — can reasonably be described as being "aggrieved" by the agency's refusal to provide it. What the respondents complain of in this suit, however, is not the refusal to provide information, but the refusal (for an allegedly improper reason) to commence an agency enforcement action against a third person. That refusal itself plainly does not render respondents "aggrieved" within the meaning of the Act, for in that case there would have been no reason for the Act to differentiate between "person" and "party aggrieved." Respondents claim that each of them is elevated to the special status of a "party aggrieved" by the fact that the requested enforcement action (if it was successful) would have had the effect, among others, of placing certain information in the agency's possession, where respondents, along with everyone else in the world, would have had access to it. It seems to me most unlikely that the failure to produce that effect — both a secondary consequence of what respondents immediately seek, and a consequence that affects respondents no more and with no greater particularity than it affects virtually the entire population — would have been meant to set apart each respondent as a "party aggrieved" (as opposed to just a rejected complainant) within the meaning of the statute.

This conclusion is strengthened by the fact that this citizen-suit provision was enacted two years after this Court's decision in United States v. Richardson, 418 U.S. 166, (1974), which, as I shall discuss at greater length below, gave Congress every reason to believe that a voter's interest in information helpful to his exercise of the franchise was constitutionally inadequate to confer standing. Richardson had said that a plaintiff's complaint that the Government was unlawfully depriving him of information he needed to "properly fulfill his obligations as a member of the electorate in voting" was "surely the kind of a generalized grievance" that does not state an Article III case or controversy.

And finally, a narrower reading of "party aggrieved" is supported by the doctrine of constitutional doubt, which counsels us to interpret statutes, if possible, in such fashion as to avoid grave constitutional questions. As I proceed to discuss, it is my view that the Court's entertainment of the present suit violates Article III. Even if one disagrees with that judgment, however, it is clear from Richardson that the question is a close one, so that the statute ought not be interpreted to present it.

II

In Richardson, we dismissed for lack of standing a suit whose "aggrieve-ment" was precisely the "aggrievement" respondents assert here: the Govern-ment's unlawful refusal to place information within the public domain. The only difference, in fact, is that the aggrievement there was more direct, since the Government already had the information within its possession, whereas here the respondents seek enforcement action that will bring information within the Gov-ernment's possession and then require the information to be made public. The plaintiff in Richardson challenged the Government's failure to disclose the ex-penditures of the Central Intelligence Agency (CIA), in alleged violation of the constitutional requirement, Art. 1, § 9, cl. 7, that "a regular Statement and Ac-count of the Receipts and Expenditures of all public Money shall be published from time to time." We held that such a claim was a nonjusticiable generalized grievance" because "the impact on [plaintiff] is plainly undifferentiated and common to all members of the public."

It was alleged in Richardson that the Government had denied a right con-ferred by the Constitution, whereas respondents here assert a right conferred by statute — but of course "there is absolutely no basis for making the Article III inquiry turn on the source of the asserted right." [Lujan] The Court today distin-guishes Richardson on a different basis — a basis that reduces it from a land-mark constitutional holding to a curio. According to the Court, "Richardson focused upon taxpayer standing, ... not voter standing." In addition to being a silly distinction, given the weighty governmental purpose underlying the "gen-eralized grievance" prohibition — viz., to avoid "something in the nature of an Athenian democracy or a New England town meeting to oversee the conduct of the National Government by means of lawsuits in federal courts," — this is also a distinction that the Court in Richardson went out of its way explicitly to elimi-nate. It is true enough that the narrow question presented in Richardson was "whether a federal taxpayer has standing." But the Richardson Court did not hold only, as the Court today suggests, that the plaintiff failed to qualify for the exception to the rule of no taxpayer standing established by the "logical nexus" test of Flast v. Cohen, 392 U.S. 83 (1968). The plaintiff's complaint in Richard-son had also alleged that he was "a member of the electorate," and he asserted injury in that capacity as well. The Richardson opinion treated that as fairly in-cluded within the taxpayer-standing question, or at least as plainly indistinguish-able from it:

> The respondent's claim is that without detailed information on CIA expenditures — and hence its activities — he cannot intelligently follow the actions of Congress or the Executive, nor can he properly fulfill his obli-

gations as a member of the electorate in voting for candidates seeking national office.

This is surely the kind of a generalized grievance described in both Frothingham and Flast since the impact on him is plainly undifferentiated and common to all members of the public.

[The] Court's opinion asserts that our language disapproving generalized grievances "invariably appears in cases where the harm at issue is not only widely shared, but is also of an abstract and indefinite nature." [If] that is so — if concrete generalized grievances (like concrete particularized grievances) are OK, and abstract generalized grievances (like abstract particularized grievances) are bad — one must wonder why we ever developed the superfluous distinction between generalized and particularized grievances at all. But of course the Court is wrong to think that generalized grievances have only concerned us when they are abstract. One need go no further than Richardson to prove that — unless the Court believes that deprivation of information is an abstract injury, in which event this case could be disposed of on that much broader ground.

What is noticeably lacking in the Court's discussion of our generalized-grievance jurisprudence is all reference to two words that have figured in it prominently: "particularized" and "undifferentiated." "Particularized" means that "the injury must affect the plaintiff in a personal and individual way." If the effect is "undifferentiated and common to all members of the public," the plaintiff has a "generalized grievance" that must be pursued by political rather than judicial means. These terms explain why it is a gross oversimplification to reduce the concept of a generalized grievance to nothing more than "the fact that [the grievance] is widely shared," thereby enabling the concept to be dismissed as a standing principle by such examples as "large numbers of individuals suffering the same common-law injury (say, a widespread mass tort), or . . . large numbers of voters suffering interference with voting rights conferred by law." The exemplified injuries are widely shared, to be sure, but each individual suffers a particularized and differentiated harm. One tort victim suffers a burnt leg, another a burnt arm — or even if both suffer burnt arms they are different arms. One voter suffers the deprivation of his franchise, another the deprivation of hers. With the generalized grievance, on the other hand, the injury or deprivation is not only widely shared but it is undifferentiated. The harm caused to Mr. Richardson by the alleged disregard of the Statement-of-Accounts Clause was precisely the same as the harm caused to everyone else: unavailability of a description of CIA expenditures. Just as the (more indirect) harm caused to Mr. Akins by the allegedly unlawful failure to enforce FECA is precisely the same as the harm caused to everyone else: unavailability of a description of AIPAC's activities.

The Constitution's line of demarcation between the Executive power and the judicial power presupposes a common understanding of the type of interest needed to sustain a "case or controversy" against the Executive in the courts. A system in which the citizenry at large could sue to compel Executive compliance with the law would be a system in which the courts, rather than the President, are given the primary responsibility to "take Care that the Laws be faithfully executed." We do not have such a system because the common understanding of the interest necessary to sustain suit has included the requirement, affirmed in Richardson, that the complained-of injury be particularized and differentiated, rather than common to all the electorate. When the Executive can be directed by the courts, at the instance of any voter, to remedy a deprivation which affects the entire electorate in precisely the same way — and particularly when that deprivation (here, the unavailability of information) is one inseverable part of a larger enforcement scheme — there has occurred a shift of political responsibility to a branch designed not to protect the public at large but to protect individual rights. "To permit Congress to convert the undifferentiated public interest in executive officers' compliance with the law into an 'individual right' vindicable in the courts is to permit Congress to transfer from the President to the courts the Chief Executive's most important constitutional duty. . . ." If today's decision is correct, it is within the power of Congress to authorize any interested person to manage (through the courts) the Executive's enforcement of any law that includes a requirement for the filing and public availability of a piece of paper. This is not the system we have had, and is not the system we should desire.

Because this statute should not be interpreted to confer upon the entire electorate the power to invoke judicial direction of prosecutions, and because if it is so interpreted the statute unconstitutionally transfers from the Executive to the courts the responsibility to "take Care that the Laws be faithfully executed," Art. II, § 3, I respectfully dissent.

For discussion of *Akins,* and of the tension between *Akins* and *Lujan,* see Sunstein, Informational Regulation and Informational Standing: Akins and Beyond, 147 U. Pa. L. Rev. 613 (1999).

F.   The Jurisdiction of the Supreme Court

Page 146.   At the end of Note 3, add the following:

4. *Not giving reasons.* In some of the areas we have discussed, the Court has, in a sense, declined to give reasons. When the Court denies certiorari, it does not explain itself. When the Court finds a case nonjusticiable, it may do so partly

because it does not want to address itself to the underlying issue. Frederick Schauer, in Giving Reasons, 47 Stan. L. Rev. 633 (1995), argues that reason-giving may have some of the problems associated with rules, and that it is some-times legitimate not to give reasons. That is, reasons may be both over-inclusive and under-inclusive, and an institution that gives reasons may later have cause for regret. "When juries deliver verdicts, when the Supreme Court denies certio-rari, when state supreme courts refuse review, when federal courts of appeals dispose of cases from the bench or without opinion, when trial judges rule on objections and frequently when they rule on motions, when lawyers exercise peremptory challenges and sometimes when judges dismiss jurors for cause, when housing and zoning authorities refuse to grant variances from their regula-tions, and sometimes when judges impose sentences, the conclusion stands alone, unsupported by reasons, justifications, or explanation." Can you think of factors that would justify a failure to give reasons? Might the answer lie partly in an assessment of the burdens of doing so and the likelihood that reasons will cause problems for the future?

2
THE POWERS OF
CONGRESS

A. *Introduction*

Page 149. At the end of the page, add the following:

For an overview of contemporary issues, see David L. Shapiro, Federalism: A Dialogue (1995).

Page 151. At the end of section 2 of the Note, add the following:

Consider the argument of Lynn A. Baker & Samuel H. Dinkin, The Senate: An Institution Whose Time Has Gone?, 13 J. L. & Pol. 21, 49-50 (1997):

[A] state's prohibition against the death penalty [could] be understood as its determination that the benefits of precluding a type of state action that some consider morally repugnant outweigh the costs of any foregone deterrence of crime. In the absence of a federal government, a state in which the death penalty is available would have only two ways to compete with a state that chose to prohibit the execution of individuals it convicts of crimes. It could continue to offer its current package of taxes and services, including the availability of the death penalty. [Or,] the state could make some adjustment(s) to its package, which may include adopting a [prohibition] against the death penalty. But the existence of our federal legislature gives states that favor the death penalty a third, competition-impeding option: their congressional representatives could enact legislation [requiring] all states to make the death penalty available. [Through] such homogenizing legislation, a majority of states can force an outlier state to disgorge any competitive gains that its uncommon choice previously afforded. [Such] legislation reduces the diversity among the states.

Consider William W. Bratton & Joseph A. McCahery, The New Economics of Jurisdictional Competition: Devolutionary Federalism in a Second-Best World, 86 Geo. L.J. 201, 260 (1997):

> The economics of jurisdictional federalism [identify] significant frictions [that] inhibit competitive lawmaking in practice. These frictions imply that regulatory subject matter requires categorization based on its degree of structural suitability to competitive influence. Accordingly, legal regulatory competition theory should avoid making a general [prediction].

John Copeland Nagle, The Commerce Clause Meets the Delhi Sands Flower-Loving Fly, 97 Mich. L. Rev. 174 (1998), examines a case in which the federal Endangered Species Act was applied to a fly whose only known habitat lies entirely within California. Applying the statute meant that construction of a public hospital could not proceed. Nagle summarizes the relevant facts: "(1) endangered species generally are substantially related to interstate commerce by virtue of the many utilitarian roles that they perform; (2) someday the Fly could have a substantial effect on interstate commerce; and (3) the county hospital [would] rely upon materials, employees, and other connections to interstate commerce. [The] Fly itself does not have an actual, substantial effect on interstate commerce. [There] appear to be many species without which the ecosystem and interstate commerce would continue unaffected, but Congress apparently concluded otherwise." Id. at 190. Under what theory might Congress have the constitutional power to protect the Fly? Nagle identifies three relevant questions: "[What] is the appropriate level of aggregation when comparing an activity to interstate commerce? [Can] a potential effect [ever] qualify as a substantial effect? [What] is the activity that must be connected to interstate commerce?" Id. at 191. Should we be concerned with the Fly, or with all endangered species, or with some other aggregation? Nagle argues that "[the] correct answer lies [between] aggregating everything and aggregating nothing, with Congress given deference to choose what activities to combine—provided it explains why." Id. at 204. Is this an adequate judicial test? Does *Lopez* explain why it answers these questions as it does? If the explanation is that the answers must be such that Congress does not have power to regulate everything, do the answers in fact explain the limits, if any, of the *Lopez* doctrine?

Page 153. At the end of section 4 of the Note, add the following:

For a follow-up, consider Edward L. Rubin, The Fundamentality and Irrelevance of Federalism, 13 Ga. St. U. L. Rev. 1009, 1057-1061 (1997):

Could federalism be [revived]? Perhaps, but why would anyone want to? Federalism requires [divided] loyalties; it requires a nation with territorial sub-groups that command political loyalty and draw support away from the central government. To render it relevant, Americans would need to work sedulously to exacerbate the differences between themselves, to generate conflicts, and to break the links that connect people to like-minded others in different parts of the nation.

[If] federalism is irrelevant, [why] is there so much talk about it? [Three] things [keep] federalism talk alive: nostalgia, opportunism, and decentralization. [Because] our current, homogenized, commercialized, media-drenched national polity is distasteful to many people, our past [serves] as a natural object of yearning. It is part of the good old days, along with bandstands in the park, horse-drawn carriages, women who acted like ladies, and wars that were fought by men and not machines. This is an understandable sentiment, but it is not a harmless one, for it addles our [minds].

[Federalism] becomes a rhetorical [weapon]. [Whenever] federal policy differs from the policies in a significant number of states, federalism will be invoked by those who agree with the state policies. [What] renders the current use of federalism opportunistic [is] that the policy variations [are] part of a national political debate, not reflections of geographically delimited views. [In] the contemporary United States, there are no states, with the possible exceptions of Utah and Hawaii, where the differing political positions are based on a generalized and distinctive culture.

Barry Friedman, Valuing Federalism, 82 Minn. L. Rev. 317 (1997), responds to the Rubin-Feeley argument. He argues that states and democracy are so "ingrained together," and that eliminating the states would therefore have adverse effects on democracy. To the point that democracy is better promoted on the local than on the state level, Friedman responds that federalism may be an incomplete solution to a contemporary "democratic deficit," but it is a partial solution. Local officials, according to Friedman, are likely to be more accountable than national ones.

Vicki C. Jackson, Federalism and the Uses and Limits of Law: *Printz* and Principle?, 111 Harv. L. Rev. 2180, 2217, 2218-19 (1998), criticizes Rubin and Feeley because "decentralization in the United States is [bound] up with federalism. [Were] the states not guaranteed existence within defined borders, [a] national government unhappy with decisionmaking in its centrally defined administrative units could simply reorganize the political boundaries of those units to create more compliant decisionmaking. [This] is [not] likely to happen, but [the] belief that it cannot happen [frames] a host of other understandings." In addition, "maintaining the significance of state governments may help foster civic identities that overlap with more deeply felt identities in ways that create cross-cutting allegiances, [which] could increase the prospects for tolerance and accommodation in the face of profound disagreements." Id. at 2121-22. Are these possibilities realized (or likely to be realized) in the contemporary United States?

Page 153. At the end of section 5 of the Note, add the following:

Consider Tom Stacy, Whose Interests Does Federalism Protect?, 45 U. Kan. L. Rev. 1185, 1190 (1997):

[Federalism] would not seem to promote limited government at all insofar as it diffuses authority into mutually exclusive state and national realms. [In] according state and national governments complete sovereignty within their own domains, the lines enforcing zones of exclusive authority will eliminate rather than create checks against the exercise of authority. In areas of concurrent authority, the electorate can check overweening exercise of state or national authority by shifting power [vertically]. A division of authority into zones of exclusive authority [eliminates] this check. [Such] lines subvert limited government.

Page 154. At the end of section 6 of the Note, add the following:

For an update on European developments, see Stephen Gardbaum, Rethinking Constitutional Federalism, 74 Tex. L. Rev. 795, 831-836 (1996).

B. The Basic Issues: Federalism and Judicial Review

Page 180. At the end of the Lopez opinion, add the following:

UNITED STATES v. MORRISON, 120 S.Ct. — (2000): The Court held the civil remedy provision of the Violence Against Women Act unconstitutional. The statute, enacted in 1994, provided a damage remedy for the victim against any person "who commits a crime of violence motivated by gender." The statute contains detailed findings, backed up by a substantial legislative history, that "gender-motivated violence affects interstate commerce 'by deterring potential victims from traveling interstate, from engaging in employment in interstate business, and from transacting with business, and in places involved in interstate commerce. . . .' "

Chief Justice Rehnquist, writing for the same justices who formed the majority in *Lopez*, wrote that "[gender]-motivated crimes of violence are not [economic] activity. While we need not adopt a categorical rule against aggregating the effects of any noneconomic activity in order to decide these cases, thus far in our Nation's history our cases have upheld Commerce Clause regulation of intrastate activity only where that activity is economic in nature." Congress's findings "are substantially weakened by the fact that they rely so heavily on a method of reasoning that we have already rejected as unworkable if we are to maintain the Constitution's enumeration of powers. [Given] these findings, [the] concern we expressed in *Lopez* that Congress might use the Commerce Clause to completely obliterate the Constitution's distinction between national and local authority seems well-founded. The reasoning [seeks] to follow the but-for causal chain from the initial occurrence of violent crime (the suppression of which has always been the prime object of the States' police power) to every attenuated effect upon interstate commerce. If accepted, petitioners' reasoning would allow Congress to regulate any crime as long as the nationwide, aggregated impact of that crime has substantial effects on employment, production, transit, or consumption." He concluded, "The Constitution requires a distinction between what is truly national and what is truly local. In recognizing this fact we preserve one of the few principles that has been consistent since the Clause was adopted."

Justice Souter, writing for the four dissenters, observed: "If we now ask why the formalistic economic/noneconomic distinction might matter today, after its rejection in *Wickard*, the answer is not that the majority fails to see causal connections in an integrated economic world. The answer is that in the minds of the majority there is a new animating theory that makes categorical formalism seem useful again. Just as the old formalism had value in the service of an economic conception, the new one is useful in serving a conception of federalism. It is the instrument by which assertions of national power are to be limited in favor of preserving a supposedly discernible, proper sphere of state autonomy to legislate or refrain from legislating as the individual States see fit. The legitimacy of the Court's current emphasis on the noncommercial nature of regulated activity, then, does not turn on any logic serving the text of the Commerce Clause or on the realism of the majority's view of the national economy. The essential issue is rather the strength of the majority's claim to have a constitutional warrant for its current conception of a federal relationship enforceable by this Court through limits on otherwise plenary commerce power. This conception is the subject of the majority's second categorical discount applied today to the facts bearing on the substantial effects test."

Justice Souter also wrote, "[In] the centuries since the framing the relative powers of the two sovereign systems have markedly changed. Nationwide economic integration is the norm, the national political power has been augmented by its vast revenues, and the power of the States has been drawn down by the Seventeenth Amendment. [Economic] growth and the burgeoning of federal revenue have not amended the Constitution, which contains no circuit breaker to preclude the political consequences of these developments. Nor is there any justification for attempts to nullify the natural political impact of the particular amendment that was adopted. [Amendments] that alter the balance of power between the National and State Governments, like the Fourteenth, or that change the way the States are represented within the Federal Government, like the Seventeenth, are not rips in the fabric of the Framers' Constitution, inviting judicial repairs. The Seventeenth Amendment may indeed have lessened the enthusiasm of the Senate to represent the States as discrete sovereignties, but the Amendment did not convert the judiciary into an alternate shield against the commerce power." His opinion concluded, "[The] practice of such ad hoc review cannot preserve the distinction between the judicial and the legislative, and this Court, in any event, lacks the institutional capacity to maintain such a regime for very long. [The] facts that cannot be ignored today are the facts of integrated national commerce and a political relationship between States and Nation much affected by their respective treasuries and constitutional modifications adopted by the people. The federalism of some earlier time is no more adequate to account for those facts today than the theory of laissez-faire was able to govern the national economy 70 years ago."

Justice Breyer also wrote a dissent. He asked, "Does the local street corner mugger engage in "economic" activity or "noneconomic" activity when he mugs for money? Would evidence that desire for economic domination underlies many brutal crimes against women save the present statute? [The] Court itself would permit Congress to aggregate, hence regulate, "noneconomic" activity taking place at economic establishments. [Can] Congress simply rewrite the present law and limit its application to restaurants, hotels, perhaps universities, and other places of public accommodation? [Can] Congress save the present law by including it, or much of it, in a broader "Safe Transport" or "Workplace Safety" act? More important, why should we give critical constitutional importance to the economic, or noneconomic, nature of an interstate-commerce-affecting cause? If chemical emanations through indirect environmental change cause identical, severe commercial harm outside a State, why should it matter whether local factories or home fireplaces release them?" He noted, "[In] a world where most everyday products or their component parts cross interstate boundaries, Congress will frequently find it possible to redraft a statute using language that ties the regulation to the interstate movement of some relevant object, thereby regulating local criminal activity or, for that matter, family affairs. Although this possibility does not give the Federal Government the power to regulate every-thing, it means that any substantive limitation will apply randomly in terms of the interests the majority seeks to protect. How much would be gained, for ex-ample, were Congress to reenact the present law in the form of "An Act Forbid-ding Violence Against Women Perpetrated at Public Accommodations or by Those Who Have Moved in, or through the Use of Items that Have Moved in, Interstate Commerce"? Complex Commerce Clause rules creating fine distinc-tions that achieve only random results do little to further the important federalist interests that called them into being." In a section of the dissent joined only by Justice Stevens, Justice Breyer emphasized that Congress had "followed proce-dures that help to protect the federalism values at stake" by providing "adequate notice to the States of its intent to legislate," and compiled a substantial factual record. "[It] tailored the law to prevent its use in certain areas of traditional state concern."

Page 181. At the end of section 1 of the Note, add the following:

Is the following a fair description of the majority's analysis?

> The actual limiting principle [on] which Chief Justice Rehnquist can be said to rely [is] the weirdly circular proposition that there must *be* a limiting prin-ciple. [There] must be some morsel of state power, however tempting, that Congress would feel compelled, in order to avoid an attack of constitutional indigestion, to leave daintily on its plate. Otherwise nothing prevents the na-tion from devouring the states. [It] could only be a matter of time until the states disappeared into the blimp-like figure of a now satiated Uncle Sam: the *consolidation catastrophe.*

Louise Weinberg, Fear and Federalism, 23 Ohio N.U. L. Rev. 1295, 1323-1324 (1997).

Consider Justice Breyer's observation in *Morrison* that the Court's doctrine, understood in light of the exceptions the Court embraces, makes the doctrine purely formal, with no connection to any functions that federalism might serve, and Justice Souter's comments in *Morrison* about the Court's formalism. Can the Court's formalism be defended, or can *Lopez* and *Morrison* be stabilized as doctrine only if the Court rethinks its commitment to *Wickard*'s approach to aggregation of commercial activity as well? Note here Justice Thomas's con-currence in *Lopez.*

41

Page 181.   At the end of section 2 of the Note, add the following:

Consider these observations about why some matters ought to be left exclusively to state control: "[State] sovereignty over family law preserves the constitutional ideal of citizenship by promoting the development of civic virtue [in] maturing children. Federalism [destroys] the federal government's power to mold the moral character of future citizens in its own uniform image. [The] communitarian nature of family law requires a level of political engagement and a sense of community identity that lie beyond the reach of national politics. [As] the bonds of community thin out, the danger that shared values will degenerate into governmentally dictated values increases. By situating communitarian politics at the state level, [localism] ensures that the civic participation, political dialogue, and shared values essential to family law will develop within the states' smaller, relatively more accessible political locales. Second, state sovereignty over family law serves to diffuse governmental power over the formation of individual values and moral aspirations. [Localism] promotes diversity [in] the name of preserving citizen choice in matters of family life." Dailey, Federalism and Families, 143 U. Pa. L. Rev. 1787, 1820, 1871-1872 (1995). To what extent can a parallel argument be made as to education? Consumer protection laws?

Page 182.   Add at the end of the Note:

5. *Social and economic change.* What effects should social and economic change have on federalism, and its judicial enforcement? Consider the argument in Thomas S. Ulen, Economic and Public-Choice Forces in Federalism, 6 Geo. Mason L. Rev. 921, 943 (1998): "The efficient structure of a federation should change when the benefits and costs of federal affiliation change in response to real forces. [Suppose] that up to a certain time air and water pollution is local so that member-state governments can optimally regulate the externality-generators. But then suppose that changes in the technology of production cause new forms of pollution to appear that stray across state borders. [The] most efficient locus of regulation [would] change from the state to the federal level. [Further,] changes in the assignment of governmental responsibility would occur only when there are changes in the strength and breadth of political interest groups. If interest groups are primarily local, [then] they will probably be content with local or state regulation. [If] the concerns of interest groups cross jurisdictional borders, [they] will prefer federal regulation."

Do these concerns justify *Lopez*? Consider the argument defending *Lopez* in Bradford R. Clark, Translating Federalism: A Structural Approach, 66 Geo.

Wash. L. Rev. 1161, 1175, 1176-77 (1998): "To the extent that changed circumstances have led us to expand our understanding of what constitutes 'commerce among the several states,' changed circumstances may also lead us to narrow our conception of which means are 'necessary and proper' to regulate such commerce. [In] 1819, the constitutional structure arguably favored broad implied power to ensure that Congress would have ample means at its disposal to further the limited objects entrusted to the federal government. [Increases] in the incidence of [interstate] commerce necessarily present Congress with greater opportunities to exercise regulatory authority. [Any] ambiguities in the text of the clause [should] now be resolved in a manner that avoids finding virtually unlimited federal power." Compare this argument to Weinberg's criticism of *Lopez* in section 1 of this Note.

Page 185. At the end of section 1 of the Note, add the following:

Larry D. Kramer, But When Exactly Was Judicially-Enforced Federalism "Born" in the First Place?, 22 Harv. J.L. & Pub. Pol'y 123, 131, 133, 134-35 (1998), argues that the Constitution's drafters and ratifiers did not expect that the Court would enforce federalism limitations on congressional power. He asserts that the Court began "to experiment with the notion that it had a role to play in setting limits on Congress's powers" in the early twentieth century, producing "indecisive, grudging acceptance" of congressional power: "[The] Court did not prevent Congress from adopting a single program that Congress really cared about during this entire period." He interprets the Court's actions during the early New Deal as involving "commitment problems": "[The] Court had been letting things develop slowly. [When] the President and Congress suddenly presented the Justices with the complete package and said 'choose,' the Justices found that they were not yet ready to say that they loved the welfare state. [Two] years later, with more time to reflect, more pressure, and a new wave of statutes that were better drafted and better defended, the Court relented."

Page 186. At the end of section 3 of the Note, add the following:

Larry D. Kramer, But When Exactly Was Judicially-Enforced Federalism "Born" in the First Place?, 22 Harv. J.L. & Pub. Pol'y 123, 127-28, 136 (1998), argues that "Congress would be restrained by politics —not politics in the sense of the sterile structural devices described by [Wechsler] but *real* politics: state officials organizing opposition among the people, establishing committees of correspondence [or] by actively campaigning to unseat unsatisfactory representatives. [The] critical feature of [the] process [that emerged in the 1790s] was a unique system of political parties that linked the fortunes of state and federal officers, and in this way, assured respect for state officers and state sovereignty. The parties dominated intergovernmental relations at least until the New Deal, and they continue to serve this function to an unexpectedly large extent today. But [they] have been supplemented by [other] mediating institutions — the most important of which is an interlocking state-federal administrative bureaucracy."

Page 188.   At the end of section 4 of the Note, add the following:

Consider this suggestion, from Regan, How to Think About the Federal Commerce Power and Incidentally Rewrite United States v. Lopez, 94 Mich. L. Rev. 554, 557, 560-561 (1995): "[In] thinking about whether the federal government has the power to do something or other, we should ask what special reason there is for the federal government to have that power. What reason is there to think the states are incapable or untrustworthy? [Is there] any reason why the regulation under consideration should come from the federal government[?]" Should this be supplemented by another question: "What reason is there to think that the courts are better able than Congress to determine whether the states are incapable or untrustworthy?"

4a. *Updating the argument.* Larry D. Kramer, Putting the Politics Back Into the Political Safeguards of Federalism, 100 Colum. L. Rev. 215 (2000), argues that, while Wechsler's argument is "flawed and unpersuasive" and has been "robbed" of force by "subsequent experience and later developments," his "core insight is still valid." Kramer agrees with Wechsler's critics that the structural safeguards he identified "(possibly) give state and local interests a greater voice in national politics, but in ways that do not necessarily protect state and local institutions." State-based apportionment, for example, may lead members of Congress to respond to state *interests* but may also "give them an incentive to reduce or minimize the role of state *government*." Kramer argues that federalism, understood as a system in which state governments hold significant governing power, is protected by the national political party system, an institution that the Constitution's framers did not anticipate. "Making state and national leaders accountable to the same constituents transformed politics by making it politically advantageous to build alliances across formal institutional boundaries. [For] most of our history, the decentralized American party systems [protected] the states by making national officials politically dependent upon state and local party organizations. [The parties] fostered a mutual dependency that induced federal lawmakers to defer to the desires of state officials and state parties." According to Kramer, this resulted from the non-programmatic and decentralized nature of American political parties. "Members of local, state, and national networks are encouraged [to] work for the election of candidates at every level. This [promotes] relationships and establishes obligations among officials that cut across governmental planes." Kramer acknowledges changes in party organization in the modern era, but concludes that these changes, often described as ones that weaken the parties, have not eliminated the party system as a safeguard of federalism. Note the difference between Wechsler's argument, which finds safeguards of federalism in specific constitutional provisions, and Kramer's, which finds them in political arrangements induced but not required by the Constitution. Should this difference matter on the question of whether (or the degree to which) the courts should overturn congressional judgments based on the courts' assessment of the impact of national legislation on constitutionally mandated allocations of power between states and nation?

4b. *A skeptical perspective.* Frank B. Cross, Realism About Federalism, 74 N.Y.U. L. Rev. 1304 (1999), argues that "federalism will be selectively invoked by courts only when ideologically convenient, so that it has no authentic restraining power of its own. [Conservative] justices [invoke] federalism to turn down prisoners' habeas corpus petitions but show no respect for federalism when striking down state redistricting plans aimed at increasing minority representation or striking down state and local affirmative action programs. [Liberals] may 'cry federalism' in [the latter context] but disregard the concept when voting to strike conservative state legislation." Cross also argues that the courts are unlikely to provide sustained support for state-oriented federalism. "For their 'rights,' [states] are supplicants before a group of courts that are agencies of the federal government. [Judges] ruling in federalism disputes are, like legislators, typically 'members of the federal government' with human concerns for 'power, prestige, and glory.' If the interests of states are not sufficiently represented in the national legislature, they are represented no better in the makeup of the federal courts. [If] the political safeguards approach to federalism is erroneous due to the hegemonic interests of the legislative and executive branches, how likely is it that those branches will place individuals on the Court who will countermand those interests?" Cross treats recent decisions invoking federalism concerns to invalidate national legislation "as mere stalking horses for an antiregulatory ideological conservative agenda."

4c. *The Seventeenth Amendment and other constitutional changes.* The Seventeenth Amendment replaced election of Senators by state legislators with direct election. Does this weaken the Wechsler-Choper argument? Justice Souter, dissenting in United States v. Morrison, argued that the Seventeenth Amendment, along with the Reconstruction amendments, fundamentally altered the assumptions about the division of power between states and nation. Consider the following argument: In 1789 the Framers believed (a) that they were creating a government of limited powers, and (b) that the grant of power to Congress to regulate commerce among the several states did not give Congress the power to regulate everything. These two beliefs were compatible in 1789. Belief (b) is no longer accurate, given transformations in the economy, but it is important to maintain the compatibility between the contemporary facts and the overall Constitution. The Seventeenth Amendment demonstrates that the underlying theory of the Constitution has changed in a way that makes it possible to reject belief (a) and make the Constitution compatible with contemporary reality. How does this argument differ from the "political safeguards" one?

Page 188. At the end of section 5 of the Note, add the following:

Paul L. Posner, Unfunded Mandate Reform: 1996 and Beyond, 27 Publius 53 (1997), reports that the Congressional Budget Office prepared 718 estimates in 1996, of which 11 exceeded the $50 million threshold in the Act. All were enacted, but only one exceeded the threshold once it was considered on the floor. According to Posner, the Act's primary impact came in deterring proposals at the drafting and early consideration stages, and in affecting the timing and structure of mandates. See also Elizabeth Garrett, Enhacing the Political Safeguards of Federalism? The Unfunded Mandates Reform Act of 1995, 45 U. Kan. L. Rev. 1113 (1997).

Page 189. After section 6 of the Note, add the following:

6a. *A comparative perspective: U.S. federalism as a model?* Alfred Stepan, Federalism and Democracy: Beyond the U.S. Model, 10 Journal of Democracy 18 (1999), describes U.S. federalism as "coming-together" (the government was created by previously independent states), "*demos*-constraining" (federalism is designed to protect individuals against encroachments by the central government), and symmetrical (each state has the same constitutional status and powers). Stepan argues that federalism is particularly appropriate for multinational democracies, but that most such systems will involve holding a democracy together by creating institutions in which one or more subunits have greater power than others. He points out that "most democratic countries that have adopted federal systems have chosen not to follow the U.S. model." That model "is bolstered by a certain normative disinclination on the part of Americans to accept the concept of collective rights." In light of Stepan's observations, what reasons might there be for students of U.S. constitutional law to consider the constitutional systems of other democracies?

D. The New Deal Crisis and the Rise of the Welfare State

Page 226.   At the end of section 1 of the Note, add the following:

For a description of the background of *Jones & Laughlin*, see Casebeer, Aliquippa: The Company Town and Contested Power in the Construction of Law, 43 Buff. L. Rev. 617 (1995).

Page 228.   After section 4 of the Note, add the following:

5. *The New Deal legacy in light of* Lopez. Consider the text and the original understanding conflict in *Lopez*: "There is little doubt that the scope of the powers now exercised by Congress far exceeds that imagined by the framers. They struggled over whether the commerce power included the power to build roads; they wouldn't have struggled over its power to reach the possession of guns near schools. But [the] language of the Constitution [plainly] supports this expanse of federal power. [As] commerce today seems plainly to reach practically every activity of social life, it would seem to follow that Congress has the power to reach, through regulation, practically every activity of social life." Lessig, Translating Federalism: United States v. Lopez, 1995 Sup. Ct. Rev. 125, 129-30.

Can the original balance between state and nation be restored through interpreting the commerce power? See Lessig, at 145: "[As] federal power increases, federalism now [becomes] an affirmative constraint on the scope of federal power. The implied balance is now made an express barrier, through the practice of deriving limits on the scope of federal power."

Robert Nagel, The Future of Federalism, 46 Case W. Res. L. Rev. 643, 649, 652 (1996), describes *Lopez* as invoking a technique of "successive validation." The technique addresses the dilemma that "our Constitution only authorizes certain enumerated powers for the national government, but also authorizes some enumerated powers that are broad enough to allow congressional control over any aspect of human affairs." In "successive validation," "one horn of the dilemma is subordinated in the case at hand but the equivalency of the competing constitutional proposition is reasserted by a stated commitment to enforce that proposition in some future case. [By] promising future enforcement, these kinds of commitments reduce the pressure to devalue either of the competing propositions. [The] great difficulty [is] that the method is inconsistent with the legalistic ideals of consistency and authoritativeness." Is the technique of successive validation a legal technique, or an observation made by, for example, a political scientist?

Krent, Turning Congress into an Agency: The Propriety of Requiring Legislative Findings, 46 Case W. Res. L. Rev. 731, 739, 745-46 (1996), describes the advantages and disadvantages of requiring findings. "Requiring legislative findings threatens to alter the delicate balance between legislative and judicial power. [Courts] might exercise the power not only to require findings, but to determine what type of findings are appropriate. [Findings] help ensure that congressional action impinging on federalism concerns are a product of reflection and deliberation. [Requiring] a record opens up the legislative process to greater public scrutiny."

E. Other Powers of Congress: Are They More (or Less) Plenary than the Commerce Power?

Page 235. At the end of section 1 of the Note, add the following:

Curtis A. Bradley, The Treaty Power and American Federalism, 97 Mich. L. Rev. 390 (1998), argues for "subject[ing] the treaty power to the same federalism restrictions that apply to Congress's legislative powers. [The] treaty power would not confer any additional regulatory powers on the federal government, just the power to bind the United States on the international plane." This appears to imply that the treaty power authorizes the national government to bind the nation to take actions that it was constitutionally barred from taking (e.g., implementing protection of religious liberty that Congress could not enact pursuant to any enumerated power).

Note that the domain covered by treaties has expanded beyond relations between nations as such to include economic relations (which might be covered by Congress's power to regulate foreign commerce) and, more interesting, human rights. Note as well that most scholars of the domestic side of international law believe that the president has the power to make binding international commitments through executive agreements, either through a delegation of authority from Congress or by agreements later endorsed by legislation enacted by both houses (but not necessarily by the supermajority in the Senate that a treaty requires). Do these developments make it more necessary to devise judicial doctrines limiting the ability of the national government to enact laws under the treaty power?

Page 251. After subsection 4b of the Note, add the following:

a. Baker, Conditional Federal Spending After Lopez, 95 Colum. L. Rev. 1911 (1995), criticizes the "political constraints" theory on the ground that it fails to deal with "the ability of some states to harness the federal lawmaking power to oppress other states." Conditional funding statutes, Baker argues, divide states into two groups, one of whose members "already willingly comply with, or favor, the stated condition." Representatives of such states may support a conditional funding statute to "garner the approval of 'single issue' voters and interest groups" or the votes of constituents who believe that activities in other state impose externalities on them. Id. at 1940-1943. Why is such action properly characterized as oppression?

Page 258. Before the Note, add the following:

City of Boerne v. Flores
117 S. Ct. 2157 (1997)

JUSTICE KENNEDY delivered the opinion of the Court.

A decision by local zoning authorities to deny a church a building permit was challenged under the Religious Freedom Restoration Act of 1993 (RFRA), 107 Stat. 1488, 42 U.S.C. § 2000bb et seq. The case calls into question the authority of Congress to enact RFRA. We conclude the statute exceeds Congress' power. . . .

II

Congress enacted RFRA in direct response to the Court's decision in Employment Div., Dept. of Human Resources of Ore. v. Smith, 494 U.S. 872 (1990)[Casebook p. 1599]. There we considered a Free Exercise Clause claim brought by members of the Native American Church who were denied unemployment benefits when they lost their jobs because they had used peyote. Their practice was to ingest peyote for sacramental purposes, and they challenged an Oregon statute of general applicability which made use of the drug criminal. In evaluating the claim, we declined to apply the balancing test set forth in Sherbert v. Verner, 374 U. S. 398 (1963), under which we would have asked whether Oregon's prohibition substantially burdened a religious practice and, if it did, whether the burden was justified by a compelling government interest. We stated:

"Government's ability to enforce generally applicable prohibitions of socially harmful conduct . . . cannot depend on measuring the effects of a governmental action on a religious objector's spiritual development. To make an individual's obligation to obey such a law contingent upon the law's coincidence with his religious beliefs, except where the State's interest is 'compelling' . . . contradicts both constitutional tradition and common sense." . . .

Four Members of the Court disagreed. They argued the law placed a substantial burden on the Native American Church members so that it could be upheld only if the law served a compelling state interest and was narrowly tailored to achieve that end. . . .

These points of constitutional interpretation were debated by Members of Congress in hearings and floor debates. Many criticized the Court's reasoning, and this disagreement resulted in the passage of RFRA. . . .

RFRA prohibits "government" from "substantially burdening" a person's exercise of religion even if the burden results from a rule of general applicability unless the government can demonstrate the burden "(1) is in furtherance of a compelling governmental interest; and (2) is the least restrictive means of furthering that compelling governmental interest." § 2000bb-1. The Act's mandate applies to any "branch, department, agency, instrumentality, and official (or other person acting under color of law) of the United States," as well as to any "State, or . . . subdivision of a State." § 2000bb-2(1). . . .

III

A . . .

[The] parties disagree over whether RFRA is a proper exercise of Congress' § 5 power "to enforce" by "appropriate legislation" the constitutional guarantee that no State shall deprive any person of "life, liberty, or property, without due process of law" nor deny any person "equal protection of the laws."

In defense of the Act respondent contends [that] RFRA is permissible enforcement legislation. Congress, it is said, is only protecting by legislation one of the liberties guaranteed by the Fourteenth Amendment's Due Process Clause, the free exercise of religion, beyond what is necessary under *Smith*. It is said the congressional decision to dispense with proof of deliberate or overt discrimination and instead concentrate on a law's effects accords with the settled understanding that § 5 includes the power to enact legislation designed to prevent as well as remedy constitutional violations. It is further contended that Congress' § 5 power is not limited to remedial or preventive legislation. . . .

[Legislation] which deters or remedies constitutional violations can fall within the sweep of Congress' enforcement power even if in the process it prohibits conduct which is not itself unconstitutional and intrudes into "legislative

50

spheres of autonomy previously reserved to the States." Fitzpatrick v. Bitzer, 427 U.S. 445, 455 (1976). . . .

It is also true, however, that "as broad as the congressional enforcement power is, it is not unlimited."[Oregon v. Mitchell] (opinion of Black, J.). In assessing the breadth of § 5's enforcement power, we begin with its text. Congress has been given the power "to enforce" the "provisions of this article." The "provisions of this article," to which § 5 refers, include the Due Process Clause of the Fourteenth Amendment. Congress' power to enforce the Free Exercise Clause follows from our holding in Cantwell v. Connecticut, 310 U.S. 296, 303 (1940), that the "fundamental concept of liberty embodied in [the Fourteenth Amendment's Due Process Clause] embraces the liberties guaranteed by the First Amendment."

Congress' power under § 5, however, extends only to "enforcing" the provisions of the Fourteenth Amendment. The Court has described this power as "remedial," [South Carolina v. Katzenbach]. The design of the Amendment and the text of § 5 are inconsistent with the suggestion that Congress has the power to decree the substance of the Fourteenth Amendment's restrictions on the States. Legislation which alters the meaning of the Free Exercise Clause cannot be said to be enforcing the Clause. Congress does not enforce a constitutional right by changing what the right is. It has been given the power "to enforce," not the power to determine what constitutes a constitutional violation. Were it not so, what Congress would be enforcing would no longer be, in any meaningful sense, the "provisions of [the Fourteenth Amendment]."

While the line between measures that remedy or prevent unconstitutional actions and measures that make a substantive change in the governing law is not easy to discern, and Congress must have wide latitude in determining where it lies, the distinction exists and must be observed. There must be a congruence and proportionality between the injury to be prevented or remedied and the means adopted to that end. Lacking such a connection, legislation may become substantive in operation and effect. . . .

*1**

The Fourteenth Amendment's history confirms the remedial, rather than substantive, nature of the Enforcement Clause. The Joint Committee on Reconstruction of the 39th Congress began drafting what would become the Fourteenth Amendment in January 1866. The objections to the Committee's first draft of the Amendment, and the rejection of the draft, have a direct bearing on the central issue of defining Congress' enforcement power. In February, Republican Representative John Bingham of Ohio reported the following draft amendment to the House of Representatives on behalf of the Joint Committee:

---

* [Justice Scalia did not join this subsection of the Court's opinion—eds.]

"The Congress shall have power to make all laws which shall be necessary and proper to secure to the citizens of each State all privileges and immunities of citizens in the several States, and to all persons in the several States equal protection in the rights of life, liberty, and property." Cong. Globe, 39th Cong., 1st Sess., 1034 (1866).

The proposal encountered immediate opposition, which continued through three days of debate. Members of Congress from across the political spectrum criticized the Amendment, and the criticisms had a common theme: The proposed Amendment gave Congress too much legislative power at the expense of the existing constitutional structure. . . .

As a result of these objections having been expressed from so many different quarters, the House voted to table the proposal until April. [The] Amendment in its early form was not again considered. Instead, the Joint Committee began drafting a new article of Amendment, which it reported to Congress on April 30, 1866.

Section 1 of the new draft Amendment imposed self-executing limits on the States. Section 5 prescribed that "the Congress shall have power to enforce, by appropriate legislation, the provisions of this article." Under the revised Amendment, Congress' power was no longer plenary but remedial. Congress was granted the power to make the substantive constitutional prohibitions against the States effective. . . .

The significance of the defeat of the Bingham proposal was apparent even then. During the debates over the Ku Klux Klan Act only a few years after the Amendment's ratification, Representative James Garfield argued there were limits on Congress' enforcement power, saying "unless we ignore both the history and the language of these clauses we cannot, by any reasonable interpretation, give to [§ 5] . . . the force and effect of the rejected [Bingham] clause." . . .

The design of the Fourteenth Amendment has proved significant also in maintaining the traditional separation of powers between Congress and the Judiciary. The first eight Amendments to the Constitution set forth self-executing prohibitions on governmental action, and this Court has had primary authority to interpret those prohibitions. The Bingham draft, some thought, departed from that tradition by vesting in Congress primary power to interpret and elaborate on the meaning of the new Amendment through legislation. Under it, "Congress, and not the courts, was to judge whether or not any of the privileges or immunities were not secured to citizens in the several States." While this separation of powers aspect did not occasion the widespread resistance which was caused by the proposal's threat to the federal balance, it nonetheless attracted the attention of various Members. [The] power to interpret the Constitution in a case or controversy remains in the Judiciary.

2

The remedial and preventive nature of Congress' enforcement power, and the limitation inherent in the power, were confirmed in our earliest cases on the Fourteenth Amendment. In the Civil Rights Cases, 109 U.S. 3 (1883), the Court invalidated sections of the Civil Rights Act of 1875 which prescribed criminal penalties for denying to any person "the full enjoyment of" public accommodations and conveyances, on the grounds that it exceeded Congress' power by seeking to regulate private conduct. The Enforcement Clause, the Court said, did not authorize Congress to pass "general legislation upon the rights of the citizen, but corrective legislation; that is, such as may be necessary and proper for counteracting such laws as the States may adopt or enforce, and which, by the amendment, they are prohibited from making or enforcing . . . ." The power to "legislate generally upon" life, liberty, and property, as opposed to the "power to provide modes of redress" against offensive state action, was "repugnant" to the Constitution. Although the specific holdings of these early cases might have been superseded or modified, see, e.g., [*Heart of Atlanta Motel*], their treatment of Congress' § 5 power as corrective or preventive, not definitional, has not been questioned.

Recent cases have continued to revolve around the question of whether § 5 legislation can be considered remedial. In South Carolina v. Katzenbach, [we] upheld various provisions of the Voting Rights Act of 1965, finding them to be "remedies aimed at areas where voting discrimination has been most flagrant," and necessary to "banish the blight of racial discrimination in voting, which has infected the electoral process in parts of our country for nearly a century." We noted evidence in the record reflecting the subsisting and pervasive discriminatory — and therefore unconstitutional — use of literacy tests. . . .

3

Any suggestion that Congress has a substantive, non-remedial power under the Fourteenth Amendment is not supported by our case law. . . .

There is language in our opinion in Katzenbach v. Morgan, 384 U. S. 641 (1966), which could be interpreted as acknowledging a power in Congress to enact legislation that expands the rights contained in § 1 of the Fourteenth Amendment. This is not a necessary interpretation, however, or even the best one. [Two] rationales for upholding § 4(e) rested on unconstitutional discrimination by New York and Congress' reasonable attempt to combat it. . . .

If Congress could define its own powers by altering the Fourteenth Amendment's meaning, no longer would the Constitution be "superior paramount law, unchangeable by ordinary means." It would be "on a level with ordinary legislative acts, and, like other acts, . . . alterable when the legislature shall please to alter it." [*Marbury.*] Under this approach, it is difficult to conceive of a principle that would limit congressional power. Shifting legislative majorities could change the Constitution and effectively circumvent the difficult and detailed amendment process contained in Article V. . . .

B

Respondent contends that RFRA is a proper exercise of Congress' remedial or preventive power. The Act, it is said, is a reasonable means of protecting the free exercise of religion as defined by Smith. It prevents and remedies laws which are enacted with the unconstitutional object of targeting religious beliefs and practices. To avoid the difficulty of proving such violations, it is said, Congress can simply invalidate any law which imposes a substantial burden on a religious practice unless it is justified by a compelling interest and is the least restrictive means of accomplishing that interest. If Congress can prohibit laws with discriminatory effects in order to prevent racial discrimination in violation of the Equal Protection Clause, then it can do the same, respondent argues, to promote religious liberty.

While preventive rules are sometimes appropriate remedial measures, there must be a congruence between the means used and the ends to be achieved. The appropriateness of remedial measures must be considered in light of the evil presented. Strong measures appropriate to address one harm may be an unwarranted response to another, lesser one.

A comparison between RFRA and the Voting Rights Act is instructive. In contrast to the record which confronted Congress and the judiciary in the voting rights cases, RFRA's legislative record lacks examples of modern instances of generally applicable laws passed because of religious bigotry. The history of persecution in this country detailed in the hearings mentions no episodes occurring in the past 40 years. [This] lack of support in the legislative record, however, is not RFRA's most serious shortcoming. Judicial deference, in most cases, is based not on the state of the legislative record Congress compiles but "on due regard for the decision of the body constitutionally appointed to decide." [Oregon v. Mitchell] (opinion of Harlan, J.). As a general matter, it is for Congress to determine the method by which it will reach a decision.

Regardless of the state of the legislative record, RFRA cannot be considered remedial, preventive legislation, if those terms are to have any meaning. RFRA is so out of proportion to a supposed remedial or preventive object that it cannot be understood as responsive to, or designed to prevent, unconstitutional behavior. It appears, instead, to attempt a substantive change in constitutional protections. Preventive measures prohibiting certain types of laws may be appropriate when there is reason to believe that many of the laws affected by the congressional enactment have a significant likelihood of being unconstitutional. . . .

The reach and scope of RFRA distinguish it from other measures passed under Congress' enforcement power, even in the area of voting rights. In South

Carolina v. Katzenbach, the challenged provisions were confined to those regions of the country where voting discrimination had been most flagrant, and affected a discrete class of state laws, i.e., state voting laws. Furthermore, to ensure that the reach of the Voting Rights Act was limited to those cases in which constitutional violations were most likely (in order to reduce the possibility of overbreadth), the coverage under the Act would terminate "at the behest of States and political subdivisions in which the danger of substantial voting discrimination has not materialized during the preceding five years." [This] is not to say, of course, that § 5 legislation requires termination dates, geographic restrictions or egregious predicates. Where, however, a congressional enactment pervasively prohibits constitutional state action in an effort to remedy or to prevent unconstitutional state action, limitations of this kind tend to ensure Congress' means are proportionate to ends legitimate under § 5.

The stringent test RFRA demands of state laws reflects a lack of proportionality or congruence between the means adopted and the legitimate end to be achieved. . . .

The substantial costs RFRA exacts, both in practical terms of imposing a heavy litigation burden on the States and in terms of curtailing their traditional general regulatory power, far exceed any pattern or practice of unconstitutional conduct under the Free Exercise Clause as interpreted in Smith. Simply put, RFRA is not designed to identify and counteract state laws likely to be unconstitutional because of their treatment of religion. . . .

When Congress acts within its sphere of power and responsibilities, it has not just the right but the duty to make its own informed judgment on the meaning and force of the Constitution. This has been clear from the early days of the Republic. In 1789, when a Member of the House of Representatives objected to a debate on the constitutionality of legislation based on the theory that "it would be officious" to consider the constitutionality of a measure that did not affect the House, James Madison explained that "it is incontrovertibly of as much importance to this branch of the Government as to any other, that the constitution should be preserved entire. It is our duty." Were it otherwise, we would not afford Congress the presumption of validity its enactments now enjoy.

Our national experience teaches that the Constitution is preserved best when each part of the government respects both the Constitution and the proper actions and determinations of the other branches. When the Court has interpreted the Constitution, it has acted within the province of the Judicial Branch, which embraces the duty to say what the law is. [*Marbury.*] When the political branches of the Government act against the background of a judicial interpretation of the Constitution already issued, it must be understood that in later cases and controversies the Court will treat its precedents with the respect due them under settled principles, including stare decisis, and contrary expectations must be disappointed. RFRA was designed to control cases and controversies, such as the one before us; but as the provisions of the federal statute here invoked are beyond congressional authority, it is this Court's precedent, not RFRA, which must control.

* * *

It is for Congress in the first instance to "determine whether and what legislation is needed to secure the guarantees of the Fourteenth Amendment," and its conclusions are entitled to much deference. Katzenbach v. Morgan, 384 U.S. at 651. Congress' discretion is not unlimited, however, and the courts retain the power, as they have since Marbury v. Madison, to determine if Congress has exceeded its authority under the Constitution. Broad as the power of Congress is under the Enforcement Clause of the Fourteenth Amendment, RFRA contradicts vital principles necessary to maintain separation of powers and the federal balance. The judgment of the Court of Appeals sustaining the Act's constitutionality is reversed.

[Justice Stevens concurred in the Court's opinion, and noted as well that he believed that RFRA violated the establishment clause of the first amendment. Justice O'Connor dissented, saying that in her view *Smith* was wrongly decided and should be overruled, but she agreed with the Court's analysis of Congress's power under § 5. Justice Breyer joined her discussion of *Smith* but did not "find it necessary" to consider the question of congressional power under § 5. Justice Souter also dissented, saying that the Court should have dismissed the writ of certiorari as improperly granted.]

Note on *Morrison*

The Court in United States v. Morrison, 120 S.Ct. — (2000), held that the civil remedy provision of the Violence Against Women Act was not a constitutionally permissible exercise of Congress's power under § 5 of the Fourteenth Amendment. The statute's defenders relied on "evidence that many participants in state justice systems are perpetuating an array of erroneous stereotypes and assumptions. Congress concluded that these discriminatory stereotypes often result in insufficient investigation and prosecution of gender-motivated crime, inappropriate focus on the behavior and credibility of the victims of that crime, and unacceptably lenient punishments for those who are actually convicted of gender-motivated violence." They argued that "this bias denies victims of gender-motivated violence the equal protection of the laws and that Congress therefore acted appropriately in enacting a private civil remedy against the perpetrators of gender-motivated violence to both remedy the States' bias and deter future instances of discrimination in the state courts." The Court rejected this argument: "[The] remedy is simply not 'corrective in its character, adapted to counteract and redress the operation of such prohibited state laws or proceedings of state officers.' Civil Rights Cases, 109 U.S. at 18. Or, as we have phrased it in more recent cases, prophylactic legislation under § 5 must have a 'congruence and proportionality between the injury to be prevented or remedied and the means adopted to that end.' [*Boerne*]. Section 13981 is not aimed at proscribing discrimination by officials which the Fourteenth Amendment might not itself proscribe; it is directed not at any State or state actor, but at individuals who have committed criminal acts motivated by gender bias." Justice Breyer's dissent asked, "[The statute] restricts private actors only by imposing liability for private conduct that is, in the main, already forbidden by state law. Why is the remedy 'disproportionate'? And given the relation between remedy and violation—the creation of a federal remedy to substitute for constitutionally inadequate state remedies—where is the lack of 'congruence'?"

Note: The Eleventh Amendment and the Constitutional Immunity of States from Certain Forms of Liability

The Supreme Court has limited congressional power not only by its construction of the Constitution's grants of substantive power, but also by limiting Congress's power to create judicial remedies for enforcing federal constitutional and statutory rights. It has relied principally on the Eleventh Amendment, which provides, "The judicial power of the United States shall not be construed to extend to any suit in law or equity, commenced or prosecuted against one of the United States by Citizens of another State, or by Citizens or Subjects of any Foreign State." The Amendment was adopted in response to the Supreme Court's ruling in Chisholm v. Georgia, 2 U.S. (2 Dall.) 419 (1793), which involved a suit by a South Carolina citizen seeking to recover a debt owed for materials supplied to Georgia during the Revolutionary War. The Supreme Court upheld federal jurisdiction by a 4 -1 vote. Congress submitted the proposed Eleventh Amendment to the states within three weeks of the decision in *Chisholm*, and the required three-quarters of the states ratified it within a year, although the official proclamation of ratification did not occur until 1797.

The Amendment's text refers only to suits against states brought by citizens of other states or foreign nations. Hans v. Louisiana, 134 U.S. 1 (1890), relied on Congress's immediate reaction to *Chisholm* to support its holding that the judicial power of the United States did not extend to suits by citizens against their own states. As the Court later explained, *Hans* adopts the view that states' immunity from suit was a presupposition of the constitutional order, not displaced by the mere adoption of the Constitution.

Does Congress have the power to eliminate the states' immunity from suit? For a period the Court held that the Constitution's grants of power to Congress, in Article I, section 8, and elsewhere, gave Congress the power to displace state immunity. See, e.g., Pennsylvania v. Union Gas, 491 U.S. 1 (1989). Seminole

Tribe of Florida v. Florida, 517 U.S. 44 (1996), rejected those decisions and held that state immunity could not be displaced by an exercise of the powers granted Congress in the unamended Constitution. The Eleventh Amendment was not directly applicable, but, according to the Court, its adoption showed that those who adopted the original Constitution did not believe that they were creating a national government authorized to eliminate state immunity. Alden v. Maine, 527 U.S. 706 (1999), held that Congress could not require state courts to entertain suits by individuals seeking damages for violation of a national statute, where the state courts refused to do so on the basis of state sovereign immunity rules that did not themselves discriminate against national claims. Again, the decision cannot be explained as relying on the Eleventh Amendment, which refers only to the judicial power of the United States.

The Court has held, however, that Section 5 of the Fourteenth Amendment does give Congress the power to displace state immunity when it develops remedies for violations of rights protected by Section 1 of that Amendment. In the Court's view, not only does the Fourteenth Amendment come later in time than the Eleventh, but it also expresses a view of the relation between the states and the nation in which state sovereign immunity must yield to congressional judgments. Congress must declare clearly that the statute imposes liability on states, and its exercise of its power under Section 5 must satisfy the requirement of *Boerne* that the remedy be a proportionate and congruent response to identified constitutional violations. The Court held unconstitutional a statute authorizing federal courts to impose monetary liability on states that violated the property rights conferred by the patent laws. Florida Prepaid, Postsecondary Ed. Expense Bd. v. College Savings Bank, 527 U.S. 626 (1999). According to the Court, the only constitutional violation was the deprivation of property without due process of law, and there was insufficient evidence that states were denying due process by, for example, making it impossible for the patent holders to obtain damages in state courts. The Court also held unconstitutional the imposition of damage liability on states for violations of the Age Discrimination in Employment Act. Kimel v. Florida Bd. of Regents, 120 S.Ct. 645 (2000). Under the Court's equal protection holdings, age discrimination by state officials is unconstitutional only when it is irrational. See Chapter 5 below. Again the Court found insufficient evidence that states were engaging in such widespread irrational (and therefore unconstitutional) age discrimination to justify a general remedy of damages for all acts of age discrimination.

The body of law dealing with state immunity is quite complex. Three other aspects of that law, stated broadly and without the qualifications needed for a complete understanding, are these: (1) States are not immune to actions filed by the United States, whether for damages or injunctive relief. (2) Individuals may obtain injunctions issued by the federal courts against continuing violations of national law, by naming as defendants the state officials engaging in unconstitutional action or enforcing the asserted unlawful state law. Ex parte Young, 209 U.S. 123 (1908). (3) Individuals may obtain damages from state officials who engage in unconstitutional action, but the officials may assert as a defense that their actions were not clearly unconstitutional at the time they acted.

The doctrines of state immunity taken together imply that the Constitution limits but does not eliminate Congress's ability to choose a scheme for remedying violations of national law. Congress may be required to select a remedial scheme that is less than completely effective, as judged by Congress itself. Is the Supreme Court justified in imposing such a limitation on Congress in the absence of specific constitutional text?

F. Implied Limits on Congress's Powers

Page 286.   At the end of subsection 4 of the Note, add the following:

Consider these observations about the politics associated with unfunded mandates: "The nonaccountability explanation of unfunded mandates also presupposes that voters will discern the state and local tax and budgetary consequences of unfunded federal mandates less well than they discern the federal tax and budgetary consequences of federally funded regulation. [If] the nonaccountability explanation of unfunded mandates is correct, one would expect that state and local politicians would do everything in their power to reduce the cost to voters of gathering information about the connections between federal action and state and local finances." Dana, The Case for Unfunded Environmental Mandates, 69 S. Cal. L. Rev. 1, 18, 20 (1995).

Page 287.   Before the Note, add the following:

Printz v. United States
117 S. Ct. 2365 (1997)

JUSTICE SCALIA delivered the opinion of the Court.

The question presented in these cases is whether certain interim provisions of the Brady Handgun Violence Prevention Act, commanding state and local law enforcement officers to conduct background checks on prospective handgun purchasers and to perform certain related tasks, violate the Constitution. [The Brady Act requires the Attorney General to establish a national instant background check system by November 1998. Until then, gun-dealers must send the "chief law enforcement officer" (CLEO) of a prospective purchaser's residence a form identifying the purchaser, unless the purchaser already has a permit or unless the state already has an instant background check system. The dealer must then wait five days to complete the sale. When the CLEO receives the form, the CLEO must "make a reasonable effort to ascertain . . . whether receipt or possession would be in violation of the law," as when the purchaser is a convicted felon. The CLEO is not required to notify the gun dealer that the purchaser is ineligible to own a gun, but if the CLEO does so, the purchaser must be notified of the reasons for that determination. Two CLEOs from Montana and Arizona challenged the Brady Act, which the court of appeals found to be constitutional.] . . .

II

From the description set forth above, it is apparent that the Brady Act purports to direct state law enforcement officers to participate, albeit only temporarily, in the administration of a federally enacted regulatory scheme. Regulated firearms dealers are required to forward Brady Forms not to a federal officer or employee, but to the CLEOs, whose obligation to accept those forms is implicit in the duty imposed upon them to make "reasonable efforts" within five days to determine whether the sales reflected in the forms are lawful. . . .

The petitioners here object to being pressed into federal service, and contend that congressional action compelling state officers to execute federal laws is unconstitutional. Because there is no constitutional text speaking to this precise question, the answer to the CLEOs' challenge must be sought in historical understanding and practice, in the structure of the Constitution, and in the jurisprudence of this Court. . . .

Petitioners contend that compelled enlistment of state executive officers for the administration of federal programs is, until very recent years at least, unprecedented. The Government contends, to the contrary, that "the earliest Congresses enacted statutes that required the participation of state officials in the implementation of federal laws." The Government's contention demands our careful consideration, since early congressional enactments "provide 'contemporaneous and weighty evidence' of the Constitution's meaning," Bowsher v. Synar, 478 U.S. 714, 723-724 (1986) (quoting Marsh v. Chambers, 463 U.S. 783, 790 (1983)). Indeed, such "contemporaneous legislative exposition of the Constitution . . . , acquiesced in for a long term of years, fixes the construction to be given its provisions." Myers v. United States, 272 U.S. 52, 175 (1926). Conversely if, as petitioners contend, earlier Congresses avoided use of this highly attractive power, we would have reason to believe that the power was thought not to exist.

The Government observes that statutes enacted by the first Congresses required state courts to record applications for citizenship, to transmit abstracts of citizenship applications and other naturalization records to the Secretary of State, and to register aliens seeking naturalization and issue certificates of registry. It may well be, however, that these requirements applied only in States that authorized their courts to conduct naturalization proceedings. Other statutes of that era apparently or at least arguably required state courts to perform functions unrelated to naturalization, such as resolving controversies between a captain and the crew of his ship concerning the seaworthiness of the vessel, hearing the claims of slave owners who had apprehended fugitive slaves and issuing certificates authorizing the slave's forced removal to the State from which he had fled, taking proof of the claims of Canadian refugees who had assisted the United States during the Revolutionary War, and ordering the deportation of alien enemies in times of war.

These early laws establish, at most, that the Constitution was originally understood to permit imposition of an obligation on state *judges* to enforce federal prescriptions, insofar as those prescriptions related to matters appropriate for the judicial power. That assumption was perhaps implicit in one of the provisions of the Constitution, and was explicit in another. In accord with the so-called Madisonian Compromise, Article III, § 1, established only a Supreme Court, and made the creation of lower federal courts optional with the Congress—even though it was obvious that the Supreme Court alone could not hear all federal cases throughout the United States. And the Supremacy Clause, Art. VI, cl. 2, announced that "the Laws of the United States . . . shall be the supreme Law of the Land; and the Judges in every State shall be bound thereby." It is understandable why courts should have been viewed distinctively in this regard; unlike legislatures and executives, they applied the law of other sovereigns all the time. . . .

For these reasons, we do not think the early statutes imposing obligations on state courts imply a power of Congress to impress the state executive into its service. Indeed, it can be argued that the numerousness of these statutes, contrasted with the utter lack of statutes imposing obligations on the States' executive (notwithstanding the attractiveness of that course to Congress), suggests an assumed *absence* of such power.[2] The only early federal law the Government

---

[2] Bereft of even a single early, or indeed even pre-20th-century, statute compelling state executive officers to administer federal laws, the dissent is driven to claim that early federal statutes compelled state judges to perform executive functions, which implies a power to compel state executive officers to do so as well. Assuming that this implication would follow (which is doubtful), the premise of the argument is in any case wrong. None of the early statutes directed to state judges or court clerks required the performance of functions more appropriately characterized as executive than judicial (bearing in

61

has brought to our attention that imposed duties on state executive officers is the Extradition Act of 1793, which required the "executive authority" of a State to cause the arrest and delivery of a fugitive from justice upon the request of the executive authority of the State from which the fugitive had fled. That was in direct implementation, however, of the Extradition Clause of the Constitution itself, see Art. IV, § 2.

Not only do the enactments of the early Congresses, as far as we are aware, contain no evidence of an assumption that the Federal Government may command the States' executive power in the absence of a particularized constitutional authorization, they contain some indication of precisely the opposite assumption. On September 23, 1789—the day before its proposal of the Bill of Rights—the First Congress enacted a law aimed at obtaining state assistance of the most rudimentary and necessary sort for the enforcement of the new Government's laws: the holding of federal prisoners in state jails at federal expense. Significantly, the law issued not a command to the States' executive, but a recommendation to their legislatures. Congress "recommended to the legislatures of the several States to pass laws, making it expressly the duty of the keepers of their goals, to receive and safe keep therein all prisoners committed under the authority of the United States," and offered to pay 50 cents per month for each prisoner. Moreover, when Georgia refused to comply with the request, Congress's only reaction was a law authorizing the marshal in any State that failed to comply with the Recommendation of September 23, 1789, to rent a temporary jail until provision for a permanent one could be made.

In addition to early legislation, the Government also appeals to other sources we have usually regarded as indicative of the original understanding of the Constitution. It points to portions of The Federalist which reply to criticisms that Congress's power to tax will produce two sets of revenue officers. ["Publius"] responded that Congress will probably "make use of the State officers and State regulations, for collecting" federal taxes, The Federalist No. 36, and predicted that "the eventual collection [of internal revenue] under the immediate authority of the Union, will generally be made by the officers, and according to the rules, appointed by the several States," No. 45. The Government also invokes the Federalist's more general observations that the Constitution would "enable the [national] government to employ the ordinary magistracy of each [State] in the

---

mind that the line between the two for present purposes is not necessarily identical with the line established by the Constitution for federal separation-of-powers purposes, see Sweezy v. New Hampshire, 354 U.S. 234, 255 (1957)). Given that state courts were entrusted with the quintessentially adjudicative task of determining whether applicants for citizenship met the requisite qualifications, it is unreasonable to maintain that the ancillary functions of recording, registering, and certifying the citizenship applications were unalterably executive rather than judicial in nature. . . .

execution of its laws," No. 27, and that it was "extremely probable that in other instances, particularly in the organization of the judicial power, the officers of the States will be clothed in the correspondent authority of the Union," No. 45. But none of these statements necessarily implies — what is the critical point here — that Congress could impose these responsibilities without the consent of the States. They appear to rest on the natural assumption that the States would consent to allowing their officials to assist the Federal Government, an assumption proved correct by the extensive mutual assistance the States and Federal Government voluntarily provided one another in the early days of the Republic, including voluntary *federal implementation of state law.*

Another passage of The Federalist reads as follows:

> "It merits particular attention . . . , that the laws of the Confederacy as to the *enumerated* and *legitimate* objects of its jurisdiction will become the SUPREME LAW of the land; to the observance of which all officers, legislative, executive, and judicial in each State will be bound by the sanctity of an oath. Thus, the legislatures, courts, and magistrates, of the respective members will be incorporated into the operations of the national government *as far as its just and constitutional authority extends;* and will be rendered auxiliary to the enforcement of its laws." [No. 27.]

The Government does not rely upon this passage, but Justice Souter [makes] it the very foundation of his position; so we pause to examine it in some detail. Justice Souter finds "the natural reading" of the phrases "will be incorporated into the operations of the national government" and "will be rendered auxiliary to the enforcement of its laws" to be that the National Government will have "authority . . . , when exercising an otherwise legitimate power (the commerce power, say), to require state 'auxiliaries' to take appropriate action." There are several obstacles to such an interpretation. First, the consequences in question [are] said in the quoted passage to flow *automatically* from the officers' oath to observe the "the laws of the Confederacy as to the *enumerated* and *legitimate* objects of its jurisdiction."[4] Thus, if the passage means that state officers must take an active role in the implementation of federal law, it means that they must do so without the necessity for a congressional directive that they implement it.

---

[4] Both the dissent and Justice Souter dispute that the consequences are said to flow automatically. They are wrong. The passage says that (1) federal laws will be supreme, and (2) all state officers will be oath-bound to observe those laws, and *thus* (3) state officers will be "incorporated" and "rendered auxiliary." The reason the progression is automatic is that there is not included between (2) and (3): "(2a) those laws will include laws compelling action by state officers." It is the mere existence of *all* federal laws that is said to make state officers "incorporated" and "auxiliary."

But no one has ever thought, and no one asserts in the present litigation, that that is the law. The second problem with Justice Souter's reading is that it makes state legislatures subject to federal direction. [We] have held, however, that state *legislatures* are not subject to federal direction. New York v. United States, 505 U.S. 144 (1992).[5]

These problems are avoided, of course, if the calculatedly vague consequences the passage recites —"incorporated into the operations of the national government" and "rendered auxiliary to the enforcement of its laws" —are taken to refer to nothing more (or less) than the duty owed to the National Government, on the part of *all* state officials, to enact, enforce, and interpret state law in such fashion as not to obstruct the operation of federal law, and the attendant reality that all state actions constituting such obstruction, even legislative acts, are ipso facto invalid. . . .

Justice Souter contends that his interpretation of Federalist No. 27 is "supported by No. 44," written by Madison, wherefore he claims that "Madison and Hamilton" together stand opposed to our view. In fact, Federalist No. 44 quite clearly contradicts Justice Souter's reading. In that Number, Madison justifies the requirement that state officials take an oath to support the Federal Constitution on the ground that they "will have an essential agency in giving effect to the federal Constitution." If the dissent's reading of Federalist No. 27 were correct (and if Madison agreed with it), one would surely have expected that "essential agency" of state executive officers (if described further) to be described as their

---

[5] Justice Souter seeks to avoid incompatibility with New York (a decision which he joined and purports to adhere to), by saying that the passage does not mean "any conceivable requirement may be imposed on any state official," and that "the essence of legislative power . . . is a discretion not subject to command," so that legislatures, at least, cannot be commanded. But then why were legislatures mentioned in the passage? It seems to us assuredly not a "natural reading" that being "rendered auxiliary to the enforcement of [the national government's] laws" means impressibility into federal service for "courts and magistrates" but something quite different for "legislatures." Moreover, the novel principle of political science that Justice Souter invokes in order to bring forth disparity of outcome from parity of language—namely, that "the essence of legislative power . . . is a discretion not subject to command"—seems to us untrue. Perhaps legislatures are inherently uncommandable as to the outcome of their legislation, but they are commanded all the time as to what subjects they shall legislate upon—commanded, that is, by the people, in constitutional provisions that require, for example, the enactment of annual budgets or forbid the enactment of laws permitting gambling. We do not think that state legislatures would be betraying their very "essence" as legislatures (as opposed to their nature as sovereigns, a nature they share with the other two branches of government) if they obeyed a federal command to enact laws, for example, criminalizing the sale of marijuana.

responsibility to execute the laws enacted under the Constitution. Instead, however, Federalist No. 44 continues with the following description:

> "The election of the President and Senate will depend, in all cases, on the legislatures of the several States. And the election of the House of Representatives will equally depend on the same authority in the first instance; and will, probably, forever *be conducted by the officers* and according to the laws *of the States.*"

It is most implausible that the person who labored for that example of state executive officers' assisting the Federal Government believed, but neglected to mention, that they had a responsibility to execute federal laws. If it was indeed Hamilton's view that the Federal Government could direct the officers of the States, that view has no clear support in Madison's writings, or as far as we are aware, in text, history, or early commentary elsewhere.[9]

To complete the historical record, we must note that there is not only an absence of executive-commandeering statutes in the early Congresses, but there is an absence of them in our later history as well, at least until very recent years. The Government points to the Act of August 3, 1882, which enlisted state officials "to take charge of the local affairs of immigration in the ports within such State, and to provide for the support and relief of such immigrants therein landing as may fall into distress or need of public aid"; to inspect arriving immigrants and exclude any person found to be a "convict, lunatic, idiot," or indigent; and to send convicts back to their country of origin "without compensation." The statute did not, however, *mandate* those duties, but merely empowered the Secretary of the Treasury "to *enter into contracts* with such State . . . officers *as may be designated* for that purpose *by the governor of any State.*"

The Government cites the World War I selective draft law that authorized the President "to utilize the service of any or all departments and any or all officers or agents of the United States *and of the several States,* Territories, and the District of Columbia, and subdivisions thereof, in the execution of this Act," and made any person who refused to comply with the President's directions guilty of a misdemeanor. However, it is far from clear that the authorization "to utilize the service" of state officers was an authorization to *compel* the service of state

---

[9] Even if we agree with Justice Souter's reading of the Federalist No. 27, it would still seem to us most peculiar to give the view expressed in that one piece, not clearly confirmed by any other writer, the determinative weight he does. That would be crediting the most expansive view of federal authority ever expressed, and from the pen of the most expansive expositor of federal power. Hamilton was "from first to last the most nationalistic of all nationalists in his interpretation of the clauses of our federal Constitution." C. Rossiter, Alexander Hamilton and the Constitution 199 (1964). . . .

officers; and the misdemeanor provision surely applied only to refusal to comply with the President's *authorized* directions, which might not have included directions to officers of States whose governors had not volunteered their services. It is interesting that in implementing the Act President Wilson did not commandeer the services of state officers, but instead requested the assistance of the States' governors, obtained the consent of each of the governors, and left it to the governors to issue orders to their subordinate state officers. It is impressive that even with respect to a wartime measure the President should have been so solicitous of state independence.

The Government points to a number of federal statutes enacted within the past few decades that require the participation of state or local officials in implementing federal regulatory schemes. Some of these are connected to federal funding measures, and can perhaps be more accurately described as conditions upon the grant of federal funding than as mandates to the States; others, which require only the provision of information to the Federal Government, do not involve the precise issue before us here, which is the forced participation of the States' executive in the actual administration of a federal program. We of course do not address these or other currently operative enactments that are not before us; it will be time enough to do so if and when their validity is challenged in a proper case. For deciding the issue before us here, they are of little relevance. Even assuming they represent assertion of the very same congressional power challenged here, they are of such recent vintage that they are no more probative than the statute before us of a constitutional tradition that lends meaning to the text. Their persuasive force is far outweighed by almost two centuries of apparent congressional avoidance of the practice. . . .

III

The constitutional practice we have examined above tends to negate the existence of the congressional power asserted here, but is not conclusive. We turn next to consideration of the structure of the Constitution, to see if we can discern among its "essential postulates," Principality of Monaco v. Mississippi, 292 U.S. 313, 322 (1934), a principle that controls the present cases.

A

It is incontestible that the Constitution established a system of "dual sovereignty." [Gregory v. Ashcroft]. Although the States surrendered many of their powers to the new Federal Government, they retained "a residuary and inviolable sovereignty," The Federalist No. 39. This is reflected throughout the Constitution's text, Lane County v. Oregon, 7 Wall. 71, 76 (1869); Texas v. White, 7 Wall. 700, 725 (1869), including (to mention only a few) the prohibition on any involuntary reduction or combination of a State's territory, Art. III, § 3; the

Judicial Power Clause, Art. III, § 2, and the Privileges and Immunities Clause, Art. IV, § 2, which speak of the "Citizens" of the States; the amendment provision, Article V, which requires the votes of three-fourths of the States to amend the Constitution; and the Guarantee Clause, Art. IV, § 4, which "pressupposes the continued existence of the state and . . . those means and instrumentalities which are the creation of their sovereign and reserved rights," Helvering v. Gerhardt, 304 U.S. 405, 414-415 (1938). Residual state sovereignty was also implicit, of course, in the Constitution's conferral upon Congress of not all governmental powers, but only discrete, enumerated ones, which implication was rendered express by the Tenth Amendment's assertion that "the powers not delegated to the United States by the Constitution, nor prohibited by it to the States, are reserved to the States respectively, or to the people."

The Framers' experience under the Articles of Confederation had persuaded them that using the States as the instruments of federal governance was both ineffectual and provocative of federal-state conflict. See The Federalist No. 15. Preservation of the States as independent political entities being the price of union, and "the practicality of making laws, with coercive sanctions, for the States as political bodies" having been, in Madison's words, "exploded on all hands," 2 Records of the Federal Convention of 1787, p. 9 (M. Farrand ed. 1911), the Framers rejected the concept of a central government that would act upon and through the States, and instead designed a system in which the state and federal governments would exercise concurrent authority over the people — who were, in Hamilton's words, "the only proper objects of government," The Federalist No. 15. [The] Constitution thus contemplates that a State's government will represent and remain accountable to its own citizens. As Madison expressed it: "The local or municipal authorities form distinct and independent portions of the supremacy, no more subject, within their respective spheres, to the general authority than the general authority is subject to them, within its own sphere." The Federalist No. 39.[11]

---

[11] Justice Breyer's dissent would have us consider the benefits that other countries, and the European Union, believe they have derived from federal systems that are different from ours. We think such comparative analysis inappropriate to the task of interpreting a constitution, though it was of course quite relevant to the task of writing one. The Framers were familiar with many federal systems, from classical antiquity down to their own time; they are discussed in Nos. 18-20 of The Federalist. Some were (for the purpose here under discussion) quite similar to the modern "federal" systems that Justice Breyer favors. Madison's and Hamilton's opinion of such systems could not be clearer. Federalist No. 20, after an extended critique of the system of government established by the Union of Utrecht for the United Netherlands, concludes:

"I make no apology for having dwelt so long on the contemplation of these federal precedents. Experience is the oracle of truth; and where its responses are unequivo-

This separation of the two spheres is one of the Constitution's structural protections of liberty. "Just as the separation and independence of the coordinate branches of the Federal Government serve to prevent the accumulation of excessive power in any one branch, a healthy balance of power between the States and the Federal Government will reduce the risk of tyranny and abuse from either front." [*Gregory*]. To quote Madison once again:

> "In the compound republic of America, the power surrendered by the people is first divided between two distinct governments, and then the portion allotted to each subdivided among distinct and separate departments. Hence a double security arises to the rights of the people. The different governments will control each other, at the same time that each will be controlled by itself." The Federalist No. 51.

The power of the Federal Government would be augmented immeasurably if it were able to impress into its service —and at no cost to itself —the police officers of the 50 States.

B

We have thus far discussed the effect that federal control of state officers would have upon the first element of the "double security" alluded to by Madison: the division of power between State and Federal Governments. It would also have an effect upon the second element: the separation and equilibration of powers between the three branches of the Federal Government itself. The Constitution does not leave to speculation who is to administer the laws enacted by Congress; the President, it says, "shall take Care that the Laws be faithfully executed." [The] Brady Act effectively transfers this responsibility to thousands of CLEOs in the 50 States, who are left to implement the program without meaningful Presidential control (if indeed meaningful Presidential control is possible without the power to appoint and remove). The insistence of the Framers upon unity in the Federal Executive —to insure both vigor and accountability —is well known. That unity would be shattered, and the power of the President would be subject to reduction, if Congress could act as effectively without the President as with him, by simply requiring state officers to execute its laws.

---

cal, they ought to be conclusive and sacred. The important truth, which it unequivocally pronounces in the present case, is that a sovereignty over sovereigns, a government over governments, a legislation for communities, as contradistinguished from individuals, as it is a solecism in theory, so in practice it is subversive of the order and ends of civil polity. . . ."

C

The dissent of course resorts to the last, best hope of those who defend ultra vires congressional action, the Necessary and Proper Clause. It reasons that the power to regulate the sale of handguns under the Commerce Clause, coupled with the power to "make all Laws which shall be necessary and proper for carrying into Execution the foregoing Powers," conclusively establishes the Brady Act's constitutional validity, because the Tenth Amendment imposes no limitations on the exercise of *delegated* powers but merely prohibits the exercise of powers "*not* delegated to the United States." What destroys the dissent's Necessary and Proper Clause argument, however, is not the Tenth Amendment but the Necessary and Proper Clause itself.[13] When a "Law . . . for carrying into Execution" the Commerce Clause violates the principle of state sovereignty reflected in the various constitutional provisions we mentioned earlier, it is not a "Law . . . *proper* for carrying into Execution the Commerce Clause," and is thus, in the words of The Federalist, "merely [an] act of usurpation" which "deserves to be treated as such." The Federalist No. 33. See Lawson & Granger, The "Proper" Scope of Federal Power: A Jurisdictional Interpretation of the Sweeping Clause, 43 Duke L. J. 267, 297-326, 330-333 (1993). We in fact answered the dissent's Necessary and Proper Clause argument in New York: "Even where Congress has the authority under the Constitution to pass laws requiring or prohibiting certain acts, it lacks the power directly to compel the States to require or prohibit those acts. . . . The Commerce Clause, for example, authorizes Congress to regulate interstate commerce directly; it does not authorize Congress to regulate state governments' regulation of interstate commerce." 505 U.S. at 166.

The dissent perceives a simple answer in that portion of Article VI which requires that "all executive and judicial Officers, both of the United States and of the several States, shall be bound by Oath or Affirmation, to support this Constitution," arguing that by virtue of the Supremacy Clause this makes "not only the Constitution, but every law enacted by Congress as well," binding on state officers, including laws requiring state-officer enforcement. The Supremacy Clause, however, makes "Law of the Land" only "Laws of the United States which shall be made in Pursuance [of the Constitution]"; so the Supremacy

---

[13] This argument also falsely presumes that the Tenth Amendment is the exclusive textual source of protection for principles of federalism. Our system of dual sovereignty is reflected in numerous constitutional provisions, and not only those, like the Tenth Amendment, that speak to the point explicitly. It is not at all unusual for our resolution of a significant constitutional question to rest upon reasonable implications. See, e.g., Myers v. United States, 272 U.S. 52 (1926) (finding by implication from Art II, §§ 1,2, that the President has the exclusive power to remove executive officers); Plaut v. Spendthrift Farm, Inc., 514 U.S. 211 (1995) (finding that Article III implies a lack of congressional power to set aside final judgments).

69

Clause merely brings us back to the question discussed earlier, whether laws conscripting state officers violate state sovereignty and are thus not in accord with the Constitution.

IV

Finally, and most conclusively in the present litigation, we turn to the prior jurisprudence of this Court. . . .

[Opinions] of ours have made clear that the Federal Government may not compel the States to implement, by legislation or executive action, federal regulatory programs [citing and discussing *Hodel*, casebook p. 226, *FREC*, casebook p. 267, and New York v. United States, casebook p. 270]. . . .

The Government contends that New York is distinguishable on the following ground: unlike the "take title" provisions invalidated there, the background-check provision of the Brady Act does not require state legislative or executive officials to make policy, but instead issues a final directive to state CLEOs. It is permissible, the Government asserts, for Congress to command state or local officials to assist in the implementation of federal law so long as "Congress itself devises a clear legislative solution that regulates private conduct" and requires state or local officers to provide only "limited, non-policymaking help in enforcing that law." "The constitutional line is crossed only when Congress compels the States to make law in their sovereign capacities."

The Government's distinction between "making" law and merely "enforcing" it, between "policymaking" and mere "implementation," is an interesting one. It is perhaps not meant to be the same as, but it is surely reminiscent of, the line that separates proper congressional conferral of Executive power from unconstitutional delegation of legislative authority for federal separation-of-powers purposes. See A. L. A. Schechter Poultry Corp. v. United States, 295 U.S. 495, 530 (1935); Panama Refining Co. v. Ryan, 293 U.S. 388, 428-429 (1935). This Court has not been notably successful in describing the latter line; indeed, some think we have abandoned the effort to do so. We are doubtful that the new line the Government proposes would be any more distinct. Executive action that has utterly no policymaking component is rare, particularly at an executive level as high as a jurisdiction's chief law-enforcement officer. Is it really true that there is no policymaking involved in deciding, for example, what "reasonable efforts" shall be expended to conduct a background check? It may well satisfy the Act for a CLEO to direct that (a) no background checks will be conducted that divert personnel time from pending felony investigations, and (b) no background check will be permitted to consume more than one-half hour of an officer's time. But nothing in the Act *requires* a CLEO to be so parsimonious; diverting at least *some* felony-investigation time, and permitting at least *some* background checks beyond one-half hour would certainly not be *un*reasonable. Is this decision whether to devote maximum "reasonable efforts" or minimum "reasonable efforts" not preeminently a matter of policy? It is quite impossible, in short, to draw the Government's proposed line at "no policymaking," and we would have to fall back upon a line of "not too much policymaking." How much is too much is not likely to be answered precisely; and an imprecise barrier against federal intrusion upon state authority is not likely to be an effective one.

Even assuming, moreover, that the Brady Act leaves no "policymaking" discretion with the States, we fail to see how that improves rather than worsens the intrusion upon state sovereignty. Preservation of the States as independent and autonomous political entities is arguably less undermined by requiring them to make policy in certain fields than (as Judge Sneed aptly described it over two decades ago) by "reducing [them] to puppets of a ventriloquist Congress," Brown v. EPA, 521 F.2d at 839. It is an essential attribute of the States' retained sovereignty that they remain independent and autonomous within their proper sphere of authority. See Texas v. White, 7 Wall at 725. It is no more compatible with this independence and autonomy that their officers be "dragooned" [into] administering federal law, than it would be compatible with the independence and autonomy of the United States that its officers be impressed into service for the execution of state laws. . . .

The Government also maintains that requiring state officers to perform discrete, ministerial tasks specified by Congress does not violate the principle of New York because it does not diminish the accountability of state or federal officials. This argument fails even on its own terms. By forcing state governments to absorb the financial burden of implementing a federal regulatory program, Members of Congress can take credit for "solving" problems without having to ask their constituents to pay for the solutions with higher federal taxes. And even when the States are not forced to absorb the costs of implementing a federal program, they are still put in the position of taking the blame for its burdensomeness and for its defects. See Merritt, Three Faces of Federalism: Finding a Formula for the Future, 47 Vand. L. Rev. 1563, 1580, n. 65 (1994). Under the present law, for example, it will be the CLEO and not some federal official who stands between the gun purchaser and immediate possession of his gun. And it will likely be the CLEO, not some federal official, who will be blamed for any error (even one in the designated federal database) that causes a purchaser to be mistakenly rejected. . . .

Finally, the Government puts forward a cluster of arguments that can be grouped under the heading: "The Brady Act serves very important purposes, is most efficiently administered by CLEOs during the interim period, and places a minimal and only temporary burden upon state officers." There is considerable disagreement over the extent of the burden, but we need not pause over that detail. Assuming all the mentioned factors were true, they might be relevant if we were evaluating whether the incidental application to the States of a federal law of general applicability excessively interfered with the functioning of state governments. See, e.g., [*National League of Cities*]. But where, as here, it is the whole object of the law to direct the functioning of the state executive, and hence to compromise the structural framework of dual sovereignty, such a "balancing" analysis is inappropriate. It is the very principle of separate state sovereignty that such a law offends, and no comparative assessment of the various interests can overcome that fundamental defect. . . .

   * * *

We held in New York that Congress cannot compel the States to enact or enforce a federal regulatory program. Today we hold that Congress cannot circumvent that prohibition by conscripting the State's officers directly. The Federal Government may neither issue directives requiring the States to address particular problems, nor command the States' officers, or those of their political subdivisions, to administer or enforce a federal regulatory program. It matters not whether policymaking is involved, and no case-by-case weighing of the burdens or benefits is necessary; such commands are fundamentally incompatible with our constitutional system of dual sovereignty. Accordingly, the judgment of the Court of Appeals for the Ninth Circuit is reversed.

[Justice O'Connor's concurring opinion is omitted.]

JUSTICE THOMAS, concurring. . . .

[Even] if we construe Congress' authority to regulate interstate commerce to encompass those intrastate transactions that "substantially affect" interstate commerce, I question whether Congress can regulate the particular transactions at issue here. The Constitution, in addition to delegating certain enumerated powers to Congress, places whole areas outside the reach of Congress' regulatory authority. The First Amendment, for example, is fittingly celebrated for preventing Congress from "prohibiting the free exercise" of religion or "abridging the freedom of speech." The Second Amendment similarly appears to contain an express limitation on the government's authority. [If], however, the Second Amendment is read to confer a personal right to "keep and bear arms," a colorable argument exists that the Federal Government's regulatory scheme, at least as it pertains to the purely intrastate sale or possession of firearms, runs afoul of that Amendment's protections. As the parties did not raise this argument, however, we need not consider it here. Perhaps, at some future date, this Court will have the opportunity to determine whether Justice Story was correct when he wrote that the right to bear arms "has justly been considered, as the palladium of the liberties of a republic." 3 J. Story, Commentaries § 1890, p. 746 (1833). . . .

JUSTICE STEVENS, with whom JUSTICE SOUTER, JUSTICE GINSBURG, and JUSTICE BREYER join, dissenting.

When Congress exercises the powers delegated to it by the Constitution, it may impose affirmative obligations on executive and judicial officers of state and local governments as well as ordinary citizens. This conclusion is firmly supported by the text of the Constitution, the early history of the Nation, decisions of this Court, and a correct understanding of the basic structure of the Federal Government.

These cases do not implicate the more difficult questions associated with congressional coercion of state legislatures addressed in New York v. United States, 505 U.S. 144 (1992). Nor need we consider the wisdom of relying on local officials rather than federal agents to carry out aspects of a federal program, or even the question whether such officials may be required to perform a federal function on a permanent basis. The question is whether Congress, acting on behalf of the people of the entire Nation, may require local law enforcement officers to perform certain duties during the interim needed for the development of a federal gun control program. It is remarkably similar to the question, heavily debated by the Framers of the Constitution, whether the Congress could require state agents to collect federal taxes. Or the question whether Congress could impress state judges into federal service to entertain and decide cases that they would prefer to ignore.

Indeed, since the ultimate issue is one of power, we must consider its implications in times of national emergency. Matters such as the enlistment of air raid wardens, the administration of a military draft, the mass inoculation of children to forestall an epidemic, or perhaps the threat of an international terrorist, may require a national response before federal personnel can be made available to respond. If the Constitution empowers Congress and the President to make an appropriate response, is there anything in the Tenth Amendment, "in historical understanding and practice, in the structure of the Constitution, [or] in the jurisprudence of this Court," that forbids the enlistment of state officers to make that response effective? More narrowly, what basis is there in any of those sources for concluding that it is the Members of this Court, rather than the elected representatives of the people, who should determine whether the Constitution contains the unwritten rule that the Court announces today?

Perhaps today's majority would suggest that no such emergency is presented by the facts of these cases. But such a suggestion is itself an expression of a policy judgment. And Congress' view of the matter is quite different from that implied by the Court today.

The Brady Act was passed in response to what Congress described as an "epidemic of gun violence." The Act's legislative history notes that 15,377 Americans were murdered with firearms in 1992, and that 12,489 of these deaths were caused by handguns. Congress expressed special concern that "the level of firearm violence in this country is, by far, the highest among developed nations." The partial solution contained in the Brady Act, a mandatory background check before a handgun may be purchased, has met with remarkable success. Between 1994 and 1996, approximately 6,600 firearm sales each month to potentially dangerous persons were prevented by Brady Act checks; over 70% of the rejected purchasers were convicted or indicted felons. Whether or not the evaluation reflected in the enactment of the Brady Act is correct as to the extent of the danger and the efficacy of the legislation, the congressional decision surely warrants more respect than it is accorded in today's unprecedented decision.

I

The text of the Constitution provides a sufficient basis for a correct disposition of this case. Article I, § 8, grants the Congress the power to regulate commerce among the States. Putting to one side the revisionist views expressed by Justice Thomas in his concurring opinion in United States v. Lopez, 514 U.S. 549, 584 (1995), there can be no question that that provision adequately supports the regulation of commerce in handguns effected by the Brady Act. Moreover, the additional grant of authority in that section of the Constitution "to make all Laws which shall be necessary and proper for carrying into Execution the foregoing Powers" is surely adequate to support the temporary enlistment of local police officers in the process of identifying persons who should not be entrusted with the possession of handguns. In short, the affirmative delegation of power in Article I provides ample authority for the congressional enactment.

Unlike the First Amendment, which prohibits the enactment of a category of laws that would otherwise be authorized by Article I, the Tenth Amendment imposes no restriction on the exercise of delegated powers. [The] Amendment confirms the principle that the powers of the Federal Government are limited to those affirmatively granted by the Constitution, but it does not purport to limit the scope or the effectiveness of the exercise of powers that are delegated to Congress. Thus, the Amendment provides no support for a rule that immunizes local officials from obligations that might be imposed on ordinary citizens.[2] In-

---

[2] Recognizing the force of the argument, the Court suggests that this reasoning is in error because—even if it is responsive to the submission that the Tenth Amendment roots the principle set forth by the majority today—it does not answer the possibility that the Court's holding can be rooted in a "principle of state sovereignty" mentioned nowhere in the constitutional text. As a ground for invalidating important federal legislation, this argument is remarkably weak. The majority's further claim that, while the Brady Act may be legislation "necessary" to Congress' execution of its undisputed Commerce Clause authority to regulate firearms sales, it is nevertheless not "proper" because it vio-

deed, it would be more reasonable to infer that federal law may impose greater duties on state officials than on private citizens because another provision of the Constitution requires that "all executive and judicial Officers, both of the United States and of the several States, shall be bound by Oath or Affirmation, to support this Constitution." U. S. Const., Art. VI, cl. 3. . . .

The reasoning in our unanimous opinion explaining why state tribunals with ordinary jurisdiction over tort litigation can be required to hear cases arising under the Federal Employers' Liability Act applies equally to local law enforcement officers whose ordinary duties parallel the modest obligations imposed by the Brady Act:

> "The suggestion that the act of Congress is not in harmony with the policy of the State, and therefore that the courts of the State are free to decline jurisdiction, is quite inadmissible, because it presupposes what in legal contemplation does not exist. When Congress, in the exertion of the power confided to it by the Constitution, adopted that act, it spoke for all the people and all the States, and thereby established a policy for all. That policy is as much the policy of Connecticut as if the act had emanated from its own legislature, and should be respected accordingly in the courts of the State." . . . Second Employers' Liability Cases, 223 U.S. 1, 57 (1912).

There is not a clause, sentence, or paragraph in the entire text of the Constitution of the United States that supports the proposition that a local police officer can ignore a command contained in a statute enacted by Congress pursuant to an express delegation of power enumerated in Article I.

II

Under the Articles of Confederation the National Government had the power to issue commands to the several sovereign states, but it had no authority to govern individuals directly. Thus, it raised an army and financed its operations by issuing requisitions to the constituent members of the Confederacy, rather than by creating federal agencies to draft soldiers or to impose taxes.

That method of governing proved to be unacceptable, not because it demeaned the sovereign character of the several States, but rather because it was

---

lates state sovereignty, is wholly circular and provides no traction for its argument. Moreover, this reading of the term "proper" gives it a meaning directly contradicted by Chief Justice Marshall in McCulloch v. Maryland, 4 Wheat. 316 (1819). As the Chief Justice explained, the Necessary and Proper Clause by "its terms purports to enlarge, not to diminish the powers vested in the government. It purports to be an additional power, not a restriction on those already granted.". . .

cumbersome and inefficient. Indeed, a confederation that allows each of its members to determine the ways and means of complying with an overriding requisition is obviously more deferential to state sovereignty concerns than a national government that uses its own agents to impose its will directly on the citizenry. The basic change in the character of the government that the Framers conceived was designed to enhance the power of the national government, not to provide some new, unmentioned immunity for state officers. Because indirect control over individual citizens ("the only proper objects of government") was ineffective under the Articles of Confederation, Alexander Hamilton explained that "we must *extend* the authority of the Union to the persons of the citizens." The Federalist No. 15.

Indeed, the historical materials strongly suggest that the Founders intended to enhance the capacity of the federal government by empowering it—as a part of the new authority to make demands directly on individual citizens—to act through local officials. Hamilton made clear that the new Constitution, "by extending the authority of the federal head to the individual citizens of the several States, will enable the government to employ the ordinary magistracy of each, in the execution of its laws." The Federalist No. 27, at 180. Hamilton's meaning was unambiguous; the federal government was to have the power to demand that local officials implement national policy programs. As he went on to explain: "It is easy to perceive that this will tend to destroy, in the common apprehension, all distinction between the sources from which [the state and federal governments] might proceed; and will give the federal government the same advantage for securing a due obedience to its authority which is enjoyed by the government of each State."

More specifically, during the debates concerning the ratification of the Constitution, it was assumed that state agents would act as tax collectors for the federal government. . . .

The Court's response to this powerful historical evidence is weak. The majority suggests that "none of these statements necessarily implies . . . Congress could impose these responsibilities without the consent of the States." No fair reading of these materials can justify such an interpretation. As Hamilton explained, the power of the government to act on "individual citizens"—including "employing the ordinary magistracy" of the States—was an answer to the problems faced by a central government that could act only directly "upon the States in their political or collective capacities." The Federalist, No. 27. The new Constitution would avoid this problem, resulting in "a regular and peaceable execution of the law of the Union."

This point is made especially clear in Hamilton's statement that "the legislatures, courts, and magistrates, of the respective members, will be incorporated into the operations of the national government *as far as its just and constitutional authority extends; and will be rendered auxiliary to the enforcement of its laws.*" It is hard to imagine a more unequivocal statement that state judicial and executive branch officials may be required to implement federal law where the National Government acts within the scope of its affirmative powers.

The Court makes two unpersuasive attempts to discount the force of this statement. First, according to the majority, because Hamilton mentioned the Supremacy Clause without specifically referring to any "congressional directive," the statement does not mean what it plainly says. But the mere fact that the Supremacy Clause is the source of the obligation of state officials to implement congressional directives does not remotely suggest that they might be "'incorporated into the operations of the national government'" before their obligations have been defined by Congress. Federal law establishes policy for the States just as firmly as laws enacted by state legislatures, but that does not mean that state or federal officials must implement directives that have not been specified in any law. Second, the majority suggests that interpreting this passage to mean what it says would conflict with our decision in New York v. United States. But since the New York opinion did not mention Federalist No. 27, it does not affect either the relevance or the weight of the historical evidence provided by No. 27 insofar as it relates to state courts and magistrates.

Bereft of support in the history of the founding, the Court rests its conclusion on the claim that there is little evidence the National Government actually exercised such a power in the early years of the Republic. This reasoning is misguided in principle and in fact. While we have indicated that the express consideration and resolution of difficult constitutional issues by the First Congress in particular "provides 'contemporaneous and weighty evidence' of the Constitution's meaning since many of [its] Members . . . 'had taken part in framing that instrument,'" Bowsher v. Synar, 478 U.S. 714, 723-724 (1986), we have never suggested that the failure of the early Congresses to address the scope of federal power in a particular area or to exercise a particular authority was an argument against its existence. That position, if correct, would undermine most of our post-New Deal Commerce Clause jurisprudence. As Justice O'Connor quite properly noted in New York, "the Federal Government undertakes activities today that would have been unimaginable to the Framers." 505 U.S. at 157.

More importantly, the fact that Congress did elect to rely on state judges and the clerks of state courts to perform a variety of executive functions, is surely evidence of a contemporary understanding that their status as state officials did not immunize them from federal service. The majority's description of these early statutes is both incomplete and at times misleading.

For example, statutes of the early Congresses required in mandatory terms that state judges and their clerks perform various executive duties with respect to applications for citizenship. The First Congress enacted a statute requiring that the state courts consider such applications, specifying that the state courts "shall administer" an oath of loyalty to the United States, and that "the clerk of such court shall record such application." Act of Mar. 26, 1790. Early legislation passed by the Fifth Congress also imposed reporting requirements relating to naturalization on court clerks, specifying that failure to perform those duties would result in a fine. Act of June 18, 1798. Not long thereafter, the Seventh Congress mandated that state courts maintain a registry of aliens seeking naturalization. Court clerks were required to receive certain information from aliens, record that data, and provide certificates to the aliens; the statute specified fees to be received by local officials in compensation. Act of Apr. 14, 1802.[9] The Court assumes that the imposition of such essentially executive duties on state judges and their clerks sheds no light on the question whether executive officials might have an immunity from federal obligations. Even assuming that the enlistment of state judges in their judicial role for federal purposes is irrelevant to the question whether executive officials may be asked to perform the same function [, the] majority's analysis is badly mistaken.

We are far truer to the historical record by applying a functional approach in assessing the role played by these early state officials. The use of state judges and their clerks to perform executive functions was, in historical context, hardly unusual. As one scholar has noted, "two centuries ago, state and local judges and associated judicial personnel performed many of the functions today performed by executive officers, including such varied tasks as laying city streets and ensuring the seaworthiness of vessels." Caminker, State Sovereignty and Subordinacy: May Congress Commandeer State Officers to Implement Federal Law?, 95 Colum. L. Rev. 1001, 1045, n. 176 (1995). And, of course, judges today continue to perform a variety of functions that may more properly be described as executive. The majority's insistence that this evidence of federal enlistment of state officials to serve executive functions is irrelevant simply because the assistance of "judges" was at issue rests on empty formalistic reasoning of the highest order.

The Court's evaluation of the historical evidence, furthermore, fails to acknowledge the important difference between policy decisions that may have

---

[9] [The] naturalization statutes at issue here, as made clear in the text, were framed in quite mandatory terms. Even the majority only goes so far as to say that "it may well be" that these facially mandatory statutes in fact rested on voluntary state participation. Any suggestion to the contrary is belied by the language of the statutes themselves. . . .

Finally, the Court suggests that the obligation set forth [that] state courts hear federal claims is "voluntary" in that States need not create courts of ordinary jurisdiction. That is true, but unhelpful to the majority. If a State chooses to have no local law enforcement officials it may avoid the Brady Act's requirements, and if it chooses to have no courts it may avoid [the argument that state courts implement Federal law]. But neither seems likely.

been influenced by respect for state sovereignty concerns, and decisions that are compelled by the Constitution.[12] Thus, for example, the decision by Congress to give President Wilson the authority to utilize the services of state officers in implementing the World War I draft surely indicates that the national legislature saw no constitutional impediment to the enlistment of state assistance during a federal emergency. The fact that the President was able to implement the program by respectfully "requesting" state action, rather than bluntly commanding it, is evidence that he was an effective statesman, but surely does not indicate that he doubted either his or Congress' power to use mandatory language if necessary. If there were merit to the Court's appraisal of this incident, one would assume that there would have been some contemporary comment on the supposed constitutional concern that hypothetically might have motivated the President's choice of language.[14]

III

[The] fact that the Framers intended to preserve the sovereignty of the several States simply does not speak to the question whether individual state employees may be required to perform federal obligations.[15]

---

[12] Indeed, an entirely appropriate concern for the prerogatives of state government readily explains Congress' sparing use of this otherwise "highly attractive" power. Congress' discretion, contrary to the majority's suggestion, indicates not that the power does not exist, but rather that the interests of the States are more than sufficiently protected by their participation in the National Government.

[14] Even less probative is the Court's reliance on the decision by Congress to authorize federal marshals to rent temporary jail facilities instead of insisting that state jailkeepers house federal prisoners at federal expense. The majority finds constitutional significance in the fact that the First Congress (apparently following practice appropriate under the Articles of Confederation) had issued a request to state legislatures rather than a command to state jailkeepers, and the further fact that it chose not to change that request to a command 18 months later. The Court does not point us to a single comment by any Member of Congress suggesting that either decision was motivated in the slightest by constitutional doubts. If this sort of unexplained congressional action provides sufficient historical evidence to support the fashioning of judge-made rules of constitutional law, the doctrine of judicial restraint has a brief, though probably colorful, life expectancy.

[15] [Despite] the exhaustive character of the Court's response to this dissent, it has failed to find even an iota of evidence that any of the Framers of the Constitution or any Member of Congress who supported or opposed the statutes discussed in the text ever expressed doubt as to the power of Congress to impose federal responsibilities on local judges or police officers. Even plausible rebuttals of evidence consistently pointing in the other direction are no substitute for affirmative evidence. In short, a neutral historian would have to conclude that the Court's discussion of history does not even begin to establish a prima facie case. [relocated footnote—eds.]

As we explained in [*Garcia*]: "The principal means chosen by the Framers to ensure the role of the States in the federal system lies in the structure of the Federal Government itself. It is no novelty to observe that the composition of the Federal Government was designed in large part to protect the States from over-reaching by Congress." Given the fact that the Members of Congress are elected by the people of the several States, with each State receiving an equivalent number of Senators in order to ensure that even the smallest States have a powerful voice in the legislature, it is quite unrealistic to assume that they will ignore the sovereignty concerns of their constituents. It is far more reasonable to presume that their decisions to impose modest burdens on state officials from time to time reflect a considered judgment that the people in each of the States will benefit therefrom.

Indeed, the presumption of validity that supports all congressional enactments has added force with respect to policy judgments concerning the impact of a federal statute upon the respective States. The majority points to nothing suggesting that the political safeguards of federalism identified in *Garcia* need be supplemented by a rule, grounded in neither constitutional history nor text, flatly prohibiting the National Government from enlisting state and local officials in the implementation of federal law.

Recent developments demonstrate that the political safeguards protecting Our Federalism are effective. The majority expresses special concern that were its rule not adopted the Federal Government would be able to avail itself of the services of state government officials "at no cost to itself. But this specific problem of federal actions that have the effect of imposing so-called "unfunded mandates" on the States has been identified and meaningfully addressed by Congress in recent legislation.[18] See Unfunded Mandates Reform Act of 1995.

---

[18] The majority also makes the more general claim that requiring state officials to carry out federal policy causes states to "take the blame" for failed programs. The Court cites no empirical authority to support the proposition, relying entirely on the speculation of a law review article. This concern is vastly overstated.

Unlike state legislators, local government executive officials routinely take action in response to a variety of sources of authority: local ordinance, state law, and federal law. It doubtless may therefore require some sophistication to discern under which authority an executive official is acting, just as it may not always be immediately obvious what legal source of authority underlies a judicial decision. In both cases, affected citizens must look past the official before them to find the true cause of their grievance. But the majority's rule neither creates nor alters this basic truth.

The problem is of little real consequence in any event, because to the extent that a particular action proves politically unpopular, we may be confident that elected officials charged with implementing it will be quite clear to their constituents where the source of the misfortune lies. These cases demonstrate the point. Sheriffs Printz and Mack have made public statements, including their decisions to serve as plaintiffs in these actions,

The statute was designed "to end the imposition, in the absence of full consideration by Congress, of Federal mandates on State . . . governments without adequate Federal funding, in a manner that may displace other essential State . . . governmental priorities." It functions, inter alia, by permitting Members of Congress to raise an objection by point of order to a pending bill that contains an "unfunded mandate," as defined by the statute, of over $50 million. The mandate may not then be enacted unless the Members make an explicit decision to proceed anyway. Whatever the ultimate impact of the new legislation, its passage demonstrates that unelected judges are better off leaving the protection of federalism to the political process in all but the most extraordinary circumstances.[20]

Perversely, the majority's rule seems more likely to damage than to preserve the safeguards against tyranny provided by the existence of vital state governments. By limiting the ability of the Federal Government to enlist state officials in the implementation of its programs, the Court creates incentives for the National Government to aggrandize itself. In the name of State's rights, the majority would have the Federal Government create vast national bureaucracies to implement its policies. This is exactly the sort of thing that the early Federalists promised would not occur, in part as a result of the National Government's ability to rely on the magistracy of the states.

With colorful hyperbole, the Court suggests that the unity in the Executive Branch of the Federal Government "would be shattered, and the power of the President would be subject to reduction, if Congress could . . . require . . . state officers to execute its laws." Putting to one side the obvious tension between the majority's claim that impressing state police officers will unduly tip the balance of power in favor of the federal sovereign and this suggestion that it will emasculate the Presidency, the Court's reasoning contradicts New York v. United States.

---

denouncing the Brady Act. Indeed, Sheriff Mack has written a book discussing his views on the issue. See R. Mack & T. Walters, From My Cold Dead Fingers: Why America Needs Guns (1994). Moreover, we can be sure that CLEOs will inform disgruntled constituents who have been denied permission to purchase a handgun about the origins of the Brady Act requirements. The Court's suggestion that voters will be confused over who is to "blame" for the statute reflects a gross lack of confidence in the electorate that is at war with the basic assumptions underlying any democratic government.

[20] The initial signs are that the Act will play an important role in curbing the behavior about which the majority expresses concern. In the law's first year, the Congressional Budget Office identified only five bills containing unfounded mandates over the statutory threshold. Of these, one was not enacted into law, and three were modified to limit their effect on the States. The fifth, which was enacted, was scarcely a program of the sort described by the majority at all; it was a generally applicable increase in the minimum wage.

That decision squarely approved of cooperative federalism programs, designed at the national level but implemented principally by state governments. New York disapproved of a particular method of putting such programs into place, not the existence of federal programs implemented locally. Indeed, nothing in the majority's holding calls into question the three mechanisms for constructing such programs that New York expressly approved. [The] majority's suggestion in response to this dissent that Congress' ability to create such programs is limited is belied by the importance and sweep of the federal statutes that meet this description, some of which we described in New York. . . .

Far more important than the concerns that the Court musters in support of its new rule is the fact that the Framers entrusted Congress with the task of creating a working structure of intergovernmental relationships around the framework that the Constitution authorized. Neither explicitly nor implicitly did the Framers issue any command that forbids Congress from imposing federal duties on private citizens or on local officials. As a general matter, Congress has followed the sound policy of authorizing federal agencies and federal agents to administer federal programs. That general practice, however, does not negate the existence of power to rely on state officials in occasional situations in which such reliance is in the national interest. Rather, the occasional exceptions confirm the wisdom of Justice Holmes' reminder that "the machinery of government would not work if it were not allowed a little play in its joints." Bain Peanut Co. of Tex. v. Pinson, 282 U. S. 499, 501 (1931). . . .

* * *

The provision of the Brady Act that crosses the Court's newly defined constitutional threshold is more comparable to a statute requiring local police officers to report the identity of missing children to the Crime Control Center of the Department of Justice than to an offensive federal command to a sovereign state. If Congress believes that such a statute will benefit the people of the Nation, and serve the interests of cooperative federalism better than an enlarged federal bureaucracy, we should respect both its policy judgment and its appraisal of its constitutional power.

Accordingly, I respectfully dissent.

JUSTICE SOUTER, dissenting. . . .

In deciding these cases, which I have found closer than I had anticipated, it is The Federalist that finally determines my position. I believe that the most straightforward reading of No. 27 is authority for the Government's position here, and that this reading is both supported by No. 44 and consistent with Nos. 36 and 45.

Hamilton in No. 27 first notes that because the new Constitution would authorize the National Government to bind individuals directly through national law, it could "employ the ordinary magistracy of each [State] in the execution of its laws." The Federalist No. 27. Were he to stop here, he would not necessarily be speaking of anything beyond the possibility of cooperative arrangements by agreement. But he then addresses the combined effect of the proposed Supremacy Clause, U.S. Const., Art. VI, cl. 2, and state officers's oath requirement, U.S. Const., Art. VI, cl. 3, and he states that "the Legislatures, Courts and Magistrates of the respective members will be incorporated into the operations of the national government, as far as its just and constitutional authority extends; and will be rendered auxiliary to the enforcement of its laws." The natural reading of this language is not merely that the officers of the various branches of state governments may be employed in the performance of national functions; Hamilton says that the state governmental machinery "will be incorporated" into the Nation's operation, and because the "auxiliary" status of the state officials will occur because they are "bound by the sanctity of an oath," I take him to mean that their auxiliary functions will be the products of their obligations thus undertaken to support federal law, not of their own, or the States', unfettered choices.[1]

---

[1] The Court offers two criticisms of this analysis. First, as the Court puts it, the consequences set forth in this passage (that is, rendering state officials "auxiliary" and "incorporating" them into the operations of the Federal Government) "are said . . . to flow automatically from the officers' oath"; from this, the Court infers that on my reading, state officers' obligations to execute federal law must follow "without the necessity for a congressional directive that they implement it." But neither Hamilton nor I use the word "automatically"; consequently, there is no reason on Hamilton's view to infer a state officer's affirmative obligation without a textual indication to that effect. This is just what Justice Stevens says.

Second, the Court reads Federalist No. 27 as incompatible with our decision in New York v. United States, 505 U.S. 144 (1992), and credits me with the imagination to devise a "novel principle of political science [in] order to bring forth disparity of outcome from parity of language"; in order, that is, to salvage New York, by concluding that congress can tell state executive officers what to execute without at the same time having the power to tell state legislators what to legislate. But the Court is too generous. I simply realize that "parity of language" (i.e., all state officials who take the oath are "incorporated" or are "auxiliaries") operates on officers of the three branches in accordance with the quite different powers of their respective branches. The core power of an executive officer is to enforce a law in accordance with its terms; that is why a state executive "auxiliary" may be told what result to bring about. The core power of a legislator acting within the legislature's subject-matter jurisdiction is to make a discretionary decision on what the law should be; that is why a legislator may not be legally ordered to exercise discretion a particular way without damaging the legislative power as such. The discretionary nature of the authorized legislative Act is probably why Madison's two examples of legislative "auxiliary" obligation address the elections of the President and Senators, not the passage of legislation to please Congress.

The Court reads Hamilton's description of state officer's role in carrying out federal law as nothing more than a way of describing the duty of state officials "not to obstruct

Madison in No. 44 supports this reading in his commentary on the oath requirement. He asks why state magistrates should have to swear to support the National Constitution, when national officials will not be required to oblige
themselves to support the state counterparts. His answer is that national officials
"will have no agency in carrying the State Constitutions into effect. The members and officers of the State Governments, on the contrary, will have an essential agency in giving effect to the Federal Constitution." The Federalist No. 44.
He then describes the state legislative "agency" as action necessary for selecting
the President and the choice of Senators. The Supremacy Clause itself, of
course, expressly refers to the state judges' obligations under federal law, and
other numbers of The Federalist give examples of state executive "agency" in
the enforcement of national revenue laws.[2] . . .

---

the operation of federal law," with the consequence that any obstruction is invalid. But I
doubt that Hamilton's English was quite as bad as all that. Someone whose virtue consists of not obstructing administration of the law is not described as "incorporated into the
operations" of a government or as an "auxiliary" to its law enforcement. One simply
cannot escape from Hamilton by reducing his prose to inapposite figures of speech.

[2] The Court reads Madison's No. 44 as supporting its view that Hamilton meant "auxiliaries" to mean merely "nonobstructors." It defends its position in what seems like a
very sensible argument, so long as one does not go beyond the terms set by the Court: if
Madison really thought state executive officials could be required to enforce federal law,
one would have expected him to say so, instead of giving examples of how state officials
(legislative and executive, the Court points out) have roles in the election of national
officials. One might indeed have expected that, save for one remark of Madison's, and a
detail of his language, that the Court ignores. When he asked why state officers should
have to take an oath to support the National Constitution, he said that "several reasons
might be assigned," but that he would "content [himself] with one which is obvious &
conclusive." The Federalist No. 44. The one example he gives describes how state officials will have "an essential agency in giving effect to the Federal Constitution." He was
not talking about executing congressional statutes; he was talking about putting the National Constitution into effect by selecting the executive and legislative members who
would exercise its powers. The answer to the Court's question (and objection), then, is
that Madison was expressly choosing one example of state officer agency, not purporting
to exhaust the examples possible.

There is, therefore, support in Madison's No. 44 for the straightforward reading of
Hamilton's No. 27 and, so, no occasion to discount the authority of Hamilton's views as
expressed in The Federalist as somehow reflecting the weaker side of a split constitutional personality. This, indeed, should not surprise us, for one of the Court's own authorities rejects the "split personality" notion of Hamilton and Madison as being at odds
in The Federalist, in favor of a view of all three Federalist writers as constituting a single
personality notable for its integration:

"In recent years it has been popular to describe Publius [the nominal author of the
Federalist] as a 'split personality' who spoke through Madison as a federalist and an

In the light of all these passages, I cannot persuade myself that the statements from No. 27 speak of anything less than the authority of the National Government, when exercising an otherwise legitimate power (the commerce power, say), to require state "auxiliaries" to take appropriate action. To be sure, it does not follow that any conceivable requirement may be imposed on any state official. I continue to agree, for example, that Congress may not require a state legislature to enact a regulatory scheme and that New York v. United States, 505 U.S. 144 (1992) was rightly decided (even though I now believe its dicta went too far toward immunizing state administration as well as state enactment of such a scheme from congressional mandate); after all, the essence of legislative power, within the limits of legislative jurisdiction, is a discretion not subject to command. But insofar as national law would require nothing from a state officer inconsistent with the power proper to his branch of tripartite state government (say, by obligating a state judge to exercise law enforcement powers), I suppose that the reach of federal law as Hamilton described it would not be exceeded.

[I] do not read any of The Federalist material as requiring the conclusion that Congress could require administrative support without an obligation to pay fair value for it. The quotation from No. 36, for example, describes the United States as paying. If, therefore, my views were prevailing in these cases, I would remand for development and consideration of petitioners' points, that they have no budget provision for work required under the Act and are liable for unauthorized expenditures.

JUSTICE BREYER, with whom JUSTICE STEVENS joins, dissenting.

I would add to the reasons Justice Stevens sets forth the fact that the United States is not the only nation that seeks to reconcile the practical need for a cen-

---

exponent of limited government, but through Hamilton as a nationalist and an admirer of energetic government. . . . Neither the diagnosis of tension between Hamilton and Madison nor the indictment of each man for self-contradiction strikes me as a useful of perhaps even fair-minded exercise. Publius was, on any large view—the only correct view to take of an effort so sprawling in size and concentrated in time— a remarkably 'whole personality,' and I am far more impressed by the large area of agreement between Hamilton and Madison than by the differences in emphasis that have been read into rather than in their papers.... The intellectual tensions of The Federalist and its creators are in fact an honest reflection of those built into the Constitution it expounds and the polity it celebrates." C. Rossiter, Alexander Hamilton and the Constitution 58 (1964).

While Hamilton and Madison went their separate ways in later years, and may have had differing personal views, the passages from The Federalist discussed here show no sign of strain.

tral authority with the democratic virtues of more local control. At least some other countries, facing the same basic problem, have found that local control is better maintained through application of a principle that is the direct opposite of the principle the majority derives from the silence of our Constitution. The federal systems of Switzerland, Germany, and the European Union, for example, all provide that constituent states, not federal bureaucracies, will themselves implement many of the laws, rules, regulations, or decrees enacted by the central "federal" body. Lenaerts, Constitutionalism and the Many Faces of   Federalism, 38 Am. J. Comp. L. 205, 237 (1990); D. Currie, The Constitution of the Federal Republic of Germany 66, 84 (1994); Mackenzie-Stuart, Foreword, Comparative Constitutional Federalism: Europe and America ix (M. Tushnet ed. 1990); Kimber, A Comparison of Environmental Federalism in the United States and the European Union, 54 Md. L. Rev. 1658, 1675-1677 (1995). They do so in part because they believe that such a system interferes less, not more, with the independent authority of the "state," member nation, or other subsidiary government, and helps to safeguard individual liberty as well.

Of course, we are interpreting our own Constitution, not those of other nations, and there may be relevant political and structural differences between their systems and our own. But their experience may nonetheless cast an empirical light on the consequences of different solutions to a common legal problem — in this case the problem of reconciling central authority with the need to preserve the liberty-enhancing autonomy of a smaller constituent governmental entity. And that experience here offers empirical confirmation of the implied answer to a question Justice Stevens asks: Why, or how, would what the majority sees as a constitutional alternative — the creation of a new federal gun-law bureaucracy, or the expansion of an existing federal bureaucracy — better promote either state sovereignty or individual liberty?

As comparative experience suggests, there is no need to interpret the Constitution as containing an absolute principle — forbidding the assignment of virtually any federal duty to any state official. Nor is there a need to read the Brady Act as permitting the Federal Government to overwhelm a state civil service. The statute uses the words "reasonable effort" — words that easily can encompass the considerations of, say, time or cost, necessary to avoid any such result. . . .

Note: Constitutional Interpretation in Printz

1. *The role of text and original understanding.* Consider the following argument: The Constitution's text should be interpreted in light of the understandings widely shared among the people of the United States, who, in ratifying the Constitution, gave it legal effect. Courts appropriately examine any materials

that shed light on those understandings. The Federalist Papers were a set of newspaper articles written by the Constitution's supporters, designed to persuade New York's voters that they should ratify the Constitution. They were not widely distributed outside of New York, but New York was a crucial state for securing the Constitution's ratification. Courts should therefore (cautiously) rely on The Federalist Papers in interpreting the Constitution. Are the Court's and Justice Souter's uses of The Federalist Papers consistent with this argument? Note that Justice Scalia did not join a section of the Court's opinion in City of Boerne v. Flores, section E supra in this Supplement,   discussing the drafting history of the Fourteenth Amendment. Is his discussion of The Federalist Papers in *Printz* consistent with the position he took there?

2. *Defending* Printz. Roderick M. Hills, Jr., The Political Economy of Cooperative Federalism: Why State Autonomy Makes Sense and Dual Sovereignty Doesn't, 96 Mich. L. Rev. 813, 819-821 (1998), defends the entitlement *Printz* gives states to refuse to comply with federal directives (unless they choose to do so), on functional grounds:

> The federal government should commandeer the services of nonfederal governments no more than it should commandeer the services of private organizations or persons. [It] is *unnecessary* [because] the federal government can purchase the services of state and local governments whenever it is cost-effective to do so. [There] is a vigorous intergovernmental marketplace in which municipalities, countries, and states [compete] with each other for the chance to obtain federal revenue. [Whenever] the national government values such services enough to pay nonfederal governments the costs of providing them, the national government can obtain the cooperation of state or local governments. [When] the government conscripts specific types of private services, [it] can inefficiently discourage private persons [from] investing resources in the production of such services. [These] same considerations suggest that the federal government ought not to conscript services [from] nonfederal governments. [One] would expect such demands inefficiently to discourage involvement in state and local politics.

Compare Vicki C. Jackson, Federalism and the Uses and Limits of Law: *Printz* and Principle?, 111 Harv. L. Rev. 2180 (1998), which argues for a strong presumption against "commandeering" state legislative action, and a much weaker presumption against commandeering state executive officials. "[Judicial] enforcement [against] collective bodies [poses] difficulties less likely to be present in the enforcement of orders against the executive or judicial officials. [There] is a close association [between voting] and speech; compelled voting by legislative representatives [bears] a disquieting similarity to governmentally compelled speech. [Legislatures] are more closely bound up with public understandings of self-government than either executive officers or courts. Compelled legislation may therefore have greater potential for voter confusion than mandates directed to other branches of state government." Id. at 2251. "[Courts] could adopt a presumption that federal directives to state legislatures are not 'Necessary and Proper' if the same goal can be accomplished through other means, such as direct federal legislation. It is hard to imagine circumstances in which national purposes could be served only by requiring state legislatures to adopt federally mandated legislation. [It] is less difficult to imagine circumstances in which a national purpose could be well served only by utilizing available state or local law enforcement officers. [An] important or legitimate governmental interest test might be imposed. [Constitutional] inquiry might consider the size of the burden or amount of state time and resources needed to perform the federally mandated tasks—thereby permitting distinctions between relatively minor recordkeeping [and] more substantial impositions on state resources involving matters that [come] close to the core of legislative responsibilities." Id. at 2253-54. Does this proposed balancing approach underestimate the benefits of the Court's clear doctrinal standard in providing guidance to Congress (and lower court judges)?

3. *The role of comparative law.* Consider the following arguments: In the absence of controlling constitutional text, courts appropriately make considerations of policy one factor in determining the Constitution's meaning. Examining constitutional experience elsewhere may illuminate the relevant policy considerations. Alternatively, in the absence of controlling constitutional text, courts should interpret the Constitution in a manner consistent with its basic structure. But structural considerations often fail to determine precisely which of many possible structures is most consistent with the U.S. Constitution. Examining constitutional experience elsewhere may illuminate the choice among alternative reasonable specifications of the U.S. Constitution's structure. Are the Court's and Justice Breyer's discussions of comparative constitutional law consistent with either of these arguments?

4. *Condon.* Reno v. Condon, 120 S.Ct. 666 (2000), upheld the federal Driver's Privacy Protection Act. The Act regulates the disclosure of personal information in the records of state motor vehicles departments. Some states had received substantial income from sales of such information to commercial enterprises. The Act prohibits state officials from disclosing "personal information" such as a person's photograph, name and address, and medical or disability information, unless the driver consents to the disclosure. The Act requires disclosure of personal information, however, in connection with "matters of motor vehicle or driver safety or threat, motor vehicle emissions," and automobile recalls, and it permits disclosure under some other circumstances. The Act also regulates the resale and redisclosure of drivers' personal information by private

entities that lawfully received the information from a state motor vehicles department.

Writing for a unanimous Court, Chief Justice Rehnquist first concluded that the information at issue was "an article of commerce." The Court rejected the argument that the statute violated the anti-commandeering principle even though the statute "will require time and effort on the part of state employees." "[The] DPPA does not require the States in their sovereign capacity to regulate their own citizens. The DPPA regulates the States as the owners of databases. It does not require the South Carolina Legislature to enact any laws or regulations, and it does not require state officials to assist in the enforcement of federal statutes regulating private individuals." The Court also concluded that the statute was "generally applicable" and did not regulate the states exclusively, because it "regulates the universe of entities that participate as suppliers to the market for motor vehicle information—the States as initial suppliers [and] private resellers."

Does *Condon* make dispositive the distinction between states acting "in their sovereign capacities" and states acting in some other capacity? If so, why is the sale of information to enhance state revenues (and reduce the need to rely on taxes) not an act taken in the states' sovereign capacity? The statute compels state officials to *refrain* from taking certain actions, in the service of a federal policy. What is there in the principles articulated in *New York* and *Printz* that supports a distinction between compelled action and compelled inaction, both in the service of federal rather than state policy?

Note: The Second Amendment

The Second Amendment, unusually for federal constitutional provisions, contains a statement of purpose as well as a guarantee of a right to bear arms. This combination has caused controversy: What is the connection between the right to bear arms and the purpose of maintaining a well-regulated militia? What is a well-regulated militia? Disputes over the amendment's interpretation can be described as centering on the choice between saying that the amendment confers an individual right, held by every person without regard to his or her participation in or connection with an organized and well-regulated militia, or saying that it confers a collective right, held by the people collectively in connection with such participation.

The Supreme Court has rarely interpreted the Second Amendment. United States v. Miller, 307 U.S. 174 (1939), the Court's most recent decision, upheld the constitutionality of a national ban on the possession of an unregistered sawed-off shotgun. The Supreme Court held that the Second Amendment did not protect possession of weapons that were not shown to have a "reasonable relationship to the preservation or efficiency of a well-regulated militia." Lower courts are essentially unanimous in holding that the Second Amendment does not confer an individual right. (How much weight should that fact have if the Supreme Court were to take up the question raised by Justice Thomas's concurrence in *Printz*?)

Proponents of the competing interpretations agree that the amendment was designed to guard against the possibility that the national government would overreach its authority and need to be checked, by military force if necessary. Proponents of the "collective right" interpretation treat the amendment as complementing federalism-based limits on national power. They argue that well-regulated militias were those under the control of state governments and that the amendment therefore does not confer individual rights. Their critics point out that the contemporary version of state-organized militias is the National Guard, which may by statute be taken over by national authority. The National Guard, they argue, therefore cannot serve the intended function of state-organized militias. Because there is no contemporary analogue of state-organized militias as the Framers understood them, the amendment should today be interpreted to confer an individual right. Is this an example of an appropriate translation of provisions written in the 18th century into modern terms?

Proponents of the "individual rights" interpretation also argue that the Second Amendment uses the same term — "the right of the people" — that the First Amendment does and that everyone agrees that the First Amendment confers an individual right. (They also point out that the phrase "the right of the people" is used in the Fourth and Ninth Amendments, where it also appears to refer to individual rights.) They also rely on the tradition of civic republicanism (see casebook p. 5), which, in their view, made the citizen's ability to join with others to resist government overreaching by force of arms a central feature of active citizenship. Their critics argue, in contrast, that the tradition of civic republicanism developed in a society lacking substantial democratic participation in government, through elected representatives responsive to the people. Under modern circumstances elections and free speech reduce the risk of governmental overreaching to the point where an individual right of armed resistance is unnecessary. Some argue, as well, that the conditions making civic republicanism a coherent theory of society, such as widespread equality in economic condition and widespread commitment to and action in accordance with ideas of civic virtue, are absent in today's society, making it inappropriate to rely on civic republicanism to justify an interpretation of the Second Amendment. Is this an example of an appropriate translation of provisions written in the 18th century into modern terms?

If the courts were to recognize an individual right to bear arms, they would then have to determine what statutes infringe the right. Should they adopt a stringent standard, analogous to the one applied to certain forms of regulation of expression, or a loose one, analogous to the one applied to other forms of regulation of expression and to regulation of economic activities? On what basis should that choice be made?

State regulations of firearms would be subject to the Second Amendment only if the Court held that its provisions were "incorporated" in the Fourteenth Amendment. If the "individual rights" interpretation rests on ideas about civic republicanism, how much weight should be placed on the fact that by the time the Fourteenth Amendment was ratified the civic republican tradition had become substantially less important in the society than it had been when the original Constitution and the Bill of Rights were ratified?

There is a substantial academic literature on the Second Amendment. Some of the leading works are J. Malcolm, To Keep and Bear Arms: The Origins of an Anglo-American Right (1994); S. Halbrook, That Every Man Be Armed, The Evolution of a Constitutional Right (1984); Van Alstyne, The Second Amendment and the Personal Right to Arms, 43 Duke L. J. 1236 (1994); Cottrol & Diamond, The Second Amendment: Toward an Afro-Americanist Reconsideration, 80 Geo. L. J. 309 (1991); Levinson, The Embarrassing Second Amendment, 99 Yale L. J. 637 (1989); Williams, Civic Republicanism and the Citizen Militia: The Terrifying Second Amendment, 101 Yale L. J. 551 (1991); Powe, Guns, Words, and Constitutional Interpretation, 38 William & Mary L.Rev. 1311 (1997).

3
JUDICIAL EFFORTS TO PROTECT THE EXPANSION OF THE MARKET AGAINST ASSERTIONS OF LOCAL POWER

A. *The Fundamental Framework*

Page 291.   The correct date for Cooley v. Board of Port Wardens is 1852.

Page 298.   At the end of the Note, add the following:

4. *A preliminary overview.* Michael A. Lawrence, Toward a More Coherent Dormant Commerce Clause: A Proposed Unitary Framework, 21 Harv. J.L. & Pub. Pol'y 395, 416-17 (1998), proposes the following analysis: If the statute is facially discriminatory, it is "virtually *per se* invalid. The State has the heavy burden of proving that the measure is virtually certain to achieve its legitimate purpose and that the purpose cannot be served as well by available *less* discriminatory means." Statutes with discriminatory purposes are per se invalid; challengers must establish the impermissible purpose. If the statutes are applied evenhandedly to both in-state and out-of-state commerce, they are constitutional unless the challenger shows that the statute's burden on interstate commerce "is clearly excessive in relation to state benefits." "Where a measure imposes a burden *mostly*, although not exclusively, on out-of-state interests, the State has the burden of justifying that the measure is likely to achieve its legitimate purpose; the challenger then has the burden of either rebutting the State's justification or of showing that the purpose can be served as well by available nondiscrimina-

tory [alternatives.] Where the measure imposes a burden *exclusively* on out-of-state interests, the State has the burden of proving that the measure is *highly* likely to achieve its legitimate purpose *and* that the purpose cannot be served as well by available nondiscriminatory alternatives." Does this accurately describe the Court's decisions, particularly those dealing with statutes that are not facially discriminatory? Are the decisions compatible with any of the theoretical approaches described in this Note?

B. Protection against Discrimination

Page 316.   At the end of section 2 of the Note, add the following:

Heinzerling, The Commercial Constitution, 1996 Sup. Ct. Rev. 217, argues that the Court's unwillingness to assess the costs of outside commerce "on account of its outsider status" distorts its cost-benefit calculations. She argues that in-state residents believe that outside commerce imposes costs because it is "intrusive" and "forced" on the in-staters, and that these are as much costs of the outside commerce as the "statistical risk of physical harm" with which the Court's analysis is exclusively concerned: "'Dangerousness' and 'cost' do not [include] the qualitative attributes of risk."

Page 319.   After section 7 of the Note, add the following:

8. *Are the regulated subjects "the same"?* General Motors Corp. v. Tracy, 117 S. Ct. 811 (1997), discussed a question the Court said often "remained dormant" in dormant commerce clause cases: whether the subjects treated differently were "substantially similar." The question matters because "the difference in products may mean that the different entities serve different markets and would continue to do so even if the supposedly discriminatory burden were removed. If in fact that should be the case, eliminating the tax or other regulatory differential would not serve the dormant Commerce Clause's fundamental objective of preserving a national market for competition undisturbed by preferential advantages conferred by a State upon its residents or resident competitors." The Court then engaged in a detailed analysis of the market for natural gas products. Can an argument be developed in each of the cases in this section that the subjects were not substantially similar because they served different markets?

Page 323.   At the end of section 1 of the Note, add the following:

Dan T. Coenen, Business Subsidies and the Dormant Commerce Clause, 107 Yale L.J. 965, 985-992 (1998), enumerates a number of functional distinctions between direct subsidies and tax breaks:

> [A] state's imposition of costs on its citizens is more visible when the state awards outright subsidies than when it doles out tax relief. [The] extent of cost [is] more readily perceptible when the state's support of local industry takes the form of a monetary subsidy [because] the total amount of subsidy payments can be determined through the easy means of tallying total payments [whereas] tax expenditures are made [passively.] [Tax] credits, exemptions, and the like are resistant to repeal because legislatures typically enact them as presumptively permanent features of state tax codes. In contrast, because subsidies involve the direct expenditure of funds, they routinely show up—and are subject to recurring reevaluation—as expense items in perennially controversial state budget bills. [Tax] breaks [have] an open-ended, unrestricted quality. [Subsidy] programs are usually more costly for the state to administer. [Cash] subsidies are less likely than discriminatory tax breaks to take hold and to persist because most people view tax structures [as] an esoteric specialty beyond their capability and willingness to understand. [Tax] breaks are more likely to gain acceptance because citizens do not perceive them as taking away that which those citizens see as already being their own or as channeling scarce state funds to competing [claimants.]

Coenen develops criteria for determining when a subsidy is closely enough linked to a discriminatory tax break to make the subsidy unconstitutional.

Consider this summary: Existing doctrine "create[s] the following modified process-reinforcing regime: When the costs of a potential state policy will be shared between an organized but out-of-state interest group and a diffuse group of local residents, the courts will presume that the diffuse locals will virtually represent the out-of-state interests against the policy when the policy requires an expenditure of tax dollars, but they will not so presume when the policy is implemented through regulation alone." Korobkin, The Local Politics of Acid Rain: Public Versus Private Decisionmaking and the Dormant Commerce Clause in a New Era of Environmental Law, 75 B.U. L. Rev. 689, 756 (1995). Why are the diffuse interests of taxpayers better able to represent out-of-state interests than the diffuse interests of consumers affected by higher prices due to regulation?

For a discussion of the distinction between tax incentives and subsidies, see Hellerstein & Coenen, Commerce Clause Restraints on State Business Development Incentives, 81 Cornell L. Rev. 789 (1996). It argues that tax incentives are unconstitutional if they "favor in-state over out-of-state activities" and "implicate the coercive powers of the state." Although subsidies are not dramatically different in economic terms from tax incentives, there should be a presumption that subsidies are constitutional. The reason is that form matters: "[Consideration] of a subsidy forces the mind of the public body to consider most pointedly the cost and consequences of moving forward."

For a related discussion, see Camps Newfound/Owatonna, Inc. v. Town of Harrison, 117 S. Ct. 1590 (1997). Holding unconstitutional a tax statute that exempted property owned by local charitable organizations but denied the exemption to organizations operated principally for nonresidents, the Court first concluded that the statute would violate the commerce clause if it were targeted at profit-making organizations because it encouraged them "to limit their out-of-state clientele" in a way that would lead to economic Balkanization. It was "functionally [an] export tariff that targets out-of-state customers by taxing the businesses that principally serve them." Relying on New Energy Co. of Ind. v. Limbach, the Court then rejected the argument that the tax exemption amounted to a permissible "discriminatory subsidy." Even if such subsidies were constitutional, discriminatory tax exemptions were not. Precedent aside, is there any reason for such a distinction? Justices Scalia and Thomas and Chief Justice Rehnquist dissented.

Walter Hellerstein, Commerce Clause Restraints on State Tax Incentives, 82 Minn. L. Rev. 413 (1997), suggests a distinction between coercive and noncoercive tax incentives, to be determined with reference to practical effects and economic realities. Is this in tension with the recent tendency to reject "balancing" and similar tests?

Page 338. After section 2 of the Note, add the following:

2A. *Recent case*: Lunding v. New York Tax Appeals Tribunal, 118 S. Ct. 766 (1988), held that a statute that effectively denied only nonresident taxpayers deduction from the state income tax for alimony they paid violated the Privileges and Immunities Clause.

D. Preemption

Page 383. As new subsection 4a of the Note, add the following:

4a. *Recent case*: Medtronic, Inc. v. Lohr, 116 S. Ct. 2240 (1996), held that the federal statute establishing a process for allowing medical devices on to the market if they were substantially equivalent to devices marketed before 1976 did not preempt state tort causes of action for injuries due to negligent design, failure to comply with federal regulations, and negligent manufacturing and labelling. The federal statute's express preemption provision states: "[No] State [may] establish or continue in effect [any] requirement which is different from, or in addition to, any requirement applicable under this chapter to the device, and [which] relates to the safety or effectiveness of the device." Justice Breyer concurred in the result. Justice O'Connor, joined by Chief Justice Rehnquist and Justices Scalia and Thomas, dissented.

See also Crosby v. National Foreign Trade Council, 530 U.S. — (2000), which relied on a statute delegating broad power to the President to devise a strategy for imposing economic sanctions on Burma to induce it to improve its human rights performance as the basis for finding preempted a Massachusetts statute barring the state government's departments from buying goods or services from companies doing business with Burma. The state statute, the Court held, stood as an obstacle to the accomplishment of the federal statute's purposes, and was inconsistent with Congress's purpose of ensuring that the President would have flexibility in devising strategies for inducing Burma to improve its performance.

4

THE DISTRIBUTION OF
NATIONAL POWERS

A. *Introduction*

Page 390.   Before section 3 of the Note, add the following:

2a. A caveat. Perhaps it is misleading to attribute any overriding function to the Constitution's separation of powers provisions that explains and rationalizes all of the choices made by the framers. Consider Tushnet, The Possibilities of Comparative Constitutional Law, 108 Yale L.J. 1225, 1299-1300 (1999):

> [The] Constitution's provisions dealing with the presidency took their shape from a series of compromises. Had the drafters had more time, some issues that had been provisionally resolved might have been reopened. But, facing the need to get the job done, the drafters simply stopped when time expired. . . .
>
> The conditions under which constitutions are written makes it likely that they will be constitutions of principle with respect to broad [themes] and constitutions of compromise with respect to the details. Under the pressure of time and the need for political compromise, a constitution's drafters are likely to latch on to whatever solution is near at hand to the immediate problems they face. [Thinking] about constitution-making [in this way] casts doubt on a form of textualism that attributes to the constitution's writers a purpose of creating a tightly integrated document governed by a form of conceptual determinism. The compromises and sheer randomness found in the constitution-making process suggests that it would be wrong to think of the writers as having so highly rationalized an understanding of their work as this form of textualism attributes to them.

Page 391.   At the end of section 4 of the Note, add
the following:

For an interesting and subtle discussion of these and other issues, see Ackerman, The New Separation of Powers, 113 Harv. L. Rev. 634 (2000). Ackerman argues in favor of what he calls "constrained parliamentarianism," which combines the British model of a unified legislative and executive branch with various constraints on parliamentary supremacy.

In Ackerman's view, the American system of separation of powers leads to various predictable pathologies. Much of the time, the legislative and executive branches will be in different hands. When this happens, the opposing parties may reach accommodation—a result that Ackerman calls the "Madisonian hope." There are other, less attractive possibilities, however. Divided government may produce a constitutional breakdown—a frequent occurrence in Latin America, where frustrated presidents disband recalcitrant legislatures and establish themselves as dictators. A less dramatic, but still pathological, outcome is a "crisis in governability," in which there is "endless backbiting, mutual recrimination, and partisan deadlock."

Of course, these pathologies can be avoided on occasions when the same party manages to control all the branches of government. On these occasions, however, the ruling party will feel pressure to enact its program quickly before it loses control. Perhaps more significantly, it will look for ways to entrench its program so that the program will survive loss of power in a branch of government. Ackerman claims that these pressures cause politicians to enact programs that emphasize symbolic statements and practical entrenchment at the expense of "middle-range efficacy." In contrast, in a parliamentary system, the ruling party knows that there is no possibility of entrenchment if it loses the next election. It will therefore feel pressure to enact programs that make a practical difference over the shorter run, thereby preventing electoral defeat.

Despite these advantages of parliamentarianism, Ackerman is uncomfortable with granting unconstrained power to the ruling party on the basis of victory in a single election. He therefore couples his endorsement of parliamentarianism with proposals for various, external methods of constraining parliamentary power. Among the devices he proposes are popular referenda (which could be enacted only if passed repeatedly in a series of electoral tests) and a constitutional court exercising a strong form of judicial review.

B. A Case Study: Presidential Seizure

Page 406. After the second full paragraph, add the following:

Consider Eskridge, Relationships between Formalism and Functionalism in Separation of Powers Cases, 22 Harv. J.L. & Pub. Pol'y 21, 24 (1998):

The warring majorities in the Steel Seizure Case suggest [that] formalism and functionalism are frequently [interconnected]. They are a "both-and" inquiry, rather than an "either-or" inquiry. Because state legitimacy depends upon both formal rule-following and functional efficacy, constitutional reasoning pervasively, and often unconsciously, melds formalist and functionalist justifications.

C. Domestic Affairs

Page 419.   Before subsection 2b of the Note, add the following:

*Clinton v. Jones**
117 S. Ct. 1636 (1997)

JUSTICE STEVENS delivered the opinion of the Court.

This case raises a constitutional and a prudential question concerning the Office of the President of the United States. Respondent, a private citizen, seeks to recover damages from the current occupant of that office based on actions allegedly taken before his term began. The President submits that in all but the most exceptional cases the Constitution requires federal courts to defer such litigation until his term ends and that, in any event, respect for the office warrants such a stay. Despite the force of the arguments supporting the President's submissions, we conclude that they must be rejected.

I

[Jones alleged that in 1991, while Clinton was Governor of Arkansas and Jones was an employee of the Arkansas Industrial Development Commission, he enticed her to a hotel room, where he made "abhorrent" sexual advances toward her. She further claimed that her superiors at work subsequently dealt with her in a hostile and rude manner and changed her duties to punish her for rejecting those advances. Her complaint alleged that this conduct violated federal and state law, and sought monetary damages. In response to Clinton's motion, the District Court held that trial of the action should be delayed until the conclusion of Clinton's term. However, the trial court held that there was no reason to delay

---

* For purposes of full disclosure, we note that one of the coauthors of this casebook represented President Clinton in this matter.

discovery in conjunction with the suit. The Court of Appeals reversed the trial court's ruling insofar as it delayed the trial.]

IV

Petitioner's principal submission—that "in all but the most exceptional cases," the Constitution affords the President temporary immunity from civil damages litigation arising out of events that occurred before he took office—cannot be sustained on the basis of precedent. . . .

The principal rationale for affording certain public servants immunity from suits for money damages arising out of their official acts is inapplicable to unofficial conduct. In cases involving prosecutors, legislators, and judges we have repeatedly explained that the immunity serves the public interest in enabling such officials to perform their designated functions effectively without fear that a particular decision may give rise to personal liability. . . .

This reasoning provides no support for an immunity for unofficial conduct. As we explained in Fitzgerald, "the sphere of protected action must be related closely to the immunity's justifying purposes." Because of the President's broad responsibilities, we recognized in that case an immunity from damages claims arising out of official acts extending to the "outer perimeter of his authority." But we have never suggested that the President, or any other official, has an immunity that extends beyond the scope of any action taken in an official capacity. . . .

VI

Petitioner's strongest argument supporting his immunity claim is based on the text and structure of the Constitution. He does not contend that the occupant of the Office of the President is "above the law," in the sense that his conduct is entirely immune from judicial scrutiny. The President argues merely for a postponement of the judicial proceedings that will determine whether he violated any law. His argument is grounded in the character of the office that was created by Article II of the Constitution, and relies on separation of powers principles that have structured our constitutional arrangement since the founding.

As a starting premise, petitioner contends that he occupies a unique office with powers and responsibilities so vast and important that the public interest demands that he devote his undivided time and attention to his public duties. He submits that—given the nature of the office—the doctrine of separation of powers places limits on the authority of the Federal Judiciary to interfere with the Executive Branch that would be transgressed by allowing this action to proceed.

We have no dispute with the initial premise of the argument. Former presidents, from George Washington to George Bush, have consistently endorsed petitioner's characterization of the office. [We] have [long] recognized the "unique position in the constitutional scheme" that this office occupies. [Fitzgerald]. Thus, while we suspect that even in our modern era there remains some truth to Chief Justice Marshall's suggestion that the duties of the Presidency are not entirely "unremitting," United States v. Burr, 25 F. Cas. 30, 34 (CC Va. 1807), we accept the initial premise of the Executive's argument.

It does not follow, however, that separation of powers principles would be violated by allowing this action to proceed. The doctrine of separation of powers is concerned with the allocation of official power among the three co-equal branches of our Government. The Framers "built into the tripartite Federal Government . . . a self-executing safeguard against the encroachment or aggrandizement of one branch at the expense of the other." Buckley v. Valeo, 424 U.S. at 122 n30. . . .

Of course the lines between the powers of the three branches are not always neatly defined. But in this case there is no suggestion that the Federal Judiciary is being asked to perform any function that might in some way be described as "executive." Respondent is merely asking the courts to exercise their core Article III jurisdiction to decide cases and controversies. Whatever the outcome of this case, there is no possibility that the decision will curtail the scope of the official powers of the Executive Branch. The litigation of questions that relate entirely to the unofficial conduct of the individual who happens to be the President poses no perceptible risk of misallocation of either judicial power or executive power.

Rather than arguing that the decision of the case will produce either an aggrandizement of judicial power or a narrowing of executive power, petitioner contends that—as a by-product of an otherwise traditional exercise of judicial power—burdens will be placed on the President that will hamper the performance of his official duties. We have recognized that "even when a branch does not arrogate power to itself . . . the separation-of-powers doctrine requires that a branch not impair another in the performance of its constitutional duties." Loving v. United States, 517 U.S. — (1996) (slip op. at 8). As a factual matter, petitioner contends that this particular case—as well as the potential additional litigation that an affirmance of the Court of Appeals judgment might spawn— may impose an unacceptable burden on the President's time and energy, and thereby impair the effective performance of his office.

Petitioner's predictive judgment finds little support in either history or the relatively narrow compass of the issues raised in this particular case. [In] the more than 200-year history of the Republic, only three sitting Presidents have been subjected to suits for their private actions. If the past is any indicator, it seems unlikely that a deluge of such litigation will ever engulf the Presidency.

As for the case at hand, if properly managed by the District Court, it appears to us highly unlikely to occupy any substantial amount of petitioner's time.

Of greater significance, petitioner errs by presuming that interactions between the Judicial Branch and the Executive, even quite burdensome interactions, necessarily rise to the level of constitutionally forbidden impairment of the Executive's ability to perform its constitutionally mandated functions. "Our . . . system imposes upon the Branches a degree of overlapping responsibility, a duty of interdependence as well as independence the absence of which 'would preclude the establishment of a Nation capable of governing itself effectively.'" [Mistretta, (quoting Buckley)]. As Madison explained, separation of powers does not mean that the branches "ought to have no partial agency in, or no control over the acts of each other." The fact that a federal court's exercise of its traditional Article III jurisdiction may significantly burden the time and attention of the Chief Executive is not sufficient to establish a violation of the Constitution. Two long-settled propositions, first announced by Chief Justice Marshall, support that conclusion.

First, we have long held that when the President takes official action, the Court has the authority to determine whether he has acted within the law. Perhaps the most dramatic example of such a case is our holding that President Truman exceeded his constitutional authority when he issued an order directing the Secretary of Commerce to take possession of and operate most of the Nation's steel mills in order to avert a national catastrophe. [Youngstown]. Despite the serious impact of that decision on the ability of the Executive Branch to accomplish its assigned mission, and the substantial time that the President must necessarily have devoted to the matter as a result of judicial involvement, we exercised our Article III jurisdiction to decide whether his official conduct conformed to the law. Our holding was an application of the principle established in Marbury that "it is emphatically the province and duty of the judicial department to say what the law is."

Second, it is also settled that the President is subject to judicial process in appropriate circumstances. Although Thomas Jefferson apparently thought otherwise, Chief Justice Marshall, when presiding in the treason trial of Aaron Burr, ruled that a subpoena duces tecum could be directed to the President. United States v. Burr, 25 F. Cas. 30 (No. 14,692d) (CC Va. 1807). We unequivocally and emphatically endorsed Marshall's position when we held that President Nixon was obligated to comply with a subpoena commanding him to produce certain tape recordings of his conversations with his aides. . . .

Sitting Presidents have responded to court orders to provide testimony and other information with sufficient frequency that such interactions between the Judicial and Executive Branches can scarcely be thought a novelty. President Monroe responded to written interrogatories, President Nixon — as noted above —produced tapes in response to a subpoena duces tecum, President Ford complied with an order to give a deposition in a criminal trial, and President Clinton has twice given videotaped testimony in criminal proceedings. Moreover, sitting Presidents have also voluntarily complied with judicial requests for testimony. President Grant gave a lengthy deposition in a criminal case under such circumstances, and President Carter similarly gave videotaped testimony for use at a criminal trial. . . .

VII

The Court of Appeals described the District Court's discretionary decision to stay the trial as the "functional equivalent" of a grant of temporary immunity. Concluding that petitioner was not constitutionally entitled to such an immunity, the court held that it was error to grant the stay. Although we ultimately conclude that the stay should not have been granted, we think the issue is more difficult than the opinion of the Court of Appeals suggests.

Strictly speaking, the stay was not the functional equivalent of the constitutional immunity that petitioner claimed, because the District Court ordered discovery to proceed. Moreover, a stay of either the trial or discovery might be justified by considerations that do not require the recognition of any constitutional immunity. The District Court has broad discretion to stay proceedings as an incident to its power to control its own docket. As we have explained, "especially in cases of extraordinary public moment, [a plaintiff] may be required to submit to delay not immoderate in extent and not oppressive in its consequences if the public welfare or convenience will thereby be promoted." Although we have rejected the argument that the potential burdens on the President violate separation of powers principles, those burdens are appropriate matters for the District Court to evaluate in its management of the case. The high respect that is owed to the office of the Chief Executive, though not justifying a rule of categorical immunity, is a matter that should inform the conduct of the entire proceeding, including the timing and scope of discovery.

Nevertheless, we are persuaded that it was an abuse of discretion for the District Court to defer the trial until after the President leaves office. Such a lengthy and categorical stay takes no account whatever of the respondent's interest in bringing the case to trial. The complaint was filed within the statutory limitations period—albeit near the end of that period—and delaying trial would increase the danger of prejudice resulting from the loss of evidence, including the inability of witnesses to recall specific facts, or the possible death of a party.

The decision to postpone the trial was, furthermore, premature. The proponent of a stay bears the burden of establishing its need. In this case, at the stage at which the District Court made its ruling, there was no way to assess whether a stay of trial after the completion of discovery would be warranted. Other than the fact that a trial may consume some of the President's time and attention, there is nothing in the record to enable a judge to assess the potential harm that may ensue from scheduling the trial promptly after discovery is concluded. We think the District Court may have given undue weight to the concern that a trial might generate unrelated civil actions that could conceivably hamper the President in conducting the duties of his office. If and when that should occur, the court's discretion would permit it to manage those actions in such fashion (including deferral of trial) that interference with the President's duties would not occur. But no such impingement upon the President's conduct of his office was shown here.

VIII

We add a final comment on two matters that are discussed at length in the briefs: the risk that our decision will generate a large volume of politically motivated harassing and frivolous litigation, and the danger that national security concerns might prevent the President from explaining a legitimate need for a continuance.

We are not persuaded that either of these risks is serious. Most frivolous and vexatious litigation is terminated at the pleading stage or on summary judgment, with little if any personal involvement by the defendant. Moreover, the availability of sanctions provides a significant deterrent to litigation directed at the President in his unofficial capacity for purposes of political gain or harassment. History indicates that the likelihood that a significant number of such cases will be filed is remote. Although scheduling problems may arise, there is no reason to assume that the District Courts will be either unable to accommodate the President's needs or unfaithful to the tradition — especially in matters involving national security — of giving "the utmost deference to Presidential responsibilities." Several Presidents, including petitioner, have given testimony without jeopardizing the Nation's security. In short, we have confidence in the ability of our federal judges to deal with both of these concerns.

If Congress deems it appropriate to afford the President stronger protection, it may respond with appropriate legislation. [If] the Constitution embodied the rule that the President advocates, Congress, of course, could not repeal it. But our holding today raises no barrier to a statutory response to these concerns.

The Federal District Court has jurisdiction to decide this case. Like every other citizen who properly invokes that jurisdiction, respondent has a right to an orderly disposition of her claims. Accordingly, the judgment of the Court of Appeals is affirmed.

JUSTICE BREYER, concurring in the judgment.

I agree with the majority that the Constitution does not automatically grant the President an immunity from civil lawsuits based upon his private conduct.

Nor does the "doctrine of separation of powers . . . require federal courts to stay" virtually "all private actions against the President until he leaves office." Rather, as the Court of Appeals stated, the President cannot simply rest upon the claim that a private civil lawsuit for damages will "interfere with the constitutionally assigned duties of the Executive Branch . . . without detailing any specific responsibilities or explaining how or the degree to which they are affected by the suit." To obtain a postponement the President must "bear the burden of establishing its need."

In my view, however, once the President sets forth and explains a conflict between judicial proceeding and public duties, the matter changes. At that point, the Constitution permits a judge to schedule a trial in an ordinary civil damages action (where postponement normally is possible without overwhelming damage to a plaintiff) only within the constraints of a constitutional principle — a principle that forbids a federal judge in such a case to interfere with the President's discharge of his public duties. I have no doubt that the Constitution contains such a principle applicable to civil suits, based upon Article II's vesting of the entire "executive Power" in a single individual, implemented through the Constitution's structural separation of powers, and revealed both by history and case precedent.

I recognize that this case does not require us now to apply the principle specifically, thereby delineating its contours; nor need we now decide whether lower courts are to apply it directly or categorically through the use of presumptions or rules of administration. Yet I fear that to disregard it now may appear to deny it. I also fear that the majority's description of the relevant precedents deemphasizes the extent to which they support a principle of the President's independent authority to control his own time and energy so as "to avoid rendering the President 'unduly cautious.'" Further, if the majority is wrong in predicting the future infrequency of private civil litigation against sitting Presidents, acknowledgement and future delineation of the constitutional principle will prove a practically necessary institutional safeguard. . . .

IV

This case is a private action for civil damages in which, as the District Court here found, it is possible to preserve evidence and in which later payment of interest can compensate for delay. The District Court in this case determined that the Constitution required the postponement of trial during the sitting President's term. It may well be that the trial of this case cannot take place without significantly interfering with the President's ability to carry out his official duties. Yet, I agree with the majority that there is no automatic temporary immunity and that the President should have to provide the District Court with a reasoned explanation of why the immunity is needed; and I also agree that, in the absence of that explanation, the court's postponement of the trial date was premature. For those reasons, I concur in the result.

In the aftermath of the impeachment of President Clinton, many people have suggested that the Court was quite naïve and that it greatly understated the effects of allowing civil suits on the President's ability to perform his duties. Do you think this experience proved the court wrong?

Page 421. Before section 3 of the Note, add the following:

(4) Protective function privilege. During the grand jury investigation of the Monica Lewinsky affair, the Independent Counsel subpoenaed several Secret Service agents to testify about what they had seen. The Secret Service asserted a "protective function" privilege that would have protected "information obtained by Secret Service personnel while performing their protective function in physical proximity to the President." The lower courts rejected the privilege, and the Supreme Court denied certiorari. See Rubin v. United States 119 S. Ct. 461 (1998). Is there a plausible argument that the privilege should be accorded constitutional status? Consider the opinion of Justice Breyer, dissenting from the denial of certiorari:

> The physical security of the President of the United States has a special legal role to play in our constitutional system. The Constitution vests the entire "Power" of one branch of Government in that single human being, the "President" of the United States. Thus, one could reasonably believe that the law should take special account of the obvious fact that serious physical harm to the President is a national calamity — by recognizing a special governmental privilege where needed to help avert that calamity.

Page 424. Before Section 2, add the following:

Note: The Clinton Impeachment

On December 19, 1998, William Jefferson Clinton became the second President in United States history to be impeached by the House of Representatives. After a trial lasting five weeks, on February 12, 1999, the Senate voted to acquit him of all charges.

The charges grew out of President Clinton's deposition testimony in a lawsuit filed by Paula Jones, alleging sexual harassment while Clinton was Governor of Arkansas. (In Clinton v. Jones, reproduced in this Supplement at the pages corresponding to Page 419 of the main text, the Supreme Court rejected Clinton's argument that the suit should be postponed until he left office. In light of the events described in this Note, reconsider the Court's conclusion that "if properly managed by the District Court, it appears to us highly unlikely [that the suit would] occupy any substantial amount of petitioner's time." Do subsequent events demonstrate that the burden of defending civil lawsuits inevitably hampers the President in the performance of his duties and that such lawsuits are bound to be politicized, or instead that President Clinton's response to this lawsuit led to an appropriate inquiry into his fitness for office and that the inquiry did no serious harm to the country?)

In his deposition testimony, on January 17, 1998, President Clinton denied having a "sexual affair," a "sexual relationship," or "sexual relations" with former White House intern, Monica Lewinsky. At the time of his testimony, Clinton was unaware that a day earlier, the Special Division of the United States Court of Appeals for the District of Columbia Circuit had expanded the jurisdiction of Independent Counsel Kenneth Starr to investigate "whether Monica Lewinsky or others suborned perjury, obstructed justice, intimidated witnesses, or otherwise violated federal law."

On January 27, 1998, the Office of Independent Counsel opened a grand jury inquiry into the Lewinsky affair. Six months later, Lewinsky entered an immunity agreement with the Independent Counsel. On the next day, President Clinton testified before the grand jury via closed circuit television. Although insisting that his testimony at the Jones deposition was accurate, he acknowledged "inappropriate contact" with Lewinsky.

On September 9, 1998, Independent Counsel Starr, acting pursuant to the Independent Counsel Act, notified the House of Representatives that he had "substantial and credible information . . . that may constitute grounds for impeachment." After hearings marked by rancorous argument and partisan division, the House Judiciary Committee approved four articles of impeachment, alleging that Clinton had perjured himself before the grand jury, that he obstructed justice by inducing others to lie in order to conceal his affair with Lewinsky, that he perjured himself in his Jones deposition, and that he abused his power by providing legalistic answers to questions put to him by the House Judiciary Committee. Three months later, the House approved two of the articles alleging perjury before the grand jury and obstruction of justice. On February 12, 1999, the Senate voted by margins of 55-45 and 50-50 to acquit Clinton of both charges. All of the relevant votes were highly partisan, that is, Democrats overwhelmingly voted against impeachment and conviction, and Republicans voted overwhelmingly for impeachment and conviction.

Consider the following issues raised by the Clinton impeachment:

1. Is false testimony in a civil lawsuit unrelated to the President's official duties a "high crime or misdemeanor" within the meaning of Article II? If the President helped to orchestrate a cover-up of his relationship with Monica Lewinsky, and also helped to ensure that the public would not find out that he had not told the truth under oath, has he committed an impeachable offense? Much of the debate in Congress involved the question of when, if ever, a President could be impeached for misconduct or criminality not involving his official duties.

Early proposals at the Constitutional Convention limited the grounds for impeachment to neglect of duty or misuse of official power. At a later point, it was proposed that the grounds for impeachment of the President be limited to "treason or bribery." George Mason opposed this limitation and moved to add "maladministration" to the list. James Madison responded that "[so] vague a term will be equivalent to a tenure during the pleasure of the Senate." Mason thereupon withdrew his motion, and substituted "bribery and other high crimes or misdemeanors against the State." This motion carried. At a later point, the Convention agreed to replace the word "State" with the words "United States." The Committee of Style and Arrangement thereupon eliminated the words "against the United States," apparently because it thought the phrase redundant.

In light of this history, consider the testimony of Professor Laurence Tribe before the Subcommittee on the Constitution of the House Judiciary Committee:

> What distinguishes certain offenses as 'high Crimes and Misdemeanors" must be *not* the fact that serious crimes are involved but the fact that those offenses are similar [to] treason and bribery. But that in turn means that [high] crimes and misdemeanors [must] refer to major offenses against our very system of government, or serious abuses of the governmental power with which a public official has been entrusted [or] grave wrongs in pursuit of governmental [power]. . . .
>
> [It] apparently did not occur to the framers or ratifiers that some sufficiently monstrous but purely private crimes against individuals might require impeachment and removal from office in order to safeguard the government and the people it serves. . . .
>
> Today [the] specter of being governed by "a common murderer" [would] lead at least some students of the English and colonial history to question whether the remedy of impeachment and removal must be withheld even from the most heinous of crimes [simply] because the crime in question involved no abuse of presidential power and did not endanger the nation as a polity. There may well be room to argue that the very continuation in office of a president who has committed a crime as heinous as murder [would] itself so gravely injure the nation and its government that such a president's decision not to resign [amounts] to [an] abuse of power.

Compare the testimony of Professor Richard Parker before the same body:

> [It] is not clear why substantial presidential misconduct should be *presumed* non-impeachable just because it "arose from" a realm of "private" life. . . .
>
> [In] terms of constitutional principle, [this claim makes] no sense. The reason is that the phrase, "other high Crimes and Misdemeanors," must be understood in light of "Bribery," one of its referents. Acts of bribery — as is well known — tend to arise from the "private" lives of actors. The fact that bribery may arise from private greed (or need) does not presumptively immunize it from impeachment. Why, then, should public acts be presumptively immunized solely on the ground that they arose from private lust?

Consider whether the following acts would be impeachable offenses: (a) wiretapping political enemies; (b) repeatedly driving drunk; (c) failing to report taxable income to the Internal Revenue Service, either before or after election to the presidency; (d) committing a murder; (e) committing a rape. What theory of impeachment underlies your responses to these questions?

2. Is the standard for impeachment the same for the President and for other civil officers? In the recent past, the House impeached, and the Senate convicted, a federal judge who committed perjury in a context unassociated with his official duties. In her testimony before the Constitutional Rights Subcommittee, Professor Susan Low Bloch argued that

> The Constitution assumes that, in general, the electorate, not the Congress will decide whether the president's behavior is acceptable. Thus, the fact that judges have been impeached for perjury does not tell us that presidents should also be removable for such behavior. While it makes sense to impeach and remove a "life-tenured" judge who commits perjury — who without impeachment will serve for life, it does not necessarily follow that we should remove a democratically elected president, who is subject to electoral accountability and a fixed term for allegedly lying, even under oath, about a consensual sexual affair.

Professor John C. Harrison disagreed:

> Under the Constitution the presidency is unique in its powers and responsibilities. While the legislative and judicial powers are vested in institutions, the executive power is vested in an individual. The public must look to the integrity of that individual alone, and not to any collegial process, to ensure that the executive power is exercised properly. Moreover, the President's powers extend to the most delicate of matters, including diplomacy and the

command of military affairs; shrouded in secrecy as those affairs necessarily often are, their conduct requires an individual in whom the people can place complete trust. . . .

It thus seems clear that if the magnitude of offense required for impeachment varies from office to office, the standard of conduct is the highest, and the threshold for impeachment the lowest, for the President.

For general discussion of the legal issues raised by the impeachment of President Clinton, compare Cass R. Sunstein, Impeaching the President, 147 U. Pa. L. Rev. 279 (1998) (concluding that impeachment was unconstitutional) with Richard Posner, The Trial and Impeachment of William Jefferson Clinton (1999) (concluding that impeachment was constitutionally permissible).

3. Throughout the proceedings, some Democrats argued that the President should be censured, rather than impeached. Is censure a constitutionally permissible alternative to impeachment? The Constitution makes no reference to censure, but both the House and the Senate regularly adopt resolutions without the force of law expressing opinions about various matters, and there are several historical precedents for the censure of presidents and federal judges. Consider the views of Professor and former Congressman Robert Drinan, who served on the House Judiciary Committee that voted articles of impeachment against Richard Nixon:

The Constitution states clearly that the House may impeach or not impeach. The separation of powers guarantees the president immunity from any other penalty.

To encourage or allow the House to "censure" the President for misconduct bypasses the only process set forth in the Constitution to penalize a president. A vote to censure a president by one or both bodies of Congress would establish a dangerous precedent which would weaken the institution of the presidency. It would invite the erosion of the separation of powers in ways which the framers sought carefully to prevent.

4. Are serious constitutional questions raised by the provision in the Independent Counsel Act requiring the Independent Counsel to "advise the House of Representatives of any substantial and credible information which such independent counsel receives, in carrying out the independent counsel's responsibilities [that] may constitute grounds for impeachment"? By the Independent Counsel filing a detailed report with the House based upon evidence gathered by a grand jury? Consider Gormley, Impeachment and the Independent Counsel: A Dysfunctional Union, 51 Stan. L. Rev. 309, 313 (1999):

[Even] if the independent counsel can prosecute a sitting President (a dubious proposition at best), the impeachment referral provision [obliterates] the prosecutor's ability to function as a prosecutor. [The provision] not only allows but mandates that the independent counsel wear two incompatible hats: one as a detached criminal prosecutor hired to conduct a neutral criminal investigation on behalf of the executive branch, and the other as a pre-impeachment deputy for the House of Representatives, gathering evidence that may be relevant to Congress' impeachment work. The latter job inevitably clashes with the prosecutor's ability to handle his or her criminal case in a responsible fashion. It also disrupts the work of the grand jury, which (in effect) is forced to accuse public officials of wrongdoing without indicting —something that is generally disfavored in American jurisprudence.

Recall that the statute requires only that the Independent Counsel "advise" the House if he discovers evidence of an impeachable offense. Would it be constitutionally troubling if an Independent Counsel happened across such evidence and so informed Congress on his own initiative? If not, why is it constitutionally objectionable for Congress to direct the Independent Counsel to so inform Congress?

Compare O'Sullivan, The Interaction between Impeachment and the Independent Counsel Statute, 86 Geo. L.J. 2193 (1998):

As a practical matter, the referral provision may permit an [independent counsel] to control the timing, scope, and content of impeachment inquiries. To the extent that an [independent counsel's] referral significantly alters the impeachment dynamic and lends the [independent counsel] credibility as the apolitical investigator of executive misconduct to impeachment inquiries, thus diminishing congressional responsibility for such inquiries, [independent counsel] referral [threatens] to disrupt the traditional balance of power between the executive and the legislative branches.

Consider whether the outcome of the Clinton impeachment proceedings tends to support, or alleviate, these worries.

5. Throughout the impeachment proceedings, public opinion polls showed that President Clinton's personal popularity remained high, and large majorities of those polled opposed impeachment. Should a conscientious member of Congress take these facts into account? Should it matter to such a member whether the impeachment resolutions achieved bipartisan support? Whether the President is, or is perceived to be, doing a good job? Are questions about presidential impeachment appropriately resolved as a matter of constitutional principle, as a matter of ordinary politics, or as some mixture of the two?

6. Consider the wisdom of the following constitutional amendment, proposed in Grossman and Yalof, The Day After: Do We Need a "Twenty-Eighth Amendment?" 17 Const. Comm. 7 (2000):

Section 1. The President, Vice President, members of the Cabinet, and federal judges, but not members of Congress or military officers, shall be removed from office on impeachment for, and conviction of, serious abuses of official power that undermine their conduct of office and threaten the integrity and legitimacy of the government. Such abuses include treason, bribery, and other serious crimes, as well as actions that are not criminal in nature.

Section 2. [No] impeachment shall survive the biennial adjournment of Congress, nor shall an impeachment or trial take place between a general election and the convening of a new congress.

Section 3. [The] president shall not be subject to criminal indictment or prosecution, or civil suit, while in [office]. Congress may [grant] to the president immunity against subsequent prosecutions or civil actions in both federal and state courts.

Section 4. Congress shall have the power to censure, rebuke, or otherwise publicly condemn official misconduct. . . .

Section 5. The President's power to grant reprieves and pardons for offenses against the United States shall not extend to cases of impeachment, nor shall a president have the power to issue a self-pardon.

Section 6. The Supreme Court, under its original jurisdiction, may review, prior to trial by the Senate, in a petition submitted by an impeached president, the procedures employed in, and the constitutional basis of, articles of impeachment voted against the president by the House of Representatives. The Court shall not have the power to review impeachments against other officers nor any action by the Senate concerning articles of impeachment. . . .

Page 425. Before the Note, add the following:

With regard to the formalist/functionalist debate, consider Flaherty, The Most Dangerous Branch, 105 Yale L.J. 1725, 1729-1730 (1996):

The Founders embraced separation of powers to further several widely agreed-upon goals [including] balance among the branches, responsibility or accountability to the electorate, and energetic, efficient government. Currently, these goals are seen to be almost necessarily in tension, with balance cutting against a unitary presidency but accountability and energy cutting in its favor. The light shed by the Founding suggests that this need not be the case. On the one hand, an examination of the period only confirms the foundational importance of balance. In this light, the emergence of the administrative state renders congressional regulation of the executive branch more crucial than ever before, especially since Congress enjoyed extensive regulatory authority even when it was still the most dangerous branch. On the other hand, a better understanding of the Founding undermines current thinking about accountability and energy. Contrary to the usual scholarly assumptions [the] Founders sought to tame, not further empower, those divisions of government that claim a special responsiveness to the electorate. On this basis, the need for congressional regulation becomes imperative precisely because of the modern presidents' claim to electoral accountability. Conversely, many of the Founders did extol separation of powers as a way to accord government greater energy, much as modern constitutional thinkers do today. Viewed in context, however, that commitment was modest, especially given the sheer scope of modern governmental activity.

These basic strategies — first, a faithful reconstruction of the doctrine's origins, and second, the attendant reconciliation of the purposes underlying separation of powers — confirm the [intuition] that there is something anomalous about the judiciary shielding what is now the most powerful office in the nation [i.e., the Presidency]. These approaches refute the idea that the Founders had developed a thoroughgoing, tripartite baseline capable of resolving modern controversies. They demonstrate that balance favors a flexible approach, that accountability bolsters this view, and that energy in the modern context is largely irrelevant. They point, finally, toward doctrinal bases for congressional regulation that are more thoroughgoing than anything currently mooted in separation of powers scholarship.

Werhan, Normalizing the Separation of Powers, 70 Tulane L. Rev. 2681, 2687, 2691, 2692 (1996), argues for an approach that would "[integrate] the formal and functional methods in a way that draws on the strength of each strategy while minimizing their respective weaknesses." The approach begins with a formal principle that "presumes that the national government may take action that affects the rights of an individual only pursuant to a process whereby Congress has enacted a law that authorizes an executive official to take that action, subject to judicial review." However, this formal principle establishes only "a *presumptive* rule, rather than one that is absolute. [The] separation norm is sufficiently flexible to allow the government to make a showing that its departure from the norm is justified and therefore legitimate." A court utilizing this approach would therefore go on to a second stage in the analysis: "Because any deviation from the separation norm is presumptively unconstitutional, [the] court would apply heightened scrutiny. A government action that violates the separation norm would survive judicial review only if it were (1) explicitly authorized by the Constitution, or (2) narrowly tailored to achieve an important, overriding government interest."

Page 428. After the first paragraph of section 3 of the Note, add the following:

For the Court's latest refusal to invoke the nondelegation doctrine, see Loving v. United States, 517 U.S. 748 (1996). After a lower court invalidated the federal statute permitting courts martial to impose the death penalty, the President attempted to meet the constitutional objections to the statute by promulgating regulations requiring consideration of aggravating and mitigating factors before a death sentence was imposed. The underlying statutes provided that "[the] punishment which a court-martial may direct for an offense may not exceed such limits as the President may prescribe for that offense," and that a court martial "may, under such limitations as the President may prescribe, adjudge any punishment not forbidden by [the statute], including the penalty of death." Loving, who had been sentenced to death under the new procedure, argued that this statutory framework failed to establish an "intelligible principle" guiding the President's discretion and therefore had violated the nondelegation doctrine. Writing for the Court, Justice Kennedy rejected the argument:

> We think [that] the question to be asked is not whether there was any explicit principle telling the President how to select aggravating factors, but whether any such guidance was needed given the nature of the delegation and the officer who is to exercise the delegated authority. First, the delegation is set within boundaries the President may not exceed. Second, the delegation here was to the President in his role as Commander in Chief. Perhaps more explicit guidance as to how to select aggravating factors would be necessary if delegation were made to a newly created entity without independent authority in the area. [The] President's duties as Commander in Chief, however, require him to take responsible and continuing action to superintend the military, including the courts-martial.

Page 428. After the second paragraph of section 3 of the Note, add the following:

For an argument in favor of "nondelegation canons" pursuant to which courts interpret statutes so as to bar delegations in certain, specified areas in the absence of a clear statement from Congress, see Sunstein, Nondelegation Canons, 67 U. Chi. L. Rev. 315 (2000).

Page 429.   At the end of section a of the Note, add the following:

In Lovell, That Sick Chicken Won't Hunt: The Limits of a Judicially Enforced Non-Delegation Doctrine, 17 Con. Comm. 79, the author responds to Schoenbrod by arguing that "even if the courts deprive Congress of the power to delegate rule-making authority to executive branch agencies, Congress would retain numerous substitute strategies that circumvent democratic controls just as capably as current forms of legislative delegation."

Page 430.   At the end of section d of the Note, add the following:

For an argument that "courts cannot be expected to set forth the proper scope of delegation or specificity of statutes because courts cannot be expected to craft a judicially administrable resolution of the rules/standards debate," see Bell, Dead Again: The Nondelegation Doctrine, the Rules/Standards Dilemma and the Line Item Veto, 44 Vill. L. Rev. 189 (1999). Consider the extent to which this argument, itself, presupposes a contestable resolution of the rules/standards debate by insisting upon a rule-like division between rules and standards.

Page 442.   Before the Note, add the following:

The House of Representatives recently initiated a "Corrections Day" to deal with relatively uncontroversial measures correcting statutory gaps and mistakes made by drafters or by administrative agencies interpreting federal statutes. Under the new procedures, the Speaker has the authority to place bills on a special, expedited calendar, to be called twice per month. The bills are subject to only very limited amendment and require a three-fifths vote for passage. See H. Res. 168, 104th Cong, 1st Sess. (1995), quoted in 141 Cong. Rec. H6104 (daily ed. June 20, 1995). Consider the extent to which this procedure serves the function of the legislative veto. For a description and defense of "Corrections Day," see Nagle, Corrections Day, 43 UCLA L. Rev. 1267 (1996).

Page 453.   Before section 3 of the Note, add the following:

In April of 1996, Congress passed and the President signed into law The Line Item Veto Act. The Act authorizes the President to "cancel in whole" any items of new spending or any "limited tax benefit." A so-called "lockbox" provision requires that savings resulting from canceled items be used to reduce the budget deficit and not to offset deficit increases arising from other laws. In identifying items for cancellation, the President is directed to consider the legislative history, purposes, and other relevant information about the canceled items. In addition, before canceling an item, the statute requires the President to find that each cancellation will "(i) reduce the Federal budget deficit; (ii) not impair any essential Government functions; and (iii) not harm the national interest."

Upon canceling an item, the President is required to transmit a special message to Congress notifying it of the cancellation. The cancellation takes effect upon receipt by Congress of the special message. However, if a "disapproval bill" is enacted, by a majority of both Houses of Congress (subject to a presidential veto), the cancellations are voided.

In the case that follows, the Supreme Court held that the statute was unconstitutional.

Clinton v. City of New York
524 U.S. 417 (1998)

JUSTICE STEVENS delivered the opinion of the Court. . . .

IV . . . .

[Under] the plain text of the statute, the two actions of the President [canceling sections of the Balanced Budget Act of 1997 and the Taxpayer Relief Act of 1997] that are challenged in these cases prevented [the sections] "from having legal force or effect." The remaining provisions of those statutes, with the exception of the second canceled item in the latter, continue to have the same force and effect as they had when signed into law.

In both legal and practical effect, the President has amended two Acts of Congress by repealing a portion of each. [There] is no provision in the Constitution that authorizes the President to enact, to amend, or to repeal statutes. . . .

There are important differences between the President's "return" of a bill pursuant to Article I, § 7, and the exercise of the President's cancellation authority pursuant to the Line Item Veto Act. The constitutional return takes place before ‗ bill becomes law; the statutory cancellation occurs after the bill becomes law. The constitutional return is of the entire bill; the statutory cancellation is of only a part. Although the Constitution expressly authorizes the President to play a role in the process of enacting statutes, it is silent on the subject of unilateral Presidential action that either repeals or amends parts of duly enacted statutes.

There are powerful reasons for construing constitutional silence on this profoundly important issue as equivalent to an express prohibition. The procedures governing the enactment of statutes set forth in the text of Article I were the product of the great debates and compromises that produced the Constitution itself. Familiar historical materials provide abundant support for the conclusion that the power to enact statutes may only "be exercised in accord with a single, finely wrought and exhaustively considered, procedure." [*Chadha*]. Our first President understood the text of the Presentment Clause as requiring that he either "approve all the parts of a Bill, or reject it in toto." What has emerged in these cases from the President's exercise of his statutory cancellation powers, however, are truncated versions of two bills that passed both Houses of Congress. They are not the product of the "finely wrought" procedure that the Framers designed.

At oral argument, the Government suggested that the cancellations at issue in these cases do not effect a "repeal" of the canceled items because under the special "lockbox" provisions of the Act, a canceled item "retains real, legal budgetary effect" insofar as it prevents Congress and the President from spending the savings that result from the cancellation. The text of the Act expressly provides, however, that a cancellation prevents a direct spending or tax benefit provision "from having legal force or effect." That a canceled item may have "real, legal budgetary effect" as a result of the lockbox procedure does not change the fact that by canceling the items at issue in these cases, the President made them entirely inoperative as to appellees. [The] cancellation of one section of a statute may be the functional equivalent of a partial repeal even if a portion of the section is not canceled.

V

The Government advances two related arguments to support its position that despite the unambiguous provisions of the Act, cancellations do not amend or repeal properly enacted statutes in violation of the Presentment Clause. First, relying primarily on Field v. Clark, 143 U.S. 649 (1892), the Government contends that the cancellations were merely exercises of discretionary authority granted to the President by the Balanced Budget Act and the Taxpayer Relief Act read in light of the previously enacted Line Item Veto Act. Second, the Government submits that the substance of the authority to cancel tax and spending items "is, in practical effect, no more and no less than the power to 'decline to spend' specified sums of money, or to 'decline to implement' specified tax measures." Neither argument is persuasive.

In Field v. Clark, the Court upheld the constitutionality of the Tariff Act of 1890. [The Act exempted some 300 specific articles from import duties, but provided that the President could suspend certain exemptions upon finding that a country exporting the products to the United States had imposed duties on United States goods that were "reciprocally unequal and unreasonable."]

119

[There are] three critical differences between the power to suspend the exemption from import duties and the power to cancel portions of a duly enacted statute. First, the exercise of the suspension power was contingent upon a condition that did not exist when the Tariff Act was passed: the imposition of "reciprocally unequal and unreasonable" import duties by other countries. In contrast, the exercise of the cancellation power within five days after the enactment of the Balanced Budget and Tax Reform Acts necessarily was based on the same conditions that Congress evaluated when it passed those statutes. Second, under the Tariff Act, when the President determined that the contingency had arisen, he had a duty to suspend; in contrast, while it is true that the President was required by the Act to make three determinations before he canceled a provision, those determinations did not qualify his discretion to cancel or not to cancel. Finally, whenever the President suspended an exemption under the Tariff Act, he was executing the policy that Congress had embodied in the statute. In contrast, whenever the President cancels an item of new direct spending or a limited tax benefit he is rejecting the policy judgment made by Congress and relying on his own policy judgment. . . .

The Government's reliance upon other tariff and import statutes, discussed in Field, that contain provisions similar to the one challenged in Field is unavailing for the same reasons. . . .

The cited statutes all relate to foreign trade, and this Court has recognized that in the foreign affairs arena, the President has "a degree of discretion and freedom from statutory restriction which would not be admissible were domestic affairs alone involved." United States v. Curtiss-Wright Export Corp., 299 U.S. 304, 320 (1936). "Moreover, he, not Congress, has the better opportunity of knowing the conditions which prevail in foreign countries." More important, when enacting the statutes discussed in Field, Congress itself made the decision to suspend or repeal the particular provisions at issue upon the occurrence of particular events subsequent to enactment, and it left only the determination of whether such events occurred up to the President. The Line Item Veto Act authorizes the President himself to effect the repeal of laws, for his own policy reasons, without observing the procedures set out in Article I, § 7. The fact that Congress intended such a result is of no moment. Although Congress presumably anticipated that the President might cancel some of the items in the Balanced Budget Act and in the Taxpayer Relief Act, Congress cannot alter the procedures set out in Article I, § 7, without amending the Constitution.[1]

---

[1] The Government argues that the Rules Enabling Act, permits this Court to "repeal" prior laws without violating Article I, § 7. Section 2072(b) provides that this Court may promulgate rules of procedure for the lower federal courts and that "all laws in conflict with such rules shall be of no further force or effect after such rules have taken effect." In

Neither are we persuaded by the Government's contention that the President's authority to cancel new direct spending and tax benefit items is no greater than his traditional authority to decline to spend appropriated funds. The Government has reviewed in some detail the series of statutes in which Congress has given the Executive broad discretion over the expenditure of appropriated funds. For example, the First Congress appropriated "sums not exceeding" specified amounts to be spent on various Government operations. In those statutes, as in later years, the President was given wide discretion with respect to both the amounts to be spent and how the money would be allocated among different functions. It is argued that the Line Item Veto Act merely confers comparable discretionary authority over the expenditure of appropriated funds. The critical difference between this statute and all of its predecessors, however, is that unlike any of them, this Act gives the President the unilateral power to change the text of duly enacted statutes. None of the Act's predecessors could even arguably have been construed to authorize such a change.

VI

Although they are implicit in what we have already written, the profound importance of these cases makes it appropriate to emphasize three points.

First, we express no opinion about the wisdom of the procedures authorized by the Line Item Veto Act. Many members of both major political parties who have served in the Legislative and the Executive Branches have long advocated the enactment of such procedures for the purpose of "ensuring greater fiscal accountability in Washington." The text of the Act was itself the product of much debate and deliberation in both Houses of Congress and that precise text was signed into law by the President. We do not lightly conclude that their action was unauthorized by the Constitution. We have, however, twice had full argument and briefing on the question and have concluded that our duty is clear.

Second, although appellees challenge the validity of the Act on alternative grounds, the only issue we address concerns the "finely wrought" procedure commanded by the Constitution. We have been favored with extensive debate about the scope of Congress' power to delegate law-making authority, or its functional equivalent, to the President. The excellent briefs filed by the parties and their amici curiae have provided us with valuable historical information that

---

enacting § 2072(b), however, Congress expressly provided that laws inconsistent with the procedural rules promulgated by this Court would automatically be repealed upon the enactment of new rules in order to create a uniform system of rules for Article III courts. As in the tariff statutes, Congress itself made the decision to repeal prior rules upon the occurrence of a particular event—here, the promulgation of procedural rules by this Court.

illuminates the delegation issue but does not really bear on the narrow issue that is dispositive of these cases. Thus, because we conclude that the Act's cancellation provisions violate Article I, § 7, of the Constitution, we find it unnecessary to consider the District Court's alternative holding that the Act "impermissibly disrupts the balance of powers among the three branches of government."

Third, our decision rests on the narrow ground that the procedures authorized by the Line Item Veto Act are not authorized by the Constitution. The Balanced Budget Act of 1997 is a 500-page document that became "Public Law 105-33" after three procedural steps were taken: (1) a bill containing its exact text was approved by a majority of the Members of the House of Representatives; (2) the Senate approved precisely the same text; and (3) that text was signed into law by the President. The Constitution explicitly requires that each of those three steps be taken before a bill may "become a law." Art. I, § 7. If one paragraph of that text had been omitted at any one of those three stages, Public Law 105-33 would not have been validly enacted. If the Line Item Veto Act were valid, it would authorize the President to create a different law—one whose text was not voted on by either House of Congress or presented to the President for signature. Something that might be known as "Public Law 105-33 as modified by the President" may or may not be desirable, but it is surely not a document that may "become a law" pursuant to the procedures designed by the Framers of Article I, §7, of the Constitution.

If there is to be a new procedure in which the President will play a different role in determining the final text of what may "become a law," such change must come not by legislation but through the amendment procedures set forth in Article V of the Constitution.

[A concurring opinion by Justice Kennedy is omitted].

JUSTICE BREYER, with whom JUSTICE O'CONNOR and JUSTICE SCALIA join as to Part III, dissenting. . . .

II

I approach the constitutional question before us with three general considerations in mind. First, the Act represents a legislative effort to provide the President with the power to give effect to some, but not to all, of the expenditure and revenue-diminishing provisions contained in a single massive appropriations bill. And this objective is constitutionally proper. . . .

[A] typical budget appropriations bill may have a dozen titles, hundreds of sections, and spread across more than 500 pages of the Statutes at Large. Congress cannot divide such a bill into thousands, or tens of thousands, of separate appropriations bills, each one of which the President would have to sign, or to veto, separately. Thus, the question is whether the Constitution permits Congress to choose a particular novel means to achieve this same, constitutionally legitimate, end.

Second, the case in part requires us to focus upon the Constitution's generally phrased structural provisions, provisions that delegate all "legislative" power to Congress and vest all "executive" power in the President. The Court, when applying these provisions, has interpreted them generously in terms of the institutional arrangements that they permit. . . .

Third, we need not here referee a dispute among the other two branches. And, as the majority points out, "When this Court is asked to invalidate a statutory provision that has been approved by both Houses of the Congress and signed by the President, particularly an Act of Congress that confronts a deeply vexing national problem, it should only do so for the most compelling constitutional reasons." (quoting [*Bowsher*] (STEVENS, J., concurring in judgment)). Cf. [*Youngstown*] (Jackson, J., concurring) ("Presidential powers are not fixed but fluctuate, depending on their disjunction or conjunction with those of Congress . . . [and when] the President acts pursuant to an express or implied authorization of Congress, his authority is at its maximum").

These three background circumstances mean that, when one measures the literal words of the Act against the Constitution's literal commands, the fact that the Act may closely resemble a different, literally unconstitutional, arrangement is beside the point. . . .

III

The Court believes that the Act violates the literal text of the Constitution. A simple syllogism captures its basic reasoning:

Major Premise: The Constitution sets forth an exclusive method for enacting, repealing, or amending laws.

Minor Premise: The Act authorizes the President to "repeal or amend" laws in a different way, namely by announcing a cancellation of a portion of a previously enacted law.

Conclusion: The Act is inconsistent with the Constitution.

I find this syllogism unconvincing, however, because its Minor Premise is faulty. When the President "canceled" the two appropriation measures now before us, he did not repeal any law nor did he amend any law. He simply followed the law, leaving the statutes, as they are literally written, intact. . . .

Literally speaking, the President has not "repealed" or "amended" anything. He has simply executed a power conferred upon him by Congress, which power is contained in laws that were enacted in compliance with the exclusive method set forth in the Constitution.

Nor can one dismiss this literal compliance as some kind of formal quibble, as if it were somehow "obvious" that what the President has done "amounts to," "comes close to," or is "analogous to" the repeal or amendment of a previously enacted law. That is because the power the Act grants the President (to render designated appropriations items without "legal force or effect") also "amounts to," "comes close to," or is "analogous to" a different legal animal, the delegation of a power to choose one legal path as opposed to [another].

This is not the first time that Congress has delegated to the President or to others this kind of power—a contingent power to deny effect to certain statutory language. [Justice Breyer cites a number of other statutes, including a statute providing that a section of the Foreign Assistance Act of 1961 "shall be of no further force and effect upon the President's determination and certification to the Congress that the resumption of full military cooperation with Turkey is in the national interest of the United States" and the Gramm-Rudman-Hollings Act, which authorized the President to issue a "final order" that has the effect of "permanently cancelling" sequestered amounts in spending statutes in order to achieve budget compliance.]

All of these examples, like the Act, delegate a power to take action that will render statutory provisions "without force or effect." Every one of these examples, like the present Act, delegates the power to choose between alternatives, each of which the statute spells out in some detail. None of these examples delegates a power to "repeal" or "amend" a statute, or to "make" a new law. Nor does the Act. Rather, the delegated power to nullify statutory language was itself created and defined by Congress, and included in the statute books on an equal footing with (indeed, as a component part of) the sections that are potentially subject to nullification. . . .

[The] Act contains a "lockbox" feature, which gives legal significance to the enactment of a particular appropriations item even if, and even after, the President has rendered it without "force or effect." [The "lockbox" provision means] that, despite the Act's use of the word "cancel," the Act does not delegate to the President the power truly to cancel a line item expenditure (returning the legal status quo to one in which the item had never been enacted). Rather, it delegates to the President the power to decide how to spend the money to which the line item refers—either for the specific purpose mentioned the item, or for general deficit reduction via the "lockbox" feature. . . .

Because one cannot say that the President's exercise of the power the Act grants is, literally speaking, a "repeal" or "amendment," the fact that the Act's procedures differ from the Constitution's exclusive procedures for enacting (or repealing) legislation is beside the point. The Act itself was enacted in accordance with these procedures, and its failure to require the President to satisfy those procedures does not make the Act unconstitutional.

IV

Because I disagree with the Court's holding of literal violation, I must consider whether the Act nonetheless violates Separation of Powers principles — principles that arise out of the Constitution's vesting of the "executive Power" in "a President," and "all legislative Powers" in "a Congress." There are three relevant Separation of Powers questions here: (1) Has Congress given the President the wrong kind of power, i.e., "non-Executive" power? (2) Has Congress given the President the power to "encroach" upon Congress' own constitutionally reserved territory? (3) Has Congress given the President too much power, violating the doctrine of "nondelegation?" [With] respect to this Act, the answer to all these questions is "no."

A

Viewed conceptually, the power the Act conveys is the right kind of power. It is "executive." As explained above, an exercise of that power "executes" the Act. Conceptually speaking, it closely resembles the kind of delegated authority — to spend or not to spend appropriations, to change or not to change tariff rates — that Congress has frequently granted the President, any differences being differences in degree, not kind. . . .

The Court has upheld congressional delegation of rulemaking power and adjudicatory power to federal agencies, guideline-writing power to a Sentencing Commission, [*Mistretta*], and prosecutor-appointment power to judges, [*Morrison*]. It is far easier conceptually to reconcile the power at issue here with the relevant constitutional description ("executive") than in many of these cases. . . .

If there is a Separation of Powers violation, then, it must rest, not upon purely conceptual grounds, but upon some important conflict between the Act and a significant Separation of Powers objective.

B

The Act does not undermine what this Court has often described as the principal function of the Separation of Powers, which is to maintain the tripartite structure of the Federal Government — and thereby protect individual liberty — by providing a "safeguard against the encroachment or aggrandizement of one branch at the expense of the other." [*Buckley*]

[One] cannot say that the Act "encroaches" upon Congress' power, when Congress retained the power to insert, by simple majority, into any future appropriations bill, into any section of any such bill, or into any phrase of any section, a provision that says the Act will not apply. And it is Congress that drafts and enacts the appropriations statutes that are subject to the Act in the first place — and thereby defines the outer limits of the President's cancellation authority. . . .

Nor can one say the Act's grant of power "aggrandizes" the Presidential office. The grant is limited to the context of the budget. It is limited to the power to spend, or not to spend, particular appropriated items, and the power to permit, or not to permit, specific limited exemptions from generally applicable tax law from taking effect. These powers [resemble] those the President has exercised in the past on other occasions. The delegation of those powers to the President may strengthen the Presidency, but any such change in Executive Branch authority seems minute when compared with the changes worked by delegations of other kinds of authority that the Court in the past has upheld.

C

The "nondelegation" doctrine represents an added constitutional check upon Congress' authority to delegate power to the Executive Branch. And it raises a more serious constitutional obstacle here. The Constitution permits Congress to "seek assistance from another branch" of Government, the "extent and character" of that assistance to be fixed "according to common sense and the inherent necessities of the governmental co-ordination." But there are limits on the way in which Congress can obtain such assistance; it "cannot delegate any part of its legislative power except under the limitation of a prescribed standard." Or, in Chief Justice Taft's more familiar words, the Constitution permits only those delegations where Congress "shall lay down by legislative act an intelligible principle to which the person or body authorized to [act] is directed to conform."

The Act before us seeks to create such a principle in three ways. The first is procedural. The Act tells the President that, in "identifying dollar amounts [or] . . . items . . . for cancellation" (which I take to refer to his selection of the amounts or items he will "prevent from having legal force or effect"), he is to "consider," among other things "the legislative history, construction, and purposes of the law which contains [those amounts or items, and] . . . any specific sources of information referenced in such law or . . . the best available information . . . ."

The second is purposive. The clear purpose behind the Act, confirmed by its legislative history, is to promote "greater fiscal accountability" and to "eliminate wasteful federal spending and . . . special tax breaks."

The third is substantive. The President must determine that, to "prevent" the item or amount "from having legal force or effect" will "reduce the Federal budget deficit; . . . not impair any essential Government functions; and . . . not harm the national interest."

The resulting standards are broad. But this Court has upheld standards that are equally broad, or broader. . . .

V

In sum, I recognize that the Act before us is novel. In a sense, it skirts a constitutional edge. But that edge has to do with means, not ends. The means chosen do not amount literally to the enactment, repeal, or amendment of a law. Nor, for that matter, do they amount literally to the "line item veto" that the Act's title announces. Those means do not violate any basic Separation of Powers principle. They do not improperly shift the constitutionally foreseen balance of power from Congress to the President. Nor, since they comply with Separation of Powers principles, do they threaten the liberties of individual citizens. They represent an experiment that may, or may not, help representative government work better. The Constitution, in my view, authorizes Congress and the President to try novel methods in this way. Consequently, with respect, I dissent.

JUSTICE SCALIA, with whom JUSTICE O'CONNOR joins, and with whom JUSTICE BREYER joins as to Part III, concurring in part and dissenting in part. . . .

III . . . .

There is no question that enactment of the Balanced Budget Act complied with [the Presentment Clause]: the House and Senate passed the bill, and the President signed it into law. It was only after the requirements of the Presentment Clause had been satisfied that the President exercised his authority under the Line Item Veto Act to cancel the spending item. Thus, the Court's problem with the Act is not that it authorizes the President to veto parts of a bill and sign others into law, but rather that it authorizes him to "cancel" — prevent from "having legal force or effect" — certain parts of duly enacted statutes.

Article I, §7 of the Constitution obviously prevents the President from cancelling a law that Congress has not authorized him to cancel. Such action cannot possibly be considered part of his execution of the law, and if it is legislative action, as the Court observes, "repeal of statutes, no less than enactment, must conform with Art. I." But that is not this case. It was certainly arguable, as an original matter, that Art. I, § 7 also prevents the President from cancelling a law which itself authorizes the President to cancel it. But as the Court acknowledges, that argument has long since been made and rejected. . . .

As much as the Court goes on about Art. I, § 7, therefore, that provision does not demand the result the Court reaches. It no more categorically prohibits the Executive reduction of congressional dispositions in the course of implementing statutes that authorize such reduction, than it categorically prohibits the Execu-

1

simplify for public comprehension, or perhaps merely to comply with the terms of a campaign pledge, has succeeded in faking out the Supreme Court. The President's action it authorizes in fact is not a line-item veto and thus does not offend Art. I, § 7; and insofar as the substance of that action is concerned, it is no different from what Congress has permitted the President to do since the formation of the Union.

Page 454. Before section 4 of the Note, add the following:

3a. *Supermajority requirement for income tax increases.* On January 4, 1995, the House of Representatives implemented a provision in the "Contract with America" by adopting a rule requiring a three-fifths majority of those present and voting to pass an increase in income tax rates. See Rules of the House of Representatives Effective for the One Hundred Fourth Congress, House Rule XXI(5)(c). Is the rule unconstitutional? Consider Comment, An Open Letter to Congressman Gingrich, 104 Yale L.J. 1539, 1541 (1995):

> On seven different occasions, [the Constitution] stipulates a supermajority requirement. [But] it never places any special obstacles in the way of the enactment of ordinary legislation signed by the President. As the *Chadha* case teaches, this carefully considered lawmaking system can only be changed by constitutional amendment. . . .
> It is true that the Constitution gives each house the right "to determine the rules of its proceedings." This sensible housekeeping provision, however, does not authorize the House to violate fundamental principles of constitutional democracy. It simply authorizes the House to organize itself for informed and efficient debate and decision.

Compare McGinnis & Rappaport, The Constitutionality of Legislative Supermajority Requirements: A Defense, 105 Yale L.J. 483, 486, 492 (1995):

> [The Constitution does not specify] the proportion of a chamber necessary to pass a bill. Rather [it] simply [refers] to a bill's passage by a house or an order's receipt of the concurrence of a house. The Constitution's failure to specify a proportion necessary to pass a bill, combined with the delegation of authority to each house under the Rules of Proceedings Clause, suggests that the Constitution permits each house to decide how many members are necessary to pass a bill. . . .
> If the Constitution contained a majority-voting requirement for legislation, Chadha would, of course, support the conclusion that Congress could not depart from the requirement. But the question here is whether the Consti-

tution contains such a requirement, and Chadha provides no guidance on this point.

Page 468. Before section 3 of the Note, add the following:

Consider Nourse, Toward a "Due Foundation" for Separation of Powers: The Federalist Papers as Political Narrative, 74 Tex. L. Rev. 447, 520 (1996):

> [The] Supreme Court was right to reject the removal argument in *Morrison*, albeit for the wrong reasons. If the separate exercise of power is our goal, then the independent counsel, like other independent agencies, poses little threat of structural collapse. By limiting the president's removal power, Congress does not gain, for itself, the ability to infiltrate the executive department. [Indeed,] it is ironic but true that the very idea of independence enshrined in the independent-counsel law replicates the underlying principles of *separation* of powers — the idea that independent persons achieve separate powers. If there is a problem with the independent counsel, it is not that it is not "separate" from other departments — it is that it is "too separate" from the people and thus raises important questions of accountability. Those questions are different in nature and kind, however, from questions about what separates the departments.

Page 469. Before section 4 of the Note, add the following:

c. *Edmond*. The Court rejected a third such challenge in Edmond v. United States, 117 S. Ct. 1573 (1997). In *Edmond*, the Court upheld the authority of the Secretary of Transportation to appoint civilian members of the Coast Guard Court of Appeals, an intermediate court that hears appeals from courts martial. According to the Court:

> Generally speaking, the term "inferior officer" connotes a relationship with some higher ranking officer or officers below the President: Whether one is an "inferior" officer depends upon whether he has a superior. ["Inferior] officers" are officers whose work is directed and supervised at some level by others who were appointed by presidential nomination with the advise and consent of the Senate.

The Court held that civilian judges on the Coast Guard Court of Appeals were inferior officers who could be appointed by a head of department because they were supervised by the Judge Advocate General, who engaged in administrative oversight and could remove judges from the court without cause, and by the Court of Appeals for the Armed Forces, which had appellate jurisdiction over the Coast Guard Court of Appeals.

Page 470. Before section 5 of the Note, add the following:

Consider whether Justice Scalia's concern about selection of "a prosecutor antagonistic to the administration, or even to the particular individual who has been selected for special treatment" was vindicated by events surrounding the Clinton impeachment. (For a brief chronology of these events, see the pages of this Supplement corresponding to Page 424 of the main volume). Following the impeachment, Congress permitted the Independent Counsel Act to expire. Should it have been renewed? For an argument that the statute should have been preserved, albeit with significant reforms, see Gormley, An Original Model of the Independent Counsel Statute, 97 Mich. L. Rev. 601 (1998).

Consider the possibility that centralization of executive power actually weakens the presidency. In The Paradox of Power in the Modern State: Why a Unitary, Centralized Presidency May Not Exhibit Effective or Legitimate Leadership, 144 U. Pa. L. Rev. 827, 837-38 (1996), Michael Fitts argues that the "president's visibility and centralization may [delegitimate] his exercise of government power [by diminishing] the president's ability to mediate conflict, [subjecting] him to an instrumentally inappropriate standard of personal moral evaluation, [resulting] in an overassessment of personal presidential error, [and leading] to an overassessment of the president's responsibility for government and social outcomes." In order to deal with these problems and strengthen the presidency, Fitts proposes "selected cutbacks in *direct* presidential oversight of agencies, and the judicious creation of commissions [that] operate with less direct presidential control."

D. Foreign Affairs

Page 476. At the bottom of the page, add the following:

For an important historical overview of the emergence of the modern position on presidential power over foreign affairs, see White, The Transformation of the Constitutional Regime of Foreign Relations, 85 U. Va. L. Rev. 1 (1999). Professor White attacks the conventional view that the growth of the President's foreign affairs power was rooted in changes in constitutional law surrounding the New Deal period. He maintains that the changes came much earlier in the twentieth century and were supported by prominent judicial opponents of the New Deal.

Page 477. At the end of the page, add the following:

Consider Sofaer, The Power over War, 50 Miami L. Rev. 33, 35-36 (1995):

Congress clearly has the upper hand with regard to war, as it controls the means of warmaking, and can punish Presidents for disregarding its instructions. On the other hand, the President has substantial powers related to war that the Constitution enables the President to use independently. The President's powers over the conduct of foreign affairs, for example, can lead the nation into conflicts, and can even cause war. Similarly, the President's power as Commander in Chief encompasses the power to utilize the troops, ships, planes, and missiles supplied by Congress to defend the territory, armed forces, citizens, and commerce of the United States, even though such actions involve the use of force and can lead to broader conflict amounting to war.

Nothing in the record of the Constitution's adoption justifies [the] view that the President's powers cannot be exercised if they involve use of force, until and unless Congress authorizes such action. [Neither] the decision to clog the road to combat, nor the determination to design a system that forces legislative review of war-related issues, establishes an intent to require the legislature to exercise the power conferred, to interfere with a decision by the President to use force, or to reach a conclusion on these issues in any respect.

Page 481. At the end of the page, add the following:

d. *The War in Kosovo.* On March 24, 1999, the United States commenced its largest military operation since the Gulf War. Americans joined a NATO air operation designed to deter and, subsequently, to reverse the "ethnic cleansing" of Kosovo, a province of Yugoslavia. Once again, the operation was undertaken without benefit of a formal congressional declaration of war.

The air strikes began after Yugoslavia's rejection of NATO demands designed to insure Kosovo's autonomy. On March 26, 1999, the President submitted a formal report to Congress which, he said, was "part of my efforts to keep Congress fully informed consistent with the War Powers Resolution." In the report, he asserted that he was undertaking the action "pursuant to my constitutional authority to conduct U.S. foreign relations and as Commander-in-Chief and Chief Executive."

Congress took a number of seemingly inconsistent actions with regard to the war. On March 23, 1999, the Senate passed a resolution authorizing the President to conduct military air operations in Yugoslavia, but the House rejected a similar measure in a tie vote on April 28, 1999. On the same day, the House defeated a measure declaring a state of war between the United States and Yugoslavia and a measure directing the President to remove all U.S. armed forces from the operations against Yugoslavia, but adopted a measure prohibiting the use of funds for the deployment of ground troops. On May 6, 1999, the House passed a measure providing emergency funding for the war.

On April 30, 1999, several members of Congress filed suit in United States District Court seeking a declaratory judgment that the Kosovo action was unconstitutional without a congressional declaration of war and that under § 1544(b) of the War Powers Resolution, the President was obligated to terminate hostilities within 60 calendar days of his report to Congress. Is this claim justiciable? If so, how should the court rule on the merits?

e. *United Nations "peacekeeping" and "peace enforcement."* In recent years, the President has authorized use of American forces in United Nations-sponsored military actions in Bosnia, Haiti, and Somalia. In each of these cases, the President did not seek prior congressional approval before troops were committed. Does the Constitution require congressional action before troops are sent as "peacekeepers" or "peace enforcers"? Consider Stromseth, Collective Force and Constitutional Responsibility: War Powers in the Post-Cold War Era, 50 Miami L. Rev. 145, 165, 166 (1995):

> [Given] the spectrum of U.N.-authorized military actions, the authority of the President to commit American forces without congressional approval will vary depending on the nature and risks of each operation. At one end of the spectrum are actions that clearly have the character and risks of "war" and are best understood as requiring prior authorization from Congress. At the other end of the spectrum are [peacekeeping] operations that enjoy the consent of all of the parties and are deployed in situations posing little risk of hostilities. Although Congress may limit American involvement in such peacekeeping operations, the President has a strong argument that sending American forces to these operations falls within well-established historical patterns of presidential peacetime troop deployments. Many if not most of the U.N.-authorized operations in which the United States is likely to participate, however, will fall into the more ambiguous middle ground. These include ["peace] enforcement" operations involving hostilities, but on a limited scale. Strong constitutional arguments in favor of congressional authorization can be made in many such cases, but grey areas and room for disagreement admittedly will exist.

For a comprehensive history of presidential warmaking, concluding that contemporary assertions of executive power "would have astonished the framers of the Constitution," see L. Fisher, Presidential War Power (1995).

Page 489.   Before section 3 of the Note, add the following:

For a detailed analysis, see Raven-Hansen & Banks, From Vietnam to Desert Shield: The Commander in Chief's Spending Power, 81 Iowa L. Rev. 79 (1995).

5
EQUALITY AND THE CONSTITUTION

A. Race and the Constitution

Page 509. After the second sentence of the second full paragraph, add the following:

The Court demonstrated renewed interest in the privileges and immunities clause in Saenz v. California Department of Social Services, 119 S. Ct. 1518 (1999), where it invalidated a California statute that limited newly arrived California residents to the welfare payments they were eligible to receive in the state from which they came. In previous cases, the Court had relied upon the equal protection clause and the constitutional right to travel when reviewing discrimination against newly arrived residents. On this occasion, however, the Court relied upon the Fourteenth Amendment's privileges and immunities clause:

> What is at issue in this case, [is] the right of the newly arrived citizen to the same privileges and immunities enjoyed by other citizens of the same State. That right is protected not only by the new arrival's status as a state citizen, but also by her status as a citizen of the United States. . . .
> Despite fundamentally differing views concerning the coverage of the Privileges or Immunities Clause of the Fourteenth Amendment, most notably expressed in the majority and dissenting opinions in the Slaughter-House Cases, it has always been common ground that this Clause protects [this] component of the right to travel.

Page 526. Before section b of the Note, add the following:

See Amar, Intratextualism, 112 Harv. L. Rev. 747, 768-773 (1999) for an argument that the Fourteenth Amendment's privileges and immunities clause, the nobility clauses, and the bill of attainder clause all justify the result in *Bolling*.

Here is how Professor Amar explains why *Bolling's* reading of the due process clause does not make the equal protection clause a redundancy:

> [For] the framers and ratifiers of the Fourteenth Amendment, the words of its Equal Protection Clause were not expressing a different idea than the words of the Due Process Clause but were elaborating the same idea: the Equal Protection Clause was in part a clarifying gloss on the due process idea. (Indeed, an early draft of the Amendment spoke of "equal protection in the rights of life, liberty, and property.") [If] equal protection really was implicit in the Fourteenth Amendment concept of "due process of law," as its framers believed and said, then after ratification of this Amendment, equal protection should also be seen as implicit in the Fifth Amendment phrase "due process of law." What's sauce for the Fourteenth Amendment should intratextually be sauce for the Fifth.

Page 528.   Before section 2 of the Note, add the following:

For a defense of the *Brown* Court's generalization concerning harm to black children caused by segregation, see Ely, If at First You Don't Succeed, Ignore the Question Next Time? Group Harm in *Brown v. Board of Education* and *Loving v. Virginia,* 15 Const. Comm. 215 (1998).

Page 558.   After the quotation from "The Hollow Hope" in the middle of the page, add the following:

For representative criticism of Rosenberg's position, see Schultz & Gottlieb, Legal Functionalism and Social Change: A Reassessment of Rosenberg's The Hollow Hope: Can Courts Bring About Social Change?, 12 J.L. & Pol. 63 (1996). Schultz and Gottlieb argue that "[if] *Brown* had not occurred, other items, such as the Cold War or McCarthyism might have filled the [legislative] agenda. *Brown* put something on the agenda and made it acceptable and legitimate to criticize segregation. It was a necessary step in the process leading to desegregation, although not a sufficient one." Id. at 77.

Page 566.   Before section 4 of the Note, add the following:

3a. *Relevant differences and a "class of one."* Suppose that the Transit Authority requires its employees to have a high school diploma, but "irrationally" concludes that a particular employee lacks such a diploma. Would this decision deprive the employee of equal protection? Would the case be meaningfully different if the Transit Authority intentionally required one employee to have a high school diploma when it required this of no one else?

Consider in this connection Village of Willowbrook v. Olech, 120 S. Ct. 1073 (2000). Plaintiffs asked the Village to connect their property to the municipal water supply, but the Village refused to do so unless plaintiffs provided it with a 33-foot easement. Plaintiffs alleged that the village required only a 15-foot easement from other property owners, that this difference of treatment was "irrational and wholly arbitrary," and that it was motivated by ill will resulting from a previous, unrelated law suit, which plaintiffs had successfully brought against the Village.

In a per curiam opinion, the Court held that the plaintiffs had stated a valid equal protection claim. According to the Court, a plaintiff belonging to a "class of one" can maintain such a claim "where [she] alleges that she has been intentionally treated differently from others similarly situated and that there is no rational basis for the difference in treatment." The majority held that these allegations were sufficient "quite apart from the Village's subjective motivation" and that it was therefore unnecessary to reach plaintiffs' alternative theory of subjective ill will.

In a concurring opinion, Justice Breyer expressed sympathy for the view that this holding might "transform many ordinary violations of city or state law into violations of the Constitution. [Zoning] decisions, for example, will often, perhaps almost always treat one landowner differently from another, and one might claim that, when a city's zoning authority takes an action that fails to conform to a city zoning regulation, it lacks a 'rational basis' for its [action]." Justice Breyer nonetheless concurred in the result on the ground that plaintiffs had also alleged "vindictive action."

Why does the majority limit its holding to plaintiffs who allege that they are *intentionally* treated differently? What does "intentionally" mean in this context?

B. *Equal Protection Methodology: Rational Basis Review*

Page 574. Before section 2 of the Note, add the following:

For another example of low-level scrutiny of the means/ends nexus, see Central State University v. American Association of University Professors, Central State University Chapter, 119 S. Ct. 1162 (1999). The Ohio Supreme Court held that a state statute requiring public universities to develop standards for professors' instructional workloads and exempting these standards from collective bargaining violated the equal protection clause. Without requesting briefs or hearing oral argument, the Supreme Court summarily reversed:

> One of the statute's objectives was to increase the time spent by faculty in the classroom; the imposition of a faculty workload policy not subject to collective bargaining was an entirely rational step to accomplish this objective. The legislature could quite reasonably have concluded that the policy animating the law would have been undercut and likely varied if it were subject to collective bargaining. The State, in effect, decided that the attainment of this goal was more important than the system of collective bargaining that had previously included university professors.

Compare Justice Stevens's dissent:

> The Court assumes that the question [is] whether collective bargaining may interfere with the attainment of a uniform workload policy. But that is not the issue, because this case involves the Equal Protection Clause, and not the principles of substantive due process.
>
> The question posed by this case is whether there is a rational basis for discriminating against faculty members by depriving them of bargaining assistance that is available to all other public employees in the State of Ohio.

Page 584.   At the end of section 2 of the Note, add the following:

Vacco v. Quill, 521 U.S. 793 (1997), applied the "rational basis" test in upholding a statute banning physician-assisted suicide against a challenge asserting that the distinction between terminating existing life support, which was permitted by statute, and providing assistance in suicide, which was not, was arbitrary and irrational. Chief Justice Rehnquist's opinion for the Court first found that the statutes banning assisted suicide and permitting termination of life support did not "[on] their faces [treat] anyone differently than anyone else or draw any distinctions between persons. Everyone, regardless of physical condition, is entitled, if competent, to refuse unwanted lifesaving medical treatment; no one is permitted to assisted a suicide." The distinction, the Court continued, "comports with fundamental legal principles of causation and intent. [When] a patient refuses life-sustaining medical treatment, he dies from an underlying fatal disease or pathology; but if a patient ingests lethal medication prescribed by a physician, he is killed by that medication. [A] physician who withdraws [life-sustaining] medical treatment purposefully intends, or may so intend, only to respect his patient's wishes. [The] same is true when a doctor provides aggressive palliative care. [A] doctor who assists a suicide ['must,] necessarily and indubitably, intend primarily that the patient be made dead.'" According to the Court, "the law distinguishes between actions taken 'because of' a given end from actions taken 'in spite of' their unintended but foreseen consequences." The distinction drawn between assisted suicide and withdrawal of life-sustaining treatment "follows a longstanding and rational distinction." The Court then stated that the state's "reasons for recognizing and acting on this distinction — including prohibiting intentional killing and preserving life; preventing suicide, [and others]" — were "valid and important" and "easily satisfy the constitutional requirement that a legislative classification bear a rational relation to some legitimate end."

Suppose philosophers demonstrate that the "common sense" distinctions on which the Court relied do not stand up under sustained analytic scrutiny. Is it nonetheless permissible for legislatures to rely on them in enacting statutes that the courts then give only "rational basis" scrutiny?

Page 588. Before section 2 of the Note, add the following:

In Saenz v. California Department of Social Services, 119 S. Ct. 1518 (1999), the Court relied upon the Fourteenth Amendment's privileges and immunities clause, rather than the equal protection clause, to invalidate a California statute providing for smaller welfare benefits for newly arrived residents.

Page 589. Before subsection 2b of the Note, add the following:

In Romer v. Evans, 517 U.S. 620 (1996), the Court relied on *Moreno* to invalidate a Colorado constitutional amendment that prohibited local measures outlawing discrimination against homosexuals. The Court stated:

Amendment 2 fails, indeed defies, [conventional rational basis] inquiry. First, the amendment has the peculiar property of imposing a broad and undifferentiated disability on a single named group, an exceptional and [invalid] form of legislation. Second, its sheer breadth is so discontinuous with the reasons offered for it that the amendment seems inexplicable by anything but animus toward the class that it affects; it lacks a rational relationship to legitimate state interests. . . .

[Laws] of the kind now before us raise the inevitable inference that the disadvantage imposed is born of animosity toward the class of persons affected. "If the constitutional conception of 'equal protection of the laws' means anything, it must at the very least mean that a bare . . . desire to harm a politically unpopular group cannot constitute a legitimate governmental interest." [*Moreno*]. Even laws enacted for broad and ambitious purposes often can be explained by reference to legitimate public policies which justify the incidental disadvantages they impose on certain persons. Amendment 2, however, in making a general announcement that gays and lesbians shall not have any particular protections from the law, inflicts on them immediate, continuing, and real injuries that outrun and belie any legitimate justifications that may be claimed for it.

Compare Justice Scalia's dissenting opinion:

The Court's opinion contains grim, disapproving hints that Coloradans have been guilty of "animus" or "animosity" toward homosexuality, as though that has been established as Unamerican. Of course it is our moral heritage that one should not hate any human being or class of human beings. But I had thought that one could consider certain conduct reprehensible—murder, for example, or polygamy, or cruelty to animals—and could exhibit even "animus" toward such conduct. Surely that is the only sort of "animus" at issue here: moral disapproval of homosexual conduct, the same sort of moral disapproval that produced the centuries-old criminal laws that we held constitutional in Bowers [v. Hardwick].

For a more detailed discussion of *Romer*, see this Supplement to page 780 of the main volume.

C. Equal Protection Methodology: Heightened Scrutiny and the Problem of Race

Page 602. Before section 2 of the Note, add the following:

For an intriguing exploration of the tensions between the colorblindness principle and originalist methodology, see Marcosson, Colorizing the Constitution of Originalism: Clarence Thomas at the Rubicon, 16 Law & Ineq. J. 429 (1998).

Page 609. After the first paragraph of section 3 of the Note, add the following:

Consider Fletcher, In God's Image: The Religious Imperative of Equality under Law, 99 Colum. L. Rev. 1608, 1624 (1999):

In [cases of caste reinforcing discrimination], where it makes sense to rely on the premise of human equality in the Declaration of Independence, [the] realization of equality under law should be treated as a categorical imperative. The courts are obligated in all cases to bring our legislation into conformity with our understanding of intrinsic human equality. No state interest can justify practices that both reflect and reenforce cultural assumptions about the intrinsic superiority of whites over blacks, men over women, "legitimate" over "illegitimate" children, or heterosexuals over homosexuals. This, at least, is the way our law of equal protection would look if the courts began to take human equality seriously.

Even if this view is correct, might not the strength of the state interest be relevant to a determination as to whether a classification does in fact "reflect and reenforce" assumptions about intrinsic superiority?

Page 614. Before section 2 of the Note, add the following:

Compare Cole, The Paradox of Race and Crime: A Comment on Randall Kennedy's "Politics of Distinction," 83 Geo. L. Rev. 2547, 2551 (1995):

The effect Kennedy has identified is attributable not to anything inherent in practices with a disparate impact, but rather to the phenomenon of intraracial crime. In this setting, anything the state does—intentional or not—that helps law-abiding African Americans is likely to burden law-violating African-Americans, and vice versa. Thus, Kennedy's argument would suggest that all discrimination in criminal law enforcement should be subject to minimal scrutiny.

Page 617. At the end of the second full paragraph, add the following:

See also Campbell v. Louisiana, — S. Ct. — (1998) (holding that a white defendant had standing to raise an equal protection claim alleging discrimination against black persons in the selection of a grand jury).

Page 618. Before section 2 of the Note, add the following:

For an interesting discussion of *Batson* and *McCollum* from the perspective of a defense attorney, see Smith, "Nice Work if You Can Get It": "Ethical" Jury Selection in Criminal Defense, 67 Fordham L. Rev. 523 (1998). On the basis of jury research and her own trial experience, Smith concludes that she would be violating her ethical obligation to provide effective assistance of counsel if she did not make race-conscious jury selection decisions.

In United States v. Armstrong, 517 U.S. 456 (1996), the Court held that, because a criminal defendant had failed to make the necessary threshold showing that the government had declined to prosecute similarly situated suspects of other races, he was not entitled to discovery from the government on a discriminatory prosecution claim. The defendant had been charged with conspiring to possess with intent to distribute "crack" cocaine. In support of his discovery motion, he offered an affidavit alleging that in every one of twenty-four similar cases closed by the Federal Public Defender Office during the year in question, the defendant was black. In addition, he submitted an affidavit from one of his attorneys alleging that an intake coordinator at a drug treatment center had told her that there were "an equal number of caucasian users and dealers to minority users and dealers," an affidavit from another criminal defense attorney alleging that in his experience many nonblacks were prosecuted in state court for crack offenses, and a newspaper article reporting that federal "crack criminals . . . are being punished far more severely than if they had been caught with powder cocaine, and almost every single one of them is black." The district court granted the defense request, and the court of appeals affirmed. In an 8-1 decision, the Court, per Chief Justice Rehnquist, reversed. The Court held that

> To establish a discriminatory effect in a race case, the claimant must show that similarly situated individuals of a different race were not prosecuted. . . .
>
> [If] the claim of selective prosecution were well founded, it should not have been an insuperable task to prove that persons of other races were being treated differently than respondents. [We] think the required threshold — a credible showing of different treatment of similarly situated persons — adequately balances the Government's interest in vigorous prosecution and the defendant's interest in avoiding selective prosecution. . . .
>
> The Court of Appeals reached its decision in part because it started "with the presumption that people of *all* races commit *all* types of crimes — not with the premise that any type of crime is the exclusive province of any particular racial or ethnic group." It cited no authority for this proposition, which seems contradicted by the most recent statistics of the United States Sentencing Commission. Those statistics show that: More than 90% of the persons sentenced in 1994 for crack cocaine trafficking were black; 93.4% of convicted LSD dealers were white; and 91% of those convicted for pornography or prostitution were white. Presumptions at war with presumably reliable statistics have no proper place in the analysis of this issue.

The Court found the defendant's study inadequate because it "failed to identify individuals who were not black, could have been prosecuted for the offenses for which respondents were charged, but were not so prosecuted." It dismissed the newspaper article as irrelevant to the allegation of discrimination in prosecutorial decisions and the other affidavits as "hearsay" and "personal conclusions based on anecdotal evidence." It distinguished *Batson* as follows:

> During jury selection, the entire *res gestae* take place in front of the trial judge. Because the judge has before him the entire venire, he is well situated to detect whether a challenge to the seating of one juror is part of a "pattern" of singling out members of a single race for peremptory challenges. He is in a position to discern whether a challenge to a black juror has evidentiary significance; the significance may differ if the venire consists mostly of blacks or of whites. Similarly, if the defendant makes out a prima facie case, the prosecutor is called upon to justify only decisions made in the very case then before the court. The trial judge need not review prosecutorial conduct in relation to other venires in other cases.

Only Justice Stevens dissented:

> The Court correctly concludes that in this case the facts presented to the District Court in support of respondents' claim that they had been singled out for prosecution because of their race were not sufficient to prove the defense. [I] am persuaded[, however,] that the District Judge did not abuse her discretion when she concluded that the factual showing was sufficiently disturbing to require some response from the United States Attorney's Office.

Note that the defendant did not allege that the statutory penalties for possession and distribution of "crack" were influenced by the racial composition of the class charged with violating the statute. How should such a claim be evaluated? In *Batson* and other cases, the Court has stated that the constitutional prohibition against race discrimination prevents the state from relying on even accurate racial generalizations. Does Chief Justice Rehnquist violate this norm when he relies on the supposedly different propensities of racial groups to commit different crimes?

Page 620. Before section c of the Note, add the following:

In Reno v. American-Arab Anti-Discrimination Committee, 119 S. Ct. 936 (1999), the Court stated the "general rule" that claims of discriminatory prosecution were not available to aliens contesting their deportation. The decision came in the context of a free speech challenge to alleged discrimination based upon the alien's affiliation with an organization claimed to be supporting terrorist activity. The Court left open the possibility that this general rule might be overcome in an "outrageous" case, but did not specify the nature of such a case. Does the general rule overcome the usual constitutional suspicion of racial and national origin discrimination, or would discriminatory deportation on these grounds be "outrageous"?

Page 622.   At the end of section c of the Note, add the following:

The Court applied the *Mt. Healthy* approach in a racial context in Texas v. Lesage, 120 S. Ct. 467 (1999). Lesage who was of Caucasian descent, was refused admission to the University of Texas and filed a suit alleging that the University's race-conscious admissions process violated the equal protection clause. In a per curiam opinion, the Supreme Court held that the District Court had appropriately granted summary judgment to the defendant on the ground that Lesage would not have been admitted even if race had not been taken into account. According to the Court, "where a plaintiff challenges a discrete governmental decision as being based on an impermissible criterion and it is undisputed that the government would have made the same decision regardless, there is no cognizable injury warranting relief." The Court distinguished circumstances where a plaintiff challenges an ongoing race-conscious program and seeks forward-looking relief. In such a case, the plaintiff "need not establish that he would receive the benefit in question if race were not considered and can rely on the injury imposed by "the inability to compete on an equal footing."

Page 631.   At the conclusion of the Note, add the following:

Compare *Hernandez* with Rice v. Cayetano, 120 S. Ct. 1044 (2000). The Hawaiian constitution establishes the Office of Hawaiian Affairs (OHA), which is vested with authority to administer revenue from land held in trust for the betterment of the conditions of the descendants of the indigenous people who inhabited the island in 1778, the date when England's Captain Cook made landfall in Hawaii. (The constitutionality of this arrangement was not before the Court, and the Court expressed no opinion on this subject). The right to vote for the nine trustees composing the governing body of the OHA is limited to persons who were descendants of people inhabiting Hawaii in 1778. Petitioner challenged this limitation on the ground that it violated the fifteenth amendment prohibition against racial restrictions on the right to vote. In a 7-2 decision, the Supreme Court, per Justice Kennedy, held that the restriction amounted to racial discrimination and, therefore, violated the amendment:

Ancestry can be a proxy for race. It is that proxy here. Even if the residents of Hawaii in 1778 had been of more diverse ethnic backgrounds and cultures, it is far from clear that a voting test favoring their descendants would not be a race-based qualification. But that is not this case. For centuries Hawaii was isolated from migration. The inhabitants shared common physical characteristics, and by 1778 they had a common culture [The] provisions before us reflect the State's effort to preserve that commonality of people to the present day. . . .

Simply because a class defined by ancestry does not include all members of the race does not suffice to make the classification race neutral. Here, the State's argument is undermined by its express racial purpose and by its actual effects.

Justice Stevens, in an opinion joined by Justice Ginsburg, dissented:

The OHA voter qualification speaks in terms of ancestry and current residence, not of race or color. . . .

Ancestry surely can be a proxy for race, or a pretext for invidious racial discrimination. But it is simply neither proxy nor pretext here. All of the persons who are eligible to vote for the trustees of OHA share two qualifications that no other person old enough to vote possesses: They are beneficiaries of the public trust created by the State and administered by OHA, and they have at least one ancestor who was a resident of Hawaii in 1778. A trust whose terms provide that the trustees shall be elected by a class including the beneficiaries is hardly a novel concept. . . .

[The] OHA election provision excludes all full-blooded Polynesians currently residing in Hawaii who are not descended from a 1778 resident of Hawaii. Conversely, [the] OHA scheme excludes no descendant of a 1778 because he or she is also part European, Asian, or African as a matter of race. The classification here is thus both too inclusive and not inclusive enough to fall strictly along racial lines.

Page 632. Before section 1 of the Note, add the following:

For a detailed analysis of the Court's different treatments of the intent requirement in different contexts and an effort to explain the differences in terms of the Court's role in policing the fairness of the political process, see Foster, Intent and Incoherence, 72 Tul. L. Rev. 1065 (1998).

Page 635.   At the end of section 2, add the following:

In Bush v. Vera, 517 U.S. 952 (1996), a plurality of the Court held that although the shape of the district was only of evidentiary significance when the issue was the triggering of heightened scrutiny, it bore directly on whether there was the "narrow tailoring" that heightened scrutiny requires:

> Our discussion in *Miller* served only to emphasize that the ultimate constitutional values at stake involve the harms caused by the use of unjustified racial classifications, and that bizarreness is not necessary to trigger strict scrutiny. Significant deviations from traditional districting principles, such as the bizarre shape and noncompactness demonstrated by the districts here, cause constitutional harm insofar as they convey the message that political identity is, or should be, predominantly racial. For example, the bizarre shaping of Districts 18 and 29, cutting across pre-existing precinct lines and other natural or traditional divisions, is not merely evidentially significant; it is part of the constitutional problem insofar as it disrupts nonracial bases of political identity and thus intensifies emphasis on race.

Bush is discussed in greater detail in Chapter 6 Section E of this Supplement.

In Hunt v. Cromartie, 119 S. Ct. 1545 (1999), the Court made clear that a bizarrely shaped district was not constitutionally vulnerable if the legislature was motivated by political, rather than racial, ends. In response to the Supreme Court's earlier decisions in Shaw v. Reno, 509 U.S. 630 (1993), and Shaw v. Hunt, 517 U.S. 899 (1996), the North Carolina legislature redrew the boundaries of District 12. The newly drawn district was no longer majority black and was somewhat less bizarrely shaped. The district court nonetheless granted a motion for summary judgment invalidating the district on the ground that race was the predominant factor motivating the drawing of district lines. The Court, per Justice Thomas, reversed, holding that there was a material dispute of fact which made the grant of summary judgment improper. The Court quoted from an affidavit by an expert witness who found a "strong correlation between racial composition and party preference" so that "in precincts with high black representation, there is a correspondingly high tendency for voters to favor the Democratic Party." Based on this affidavit, the Court held that

> Accepting appellants' political motivation explanation as true, as the District Court was required to do in ruling on appellees' motion for summary judgment, appellees were not entitled to judgment as a matter of law. Our prior decisions have made clear that a jurisdiction may engage in constitutional

political gerrymandering, even if it so happens that the most loyal Democrats happen to be black Democrats and even if the State were conscious of that fact. Evidence that blacks constitute even a supermajority in one congressional district while amounting to less than a plurality in a neighboring district will not, by itself, suffice to prove that a jurisdiction was motivated by race in drawing its district lines when the evidence also shows a high correlation between race and party preference.

Does *Hunt* mean that the legislature may constitutionally rely on an empirically supported racial generalization, like the generalization that most African-Americans will vote for Democratic candidates? Is such reliance consistent with the Court's holding in Batson v. Kentucky, discussed at page 617 of the main volume?

Page 646.   Before section 2 of the Note, add the following:

For a thoughtful discussion of the various strands of the *Loving* opinion, see Moore, *Loving*'s Legacy: The Other Antidiscrimination Principle, 34 Harv. C.R.-C.L. L. Rev. 163 (1999).

Moore argues that the result in *Loving* is supported by three different principles: the "neutrality" principle; the "consistency" principle, and the "impartiality" principle. The neutrality principle prohibits the government from making distinctions solely according to race. As applied to *Loving*, the principle was violated because the substance of the criminal act turned on the defendant's race. (Mr. Loving was punished for an act (marrying a black woman) that would not have been criminal but for the fact that Mr. Loving was white.) In contrast, the consistency principle prohibits the government from regulating matters touching on race when other, comparable matters are left unregulated. As applied to *Loving*, the principle was violated because of special constraints placed on the racial aspect of marriage that are not placed on other aspects of marital choice. Finally, the impartiality principle prohibits statutes motivated by animus toward racial groups. In *Loving*, the animus was demonstrated by the prohibition of interracial marriages involving whites, but not on interracial marriages exclusively involving nonwhites.

Moore argues that the second and third principles have "largely disappeared from conventional equal protection analysis today" and that "[a] more robust antidiscrimination analysis must reincorporate the principles of consistency and impartiality that animated cases such as *Loving*."

Page 648.   At the end of section 4 of the Note, add the following:

In Romer v. Evans, 517 U.S. 620 (1996), the Court utilized rational basis review to invalidate an amendment to the Colorado constitution that prohibited localities from enacting laws that protected homosexuals from discrimination. The Court stated:

> It is not within our constitutional tradition to enact laws of this sort. Central both to the idea of the rule of law and to our own Constitution's guarantee of equal protection is the principle that government and each of its parts remain open on impartial terms to all who seek its assistance. "'Equal protection of the laws is not achieved through indiscriminate imposition of inequalities.'" Sweatt v. Painter (quoting Shelley v. Kraemer). Respect for this principle explains why laws singling out a certain class of citizens for disfavored legal status or general hardships are rare. A law declaring that in general it shall be more difficult for one group of citizens than for all others to seek aid from the government is itself a denial of equal protection of the laws in the most literal sense. "The guaranty of 'equal protection of the laws is a pledge of the protection of equal laws.'" Skinner v. Oklahoma ex rel. Williamson, (quoting Yick Wo v. Hopkins).

Compare Justice Scalia's dissent:

> The central thesis of the Court's reasoning is that any group is denied equal protection when, to obtain advantage (or, presumably, to avoid disadvantage), it must have recourse to a more general and hence more difficult level of political decisionmaking than others. The world has never heard of such a principle, which is why the Court's opinion is so long on emotive utterance and so short on relevant legal citation. And it seems to me most unlikely that any multilevel democracy can function under such a principle. For whenever a disadvantage is imposed, or conferral of a benefit is prohibited, at one of the higher levels of democratic decisionmaking (i.e., by the state legislature rather than local government, or by the people at large in the state constitution rather than the legislature), the affected group has (under this theory) been denied equal protection. To take the simplest of examples, consider a state law prohibiting the award of municipal contracts to relatives of mayors or city councilmen. Once such a law is passed, the group composed of such relatives must, in order to get the benefit of city contracts, persuade the state legislature — unlike all other citizens, who need only persuade the municipality. It is ridiculous to consider this a denial of equal protection, which is why the Court's theory is unheard-of.

In The Promise of Cooley's City: Traces of Local Constitutionalism, 147 U. Pa. L. Rev. 487, 568, 578, 589 (1999), David Barron argues that *Seattle, Crawford,* and *Romer* can all be explained by what he calls "local constitutionalism." This principle holds that "as a matter of federal constitutional structure, states may not preclude their local political institutions from promoting a norm of constitutional equality that lies beyond direct judicial enforcement." Thus, in *Seattle*, the Court's unwillingness to saddle localities with burdensome remedies for school segregation rested on the supposition that "states would not [restrict] the remedial power of the very public institutions to which [the Supreme Court] had instructed the federal courts to defer." On this view, *Crawford* is distinguishable because the California constitutional amendment, unlike the Washington measure, "[restricted] central judicial interference with local educational processes. [*Crawford*] simply followed [*Seattle School District*] in preserving local discretion to remedy segregation." *Romer*, too, can be understood as resting on the proposition that local governments must be left free to enforce constitutional principles that federal courts are ill-equipped to implement.

> Federal courts are necessarily poorly positioned to assess the degree of affirmative "protection" that citizens are owed from private power. Federal courts could directly enforce a broad constitutional norm that prohibited private discrimination only by intruding deeply into the practices and functions of local self-government, and thereby calling their own legitimacy into substantial doubt. Such a declaration would obliterate the line between the public and private and threaten to make any private action subject to constitutional challenge. . . .
>
> The constitutional obligation to provide public protection from private harms, therefore, was left, as a matter of federal constitutional structure, to the states and their local governments. . . .
>
> Given this background, Colorado's blanket action to bar all of its local political institutions from determining that a certain class of persons needed statutory protection appeared to upset the careful structure of the federal constitutional framework.

For a more detailed discussion of *Romer*, see this Supplement to page 780 of the main volume.

Page 688.   At the end of subsection e of the Note, add the following:

In connection with the political process argument, consider Strauss, Affirmative Action and the Public Interest, 1995 Sup. Ct. Rev. 1, 12-13:

In general, the notion of "consistency" used in Adarand and Croson would lead to implausible, even bizarre, conclusions. . . .

The Court has never ruled, for example, that homosexuals are a suspect class. Today, therefore, affirmative action legislation favoring homosexuals would be treated the same as legislation favoring, say, optometrists or any other group: all such legislation is almost automatically constitutional under the rational basis standard. But suppose the Court were to decide that the extent of prejudice against homosexuals is sufficiently great, and their political power sufficiently limited, to warrant declaring homosexuality a suspect classification. Under *Adarand* and *Croson*, that decision would automatically make it much more difficult to enact legislation favoring homosexuals than to favor optometrists or tobacco farmers. In other words, under the "consistency" principle, the decision that homosexuals have historically been discriminated against, are currently the victims of prejudice, and lack political power would yield the conclusion that legislation seeking to aid homosexuals is subject to strict scrutiny and generally unconstitutional. This cannot possibly be the right approach.

Page 691.   At the bottom of the page, add the following:

For an argument that *Croson* permits extensive affirmative action to remedy private discrimination, see Ayers & Vars, When Does Private Discrimination Justify Public Affirmative Action, 98 Colum. L. Rev. 1577 (1998). The authors argue that *Croson* permits government affirmative action to remedy private discrimination in three circumstances: (1) The causal justification. When government spending causes private discrimination, the government has a compelling justification for remedying it. For example, if prime contractors working for the government discriminate against minority subcontractors, the government can use affirmative action on behalf of these subcontractors. (2) The but-for justification. Even if the government does not cause private discrimination, it can utilize affirmative action so as to make certain that its procurements are not distorted by private discrimination. For example, if a private association refuses to accredit minority businesses and the government relied upon this accreditation, it can utilize affirmative action to remove this distortion. (3) The single market justification. On this theory, the government can use affirmative action not just to correct shortfalls in government purchasing caused by private discrimination, but also to compensate for shortfalls in private purchasing caused by private discrimination. Although the government cannot use affirmative action in one market to remedy discrimination in another, the government should be able to remedy private discrimination against sellers of the same product.

Page 692.   At the end of section b of the Note, add the following:

Does the diversity argument for affirmative action survive Croson and Adarand? Consider Amar & Katyal, Bakke's Fate, 43 U.C.L.A. L. Rev. 1745, 1746 (1996):

> [One] can agree with [Croson and Adarand] and still share the vision of *Bakke*: Because our public universities should be places where persons from different walks of life and diverse backgrounds come together to talk with, to learn from, and to teach each other, each person's unique background and life experience may be relevant in the admissions [process]. . . .
>
> If a university wants to teach people about France, the university should admit students from France; if a university wants to teach people about the South, it should admits students from the South. The university experience is thus quite different from the very attenuated interaction between the minority "owner" of a broadcast station and the public in *Metro Broadcasting,* and even more different from the largely nonexistent contact between the minority and nonminority contractors in *Croson* and *Adarand.* Integrated education democratically benefits students of all races, including white students, by [providing] a space for people of all races to grow together.

Page 692.   At the end of the page, add the following:

Consider Addis, Role Models and the Politics of Recognition, 144 U. Pa. L. Rev. 1377, 1442-1443 (1996):

> Ironically, while the Supreme Court rejected the role model theory as an "amorphous" remedial measure in one context, it considered the notion sufficiently precise to justify exclusion and discrimination in another context. Thus, in Ambach v. Norwick, [441 U.S. 68 (1979)], the Supreme Court upheld a New York statute that permitted only United States citizens or persons who intended to apply for citizenship to receive a public school teaching certificate on the ground that "a teacher serves as a role model for his students, exerting a subtle but important influence over their perceptions and values." Justice Powell, the same Justice who, in *Wygant*, deemed the role model theory too ambiguous to justify race-based decisionmaking, seemed quite confident that the notion was precise enough to justify the state's exclusion of resident aliens from the teaching profession and to prevent that exclusion from violating the Equal Protection Clause of the Fourteenth Amendment.

d. *The public interest.* Can strict scrutiny for affirmative action measures be justified on the ground that it is designed to insure that such measures are really in the "public interest" rather than simply a part of a "racial spoils system"? Consider Strauss, Affirmative Action and the Public Interest, 1995 Sup. Ct. Rev. 1, 3-4:

> [What] the Court has done is to revive, in the area of affirmative action, one of the noble dreams of American public law—that courts should try to ensure that legislation does not just benefit narrow interest groups but instead serves a public interest. This dream has at times turned into what would generally be thought a nightmare, as in the *Lochner* era. The Court's selectivity, in dealing only with affirmative action laws (and perhaps a few others) in this way, is hard to defend. There are enormous theoretical and practical problems in trying to define a public interest, as distinguished from special interests. But however questionable, the Court's approach to affirmative action should be understood and evaluated, as the latest display of this undeniably attractive leitmotif of American law.

e. *The "special" case of American Indians.* Are the many statutes providing special treatment for American Indians consistent with the strict scrutiny supposedly accorded race-specific statutes? In his dissenting opinion in Rice v. Cayetano, 120 S. Ct. 1044 (2000), Justice Stevens summarized the current state of the law:

> Throughout our Nation's history, this Court has recognized both the plenary power of Congress over the affairs of native Americans and the fiduciary character of the special federal relationship with descendants of those once sovereign peoples. . . . As our cases have consistently recognized, Congress' plenary power over these peoples has been exercised time and again to implement a federal duty to provide native peoples with special 'care and protection.' [Today], the Federal Bureau of Indian Affairs [administers] countless modern programs responding to [pragmatic] concerns, including health, education, housing, and impoverishment. Federal regulation in this area is not limited to the strictly practical but has encompassed as well the protection of cultural values. . . .
>
> [This] Court has taken account of the 'numerous occasions' on which 'legislation that singles out Indians for particular and special treatment' has been upheld, and has concluded that as 'long as the special treatment can be tied rationally to fulfillment of Congress' unique obligations towards the Indians, such legislative judgments will not be disturbed.

Can this body of law be reconciled with the Court's treatment of race-based affirmative action in other contexts? What is it about sovereignty—as distinct from individual liberty—that justifies placing unique obligations on Congress with respect to Native Americans but not with respect to African Americans?

Consider in this regard, the Court's treatment of a statute restricting the franchise to descendants of native Hawaiians in Rice v. Cayetano, supra. Hawaii's constitution charges the Office of Hawaiian Affairs (OHA) with the task of managing huge plots of land held in trust for the descendants of the Polynesians who occupied the Hawaiian Islands before the 1778 arrival of Captain Cook. Among its other tasks, OHA is charged with carrying out the duties of the trust relationship between the Islands' indigenous peoples and the Government of the United States, compensating for past wrongs to the ancestors of those people, and helping to preserve the indigenous culture that existed before 1778.

In a 7-2 decision, the Court assumed, without deciding, that the substantive activities of OHA were constitutional. It found, however, that the method by which the trustees who administered OHA were elected violated the fifteenth amendment because the franchise was limited to descendants of people inhabiting the Islands in 1778. Writing for the Court, Justice Kennedy rejected the analogy to statutes dealing specially with American Indians:

> The decisions of this Court, interpreting the effect of treaties and congressional enactments on the subject, have held that various tribes retained some elements of quasi-sovereign authority, even after cession of their lands to the United States. In reliance on that theory the Court has sustained a federal provision giving employment preferences to persons of tribal ancestry. [Morton v. Mancari, 417 U.S. 535 (1974)]....
>
> It does not follow from Mancari, however, that Congress may authorize a State to establish a voting scheme that limits the electorate for its public officials to a class of tribal Indians, to the exclusion of all non-Indian citizens.
>
> [If] a non-Indian lacks the right to vote in tribal elections, it is for the reason that such elections are the internal affair of a quasi-sovereign. The OHA elections, by contrast, are the affair of the State of Hawaii. . . .
>
> To extend Mancari to this context would be to permit a State, by racial classification, to fence out whole classes of its citizens from decisionmaking in critical state affairs.

Justice Stevens, joined by Justice Ginsburg, dissented:

> The descendants of the native Hawaiians share with the descendants of the Native Americans on the mainland or in the Aleutian islands not only a history of subjugation at the hands of colonial forces, but also a purposefully created and specialized 'guardian-ward' relationship with the Government of the United States. It follows that legislation targeting the native Hawaiians must be evaluated according to the same understanding of equal protection

that this Court has long applied to the Indians on the continental United States: that 'special treatment . . . be tied rationally to the fulfillment of Congress' unique obligation' toward the native peoples . . . .

[The] Federal Government [has] not been limited in its special dealings with the native peoples to laws affecting tribes or tribal Indians alone. In light of this precedent, it is a painful irony indeed to conclude that native Hawaiians are not entitled to special benefits designed to restore a measure of native self-governance because they currently lack any vestigial native government—a possibility of which history and the actions of this Nation have deprived them.

Consider the extent to which the last paragraph of Justice Stevens opinion might apply to African Americans as well.

Page 694. At the end of section 3 of the Note, add the following:

In Bush v. Vera, 517 U.S. 952 (1996), a three-Justice plurality of the Court assumed, without deciding, that compliance with section 2 of the Voting Rights Act was a compelling state interest justifying using race as a predominant factor in drawing district lines. Section 2 goes beyond prohibiting discriminatory intent in districting by imposing a "results" test: districts are illegal when protected groups "have less opportunity than other members of the electorate to [elect] representatives of their choice." The plurality nonetheless held that the districts in question were unconstitutional because they were "bizarrely shaped" and "far from compact" and because section 2 as previously interpreted by the Court did not "require race-based creation of a district that is far from compact." The plurality noted, however, that

[i]f the State has a "strong basis in evidence" for concluding that creation of a majority-minority district is reasonably necessary to comply with §2, and the districting that is based on race "substantially addresses the §2 violation," it satisfies strict scrutiny. . . . A §2 district that is reasonably compact and regular, taking into account traditional districting principles such as maintaining communities of interest and traditional boundaries, may pass strict scrutiny without having to defeat rival compact districts designed by plaintiffs' experts in endless "beauty contests." [Under] our cases, the States retain a flexibility that federal courts enforcing §2 lack [insofar] as deference is due to their reasonable fears of, and to their reasonable efforts to avoid, §2 liability.

In an unusual concurrence to her own plurality opinion, Justice O'Connor wrote that in her judgment, compliance with the "results" requirement of section

2 was a compelling state interest. In a separate concurrence, Justice Thomas, joined by Justice Scalia, "[assumed] without deciding" that the State had asserted a compelling state interest. "Given that assumption, I agree that the State's redistricting attempts were not narrowly tailored to achieve its asserted interest." Justice Stevens, joined by Justices Ginsburg and Breyer, and Justice Souter, also joined by Justices Ginsburg and Breyer, filed dissenting opinions.

In Shaw v. Hunt, 517 U.S. 899 (1996), decided on the same day as Bush, the Court, in a 5-4 decision written by Chief Justice Rehnquist,

> [assumed] *arguendo* for the purpose of resolving this case, that compliance with §2 could be a compelling interest, and we likewise assume, *arguendo*, that the General Assembly believed a second majority-minority district was needed in order not to violate §2, and that the legislature at the time it acted had a strong basis in evidence to support that conclusion.

The Court nonetheless found the district unconstitutional because it was not narrowly tailored to meet the asserted end. This was so because a district that was not "narrowly compact" would not avoid a section 2 violation.

> If a §2 violation is proven for a particular area, it flows from the fact that individuals in this area "have less opportunity than other members of the electorate to participate in the political process and elect representatives of their choice" [quoting from section 2]. The vote dilution injuries suffered by these persons are not remedied by creating a safe majority-black district somewhere else in the State. For example, if a geographically compact, cohesive minority poulation lives in south-central to southeastern North Carolina, . . . [a district] which spans the Piedmont Crescent would not address that §2 violation. The black voters of the south-central to southeastern region would still be suffering precisely the same injury that they suffered before [the district] was drawn.

Bush and Shaw v. Hunt are discussed in more detail in this Supplement to Chapter 6 Section E of the main volume.

Consider the possibility that the "narrow tailoring" requirement might actually support explicit racial quotas. In Ayres, Narrow Tailoring, 43 U.C.L.A. L. Rev. 1781, 1782 (1996), the author argues that:

> [extending] affirmative action subsidies to non-victim whites produces less-tailored, over-inclusive programs. And because both race-neutral and explicitly racial means share the same race-conscious motivation of remedying past discrimination, it is not clear that race-neutral means represent a less restrictive alternative.

[Quotas] may be more narrowly tailored to achieve the government's remedial interest than many racial preferences. While quotas are imperfectly tailored because they mandate an inflexible level of minority participation, bidding credits (and other preferences) may be poorly tailored because they induce *too much uncertainty and volatility* in minority participation. More narrowly tailored programs will exhibit a "sliding scale" of racial preferences in which the size of the preference will vary inversely with the degree of successful minority participation in the program. Under a narrowly tailored program, the farther minority participation falls below what it would be in the absence of discrimination, the larger the racial preference government might legitimately confer.

Page 694. Before section 5 of the Note, add the following:

Do *Croson* and *Adarand* raise questions about "soft" affirmative action designed to encourage employers to "reach out" to minority communities through race-conscious recruitment devices? For a strong defense of such measures, see Adams, The Last Wave of Affirmative Action, 1998 Wis. L. Rev. 1395.

Page 696. Before section 6 of the Note, add the following:

For the Court's latest holdings regarding race-based congressional districting, see Shaw v. Hunt, 517 U.S. 899 (1996) and Bush v. Vera, 517 U.S. 952 (1996), discussed in Chapter 6 Section E of this Supplement to the main volume.

Consider Spann, Affirmative Action and Discrimination, 39 How. L. Rev. 1, 72 (1995):

[The] consequence of *Adarand* will necessarily be to divert some societal resources from racial minorities to whites. The racial minorities who would have received societal resources under an affirmative action program that *Adarand* invalidates will no longer receive them; they will instead go to members of the white majority.

This diversion of resources [is] good, old-fashioned racial discrimination, pure and simple. It disadvantages racial minorities to advance the interests of whites. It does so through the use of an explicit racial classification that distinguishes affirmative action programs from other resource allocation programs. It is the product of an official government body taking an official government action, with full knowledge of the adverse impact that its action will have on the interests of racial minorities. It inflicts a type of harm on racial minorities that, by design and effect, is both widespread and pervasive.

And it ultimately stigmatizes racial minorities in a way that brands them as inferior to whites.

5a. *The Empirical Dimension.* Consider the extent to which the dispute about affirmative action turns on disagreement about empirical questions. For example, opponents and proponents of affirmative action may disagree about whether affirmative action helps or hurts its intended beneficiaries, about whether it increases or decreases racial antagonism, and about whether a "colorblind" regime eliminates or perpetuates discrimination.

For an excellent summary of the social psychological literature bearing on these and other questions, see Krieger, Civil Rights Perestroika: Intergroup Relations after Affirmative Action, 86 Cal. L. Rev. 1251, 1264, 1267-68, 1294, 1331 (1998). According to Krieger, there is reason for concern that at least certain types of affirmative action may harm intended beneficiaries. The evidence that affirmative action produces self-derogating effects is mixed and largely depends on how the program is described and implemented. The effects of such programs on nonbeneficiaries is more troublesome. For example:

> In one group of studies, experimenters asked subjects to evaluate the qualifications of people supposedly selected for employment or admission to programs of higher education. Researchers indirectly informed subjects in one condition that the selecting institution had an affirmative action program. In a second condition, researchers made no mention of affirmative action. Subjects in the "affirmative action" condition consistently rated the files of selected women and minorities as reflecting lower levels of competence, qualification, and accomplishment than did subjects evaluating identical files in the "non-affirmative action" condition.

Researchers have also found that

> there are serious bases for concern that preferential forms of affirmative action might reinforce subtle negative expectancies relating to members of beneficiary groups. For example, using overt preferences in selection decision making can increase the salience of race or gender in those institutions. As many social cognition researchers have demonstrated, the more salient a particular characteristic in the mind of the observer, the more likely that observer will use it in making causal attributions. . . .
>
> Absent some explanatory theory, the presence of women or minorities [in positions] [indicating] high levels of ability and accomplishment would disconfirm a variety of inconsistent, negative racial or gender stereotypes. [Preferential] selection, however, provides a plausible situational attribution

for the stereotype-inconsistent information. Once female or minority presence in "high places" is attributed to preferential selection rather than to merit-related factors, pre-existing negative stereotypes are insulated from the potentially disconfirming effect of the otherwise stereotype disconfirming data.

To some degree these negative effects can be mitigated by programs that take into account both "merit" and group membership, by emphasizing a pattern of discrimination against the group in describing the programs, and by avoiding numerical quotas. Moreover, Krieger claims, that a "colorblind" approach is unlikely to eliminate discrimination.

> [Research] strongly suggests that cognitive biases in social judgment operate automatically, without intention or awareness, and can be controlled only through subsequent, deliberate "mental correction" that takes group status squarely into account. . . .
>
> When we encounter a person in our social environment, we automatically place that person into pre-existing categorical structures. [Admonitions] to refrain from categorizing the social environment in a particular way will prove ineffective if those categories reflect patterns made salient by history, culture, or observable patterns of economic, demographic, or political distribution. Whether we like it or not, it is highly implausible to assume that an American of one race encountering an American of another race would not notice racial attributes or use those attributes in initially categorizing the person perceived. [Nothing] in the colorblindness approach to nondiscrimination provides social decision makers with the tools required to recognize or to correct for biases of this sort. . . .
>
> [Only] the application of deliberate, controlled, corrective processes can prevent stereotypes and subtle ingroup priming valences from biasing interpersonal judgment. . . .
>
> [A] professor considering which student to hire as a research assistant, may know the rule, "don't discriminate against the black guy." But [colorblindness] cannot be applied in the same way as cost-benefit [analysis]. It can be applied to eliminate facial [discrimination]. But it cannot be applied to prevent or correct biases caused by emotional discomfort, the subconscious effects of stereotypes, causal attribution, or spontaneous trait inference, because it fails to provide a specific set of procedures or techniques which can be applied to the evaluation or decision task at hand.

According to Krieger, this problem is aggravated by subtle biases in the construction of "merit."

Social identity research [has] shown that we undervalue the product of an outgroup in relation to our own group's products. Accordingly, if those who control the definition of merit in a particular social context belong to the same social reference group, and if members of that group tend to excel on one of the relevant performance dimensions in relation to the others, social identity theory predicts that those who determine merit will tend to over-value performance in the domain where they collectively excel.

Krieger concludes that

For better or for worse, the application of insights from social cognition and social identity theory complicates rather than simplifies the affirmative action debate. On the one hand, there is reason to fear that preferential forms of affirmative action, at least in some contexts, may indeed exacerbate intergroup tensions and perpetuate rather than reduce subtle forms of intergroup bias. [On] the other hand, insights derived from these fields suggest that we are not yet ready to abandon preferential forms of affirmative action for the simple reason that we have nothing adequate with which to replace them.

For a detailed and mostly positive empirical study of the effects of affirmative action in higher education, see William Bowen and Derek Bok, The Shape of the River (1998). How, if at all, do you think that such studies should affect the constitutional issue?

Page 697.   At the conclusion of the Note, add the following:

For an insightful examination of American affirmative action through the lens of Indian experience, see Cunningham & Menon, Race, Class, Caste . . . ? Rethinking Affirmative Action, 97 Mich. L. Rev. 1296 (1999). According to Cunningham and Menon, if the United States followed the Indian model of directing affirmative action against caste-like structures, it would result in

[a reduction in] the absolute number of persons eligible for affirmative action [even] if the number of identified groups was expanded somewhat beyond the four commonly listed: black, Hispanic, Native American and Asian. [The] Indian approach has been to create artificial groups [that] use intersecting cultural, social and economic factors to narrow, not expand the number of potentially eligible persons. The first limiting principle is that [a] group that intermarries freely with other groups, although identifiable in other way, would not be eligible. The second limitation would be that the [group] be significantly below average levels of educational [attainment].

The third factor would consist of a mix of socioeconomic factors indicative of continuing effects of past discrimination. It is likely that such heterogenous categories as "Asian" and "Hispanic" would break into much more discrete units, some of which would present more compelling cases for affirmative action than others; such a process might even take place within the group now called African-American, which [might] also be quite heterogenous.

Would this approach to affirmative action be preferable to methods used in the United States? Under current doctrine, would it be constitutionally permissible?

D. Equal Protection Methodology: Heightened Scrutiny and the Problem of Gender

Page 713.   Before section 4 of the Note, add the following:

United States v. Virginia
518 U.S. 515 (1996)

JUSTICE GINSBURG delivered the opinion of the Court.

Virginia's public institutions of higher learning include an incomparable military college, Virginia Military Institute (VMI). The United States maintains that the Constitution's equal protection guarantee precludes Virginia from reserving exclusively to men the unique educational opportunities VMI affords. We agree.

I

Founded in 1839, VMI is today the sole single-sex school among Virginia's 15 public institutions of higher learning. VMI's distinctive mission is to produce "citizen-soldiers," men prepared for leadership in civilian life and in military service. VMI pursues this mission through pervasive training of a kind not available anywhere else in Virginia. Assigning prime place to character development, VMI uses an "adversative method" modeled on English public schools and once characteristic of military instruction. VMI constantly endeavors to instill physical and mental discipline in its cadets and impart to them a strong moral code. The school's graduates leave VMI with heightened comprehension of their capacity to deal with duress and stress, and a large sense of accomplishment for completing the hazardous course.

VMI has notably succeeded in its mission to produce leaders; among its alumni are military generals, Members of Congress, and business executives. The school's alumni overwhelmingly perceive that their VMI training helped them to realize their personal goals. VMI's endowment reflects the loyalty of its graduates; VMI has the largest per-student endowment of all undergraduate institutions in the Nation.

Neither the goal of producing citizen-soldiers nor VMI's implementing methodology is inherently unsuitable to women. And the school's impressive record in producing leaders has made admission desirable to some women. Nevertheless, Virginia has elected to preserve exclusively for men the advantages and opportunities a VMI education affords. . . .

II

A . . .

VMI produces its "citizen-soldiers" through "an adversative, or doubting, model of education" which features "physical rigor, mental stress, absolute equality of treatment, absence of privacy, minute regulation of behavior, and indoctrination in desirable values.". . . .

VMI cadets live in spartan barracks where surveillance is constant and privacy nonexistent; they wear uniforms, eat together in the mess hall, and regularly participate in drills. Entering students are incessantly exposed to the rat line, "an extreme form of the adversative model," comparable in intensity to Marine Corps boot camp. Tormenting and punishing, the rat line bonds new cadets to their fellow sufferers and, when they have completed the 7-month experience, to their former tormentors.

VMI's "adversative model" is further characterized by a hierarchical "class system" of privileges and responsibilities, a "dyke system" for assigning a senior class mentor to each entering class "rat," and a stringently enforced "honor code," which prescribes that a cadet " 'does not lie, cheat, steal nor tolerate those who do.' "

VMI attracts some applicants because of its reputation as an extraordinarily challenging military school, and "because its alumni are exceptionally close to the school." "Women have no opportunity anywhere to gain the benefits of [the system of education at VMI]."

B

[In 1990, the United States sued Virginia and VMI, alleging that VMI's admission policy violated the Equal Protection Clause. At the conclusion of a trial, the District Court found that "some women, at least" would want to attend VMI and were capable of all the activities required of VMI cadets. The district court nonetheless ruled in favor of VMI. The court acknowledged that women were denied a unique education opportunity available only at VMI, but held that if women were admitted "some aspects of the [school's] distinctive method would be altered." Specifically, allowance for personal privacy would have to be made, physical education requirements would have to be altered, and the adversative environment could not survive unmodified. The court found that these changes would impinge upon the state interest in diversity in public education.

[The Court of Appeals reversed, holding that "neither the goal of producing citizen soldiers nor VMI's implementing methodology is inherently unsuitable to women." It remanded the case to the district court for purposes of selecting a remedy.]

C

In response to the Fourth Circuit's ruling, Virginia proposed a parallel program for women: Virginia Women's Institute for Leadership (VWIL). The 4-year, state-sponsored undergraduate program would be located at Mary Baldwin College, a private liberal arts school for women, and would be open, initially, to about 25 to 30 students. Although VWIL would share VMI's mission—to produce "citizen-soldiers"—the VWIL program would differ, as does Mary Baldwin College, from VMI in academic offerings, methods of education, and financial resources.

The average combined SAT score of entrants at Mary Baldwin is about 100 points lower than the score for VMI freshmen. Mary Baldwin's faculty holds "significantly fewer Ph.D.'s than the faculty at VMI," and receives significantly lower salaries, While VMI offers degrees in liberal arts, the sciences, and engineering, Mary Baldwin, at the time of trial, offered only bachelor of arts degrees. A VWIL student seeking to earn an engineering degree could gain one, without public support, by attending Washington University in St. Louis, Missouri, for two years, paying the required private tuition.

Experts in educating women at the college level composed the Task Force charged with designing the VWIL program; Task Force members were drawn from Mary Baldwin's own faculty and staff. Training its attention on methods of instruction appropriate for "most women," the Task Force determined that a military model would be "wholly inappropriate" for VWIL. . . .

In lieu of VMI's adversative method, the VWIL Task Force favored "a cooperative method which reinforces self-esteem." In addition to the standard bachelor of arts program offered at Mary Baldwin, VWIL students would take courses in leadership, complete an off-campus leadership externship, participate in community service projects, and assist in arranging a speaker series.

Virginia represented that it will provide equal financial support for in-state VWIL students and VMI cadets, and the VMI Foundation agreed to supply a $5.4625 million endowment for the VWIL program, Mary Baldwin's own endowment is about $19 million; VMI's is $131 million. Mary Baldwin will add $35 million to its endowment based on future commitments; VMI will add $220 million. The VMI Alumni Association has developed a network of employers interested in hiring VMI graduates. The Association has agreed to open its network to VWIL graduates, but those graduates will not have the advantage afforded by a VMI degree.

D

[The district court approved this remedial plan, and the court of appeals affirmed.]

III

The cross-petitions in this case present two ultimate issues. First, does Virginia's exclusion of women from the educational opportunities provided by VMI—extraordinary opportunities for military training and civilian leadership development—deny to women "capable of all of the individual activities required of VMI cadets," the equal protection of the laws guaranteed by the Fourteenth Amendment? Second, if VMI's "unique" situation,—as Virginia's sole single-sex public institution of higher education—offends the Constitution's equal protection principle, what is the remedial requirement?

IV

We note, once again, the core instruction of this Court's pathmarking decisions in J. E. B. v. Alabama ex rel. T. B. [page 726 of the main volume] and *Mississippi Univ. for Women*: Parties who seek to defend gender-based government action must demonstrate an "exceedingly persuasive justification" for that action. . . .

Since *Reed*, the Court has repeatedly recognized that neither federal nor state government acts compatibly with the equal protection principle when a law or official policy denies to women, simply because they are women, full citizenship stature—equal opportunity to aspire, achieve, participate in and contribute to society based on their individual talents and capacities.

Without equating gender classifications, for all purposes, to classifications based on race or national origin,[6] the Court, in post-Reed decisions, has carefully inspected official action that closes a door or denies opportunity to women (or to men). To summarize the Court's current directions for cases of official classifi-

---

[6] The Court has thus far reserved most stringent judicial scrutiny for classifications based on race or national origin, but last Term observed that strict scrutiny of such classifications is not inevitably "fatal in fact." [Adarand]

cation based on gender: Focusing on the differential treatment or denial of opportunity for which relief is sought, the reviewing court must determine whether the proffered justification is "exceedingly persuasive." The burden of justification is demanding and it rests entirely on the State. The State must show "at least that the [challenged] classification serves 'important governmental objectives and that the discriminatory means employed' are 'substantially related to the achievement of those objectives.'" The justification must be genuine, not hypothesized or invented post hoc in response to litigation. And it must not rely on overbroad generalizations about the different talents, capacities, or preferences of males and females.

The heightened review standard our precedent establishes does not make sex a proscribed classification. Supposed "inherent differences" are no longer accepted as a ground for race or national origin classifications. See Loving v. Virginia. Physical differences between men and women, however, are enduring. . . .

"Inherent differences" between men and women, we have come to appreciate, remain cause for celebration, but not for denigration of the members of either sex or for artificial constraints on an individual's opportunity. Sex classifications may be used to compensate women "for particular economic disabilities [they have] suffered," to "promote equal employment opportunity," to advance full development of the talent and capacities of our Nation's people.[7] But such classifications may not be used, as they once were, to create or perpetuate the legal, social, and economic inferiority of women.

Measuring the record in this case against the review standard just described, we conclude that Virginia has shown no "exceedingly persuasive justification" for excluding all women from the citizen-soldier training afforded by VMI. We therefore affirm the Fourth Circuit's initial judgment, which held that Virginia had violated the Fourteenth Amendment's Equal Protection Clause. Because the remedy proffered by Virginia — the Mary Baldwin VWIL program — does not cure the constitutional violation, i.e., it does not provide equal opportunity, we reverse the Fourth Circuit's final judgment in this case.

---

[7] Several amici have urged that diversity in educational opportunities is an altogether appropriate governmental pursuit and that single-sex schools can contribute importantly to such diversity. Indeed, it is the mission of some single-sex schools "to dissipate, rather than perpetuate, traditional gender classifications." We do not question the State's prerogative even-handedly to support diverse educational opportunities. We address specifically and only an educational opportunity recognized by the District Court and the Court of Appeals as "unique," an opportunity available only at Virginia's premier military institute, the State's sole single-sex public university or college.

V

[Virginia] asserts two justifications in defense of VMI's exclusion of women. First, the Commonwealth contends, "single-sex education provides important educational benefits," and the option of single-sex education contributes to "diversity in educational approaches." Second, the Commonwealth argues, "the unique VMI method of character development and leadership training," the school's adversative approach, would have to be modified were VMI to admit women. We consider these two justifications in turn.

A

Single-sex education affords pedagogical benefits to at least some students, Virginia emphasizes, and that reality is uncontested in this litigation. Similarly, it is not disputed that diversity among public educational institutions can serve the public good. But Virginia has not shown that VMI was established, or has been maintained, with a view to diversifying, by its categorical exclusion of women, educational opportunities within the State. In cases of this genre, our precedent instructs that "benign" justifications proffered in defense of categorical exclusions will not be accepted automatically; a tenable justification must describe actual state purposes, not rationalizations for actions in fact differently grounded. . . .

Neither recent nor distant history bears out Virginia's alleged pursuit of diversity through single-sex educational options. In 1839, when the State established VMI, a range of educational opportunities for men and women was scarcely contemplated. Higher education at the time was considered dangerous for women; reflecting widely held views about women's proper place, the Nation's first universities and colleges — for example, Harvard in Massachusetts, William and Mary in Virginia — admitted only men. . . .

Virginia describes the current absence of public single-sex higher education for women as "an historical anomaly." But the historical record indicates action more deliberate than anomalous: First, protection of women against higher education; next, schools for women far from equal in resources and stature to schools for men; finally, conversion of the separate schools to coeducation. The state legislature, prior to the advent of this controversy, had repealed "all Virginia statutes requiring individual institutions to admit only men or women." And in 1990, an official commission, "legislatively established to chart the future goals of higher education in Virginia," reaffirmed the policy "of affording broad access" while maintaining "autonomy and diversity." Significantly, the Commission reported:

> "Because colleges and universities provide opportunities for students to develop values and learn from role models, it is extremely important that they

deal with faculty, staff, and students without regard to sex, race, or ethnic origin."

This statement, the Court of Appeals observed, "is the only explicit one that we have found in the record in which the Commonwealth has expressed itself with respect to gender distinctions."

Our 1982 decision in *Mississippi Univ. for Women* prompted VMI to reexamine its male-only admission policy. Virginia relies on that reexamination as a legitimate basis for maintaining VMI's single-sex character. A Mission Study Committee, appointed by the VMI Board of Visitors, studied the problem from October 1983 until May 1986, and in that month counseled against "change of VMI status as a single-sex college." Whatever internal purpose the Mission Study Committee served — and however well-meaning the framers of the report — we can hardly extract from that effort any state policy evenhandedly to advance diverse educational options. As the District Court observed, the Committee's analysis "primarily focused on anticipated difficulties in attracting females to VMI," and the report, overall, supplied "very little indication of how the conclusion was reached."

In sum, we find no persuasive evidence in this record that VMI's male-only admission policy "is in furtherance of a state policy of 'diversity.'" No such policy, the Fourth Circuit observed, can be discerned from the movement of all other public colleges and universities in Virginia away from single-sex education. That court also questioned "how one institution with autonomy, but with no authority over any other state institution, can give effect to a state policy of diversity among institutions." A purpose genuinely to advance an array of educational options, as the Court of Appeals recognized, is not served by VMI's historic and constant plan—a plan to "afford a unique educational benefit only to males." However "liberally" this plan serves the State's sons, it makes no provision whatever for her daughters. That is not equal protection.

B

Virginia next argues that VMI's adversative method of training provides educational benefits that cannot be made available, unmodified, to women. Alterations to accommodate women would necessarily be "radical," so "drastic," Virginia asserts, as to transform, indeed "destroy," VMI's program. Neither sex would be favored by the transformation, Virginia maintains: Men would be deprived of the unique opportunity currently available to them; women would not gain that opportunity because their participation would "eliminate the very aspects of [the] program that distinguish [VMI] from . . . other institutions of higher education in Virginia."

[It] is uncontested that women's admission would require accommodations, primarily in arranging housing assignments and physical training programs for female cadets. It is also undisputed, however, that "the VMI methodology could be used to educate women." ["Some] women," the expert testimony established, "are capable of all of the individual activities required of VMI cadets." The parties, furthermore, agree that "some women can meet the physical standards [VMI] now imposes on men." . . .

In support of its initial judgment for Virginia, a judgment rejecting all equal protection objections presented by the United States, the District Court made "findings" on "gender-based developmental differences." . . .

The United States does not challenge any expert witness estimation on average capacities or preferences of men and women. Instead, the United States emphasizes that time and again since this Court's turning point decision in Reed v. Reed, we have cautioned reviewing courts to take a "hard look" at generalizations or "tendencies" of the kind pressed by Virginia, and relied upon by the District Court. State actors controlling gates to opportunity, we have instructed, may not exclude qualified individuals based on "fixed notions concerning the roles and abilities of males and females." [*Mississippi Univ. for Women*]

It may be assumed, for purposes of this decision, that most women would not choose VMI's adversative method. As Fourth Circuit Judge Motz observed, however, in her dissent from the Court of Appeals' denial of rehearing en banc, it is also probable that "many men would not want to be educated in such an environment." (On that point, even our dissenting colleague might agree.) Education, to be sure, is not a "one size fits all" business. The issue, however, is not whether "women—or men—should be forced to attend VMI"; rather, the question is whether the State can constitutionally deny to women who have the will and capacity, the training and attendant opportunities that VMI uniquely affords.

The notion that admission of women would downgrade VMI's stature, destroy the adversative system and, with it, even the school, is a judgment hardly proved, a prediction hardly different from other "self-fulfilling prophecies," once routinely used to deny rights or opportunities. When women first sought admission to the bar and access to legal education, concerns of the same order were expressed. For example, in 1876, the Court of Common Pleas of Hennepin County, Minnesota, explained why women were thought ineligible for the practice of law. Women train and educate the young, the court said, which "forbids that they shall bestow that time (early and late) and labor, so essential in attaining to the eminence to which the true lawyer should ever aspire. It cannot therefore be said that the opposition of courts to the admission of females to practice . . . is to any extent the outgrowth of . . . 'old fogyism[.]' . . . It arises rather from a comprehension of the magnitude of the responsibilities connected with the successful practice of law, and a desire to grade up the profession." A like fear, according to a 1925 report, accounted for Columbia Law School's resistance to women's admission, although

the faculty . . . never maintained that women could not master legal learning. . . . No, its argument has been . . . more practical. If women were admitted to the Columbia Law School, [the faculty] said, then the choicer, more
manly and red-blooded graduates of our great universities would go to the
Harvard Law School!" The Nation, Feb. 18, 1925, p.173. . . .

Women's successful entry into the federal military academies, and their participation in the Nation's military forces, indicate that Virginia's fears for the
future of VMI may not be solidly grounded. The State's justification for excluding all women from "citizen-soldier" training for which some are qualified, in
any event, cannot rank as "exceedingly persuasive," as we have explained and
applied that standard.

Virginia and VMI trained their argument on "means" rather than "end," and
thus misperceived our precedent. Single-sex education at VMI serves an "important governmental objective," they maintained, and exclusion of women is not
only "substantially related," it is essential to that objective. By this notably circular argument, the "straightforward" test *Mississippi Univ. for Women* described was bent and bowed.

The State's misunderstanding and, in turn, the District Court's, is apparent
from VMI's mission: to produce "citizen-soldiers," individuals "'imbued with
love of learning, confident in the functions and attitudes of leadership, possess-
ing a high sense of public service, advocates of the American democracy and
free enterprise system, and ready . . . to defend their country in time of national
peril.'"

Surely that goal is great enough to accommodate women, who today count
as citizens in our American democracy equal in stature to men. Just as surely,
the State's great goal is not substantially advanced by women's categorical exclusion, in total disregard of their individual merit, from the State's premier
"citizen-soldier" corps.[16] Virginia, in sum, "has fallen far short of establishing
the 'exceedingly persuasive justification,'" that must be the solid base for any
gender-defined classification.

VI . . .

A . . .

Virginia chose not to eliminate, but to leave untouched, VMI's exclusionary
policy. For women only, however, Virginia proposed a separate program, differ-

---

[16] VMI has successfully managed another notable change. The school admitted its first
African-American cadets in 1968. See The VMI Story 347-349 (students no longer sing
"Dixie," salute the Confederate flag or the tomb of General Robert E. Lee at ceremonies
and sports events).

ent in kind from VMI and unequal in tangible and intangible facilities. Having violated the Constitution's equal protection requirement, Virginia was obliged to show that its remedial proposal "directly addressed and related to" the violation, i.e., the equal protection denied to women ready, willing, and able to benefit from educational opportunities of the kind VMI offers. . . .

VWIL affords women no opportunity to experience the rigorous military training for which VMI is famed. Instead, the VWIL program "deemphasizes" military education, and uses a "cooperative method" of education "which reinforces self-esteem." . . .

Virginia maintains that these methodological differences are "justified pedagogically," based on "important differences between men and women in learning and developmental needs," "psychological and sociological differences" Virginia describes as "real" and "not stereotypes." . . .

As earlier stated, generalizations about "the way women are," estimates of what is appropriate for most women, no longer justify denying opportunity to women whose talent and capacity place them outside the average description. Notably, Virginia never asserted that VMI's method of education suits most men. It is also revealing that Virginia accounted for its failure to make the VWIL experience "the entirely militaristic experience of VMI" on the ground that VWIL "is planned for women who do not necessarily expect to pursue military careers." By that reasoning, VMI's "entirely militaristic" program would be inappropriate for men in general or as a group, for "only about 15% of VMI cadets enter career military service."[19]. . .

B

In myriad respects other than military training, VWIL does not qualify as VMI's equal. VWIL's student body, faculty, course offerings, and facilities

---

[19] Admitting women to VMI would undoubtedly require alterations necessary to afford members of each sex privacy from the other sex in living arrangements, and to adjust aspects of the physical training programs. Cf. note following 10 U.S.C. §4342 (academic and other standards for women admitted to the Military, Naval, and Air Force Academies "shall be the same as those required for male individuals, except for those minimum essential adjustments in such standards required because of physiological differences between male and female individuals"). Experience shows such adjustments are manageable. See U.S. Military Academy, A. Vitters, N. Kinzer, & J. Adams, Report of Admission of Women (Project Athena I-IV) (1977-1980) (4-year longitudinal study of the admission of women to West Point); Defense Advisory Committee on Women in the Services, Report on the Integration and Performance of Women at West Point 17-18 (1992). [Relocated footnote]

hardly match VMI's. Nor can the VWIL graduate anticipate the benefits associated with VMI's 157-year history, the school's prestige, and its influential alumni network. . . .

Virginia, in sum, while maintaining VMI for men only, has failed to provide any "comparable single-gender women's institution." Instead, the Commonwealth has created a VWIL program fairly appraised as a "pale shadow" of VMI in terms of the range of curricular choices and faculty stature, funding, prestige, alumni support and influence.

Virginia's VWIL solution is reminiscent of the remedy Texas proposed 50 years ago, in response to a state trial court's 1946 ruling that, given the equal protection guarantee, African Americans could not be denied a legal education at a state facility. See Sweatt v. Painter. Reluctant to admit African Americans to its flagship University of Texas Law School, the State set up a separate school for Herman Sweatt and other black law students. . . .

More important than the tangible features, the [Sweatt] Court emphasized, are "those qualities which are incapable of objective measurement but which make for greatness" in a school, including "reputation of the faculty, experience of the administration, position and influence of the alumni, standing in the community, traditions and prestige." Facing the marked differences reported in the Sweatt opinion, the Court unanimously ruled that Texas had not shown "substantial equality in the [separate] educational opportunities" the State offered. Accordingly, the Court held, the Equal Protection Clause required Texas to admit African Americans to the University of Texas Law School. In line with Sweatt, we rule here that Virginia has not shown substantial equality in the separate educational opportunities the State supports at VWIL and VMI.

C . . .

Valuable as VWIL may prove for students who seek the program offered, Virginia's remedy affords no cure at all for the opportunities and advantages withheld from women who want a VMI education and can make the grade.[20] In

---

[20] Virginia's prime concern, it appears, is that "placing men and women into the adversative relationship inherent in the VMI program ... would destroy, at least for that period of the adversative training, any sense of decency that still permeates the relationship between the sexes." It is an ancient and familiar fear. Compare In re Lavinia Goodell, 39 Wis. 232, 246 (1875) (denying female applicant's motion for admission to the bar of its court, Wisconsin Supreme Court explained: "Discussions are habitually necessary in courts of justice, which are unfit for female ears. The habitual presence of women at these would tend to relax the public sense of decency and propriety."), with Levine, Closing Comments, 6 Law & Inequality 41, 41 (1988) (presentation at Eighth Circuit Judicial Conference, Colorado Springs, Colorado, July 17, 1987) (footnotes omitted): "Plato questioned whether women should be afforded equal opportunity to become

sum, Virginia's remedy does not match the constitutional violation; the State has shown no "exceedingly persuasive justification" for withholding from women qualified for the experience premier training of the kind VMI affords.

VII . . .

A prime part of the history of our Constitution, historian Richard Morris recounted, is the story of the extension of constitutional rights and protections to people once ignored or excluded. [R. Morris, The Forging of the Union, 1781-1789 (1989).] VMI's story continued as our comprehension of "We the People" expanded. There is no reason to believe that the admission of women capable of all the activities required of VMI cadets would destroy the Institute rather than enhance its capacity to serve the "more perfect Union."

For the reasons stated, the initial judgment of the Court of Appeals is affirmed, the final judgment of the Court of Appeals is reversed, and the case is remanded for further proceedings consistent with this opinion.

It is so ordered.

Justice Thomas took no part in the consideration or decision of this case.

CHIEF JUSTICE REHNQUIST, concurring in judgment.

The Court holds first that Virginia violates the Equal Protection Clause by maintaining [VMI's] all-male admissions policy, and second that establishing the [VWIL] program does not remedy that violation. While I agree with these conclusions, I disagree with the Court's analysis and so I write separately.

---

guardians, those elite Rulers of Platonic society. Ironically, in that most undemocratic system of government, the Republic, women's native ability to serve as guardians was not seriously questioned. The concern was over the wrestling and exercise class in which all candidates for guardianship had to participate, for rigorous physical and mental training were prerequisites to attain the exalted status of guardian. And in accord with Greek custom, those exercise classes were conducted in the nude. Plato concluded that their virtue would cloth the women's nakedness and that Platonic society would not thereby be deprived of the talent of qualified citizens for reasons of mere gender."

[Virginia,] not bound to ancient Greek custom in its "rigorous physical and mental training" programs, could more readily make the accommodations necessary to draw on "the talent of [all] qualified citizens."

I

Two decades ago in Craig v. Boren, we announced that "to withstand constitutional challenge, . . . classifications by gender must serve important governmental objectives and must be substantially related to achievement of those objectives." We have adhered to that standard of scrutiny ever since. While the majority adheres to this test today, it also says that the State must demonstrate an " 'exceedingly persuasive justification' " to support a gender-based classification. It is unfortunate that the Court thereby introduces an element of uncertainty respecting the appropriate test.

While terms like "important governmental objective" and "substantially related" are hardly models of precision, they have more content and specificity than does the phrase "exceedingly persuasive justification." That phrase is best confined, as it was first used, as an observation on the difficulty of meeting the applicable test, not as a formulation of the test itself. See, e.g., [Massachusetts v. Feeney] ("These precedents dictate that any state law overtly or covertly designed to prefer males over females in public employment require an exceedingly persuasive justification"). . . .

Our cases dealing with gender discrimination also require that the proffered purpose for the challenged law be the actual purpose. It is on this ground that the Court rejects the first of two justifications Virginia offers for VMI's single-sex admissions policy, namely, the goal of diversity among its public educational institutions. While I ultimately agree that the State has not carried the day with this justification, I disagree with the Court's method of analyzing the issue. . . .

I agree with the Court that there is scant evidence in the record that this was the real reason that Virginia decided to maintain VMI as men only. But, unlike the majority, I would consider only evidence that postdates our decision in *Hogan*, and would draw no negative inferences from the State's actions before that time. I think that after *Hogan*, the State was entitled to reconsider its policy with respect to VMI, and to not have earlier justifications, or lack thereof, held against it.

Even if diversity in educational opportunity were the State's actual objective, the State's position would still be problematic. The difficulty with its position is that the diversity benefited only one sex; there was single-sex public education available for men at VMI, but no corresponding single-sex public education available for women. When *Hogan* placed Virginia on notice that VMI's admissions policy possibly was unconstitutional, VMI could have dealt with the problem by admitting women; but its governing body felt strongly that the admission of women would have seriously harmed the institution's educational approach. Was there something else the State could have done to avoid an equal protection violation? Since the State did nothing, we do not have to definitively answer that question.

I do not think, however, that the State's options were as limited as the majority may imply. [VMI] had been in operation for over a century and a half, and had an established, successful and devoted group of alumni. No legislative wand could instantly call into existence a similar institution for women; and it would be a tremendous loss to scrap VMI's history and tradition. In the words of Grover Cleveland's second inaugural address, the State faced a condition, not a theory. And it was a condition that had been brought about, not through defiance of decisions construing gender bias under the Equal Protection Clause, but, until the decision in *Hogan*, a condition which had not appeared to offend the Constitution. Had Virginia made a genuine effort to devote comparable public resources to a facility for women, and followed through on such a plan, it might well have avoided an equal protection violation. I do not believe the State was faced with the stark choice of either admitting women to VMI, on the one hand, or abandoning VMI and starting from scratch for both men and women, on the other.

But [neither] the governing board of VMI nor the State took any action after 1982. If diversity in the form of single-sex, as well as coeducational, institutions of higher learning were to be available to Virginians, that diversity had to be available to women as well as to men. . . .

Virginia offers a second justification for the single-sex admissions policy: maintenance of the adversative method. I agree with the Court that this justification does not serve an important governmental objective. A State does not have substantial interest in the adversative methodology unless it is pedagogically beneficial. While considerable evidence shows that a single-sex education is pedagogically beneficial for some students, and hence a State may have a valid interest in promoting that methodology, there is no similar evidence in the record that an adversative method is pedagogically beneficial or is any more likely to produce character traits than other methodologies.

II

An adequate remedy in my opinion might be a demonstration by Virginia that its interest in educating men in a single-sex environment is matched by its interest in educating women in a single-sex institution. To demonstrate such, the State does not need to create two institutions with the same number of faculty PhD's, similar SAT scores, or comparable athletic fields. Nor would it necessarily require that the women's institution offer the same curriculum as the men's; one could be strong in computer science, the other could be strong in liberal arts. It would be a sufficient remedy, I think, if the two institutions offered the same quality of education and were of the same overall calibre.

If a state decides to create single-sex programs, the state would, I expect, consider the public's interest and demand in designing curricula. And rightfully so. But the state should avoid assuming demand based on stereotypes; it must not assume a priori, without evidence, that there would be no interest in a women's school of civil engineering, or in a men's school of nursing.

In the end, the women's institution Virginia proposes, VWIL, fails as a remedy, because it is distinctly inferior to the existing men's institution and will continue to be for the foreseeable future. VWIL simply is not, in any sense, the institution that VMI is. In particular, VWIL is a program appended to a private college, not a self-standing institution; and VWIL is substantially underfunded as compared to VMI. I therefore ultimately agree with the Court that Virginia has not provided an adequate remedy.

JUSTICE SCALIA, dissenting.

Today the Court shuts down an institution that has served the people of the Commonwealth of Virginia with pride and distinction for over a century and a half. To achieve that desired result, it rejects (contrary to our established practice) the factual findings of two courts below, sweeps aside the precedents of this Court, and ignores the history of our people. As to facts: it explicitly rejects the finding that there exist "gender-based developmental differences" supporting Virginia's restriction of the "adversative" method to only a men's institution, and the finding that the all-male composition of the Virginia Military Institute (VMI) is essential to that institution's character. As to precedent: it drastically revises our established standards for reviewing sex-based classifications. And as to history: it counts for nothing the long tradition, enduring down to the present, of men's military colleges supported by both States and the Federal Government.

Much of the Court's opinion is devoted to deprecating the closed-mindedness of our forebears with regard to women's education, and even with regard to the treatment of women in areas that have nothing to do with education. Closed-minded they were—as every age is, including our own, with regard to matters it cannot guess, because it simply does not consider them debatable. The virtue of a democratic system with a First Amendment is that it readily enables the people, over time, to be persuaded that what they took for granted is not so, and to change their laws accordingly. That system is destroyed if the smug assurances of each age are removed from the democratic process and written into the Constitution. So to counterbalance the Court's criticism of our ancestors, let me say a word in their praise: they left us free to change. The same cannot be said of this most illiberal Court, which has embarked on a course of inscribing one after another of the current preferences of the society (and in some cases only the counter-majoritarian preferences of the society's law-trained elite) into our Basic Law. Today it enshrines the notion that no substantial educational value is to be served by an all-men's military academy — so that the decision by the people of Virginia to maintain such an institution denies equal protection to women who cannot attend that institution but can attend others. Since it is entirely clear that the Constitution of the United States — the old one — takes no sides in this educational debate, I dissent.

I

I shall devote most of my analysis to evaluating the Court's opinion on the basis of our current equal-protection jurisprudence, which regards this Court as free to evaluate everything under the sun by applying one of three tests: "rational basis" scrutiny, intermediate scrutiny, or strict scrutiny. These tests are no more scientific than their names suggest, and a further element of randomness is added by the fact that it is largely up to us which test will be applied in each case. . . .

I have no problem with a system of abstract tests such as rational-basis, intermediate, and strict scrutiny (though I think we can do better than applying strict scrutiny and intermediate scrutiny whenever we feel like it). Such formulas are essential to evaluating whether the new restrictions that a changing society constantly imposes upon private conduct comport with that "equal protection" our society has always accorded in the past. But in my view the function of this Court is to preserve our society's values regarding (among other things) equal protection, not to revise them; to prevent backsliding from the degree of restriction the Constitution imposed upon democratic government, not to prescribe, on our own authority, progressively higher degrees. For that reason it is my view that, whatever abstract tests we may choose to devise, they cannot supersede — and indeed ought to be crafted so as to reflect — those constant and unbroken national traditions that embody the people's understanding of ambiguous constitutional texts. More specifically, it is my view that "when a practice not expressly prohibited by the text of the Bill of Rights bears the endorsement of a long tradition of open, widespread, and unchallenged use that dates back to the beginning of the Republic, we have no proper basis for striking it down." Rutan v. Republican Party of Ill., (Scalia, J., dissenting). . . .

The all-male constitution of VMI comes squarely within such a governing tradition. Founded by the Commonwealth of Virginia in 1839 and continuously maintained by it since, VMI has always admitted only men. And in that regard it has not been unusual. For almost all of VMI's more than a century and a half of existence, its single-sex status reflected the uniform practice for government-supported military colleges. [In] other words, the tradition of having government-funded military schools for men is as well rooted in the traditions of this country as the tradition of sending only men into military combat. The people may decide to change the one tradition, like the other, through democratic processes; but the assertion that either tradition has been unconstitutional through the centuries is not law, but politics-smuggled-into-law.

And the same applies, more broadly, to single-sex education in general, which, as I shall discuss, is threatened by today's decision with the cut-off of all state and federal support. . . .

Today, however, change is forced upon Virginia, and reversion to single-sex education is prohibited nationwide, not by democratic processes but by order of this Court. Even while bemoaning the sorry, bygone days of "fixed notions" concerning women's education, and the Court favors current notions so fixedly that it is willing to write them into the Constitution of the United States by application of custom-built "tests." This is not the interpretation of a Constitution, but the creation of one.

II

To reject the Court's disposition today, however, it is not necessary to accept my view that the Court's made-up tests cannot displace longstanding national traditions as the primary determinant of what the Constitution means. It is only necessary to apply honestly the test the Court has been applying to sex-based classifications for the past two decades. It is well settled, as Justice O'Connor stated some time ago for a unanimous Court, that we evaluate a statutory classification based on sex under a standard that lies "between the extremes of rational basis review and strict scrutiny." Clark v. Jeter. We have denominated this standard "intermediate scrutiny" and under it have inquired whether the statutory classification is "substantially related to an important governmental objective."

Before I proceed to apply this standard to VMI, I must comment upon the manner in which the Court avoids doing so. Notwithstanding our above-described precedents and their "'firmly established principles,'" the United States urged us to hold in this case "that strict scrutiny is the correct constitutional standard for evaluating classifications that deny opportunities to individuals based on their sex." [The] Court, while making no reference to the Government's argument, effectively accepts it. . . .

Only the amorphous "exceedingly persuasive justification" phrase, and not the standard elaboration of intermediate scrutiny, can be made to yield [the] conclusion that VMI's single-sex composition is unconstitutional because there exist several women (or, one would have to conclude under the Court's reasoning, a single woman) willing and able to undertake VMI's program. Intermediate scrutiny has never required a least-restrictive-means analysis, but only a "substantial relation" between the classification and the state interests that it serves. . . .

III . . .

A

It is beyond question that Virginia has an important state interest in providing effective college education for its citizens. That single-sex instruction is an approach substantially related to that interest should be evident enough from the long and continuing history in this country of men's and women's colleges. But beyond that, as the Court of Appeals here stated: "That single-gender education at the college level is beneficial to both sexes is a fact established in this case."

The evidence establishing that fact was overwhelming—indeed, "virtually uncontradicted" in the words of the court that received the evidence. [Virginia] demonstrated at trial that "[a] substantial body of contemporary scholarship and research supports the proposition that, although males and females have significant areas of developmental overlap, they also have differing developmental needs that are deep-seated." While no one questioned that for many students a coeducational environment was nonetheless not inappropriate, that could not obscure the demonstrated benefits of single-sex colleges. . . .

But besides its single-sex constitution, VMI is different from other colleges in another way. It employs a "distinctive educational method," sometimes referred to as the "adversative, or doubting, model of education." [It] was uncontested that "if the state were to establish a women's VMI-type [i.e., adversative] program, the program would attract an insufficient number of participants to make the program work," and it was found by the District Court that if Virginia were to include women in VMI, the school "would eventually find it necessary to drop the adversative system altogether." Thus, Virginia's options were an adversative method that excludes women or no adversative method at all.

[As] a theoretical matter, Virginia's educational interest would have been best served [by] six different types of public colleges—an all-men's, an all-women's, and a coeducational college run in the "adversative method," and an all-men's, an all-women's, and a coeducational college run in the "traditional method." But as a practical matter, of course, Virginia's financial resources, like any State's, are not limitless, and the Commonwealth must select among the available options. Virginia thus has decided to fund, in addition to some 14 coeducational 4-year colleges, one college that is run as an all-male school on the adversative model: the Virginia Military Institute. . . .

B

The Court today has no adequate response to this clear demonstration of the conclusion produced by application of intermediate scrutiny. Rather, it relies on a series of contentions that are irrelevant or erroneous as a matter of law, foreclosed by the record in this case, or both. . . .

[The] Court suggests that Virginia's claimed purpose in maintaining VMI as an all-male institution — its asserted interest in promoting diversity of educational options — is not "genuine," but is a pretext for discriminating against women. To support this charge, the Court would have to impute that base motive to VMI's Mission Study Committee, which conducted a 3-year study from 1983 to 1986 and recommended to VMI's Board of Visitors that the school remain all-male. The Committee, a majority of whose members consisted of non-VMI graduates, "read materials on education and on women in the military," "made site visits to single-sex and newly coeducational institutions" including West Point and the Naval Academy, and "considered the reasons that other institutions had changed from single-sex to coeducational status"; its work was praised as "thorough" in the accreditation review of VMI conducted by the Southern Association of Colleges and Schools. [The] relevance of the Mission Study Committee is that its very creation, its sober 3-year study, and the analysis it produced, utterly refute the claim that VMI has elected to maintain its all-male student-body composition for some misogynistic reason. . . .

[In] addition to disparaging Virginia's claim that VMI's single-sex status serves a state interest in diversity, the Court finds fault with Virginia's failure to offer education based on the adversative training method to women. . . .

Ultimately, [the] Court does not deny the evidence supporting [the District Court's findings on gender-based developmental differences]. It instead makes evident that the parties to this case could have saved themselves a great deal of time, trouble, and expense by omitting a trial. The Court simply dispenses with the evidence submitted at trial — it never says that a single finding of the District Court is clearly erroneous — in favor of the Justices' own view of the [world].

It is not too much to say that this approach to the case has rendered the trial a sham. But treating the evidence as irrelevant is absolutely necessary for the Court to reach its conclusion. Not a single witness contested, for example, Virginia's "substantial body of 'exceedingly persuasive' evidence . . . that some students, both male and female, benefit from attending a single-sex college" and "[that] for those students, the opportunity to attend a single-sex college is a valuable one, likely to lead to better academic and professional achievement." Even the United States' expert witness "called himself a 'believer in single-sex education,'" although it was his "personal, philosophical preference," not one "born of educational-benefit considerations," "that single-sex education should be provided only by the private sector." . . .

[The] Court argues that VMI would not have to change very much if it were to admit women. The principal response to that argument is that it is irrelevant: If VMI's single-sex status is substantially related to the government's important educational objectives, as I have demonstrated above and as the Court refuses to discuss, that concludes the inquiry. There should be no debate in the federal judiciary over "how much" VMI would be required to change if it admitted women and whether that would constitute "too much" change.

But if such a debate were relevant, the Court would certainly be on the losing side. The District Court found as follows: "The evidence establishes that key elements of the adversative VMI educational system, with its focus on barracks life, would be fundamentally altered, and the distinctive ends of the system would be thwarted, if VMI were forced to admit females and to make changes necessary to accommodate their needs and interests." Changes that the District Court's detailed analysis found would be required include new allowances for personal privacy in the barracks, such as locked doors and coverings on windows, which would detract from VMI's approach of regulating minute details of student behavior, "contradict the principle that everyone is constantly subject to scrutiny by everyone else," and impair VMI's "total egalitarian approach" under which every student must be "treated alike"; changes in the physical training program, which would reduce "the intensity and aggressiveness of the current program"; and various modifications in other respects of the adversative training program which permeates student life. . . .

[Finally,] the absence of a precise "all-women's analogue" to VMI is irrelevant. In Mississippi Univ. for Women v. Hogan, we attached no constitutional significance to the absence of an all-male nursing school. . . .

Although there is no precise female-only analogue to VMI, Virginia has created during this litigation the Virginia Women's Institute for Leadership (VWIL), a state-funded all-women's program run by Mary Baldwin College. I have thus far said nothing about VWIL because it is, under our established test, irrelevant, so long as VMI's all-male character is "substantially related" to an important state goal. But VWIL now exists, and the Court's treatment of it shows how far-reaching today's decision is.

VWIL was carefully designed by professional educators who have long experience in educating young women. The program rejects the proposition that there is a "difference in the respective spheres and destinies of man and woman," Bradwell v. State, and is designed to "provide an all-female program that will achieve substantially similar outcomes [to VMI's] in an all-female environment," After holding a trial where voluminous evidence was submitted and making detailed findings of fact, the District Court concluded that "there is a legitimate pedagogical basis for the different means employed [by VMI and VWIL] to achieve the substantially similar ends." . . .

IV

As is frequently true, the Court's decision today will have consequences that extend far beyond the parties to the case. What I take to be the Court's unease with these consequences, and its resulting unwillingness to acknowledge them, cannot alter the reality.

A

Under the constitutional principles announced and applied today, single-sex public education is unconstitutional. . . .

[The] rationale of today's decision is sweeping: for sex-based classifications, a redefinition of intermediate scrutiny that makes it indistinguishable from strict scrutiny. Indeed, the Court indicates that if any program restricted to one sex is "unique," it must be opened to members of the opposite sex "who have the will and capacity" to participate in it. I suggest that the single-sex program that will not be capable of being characterized as "unique" is not only unique but non-existent.[8]

In any event, regardless of whether the Court's rationale leaves some small amount of room for lawyers to argue, it ensures that single-sex public education is functionally dead. The costs of litigating the constitutionality of a single-sex education program, and the risks of ultimately losing that litigation, are simply too high to be embraced by public officials. [The] enemies of single-sex education have won; by persuading only seven Justices (five would have been enough) that their view of the world is enshrined in the Constitution, they have effectively imposed that view on all 50 States.

This is especially regrettable because, as the District Court here determined, educational experts in recent years have increasingly come to "support [the] view that substantial educational benefits flow from a single-gender environment, be it male or female, that cannot be replicated in a coeducational setting." "The evidence in this case," for example, "is virtually uncontradicted" to that effect. Until quite recently, some public officials have attempted to institute new single-sex programs, at least as experiments. In 1991, for example, the Detroit Board of Education announced a program to establish three boys-only schools for inner-city youth; it was met with a lawsuit, a preliminary injunction was swiftly entered by a District Court that purported to rely on Hogan, and the Detroit Board of Education voted to abandon the litigation and thus abandon the plan. Today's opinion assures that no such experiment will be tried again.

---

[8] In this regard, I note that the Court—which I concede is under no obligation to do so—provides no example of a program that would pass muster under its reasoning today: not even, for example, a football or wrestling program. On the Court's theory, any woman ready, willing, and physically able to participate in such a program would, as a constitutional matter, be entitled to do so.

B

There are few extant single-sex public educational programs. The potential of today's decision for widespread disruption of existing institutions lies in its application to private single-sex education. Government support is immensely important to private educational institutions. [Charitable] status under the tax laws is also highly significant for private educational institutions, and it is certainly not beyond the Court that rendered today's decision to hold that a donation to a single-sex college should be deemed contrary to public policy and therefore not deductible if the college discriminates on the basis of sex. . . .

The only hope for state-assisted single-sex private schools is that the Court will not apply in the future the principles of law it has applied today. That is a substantial hope, I am happy and ashamed to say. After all, did not the Court today abandon the principles of law it has applied in our earlier sex-classification cases? And does not the Court positively invite private colleges to rely upon our ad-hocery by assuring them this case is "unique"? I would not advise the foundation of any new single-sex college (especially an all-male one) with the expectation of being allowed to receive any government support; but it is too soon to abandon in despair those single-sex colleges already in existence. It will certainly be possible for this Court to write a future opinion that ignores the broad principles of law set forth today, and that characterizes as utterly dispositive the opinion's perceptions that VMI was a uniquely prestigious all-male institution, conceived in chauvinism, etc., etc. I will not join that opinion.

Justice Brandeis said it is "one of the happy incidents of the federal system that a single courageous State may, if its citizens choose, serve as a laboratory; and try novel social and economic experiments without risk to the rest of the country." New State Ice Co. v. Liebmann (dissenting opinion). But it is one of the unhappy incidents of the federal system that a self-righteous Supreme Court, acting on its Members' personal view of what would make a "more perfect Union," (a criterion only slightly more restrictive than a "more perfect world"), can impose its own favored social and economic dispositions nationwide. As today's disposition, and others this single Term, show, this places it beyond the power of a "single courageous State," not only to introduce novel dispositions that the Court frowns upon, but to reintroduce, or indeed even adhere to, disfavored dispositions that are centuries old. See, Romer v. Evans, 517 U.S. — [116 S. Ct. 1620] (1996). The sphere of self-government reserved to the people of the Republic is progressively narrowed.

In the course of this dissent, I have referred approvingly to the opinion of my former colleague, Justice Powell, in Mississippi Univ. for Women v. Hogan. Many of the points made in his dissent apply with equal force here — in particular, the criticism of judicial opinions that purport to be "narrow" but whose "logic" is "sweeping." But there is one statement with which I cannot agree. Justice Powell observed that the Court's decision in Hogan, which struck down a single-sex program offered by the Mississippi University for Women, had thereby "left without honor . . . an element of diversity that has characterized much of American education and enriched much of American life." Today's decision does not leave VMI without honor; no court opinion can do that.

In an odd sort of way, it is precisely VMI's attachment to such old-fashioned concepts as manly "honor" that has made it, and the system it represents, the target of those who today succeed in abolishing public single-sex education. The record contains a booklet that all first-year VMI students (the so-called "rats") were required to keep in their possession at all times. Near the end there appears the following period-piece, entitled "The Code of a Gentleman":

> Without a strict observance of the fundamental Code of Honor, no man, no matter how "polished," can be considered a gentleman. The honor of a gentleman demands the inviolability of his word, and the incorruptibility of his principles. He is the descendant of the knight, the crusader; he is the defender of the defenseless and the champion of justice . . . or he is not a Gentleman.
>
> A Gentleman . . .
>
> Does not discuss his family affairs in public or with acquaintances.
>
> Does not speak more than casually about his girl friend.
>
> Does not go to a lady's house if he is affected by alcohol. He is temperate in the use of alcohol.
>
> Does not lose his temper; nor exhibit anger, fear, hate, embarrassment, ardor or hilarity in public.
>
> Does not hail a lady from a club window.
>
> A gentleman never discusses the merits or demerits of a lady.
>
> Does not mention names exactly as he avoids the mention of what things cost.
>
> Does not borrow money from a friend, except in dire need. Money borrowed is a debt of honor, and must be repaid as promptly as possible. Debts incurred by a deceased parent, brother, sister or grown child are assumed by honorable men as a debt of honor.
>
> Does not display his wealth, money or possessions.
>
> Does not put his manners on and off, whether in the club or in a ballroom. He treats people with courtesy, no matter what their social position may be.
>
> Does not slap strangers on the back nor so much as lay a finger on a lady.
>
> Does not "lick the boots of those above" nor "kick the face of those below him on the social ladder."

Does not take advantage of another's helplessness or ignorance and assumes that no gentleman will take advantage of him.

A Gentleman respects the reserves of others, but demands that others respect those which are his.

A Gentleman can become what he wills to be. . . .

I do not know whether the men of VMI lived by this Code; perhaps not. But it is powerfully impressive that a public institution of higher education still in existence sought to have them do so. I do not think any of us, women included, will be better off for its destruction.

Page 721.   At the end of section 1 of the Note, add the following:

Compare with this approach, a "sociological" approach proposed in Post, Prejudicial Appearances: The Logic of American Antidiscrimination Law, 88 Cal. L. Rev. 1, 17, 31 (2000):

The law is itself a social institution. [Law] is made by the very persons who participate in the social practices that constitute [gender]. It would be astonishing, therefore, if American antidiscrimination law could transcend [this category], if it could operate in a way that rendered [gender] truly irrelevant. . . .

Because the dominant conception offers an implausible story about the actual shape of antidiscrimination law, I [propose] an alternative perspective [in] which antisdiscrimination law is understood as a social practice that acts on other social practices. [Antidiscrimination] law [transforms] preexisting social practices [by] reconstructing the social identity of persons. The sociological account does not ask whether "stereotypic impressions" can be [totally] eliminated, [but] rather how the law alters and modifies such impressions.

Page 726.   Before section 5 of the Note, add the following:

5a. Miller. Federal naturalization law provides that an out-of-wedlock child born outside the United States to a citizen mother and non-citizen father is a United States citizen if the mother has previously been physically present in the United States for one year. In contrast, an out-of-wedlock child born to a citizen father and noncitizen mother is a United States citizen only if the child obtains formal proof of paternity before the age of 18, either through legitimation, written acknowledgment by the father under oath, or adjudication by a competent court.

In Miller v. Albright, 523 U.S. 420 (1998), petitioner was born in the Philippines to a Filipino mother. The government conceded that her father was an American citizen, and indeed, a "Voluntary Paternity Decree" entered by a Texas court established that he was the biological father. The government nonetheless refused to recognize her citizenship because she had not been legitimated before the age of 18 as required by the statute. Petitioner claimed that the statutory distinctions based upon the gender of her parents violated equal protection principles. Although the Supreme Court ultimately ruled against her, only Justice Stevens, who announced the Court's judgment, and Chief Justice Rehnquist, who joined Justice Stevens' opinion, specifically rejected her gender discrimination claim.

Justice Stevens argued that unmarried fathers and mothers were differently situated:

> If the citizen is the unmarried female, she must first choose to carry the pregnancy to term and reject the alternative of abortion. [She] must actually give birth to the child. [The statute] rewards that choice and that labor by conferring citizenship on her child.
>
> If the citizen is the unmarried male, he need not participate in the decision to give birth rather than to choose an abortion; he need not be present at the birth; and for at least 17 years thereafter he need not provide any parental support, either moral or financial to either the mother or the child, in order to preserve his right to confer citizenship on the child.
>
> [There] is thus a vast difference between the burdens imposed on the respective parents of potential citizens born out of wedlock in a foreign land. It seems obvious that the burdens imposed on the female citizen are more severe than those imposed on the male citizen.

In Justice Stevens' view, the statutory requirement for male citizens served the purpose of "ensur[ing] that a person born out of wedlock who claims citizenship by birth actually shares a blood relationship with an American citizen."

> [It cannot] be denied that the male and female parents are differently situated in this respect. The blood relationship to the birth mother is immediately obvious and is typically established by hospital records and birth certificates; the relationship to the unmarried father may often be undisclosed and unrecorded in any contemporary public record. Thus, the requirement that the father make a timely written acknowledgment under oath, or that the child obtain a court adjudication of paternity, produces the rough equivalent of the

documentation that is already available to evidence the blood relationship [between] the mother and the child.

Moreover, two other interests, unrelated to the determination of paternity, were also served by the statute: the interest in encouraging the development of a healthy relationship between the citizen parent and the child while the child is a minor; and the related interest in fostering ties between the foreign-born child and the United States.

When a child is born out of wedlock outside the United States, the citizen mother, unlike the citizen father, certainly knows of her child's existence and typically will have custody of the child immediately after the birth. Such a child thus has the opportunity to develop ties with its citizen mother at an early age, and may even grow up in the United States if the mother returns. By contrast, due to the normal interval of nine months between conception and birth, the unmarried father may not even know that his child exists, and the child may not know the father's identity. [The statute] requires a relatively easy, formal step by either the citizen father or his child that shows beyond doubt that at least one of the two knows of their blood relationship, thus assuring at least the opportunity for them to develop a personal relationship.

Finally, Justice Stevens rejected the argument that the Court's prior decisions condemning statutes based upon gender stereotypes were relevant.

[The statute] is not concerned with either the average father or even the average father of a child born out of wedlock. It is concerned with a father (a) whose child was born in a foreign country, and (b) who is unwilling or unable to acknowledge his paternity, and whose child is unable or unwilling to obtain a court paternity adjudication. A congressional assumption that such a father and his child are especially unlikely to develop a relationship, and thus to foster the child's ties with this country, has a solid basis even if we assume that all fathers who have made some effort to become acquainted with their children are as good, if not better, parents than members of the opposite sex.

Nor does the statute assume that all mothers of illegitimate children will necessarily have a closer relationship with their children than will fathers. It does assume that all of them will be present at the event that transmits their citizenship to the child, that hospital records and birth certificates will normally make a further acknowledgment and formal proof of parentage unnecessary, and that their initial custody will at least give them the opportunity to develop a caring relationship with the child.

The remaining votes necessary to support the Court's judgment were supplied by Justice O'Connor, in an opinion joined by Justice Kennedy, and Justice Scalia, in an opinion joined by Justice Thomas.

Justice O'Connor would have held that petitioner lacked standing to raise the gender discrimination claim that might have been brought by her father. (She took this position even though, at an earlier stage in the litigation, her father, on the government's motion, had been dismissed from the suit for lack of standing). As applied to petitioner, the statute was gender neutral, since the standards for citizenship were the same for male and female out-of-wedlock children.

> Given that petitioner cannot raise a claim of discrimination triggering heightened scrutiny, she can argue only that [the statute] irrationally discriminates between illegitimate children of citizen fathers and citizen mothers. Although I do not share JUSTICE STEVENS' assessment that the provision withstands heightened scrutiny, I believe it passes rational scrutiny for the reasons he gives for sustaining it under the higher standard. It is unlikely, in my opinion, that any gender classification based on stereotypes can survive heightened scrutiny, but under rational scrutiny, a statute may be defended based on generalized classifications unsupported by empirical evidence.

Justice Scalia also concurred in the judgment but argued that "it makes no difference whether or not [the statute] passes 'heightened scrutiny' or any other test members of this Court may choose to apply." Instead, in his judgment,

> the complaint must be dismissed because the Court has no power to provide the relief requested: conferral of citizenship on a basis other than that prescribed by Congress. . . .
>
> [Because] only Congress has the power to set the requirements for acquisition of citizenship by persons not born within the territory of the United States, federal courts cannot exercise that power under the guise of their remedial authority. . . .
>
> I know of no instance [in] which this Court has severed an unconstitutional restriction upon the grant of immigration or citizenship. It is in my view incompatible with the plenary power of Congress over those fields for judges to speculate as to what Congress would have enacted if it had not enacted what it did—whether it would, for example have preferred to extend the requirements of [the statute] to mothers instead of eliminating them for fathers, or even to deny citizenship to illegitimate children entirely.

Justice Breyer, in an opinion joined by Justices Souter and Ginsburg, dissented:

186

Distinctions of this kind — based upon gender — are subject to a "strong presumption" of constitutional invalidity. [United States v. Virginia]. The Equal Protection Clause permits them only if the Government meets the "demanding" burden of showing an "exceedingly persuasive" justification for the distinction. [*Virginia*]. . . .

The statutory distinctions here violate these standards. They depend for their validity upon the generalization that mothers are significantly more likely than fathers to care for their children, or to develop caring relationships with their children. But consider how the statutes work once one abandons that generalization as the illegitimate basis for legislative linedrawing we have held it to be. First, assume that the American citizen is also the Caretaker Parent. The statute would then require a Male Caretaker Parent to acknowledge his child prior to the child's 18th birthday. [It] would not require a Female Caretaker Parent to do [so]. The gender-based distinction that would impose added burdens only upon the Male Caretaker Parent would serve no purpose at all. Second, assume that the American citizen is the NonCaretaker Parent. In that circumstance, the statute would forgive a Female NonCaretaker Parent from complying with the requirements [that] it would impose upon a Male non-Caretaker Parent. Again, the gender based distinction that would impose lesser burdens only upon the Female Non-Caretaker Parent would serve no purpose.

Justice Ginsburg also filed a dissenting opinion that was joined by Justices Souter and Breyer.

Given *Miller,* what result should a lower court reach in a suit brought by a citizen-father challenging the statute?

E. Equal Protection Methodology: Other Candidates for Heightened Scrutiny

Page 754. Before section 2 of the Note, add the following:

In Reno v. American-Arab Anti-Discrimination Committee, 119 S. Ct. 936 (1999), the Court held that in general aliens could not challenge their deportations on the ground that they were being selectively prosecuted. The Court's decision came in the context of alleged discrimination impinging on free speech rights, and the opinion suggested without elaboration that a different result might follow in an "outrageous" case.

Page 758.   Before the last paragraph, add the following:

See also M.L.B. v. S.L.J., 117 S. Ct. 555 (1996) (holding that the due process and equal protection clauses prohibit the state from conditioning appeals from trial court decrees terminating parental rights on the parent's ability to pay record preparation fees).

Page 761.   Before section 3 of the Note, add the following:

In M.L.B. v. S.L.J., 117 S. Ct. 555 (1996), the state relied upon Washington v. Davis to defend its requirement that litigants pay record preparation fees before appealing from decisions terminating parental rights. The state reasoned that this requirement, like the practice at issue in Washington v. Davis, had no more than a disproportionate impact on the affected class. In a 6-3 decision, the Court rejected this argument:

> To comprehend the difference between the case at hand and cases controlled by Washington v. Davis, one need look no further than this Court's opinion in Williams v. Illinois. *Williams* held unconstitutional an Illinois law under which an indigent offender could be continued in confinement beyond the maximum prison term specified by statute if his indigency prevented him from satisfying the monetary portion of the sentence. The Court described that law as "nondiscriminatory on its face," and recalled that the law found incompatible with the Constitution in *Griffin* had been so characterized. But the *Williams* Court went on to explain that the "Illinois statute in operative effect exposes *only indigents* to the risk of imprisonment beyond the statutory maximum" (emphasis added). Sanctions of the *Williams* genre, like the Mississippi prescription here at issue, are not merely *disporportionate* in impact. Rather, they are wholly contingent on one's ability to pay, and thus "visi[t] different consequences on two categories of persons," [*Williams*]; they apply to all indigents and do not reach anyone outside that class.

Page 779.   Before section 4 of the Note, add the following:

Consider in this connection whether the Court's criteria for heightened scrutiny reveal an "assimilationist bias." See Yoshino, Assimilationist Bias in Equal Protection: The Visibility Presumption and the Case of "Don't Ask, Don't Tell," 108 Yale L.J. 487, 492 (1998):

> By withholding protection from [classifications if their defining traits can be altered or concealed], the judiciary is subtly encouraging groups comprised

by such classifications to assimilate by changing or hiding their defining characteristic. . . .

When the state has animus against an invisible group, it can manipulate the context in which the group functions to ensure that the net effects of its invisibility are disempowering. The most egregious injustice of the visibility bias manifests itself in these scenarios, in which courts defer to such state action because they assume that invisibility is empowering, even as the state is banking on the opposite presumption.

This dynamic is illustrated by the case of gays in the military. [The] military's "don't ask, don't tell" policy manipulates the context in which gays operate, amplifying and disempowering aspects (and dampening the empowering aspects) of their invisibility. [The] judicial assumption that invisibility is always empowering [is untenable given] the military's investment in precisely the opposite dynamic.

Page 780. Before Section 4, add the following:

Compare the views of Sunstein and Fajer with Massaro, Gay Rights, Thick and Thin, 49 Stan. L. Rev. 45 (1996). Massaro shares some of Sunstein's skepticism about the utility of judicial intervention, albeit for somewhat different reasons:

Legal categories, [tend] to repress or problematize nuances. These sophisticated shadings are the underpinnings of the more complex constitutional framework that [many] deem critical to any gay rights worth the candle. The very nature of legal reasoning, especially its reliance on analogical reasoning, demands that lawyers hew to heterosexual norms when arguing for gay rights. However, this strategy, in flattening crucial nuances, produces marginality instead of equality.

For Massaro, however, these and other arguments against a litigation strategy are beside the point.

The problem with these arguments [is] that litigation continues despite the many good reasons not to pursue it. . . .

[The] pertinent question is neither whether to pursue litigation at all, nor whether change ever happens. The important question is how advocates who do pursue litigation can make the best of a legal structure that is [shaped] by "an implicit, trans-individual Western project or fantasy of eradicating [gay] identity," but that is also evolving. How might theories and advocates best mitigate the harsh effects of what may be unavoidable double-binds? Which legal cord should they attempt to cut first, and with what tools?

Massaro answers this question by advocating rational basis analysis, or what she calls "the thin constitutional rights approach."

> Unlike strict scrutiny, privacy, free speech, or other doctrinally thick rivals, the thin rights approach minimizes doctrinal props. It forces to the foreground the central issue—whether homosexuality is wrong—and enables judges to hear, free of jargon, the nondoctrinal material that is so crucial to influencing judges on matters of sexuality.

In the case that follows, the Court, for the first time in its history, invalidated a measure on the ground that it discriminated against homosexuals. Consider the extent to which the Court's decision requires rethinking of lower court decisions about homosexual marriage, criminalization of homosexual sodomy, and service by homosexuals in the military.

Romer v. Evans
517 U.S. 620 (1996)

JUSTICE KENNEDY delivered the opinion of the Court.

One century ago, the first Justice Harlan admonished this Court that the Constitution "neither knows nor tolerates classes among citizens." Plessy v. Ferguson (dissenting opinion). Unheeded then, those words now are understood to state a commitment to the law's neutrality where the rights of persons are at stake. The Equal Protection Clause enforces this principle and today requires us to hold invalid a provision of Colorado's Constitution.

I

["Amendment 2" was added to the state constitution by a statewide referendum held in 1992. It was enacted after a number of Colorado municipalities had adopted ordinances prohibiting discrimination on the basis of sexual orientation in many transactions and activities such as housing, employment, education, public accommodations, and health and welfare services. It provided:

No Protected Status Based on Homosexual, Lesbian, or Bisexual Orientation

Neither the State of Colorado, through any of its branches or departments, nor any of its agencies, political subdivisions, municipalities or school districts, shall enact, adopt or enforce any statute, regulation, ordinance or policy whereby homosexual, lesbian or bisexual orientation, conduct, practices or relationships shall constitute or otherwise be the basis of or entitle any person or class of persons to have or claim any minority status, quota preferences, protected status or claim of discrimination. This Section of the Constitution shall be in all respects self-executing.

[The Colorado Supreme Court held that Amendment 2 was subject to strict scrutiny under the equal protection clause on the ground that it impinged on the right of homosexuals to participate in the political process.] On remand, the State advanced various arguments in an effort to show that Amendment 2 was narrowly tailored to serve compelling interests, but the trial court found none sufficient. It enjoined enforcement of Amendment 2, and the Supreme Court of Colorado, in a second opinion, affirmed the ruling. We granted certiorari and now affirm the judgment, but on a rationale different from that adopted by the State Supreme Court.

II

The State's principal argument in defense of Amendment 2 is that it puts gays and lesbians in the same position as all other persons. So, the State says, the measure does no more than deny homosexuals special rights. This reading of the amendment's language is implausible. We rely not upon our own interpretation of the amendment but upon the authoritative construction of Colorado's Supreme Court. The state court, deeming it unnecessary to determine the full extent of the amendment's reach, found it invalid even on a modest reading of its implications. The critical discussion of the amendment [is] as follows:

The immediate objective of Amendment 2 is, at a minimum, to repeal existing statutes, regulations, ordinances, and policies of state and local entities that barred discrimination based on sexual orientation.

The "ultimate effect" of Amendment 2 is to prohibit any governmental entity from adopting similar, or more protective statutes, regulations, ordinances, or policies in the future unless the state constitution is first amended to permit such measures.

Sweeping and comprehensive is the change in legal status effected by this law. So much is evident from the ordinances that the Colorado Supreme Court declared would be void by operation of Amendment 2. Homosexuals, by state decree, are put in a solitary class with respect to transactions and relations in both the private and governmental spheres. The amendment withdraws from homosexuals, but no others, specific legal protection from the injuries caused by discrimination, and it forbids reinstatement of these laws and policies.

The change that Amendment 2 works in the legal status of gays and lesbians in the private sphere is far-reaching, both on its own terms and when considered

191

in light of the structure and operation of modern anti-discrimination laws. That structure is well illustrated by contemporary statutes and ordinances prohibiting discrimination by providers of public accommodations. "At common law, inn-keepers, smiths, and others who 'made profession of a public employment,' were prohibited from refusing, without good reason, to serve a customer." Hurley v. Irish-American Gay, Lesbian and Bisexual Group of Boston, Inc., 515 U.S. 557 (1995). The duty was a general one and did not specify protection for particular groups. The common law rules, however, proved insufficient in many instances, and it was settled early that the Fourteenth Amendment did not give Congress a general power to prohibit discrimination in public accommodations. In consequence, most States have chosen to counter discrimination by enacting detailed statutory schemes.

Colorado's state and municipal laws typify this emerging tradition of statutory protection and follow a consistent pattern. The laws first enumerate the persons or entities subject to a duty not to discriminate. The list goes well beyond the entities covered by the common law. The Boulder ordinance, for example, has a comprehensive definition of entities deemed places of "public accommodation." They include "any place of business engaged in any sales to the general public and any place that offers services, facilities, privileges, or advantages to the general public or that receives financial support through solicitation of the general public or through governmental subsidy of any kind." . . .

These statutes and ordinances also depart from the common law by enumerating the groups or persons within their ambit of protection. Enumeration is the essential device used to make the duty not to discriminate concrete and to provide guidance for those who must comply. In following this approach, Colorado's state and local governments have not limited anti-discrimination laws to groups that have so far been given the protection of heightened equal protection scrutiny under our cases. Rather, they set forth an extensive catalogue of traits which cannot be the basis for discrimination, including age, military status, marital status, pregnancy, parenthood, custody of a minor child, political affiliation, physical or mental disability of an individual or of his or her associates and, in recent times, sexual orientation.

Amendment 2 bars homosexuals from securing protection against the injuries that these public-accommodations laws address. That in itself is a severe consequence, but there is more. Amendment 2, in addition, nullifies specific legal protections for this targeted class in all transactions in housing, sale of real estate, insurance, health and welfare services, private education, and employment.

Not confined to the private sphere, Amendment 2 also operates to repeal and forbid all laws or policies providing specific protection for gays or lesbians from discrimination by every level of Colorado government. The State Supreme

Court cited two examples of protections in the governmental sphere that are now rescinded and may not be reintroduced. The first is Colorado Executive Order D0035 (1990), which forbids employment discrimination against "'all state employees, classified and exempt' on the basis of sexual orientation." Also repealed, and now forbidden, are "various provisions prohibiting discrimination based on sexual orientation at state colleges." The repeal of these measures and the prohibition against their future reenactment demonstrates that Amendment 2 has the same force and effect in Colorado's governmental sector as it does elsewhere and that it applies to policies as well as ordinary legislation.

Amendment 2's reach may not be limited to specific laws passed for the benefit of gays and lesbians. It is a fair, if not necessary, inference from the broad language of the amendment that it deprives gays and lesbians even of the protection of general laws and policies that prohibit arbitrary discrimination in governmental and private settings. At some point in the systematic administration of these laws, an official must determine whether homosexuality is an arbitrary and thus forbidden basis for decision. Yet a decision to that effect would itself amount to a policy prohibiting discrimination on the basis of homosexuality, and so would appear to be no more valid under Amendment 2 than the specific prohibitions against discrimination the state court held invalid.

If this consequence follows from Amendment 2, as its broad language suggests, it would compound the constitutional difficulties the law creates. The state court did not decide whether the amendment has this effect, however, and neither need we. In the course of rejecting the argument that Amendment 2 is intended to conserve resources to fight discrimination against suspect classes, the Colorado Supreme Court made the limited observation that the amendment is not intended to affect many anti-discrimination laws protecting non-suspect classes, In our view that does not resolve the issue. In any event, even if, as we doubt, homosexuals could find some safe harbor in laws of general application, we cannot accept the view that Amendment 2's prohibition on specific legal protections does no more than deprive homosexuals of special rights. To the contrary, the amendment imposes a special disability upon those persons alone. Homosexuals are forbidden the safeguards that others enjoy or may seek without constraint. They can obtain specific protection against discrimination only by enlisting the citizenry of Colorado to amend the state constitution or perhaps, on the State's view, by trying to pass helpful laws of general applicability. This is so no matter how local or discrete the harm, no matter how public and widespread the injury. We find nothing special in the protections Amendment 2 withholds. These are protections taken for granted by most people either because they already have them or do not need them; these are protections against exclusion from an almost limitless number of transactions and endeavors that constitute ordinary civic life in a free society.

193

III

The Fourteenth Amendment's promise that no person shall be denied the equal protection of the laws must co-exist with the practical necessity that most legislation classifies for one purpose or another, with resulting disadvantage to various groups or persons. We have attempted to reconcile the principle with the reality by stating that, if a law neither burdens a fundamental right nor targets a suspect class, we will uphold the legislative classification so long as it bears a rational relation to some legitimate end.

Amendment 2 fails, indeed defies, even this conventional inquiry. First, the amendment has the peculiar property of imposing a broad and undifferentiated disability on a single named group, an exceptional and, as we shall explain, invalid form of legislation. Second, its sheer breadth is so discontinuous with the reasons offered for it that the amendment seems inexplicable by anything but animus toward the class that it affects; it lacks a rational relationship to legitimate state interests.

Taking the first point, even in the ordinary equal protection case calling for the most deferential of standards, we insist on knowing the relation between the classification adopted and the object to be attained. The search for the link between classification and objective gives substance to the Equal Protection Clause; it provides guidance and discipline for the legislature, which is entitled to know what sorts of laws it can pass; and it marks the limits of our own authority. In the ordinary case, a law will be sustained if it can be said to advance a legitimate government interest, even if the law seems unwise or works to the disadvantage of a particular group, or if the rationale for it seems tenuous. See New Orleans v. Dukes (tourism benefits justified classification favoring push-cart vendors of certain longevity); Williamson v. Lee Optical of Okla., Inc., (assumed health concerns justified law favoring optometrists over opticians); Railway Express Agency, Inc. v. New York (potential traffic hazards justified exemption of vehicles advertising the owner's products from general advertising ban); Kotch v. Board of River Port Pilot Comm'rs for Port of New Orleans, (licensing scheme that disfavored persons unrelated to current river boat pilots justified by possible efficiency and safety benefits of a closely knit pilotage system). The laws challenged in the cases just cited were narrow enough in scope and grounded in a sufficient factual context for us to ascertain that there existed some relation between the classification and the purpose it served. By requiring that the classification bear a rational relationship to an independent and legitimate legislative end, we ensure that classifications are not drawn for the purpose of disadvantaging the group burdened by the law.

Amendment 2 confounds this normal process of judicial review. It is at once too narrow and too broad. It identifies persons by a single trait and then denies them protection across the board. The resulting disqualification of a class of persons from the right to seek specific protection from the law is unprecedented in our jurisprudence. The absence of precedent for Amendment 2 is itself instructive; "discriminations of an unusual character especially suggest careful consideration to determine whether they are obnoxious to the constitutional provision." Louisville Gas & Elec. Co. v. Coleman, 277 U.S. 32, 37-38, (1928).

It is not within our constitutional tradition to enact laws of this sort. Central both to the idea of the rule of law and to our own Constitution's guarantee of equal protection is the principle that government and each of its parts remain open on impartial terms to all who seek its assistance. "'Equal protection of the laws is not achieved through indiscriminate imposition of inequalities.'" Sweatt v. Painter, (quoting Shelley v. Kraemer). Respect for this principle explains why laws singling out a certain class of citizens for disfavored legal status or general hardships are rare. A law declaring that in general it shall be more difficult for one group of citizens than for all others to seek aid from the government is itself a denial of equal protection of the laws in the most literal sense. "The guaranty of 'equal protection of the laws is a pledge of the protection of equal laws.'" Skinner v. Oklahoma ex rel. Williamson, (quoting Yick Wo v. Hopkins).

Davis v. Beason, 133 U.S. 333, (1890), not cited by the parties but relied upon by the dissent, is not evidence that Amendment 2 is within our constitutional tradition, and any reliance upon it as authority for sustaining the amendment is misplaced. In Davis, the Court approved an Idaho territorial statute denying Mormons, polygamists, and advocates of polygamy the right to vote and to hold office because, as the Court construed the statute, it "simply excludes from the privilege of voting, or of holding any office of honor, trust or profit, those who have been convicted of certain offences, and those who advocate a practical resistance to the laws of the Territory and justify and approve the commission of crimes forbidden by it." To the extent Davis held that persons advocating a certain practice may be denied the right to vote, it is no longer good law. Brandenburg v. Ohio, 395 U.S. 444, (1969) (per curiam). To the extent it held that the groups designated in the statute may be deprived of the right to vote because of their status, its ruling could not stand without surviving strict scrutiny, a most doubtful outcome. Dunn v. Blumstein, 405 U.S. 330, 337, (1972). To the extent Davis held that a convicted felon may be denied the right to vote, its holding is not implicated by our decision and is unexceptionable. See Richardson v. Ramirez, 418 U.S. 24 (1974).

A second and related point is that laws of the kind now before us raise the inevitable inference that the disadvantage imposed is born of animosity toward the class of persons affected. "If the constitutional conception of 'equal protection of the laws' means anything, it must at the very least mean that a bare . . . desire to harm a politically unpopular group cannot constitute a legitimate governmental interest." Department of Agriculture v. Moreno. Even laws enacted for broad and ambitious purposes often can be explained by reference to legitimate public policies which justify the incidental disadvantages they impose on certain persons. Amendment 2, however, in making a general announcement that gays and lesbians shall not have any particular protections from the law, inflicts on them immediate, continuing, and real injuries that outrun and belie any legitimate justifications that may be claimed for it. We conclude that, in addition to the far-reaching deficiencies of Amendment 2 that we have noted, the principles it offends, in another sense, are conventional and venerable; a law must bear a rational relationship to a legitimate governmental purpose, and Amendment 2 does not.

The primary rationale the State offers for Amendment 2 is respect for other citizens' freedom of association, and in particular the liberties of landlords or employers who have personal or religious objections to homosexuality. Colorado also cites its interest in conserving resources to fight discrimination against other groups. The breadth of the Amendment is so far removed from these particular justifications that we find it impossible to credit them. We cannot say that Amendment 2 is directed to any identifiable legitimate purpose or discrete objective. It is a status-based enactment divorced from any factual context from which we could discern a relationship to legitimate state interests; it is a classification of persons undertaken for its own sake, something the Equal Protection Clause does not permit. "Class legislation . . . [is] obnoxious to the prohibitions of the Fourteenth Amendment. . . ." Civil Rights Cases, 109 U.S. at 24.

We must conclude that Amendment 2 classifies homosexuals not to further a proper legislative end but to make them unequal to everyone else. This Colorado cannot do. A State cannot so deem a class of persons a stranger to its laws. Amendment 2 violates the Equal Protection Clause, and the judgment of the Supreme Court of Colorado is affirmed.

JUSTICE SCALIA, with whom [CHIEF JUSTICE REHNQUIST] and JUSTICE THOMAS join, dissenting.

The Court has mistaken a Kulturkampf for a fit of spite. The constitutional amendment before us here is not the manifestation of a "'bare . . . desire to harm'" homosexuals, but is rather a modest attempt by seemingly tolerant Coloradans to preserve traditional sexual mores against the efforts of a politically powerful minority to revise those mores through use of the laws. That objective, and the means chosen to achieve it, are not only unimpeachable under any constitutional doctrine hitherto pronounced (hence the opinion's heavy reliance upon principles of righteousness rather than judicial holdings); they have been specifically approved by the Congress of the United States and by this Court.

In holding that homosexuality cannot be singled out for disfavorable treatment, the Court contradicts a decision, unchallenged here, pronounced only 10 years ago, see Bowers v. Hardwick, and places the prestige of this institution behind the proposition that opposition to homosexuality is as reprehensible as racial or religious bias. Whether it is or not is precisely the cultural debate that gave rise to the Colorado constitutional amendment (and to the preferential laws against which the amendment was directed). Since the Constitution of the United States says nothing about this subject, it is left to be resolved by normal democratic means, including the democratic adoption of provisions in state constitutions. This Court has no business imposing upon all Americans the resolution favored by the elite class from which the Members of this institution are selected, pronouncing that "animosity" toward homosexuality, is evil. I vigorously dissent.

I

Let me first discuss Part II of the Court's opinion, its longest section, which is devoted to rejecting the State's arguments that Amendment 2 "puts gays and lesbians in the same position as all other persons," and "does no more than deny homosexuals special rights." The Court concludes that this reading of Amendment 2's language is "implausible" under the "authoritative construction" given Amendment 2 by the Supreme Court of Colorado.

In reaching this conclusion, the Court considers it unnecessary to decide the validity of the State's argument that Amendment 2 does not deprive homosexuals of the "protection [afforded by] general laws and policies that prohibit arbitrary discrimination in governmental and private settings." I agree that we need not resolve that dispute, because the Supreme Court of Colorado has resolved it for us. [The] Colorado court stated:

> It is significant to note that Colorado law currently proscribes discrimination against persons who are not suspect classes, including discrimination based on age, marital or family status, veterans' status, and for any legal, off-duty conduct such as smoking tobacco. Of course Amendment 2 is not intended to have any effect on this legislation, but seeks only to prevent the adoption of anti-discrimination laws intended to protect gays, lesbians, and bisexuals.

The Court utterly fails to distinguish this portion of the Colorado court's opinion. [The] clear import of the Colorado court's conclusion [is] that "general laws and policies that prohibit arbitrary discrimination" would continue to prohibit discrimination on the basis of homosexual conduct as well. This analysis, which is fully in accord with (indeed, follows inescapably from) the text of the constitutional provision, lays to rest such horribles, raised in the course of oral argument, as the prospect that assaults upon homosexuals could not be prosecuted. The amendment prohibits special treatment of homosexuals, and nothing more. It would not affect, for example, a requirement of state law that pensions be paid to all retiring state employees with a certain length of service; homosexual employees, as well as others, would be entitled to that benefit. But it would prevent the State or any municipality from making death-benefit payments to the "life partner" of a homosexual when it does not make such payments to the long-time roommate of a nonhomosexual employee. Or again, it does not affect the requirement of the State's general insurance laws that customers be afforded coverage without discrimination unrelated to anticipated risk. Thus, homosexuals could not be denied coverage, or charged a greater premium, with respect to auto collision insurance; but neither the State nor any municipality could require that distinctive health insurance risks associated with homosexuality (if there are any) be ignored.

Despite all of its hand-wringing about the potential effect of Amendment 2 on general antidiscrimination laws, the Court's opinion ultimately does not dispute all this, but assumes it to be true. The only denial of equal treatment it contends homosexuals have suffered is this: They may not obtain preferential treatment without amending the state constitution. That is to say, the principle underlying the Court's opinion is that one who is accorded equal treatment under the laws, but cannot as readily as others obtain preferential treatment under the laws, has been denied equal protection of the laws. If merely stating this alleged "equal protection" violation does not suffice to refute it, our constitutional jurisprudence has achieved terminal silliness.

The central thesis of the Court's reasoning is that any group is denied equal protection when, to obtain advantage (or, presumably, to avoid disadvantage), it must have recourse to a more general and hence more difficult level of political decisionmaking than others. The world has never heard of such a principle, which is why the Court's opinion is so long on emotive utterance and so short on relevant legal citation. And it seems to me most unlikely that any multilevel democracy can function under such a principle. For whenever a disadvantage is imposed, or conferral of a benefit is prohibited, at one of the higher levels of democratic decisionmaking (i.e., by the state legislature rather than local government, or by the people at large in the state constitution rather than the legislature), the affected group has (under this theory) been denied equal protection. To take the simplest of examples, consider a state law prohibiting the award of municipal contracts to relatives of mayors or city councilmen. Once such a law is passed, the group composed of such relatives must, in order to get the benefit of city contracts, persuade the state legislature — unlike all other citizens, who need only persuade the municipality. It is ridiculous to consider this a denial of equal protection, which is why the Court's theory is unheard-of.

The Court might reply that the example I have given is not a denial of equal protection only because the same "rational basis" (avoidance of corruption) which renders constitutional the substantive discrimination against relatives (i.e., the fact that they alone cannot obtain city contracts) also automatically suffices to sustain what might be called the electoral-procedural discrimination against them (i.e., the fact that they must go to the state level to get this changed). This is of course a perfectly reasonable response, and would explain why "electoral-procedural discrimination" has not hitherto been heard of: a law that is valid in its substance is automatically valid in its level of enactment. But the Court cannot afford to make this argument, for as I shall discuss next, there is no doubt of a rational basis for the substance of the prohibition at issue here. The Court's entire novel theory rests upon the proposition that there is something special — something that cannot be justified by normal "rational basis" analysis — in making a disadvantaged group (or a nonpreferred group) resort to a higher decision-making level. That proposition finds no support in law or logic.

II

I turn next to whether there was a legitimate rational basis for the substance of the constitutional amendment — for the prohibition of special protection for homosexuals. It is unsurprising that the Court avoids discussion of this question, since the answer is so obviously yes. The case most relevant to the issue before us today is not even mentioned in the Court's opinion: In Bowers v. Hardwick, we held that the Constitution does not prohibit what virtually all States had done from the founding of the Republic until very recent years — making homosexual conduct a crime. That holding is unassailable, except by those who think that the Constitution changes to suit current fashions. But in any event it is a given in the present case: Respondents' briefs did not urge overruling Bowers, and at oral argument respondents' counsel expressly disavowed any intent to seek such overruling. If it is constitutionally permissible for a State to make homosexual conduct criminal, surely it is constitutionally permissible for a State to enact other laws merely disfavoring homosexual conduct. [And] a fortiori it is constitutionally permissible for a State to adopt a provision not even disfavoring homosexual conduct, but merely prohibiting all levels of state government from bestowing special protections upon homosexual conduct. Respondents (who, unlike the Court, cannot afford the luxury of ignoring inconvenient precedent) counter *Bowers* with the argument that a greater-includes-the-lesser rationale cannot justify Amendment 2's application to individuals who do not engage in homosexual acts, but are merely of homosexual "orientation." . . .

But assuming that, in Amendment 2, a person of homosexual "orientation" is someone who does not engage in homosexual conduct but merely has a tendency or desire to do so, *Bowers* still suffices to establish a rational basis for the provision. If it is rational to criminalize the conduct, surely it is rational to deny special favor and protection to those with a self-avowed tendency or desire to engage in the conduct. Indeed, where criminal sanctions are not involved, homosexual "orientation" is an acceptable stand-in for homosexual conduct. A State "does not violate the Equal Protection Clause merely because the classifications

199

made by its laws are imperfect," Dandridge v. Williams. Just as a policy barring the hiring of methadone users as transit employees does not violate equal protection simply because some methadone users pose no threat to passenger safety, see New York City Transit Authority v. Beazer, and just as a mandatory retirement age of 50 for police officers does not violate equal protection even though it prematurely ends the careers of many policemen over 50 who still have the capacity to do the job, see Massachusetts Bd. of Retirement v. Murgia, Amendment 2 is not constitutionally invalid simply because it could have been drawn more precisely so as to withdraw special antidiscrimination protections only from those of homosexual "orientation" who actually engage in homosexual conduct. As Justice Kennedy wrote, when he was on the Court of Appeals, in a case involving discharge of homosexuals from the Navy: "Nearly any statute which classifies people may be irrational as applied in particular cases. Discharge of the particular plaintiffs before us would be rational, under minimal scrutiny, not because their particular cases present the dangers which justify Navy policy, but instead because the general policy of discharging all homosexuals is rational." Beller v. Middendorf, 632 F.2d 788, 808-809, n.20 (CA9 1980) (citation omitted). . . .

III

The foregoing suffices to establish what the Court's failure to cite any case remotely in point would lead one to suspect: No principle set forth in the Constitution, nor even any imagined by this Court in the past 200 years, prohibits what Colorado has done here. But the case for Colorado is much stronger than that. What it has done is not only unprohibited, but eminently reasonable, with close, congressionally approved precedent in earlier constitutional practice.

First, as to its eminent reasonableness. The Court's opinion contains grim, disapproving hints that Coloradans have been guilty of "animus" or "animosity" toward homosexuality, as though that has been established as Unamerican. Of course it is our moral heritage that one should not hate any human being or class of human beings. But I had thought that one could consider certain conduct reprehensible—murder, for example, or polygamy, or cruelty to animals—and could exhibit even "animus" toward such conduct. Surely that is the only sort of "animus" at issue here: moral disapproval of homosexual conduct, the same sort of moral disapproval that produced the centuries-old criminal laws that we held constitutional in Bowers. The Colorado amendment does not, to speak entirely precisely, prohibit giving favored status to people who are homosexuals; they can be favored for many reasons—for example, because they are senior citizens or members of racial minorities. But it prohibits giving them favored status because of their homosexual conduct—that is, it prohibits favored status for homosexuality.

Trouble some

But though Coloradans are, as I say, entitled to be hostile toward homosexual conduct, the fact is that the degree of hostility reflected by Amendment 2 is the smallest conceivable. The Court's portrayal of Coloradans as a society fallen victim to pointless, hate-filled "gay-bashing" is so false as to be comical. Colorado not only is one of the 25 States that have repealed their antisodomy laws, but was among the first to do so. But the society that eliminates criminal punishment for homosexual acts does not necessarily abandon the view that homosexuality is morally wrong and socially harmful; often, abolition simply reflects the view that enforcement of such criminal laws involves unseemly intrusion into the intimate lives of citizens.

There is a problem, however, which arises when criminal sanction of homosexuality is eliminated but moral and social disapprobation of homosexuality is meant to be retained. The Court cannot be unaware of that problem; it is evident in many cities of the country, and occasionally bubbles to the surface of the news, in heated political disputes over such matters as the introduction into local schools of books teaching that homosexuality is an optional and fully acceptable "alternate life style." The problem (a problem, that is, for those who wish to retain social disapprobation of homosexuality) is that, because those who engage in homosexual conduct tend to reside in disproportionate numbers in certain communities, have high disposable income, and of course care about homosexual-rights issues much more ardently than the public at large, they possess political power much greater than their numbers, both locally and statewide. Quite understandably, they devote this political power to achieving not merely a grudging social toleration, but full social acceptance, of homosexuality.

By the time Coloradans were asked to vote on Amendment 2, their exposure to homosexuals' quest for social endorsement was not limited to newspaper accounts of happenings in places such as New York, Los Angeles, San Francisco, and Key West. Three Colorado cities — Aspen, Boulder, and Denver — had enacted ordinances that listed "sexual orientation" as an impermissible ground for discrimination, equating the moral disapproval of homosexual conduct with racial and religious bigotry. The phenomenon had even appeared statewide: the Governor of Colorado had signed an executive order pronouncing that "in the State of Colorado we recognize the diversity in our pluralistic society and strive to bring an end to discrimination in any form," and directing state agency-heads to "ensure non-discrimination" in hiring and promotion based on, among other things, "sexual orientation." I do not mean to be critical of these legislative successes; homosexuals are as entitled to use the legal system for reinforcement of their moral sentiments as are the rest of society. But they are subject to being countered by lawful, democratic countermeasures as well.

That is where Amendment 2 came in. It sought to counter both the geographic concentration and the disproportionate political power of homosexuals by (1) resolving the controversy at the statewide level, and (2) making the election a single-issue contest for both sides. It put directly, to all the citizens of the State, the question: Should homosexuality be given special protection? They answered no. The Court today asserts that this most democratic of procedures is unconstitutional. Lacking any cases to establish that facially absurd proposition, it simply asserts that it must be unconstitutional, because it has never happened before. . . .

What the Court says is even demonstrably false at the constitutional level. The Eighteenth Amendment to the Federal Constitution, for example, deprived those who drank alcohol not only of the power to alter the policy of prohibition locally or through state legislation, but even of the power to alter it through state constitutional amendment or federal legislation. The Establishment Clause of the First Amendment prevents theocrats from having their way by converting their fellow citizens at the local, state, or federal statutory level; as does the Republican Form of Government Clause prevent monarchists.

But there is a much closer analogy, one that involves precisely the effort by the majority of citizens to preserve its view of sexual morality statewide, against the efforts of a geographically concentrated and politically powerful minority to undermine it. The constitutions of the States of Arizona, Idaho, New Mexico, Oklahoma, and Utah to this day contain provisions stating that polygamy is "forever prohibited." Polygamists, and those who have a polygamous "orientation," have been "singled out" by these provisions for much more severe treatment than merely denial of favored status; and that treatment can only be changed by achieving amendment of the state constitutions. The Court's disposition today suggests that these provisions are unconstitutional, and that polygamy must be permitted in these States on a state-legislated, or perhaps even local-option, basis—unless, of course, polygamists for some reason have fewer constitutional rights than homosexuals.

The United States Congress, by the way, required the inclusion of these anti-polygamy provisions in the constitutions of Arizona, New Mexico, Oklahoma, and Utah, as a condition of their admission to statehood. (For Arizona, New Mexico, and Utah, moreover, the Enabling Acts required that the antipolygamy provisions be "irrevocable without the consent of the United States and the people of said State"—so that not only were "each of [the] parts" of these States not "open on impartial terms" to polygamists, but even the States as a whole were not; polygamists would have to persuade the whole country to their way of thinking.) [Thus], this "singling out" of the sexual practices of a single group for statewide, democratic vote — so utterly alien to our constitutional system, the Court would have us believe — has not only happened, but has received the explicit approval of the United States Congress.

I cannot say that this Court has explicitly approved any of these state constitutional provisions; but it has approved a territorial statutory provision that went even further, depriving polygamists of the ability even to achieve a constitutional amendment, by depriving them of the power to vote. In Davis v. Beason, 133 U.S. 333, (1890), Justice Field wrote for a unanimous Court:

> In our judgment, §501 of the Revised Statutes of Idaho Territory, which provides that "no person . . . who is a bigamist or polygamist or who teaches, advises, counsels, or encourages any person or persons to become bigamists or polygamists, or to commit any other crime defined by law, or to enter into what is known as plural or celestial marriage, or who is a member of any order, organization or association which teaches, advises, counsels, or encourages its members or devotees or any other persons to commit the crime of bigamy or polygamy, or any other crime defined by law . . . is permitted to vote at any election, or to hold any position or office of honor, trust, or profit within this Territory," is not open to any constitutional or legal objection.

To the extent, if any, that this opinion permits the imposition of adverse consequences upon mere abstract advocacy of polygamy, it has of course been overruled by later cases. See Brandenburg v. Ohio, 395 U.S. 444 (1969) (per curiam). But the proposition that polygamy can be criminalized, and those engaging in that crime deprived of the vote, remains good law. See Richardson v. Ramirez, 418 U.S. 24, 53, (1974). Beason rejected the argument that "such discrimination is a denial of the equal protection of the laws." Among the Justices joining in that rejection were the two whose views in other cases the Court today treats as equal-protection lodestars — Justice Harlan, who was to proclaim in Plessy v. Ferguson, (dissenting opinion), that the Constitution "neither knows nor tolerates classes among citizens," and Justice Bradley, who had earlier declared that "class legislation . . . [is] obnoxious to the prohibitions of the Fourteenth Amendment," Civil Rights Cases.

This Court cited *Beason* with approval as recently as 1993, in an opinion authored by the same Justice who writes for the Court today. That opinion said: "Adverse impact will not always lead to a finding of impermissible targeting. For example, a social harm may have been a legitimate concern of government for reasons quite apart from discrimination. . . . See, e.g., . . . Davis v. Beason." Church of Lukumi Babalu Aye, Inc. v. Hialeah, 508 U.S. 520, 535, (1993). It remains to be explained how §501 of the Idaho Revised Statutes was not an "impermissible targeting" of polygamists, but (the much more mild) Amendment 2 is an "impermissible targeting" of homosexuals. Has the Court concluded that the perceived social harm of polygamy is a "legitimate concern of government," and the perceived social harm of homosexuality is not?

IV

I strongly suspect that the answer to the last question is yes, which leads me to the last point I wish to make: The Court today, announcing that Amendment 2 "defies . . . conventional [constitutional] inquiry," and "confounds [the] normal process of judicial review," employs a constitutional theory heretofore unknown to frustrate Colorado's reasonable effort to preserve traditional American moral values. The Court's stern disapproval of "animosity" towards homosexuality might be compared with what an earlier Court (including the revered Justices Harlan and Bradley) said in Murphy v. Ramsey, 114 U.S. 15 (1885), rejecting a constitutional challenge to a United States statute that denied the franchise in federal territories to those who engaged in polygamous cohabitation:

> Certainly no legislation can be supposed more wholesome and necessary in the founding of a free, self-governing commonwealth, fit to take rank as one of the co-ordinate States of the Union, than that which seeks to establish it on the basis of the idea of the family, as consisting in and springing from the union for life of one man and one woman in the holy estate of matrimony; the sure foundation of all that is stable and noble in our civilization; the best guaranty of that reverent morality which is the source of all beneficent progress in social and political improvement.

I would not myself indulge in such official praise for heterosexual monogamy, because I think it no business of the courts (as opposed to the political branches) to take sides in this culture war.

But the Court today has done so, not only by inventing a novel and extravagant constitutional doctrine to take the victory away from traditional forces, but even by verbally disparaging as bigotry adherence to traditional attitudes. To suggest, for example, that this constitutional amendment springs from nothing more than "'a bare . . . desire to harm a politically unpopular group'" is nothing short of insulting. (It is also nothing short of preposterous to call "politically unpopular" a group which enjoys enormous influence in American media and politics, and which, as the trial court here noted, though composing no more than 4% of the population had the support of 46% of the voters on Amendment 2.

When the Court takes sides in the culture wars, it tends to be with the knights rather than the villeins—and more specifically with the Templars, reflecting the views and values of the lawyer class from which the Court's Members are drawn. How that class feels about homosexuality will be evident to anyone who wishes to interview job applicants at virtually any of the Nation's law schools. The interviewer may refuse to offer a job because the applicant is a Republican; because he is an adulterer; because he went to the wrong prep school or belongs to the wrong country club; because he eats snails; because he is a womanizer; because she wears real-animal fur; or even because he hates the Chicago Cubs. But if the interviewer should wish not to be an associate or partner of an applicant because he disapproves of the applicant's homosexuality, then he will have violated the pledge which the Association of American Law Schools requires all its member-schools to exact from job interviewers: "assurance of the employer's willingness" to hire homosexuals. This law-school view of what "prejudices" must be stamped out may be contrasted with the more plebeian attitudes that apparently still prevail in the United States Congress, which has been unresponsive to repeated attempts to extend to homosexuals the protections of federal civil rights laws, and which took the pains to exclude them specifically from the Americans With Disabilities Act of 1990.

Today's opinion has no foundation in American constitutional law, and barely pretends to. The people of Colorado have adopted an entirely reasonable provision which does not even disfavor homosexuals in any substantive sense, but merely denies them preferential treatment. Amendment 2 is designed to prevent piecemeal deterioration of the sexual morality favored by a majority of Coloradans, and is not only an appropriate means to that legitimate end, but a means that Americans have employed before. Striking it down is an act, not of judicial judgment, but of political will. I dissent.

Note: The Meaning of Romer

1. *Rational basis review?* The Court asserts that it is utilizing rational basis review to invalidate Amendment 2. Is this claim plausible? Recall Reed v. Reed, page 699 of the main volume, where the Court inaugurated its modern encounter with gender discrimination by purporting to utilize rational basis review to invalidate gender-specific laws. Only later did the Court acknowledge that it was utilizing heightened scrutiny. See Craig v. Boren, at page 703 of the main volume. Does *Romer* mark the beginning of an analogous transformation of the Court's jurisprudence regarding sexual preference? If so, what institutional interests are served by insisting on rational-basis review at the beginning of this process?

Note that Amendment 2 was unusually broad in scope. Unlike state constitutional provisions that simply outlaw certain practices, such as polygamy, or the "don't ask/don't tell" policy, which disadvantages homosexuals in a particular context, this provision deprived a class of citizens of access to *any* protection against discrimination, regardless of context, on the basis of a single trait. Even if the denial of protection to homosexuals is rational in *some* contexts, might not the general denial of such protection *regardless of context* be irrational?

2. *Baselines again.* The Court claims that its decision guarantees for homosexuals only "equal" and not "special protection. This is so, the Court asserts,

because under modern conditions, the baseline is a general right to be free from discrimination. Protections against discrimination are "taken for granted by most people either because they already have them or do not need them; these are protections against exclusion from an almost limitless number of transactions and endeavors that constitute ordinary civic life in a free society." Suppose Colorado had never enacted Amendment 2, but had simply failed to enact measures protecting homosexuals from discrimination. Does it follow from the Court's analysis that a state acts "irrationally" and therefore violates the Constitution if it provides general protection against discrimination for a wide range of groups but fails to provide such protection for gays? Is this position consistent with Washington v. Davis?

3. *The future of* Bowers. The Court asserts that Amendment 2 raises "the inevitable inference that the disadvantage imposed is born of animosity toward the class of persons affected" and relies on *Moreno* for the proposition that "[if] the constitutional conception of 'equal protection of the laws' means anything, it must at the very least mean that a bare . . . desire to harm a politically unpopular group cannot constitute a legitimate governmental interest." Can this argument against Amendment 2 be squared with the Court's holding in *Bowers* that moral opposition to homosexuality is a sufficiently strong government interest to justify criminalization of homosexual sodomy? Note that the Court fails to cite *Bowers*, although the decision is surely at least tangentially relevant to the Court's analysis. What message does this failure send?

Does it follow from the government's ability to criminalize certain activity that any other disadvantage the government imposes on those who engage in it is automatically permissible under the equal protection clause? Could the government deny a driver's license to a person caught smoking cigarettes?

4. *Justice Scalia's dissent.* What is the meaning of the first sentence of Justice Scalia's opinion? "Kulturkampf" is the German word for "culture war." The term refers to the effort by the German government in the late 19th century, under the leadership of Count Bismarck, to reduce the influence of the Roman Catholic Church. Among other things, Bismarck insisted that the state train and license priests and imprisoned priests and bishops who disobeyed his orders. Consider the possibility that our Constitution outlaws state-supported "Kulturkampfs" and that Amendment 2 violated the Constitution precisely because it formed part of an official "culture war" against a particular subsection of the population. Note that the majority and dissenting opinions each accuse the other of departing from a position of state neutrality in this conflict. The majority disclaims any effort to give homosexuals "special" rights and claims that Colorado has failed to treat them "equally." The dissent, in turn, accuses the majority of siding with homosexuals against their adversaries. What does state neutrality mean in this context? Is neutrality a desirable or constitutionally required objective?

For a discussion of the equal rights/special rights distinction, see Rubin, Equal Rights, Special Rights, and the Nature of Antidiscrimination Law, 97 Mich. L. Rev. 564 (1998). Professor Rubin identifies three reasons why laws and constitutional provisions providing for "equal" rights are sometimes perceived as requiring "special" rights. First, although antidiscrimination law prohibits actions taken on the basis of group membership, it cannot create a world where the impulse to discriminate is eliminated. Because this impulse continues to exist, those subject to the law's constraint may feel that they are required to provide special treatment to the protected group. Second, the possibility of error in applying antidiscrimination law may lead those subject to it to act differently toward members of the protected class. Finally, those who disagree with the view that members of the protected class are morally similar to others will see a prohibition against discrimination as providing special rights.

5. *Romer's Reach.* Commentators have offered a variety of different opinions concerning the meaning and scope of *Romer.* On the decision's reach, compare Sunstein, Forward, Leaving Things Undecided, 110 Harv. L. Rev. 4 (1996) (defending a "minimalist" interpretation) with Seidman, *Romer's* Radicalism: The Unexpected Revival of Warren Court Activism, 1996 Sup. Ct. Rev. 67 (defending a "radical" interpretation). On its meaning, see, e.g., Jeffries & Levinson, The Non-Retrogression Principle in Constitutional Law, 86 Cal. L. Rev. 1211 (1998) (analyzing and criticizing *Romer* as embodying a nonretrogression principle); Amar, Attainment and Amendment 2: *Romer's* Rightness, 95 Mich. L. Rev. 203 (1996) (analyzing *Romer* under the Bill of Attainder Clause); Farber & Sherry, The Pariah Principle, 13 Con. Comm. 257 (1996) (analyzing *Romer* under the principle that "forbids government from designating any societal group as untouchable, regardless of whether the group in question is generally entitled to some special degree of judicial protection"); Alexander, Sometimes Better Boring and Correct: Romer v. Evans as an Exercise of Ordinary Equal Protection Analysis, 68 U. Col . L. Rev. 335 (1996) (analyzing *Romer* in terms of "ordinary" equal protection principles). See generally Symposium, Gay Rights and the Courts: The Amendment 2 Controversy, 68 U. Colo. L. Rev. 285 (1996).

6
IMPLIED FUNDAMENTAL RIGHTS

E. Fundamental Interests and the Equal Protection Clause

Page 892. Before "c. Denial of 'Access to the Ballot,'" add the following:

Bush v. Vera
517 U.S. 952 (1996)

JUSTICE O'CONNOR announced the judgment of the Court and delivered an opinion, in which THE CHIEF JUSTICE and JUSTICE KENNEDY join.

This is the latest in a series of appeals involving racial gerrymandering challenges to state redistricting efforts in the wake of the 1990 census. That census revealed a population increase, largely in urban minority populations, that entitled Texas to three additional congressional seats. In response, and with a view to complying with the Voting Rights Act of 1965 (VRA), the Texas Legislature promulgated a redistricting plan that, among other things: created District 30, a new majority-African-American district in Dallas County; created District 29, a new majority-Hispanic district in and around Houston in Harris County; and reconfigured District 18, which is adjacent to District 29, to make it a majority-African-American district. The Department of Justice precleared that plan under VRA § 5 in 1991, and it was used in the 1992 congressional elections.

The plaintiffs, six Texas voters, challenged the plan, alleging that 24 of Texas' 30 congressional districts constitute racial gerrymanders in violation of the Fourteenth Amendment. The three-judge United States District Court for the Southern District of Texas held Districts 18, 29, and 30 unconstitutional. . . . The Governor of Texas, private intervenors, and the United States (as intervenor) now appeal. Finding that, under this Court's decisions in *Shaw I* and *Miller*, the district lines at issue are subject to strict scrutiny, and that they are not narrowly tailored to serve a compelling state interest, we affirm. . . .

II

We must now determine whether those districts are subject to strict scrutiny. Our precedents have used a variety of formulations to describe the threshold for the application of strict scrutiny. . . .

Strict scrutiny does not apply merely because redistricting is performed with consciousness of race. Nor does it apply to all cases of intentional creation of majority-minority districts. Electoral district lines are "facially race neutral," so a more searching inquiry is necessary before strict scrutiny can be found applicable in redistricting cases than in cases of "classifications based explicitly on race." For strict scrutiny to apply, the plaintiffs must prove that other, legitimate districting principles were "subordinated" to race. By that, we mean that race must be "the predominant factor motivating the legislature's [redistricting] decision." We thus differ from Justice Thomas, who would apparently hold that it suffices that racial considerations be a motivation for the drawing of a majority-minority district.

The present case is a mixed motive case. The appellants concede that one of Texas' goals in creating the three districts at issue was to produce majority-minority districts, but they also cite evidence that other goals, particularly incumbency protection (including protection of "functional incumbents," i.e., sitting members of the Texas Legislature who had declared an intention to run for open congressional seats), also played a role in the drawing of the district lines. [A] careful review is, therefore, necessary to determine whether these districts are subject to strict scrutiny. But review of the District Court's findings of primary fact and the record convinces us that the District Court's determination that race was the "predominant factor" in the drawing of each of the districts must be sustained.

We begin with general findings and evidence regarding the redistricting plan's respect for traditional districting principles, the legislators' expressed motivations, and the methods used in the redistricting process. The District Court began its analysis by rejecting the factual basis for appellants' claim that Texas' challenged "districts cannot be unconstitutionally bizarre in shape because Texas does not have and never has used traditional redistricting principles such as natural geographical boundaries, contiguity, compactness, and conformity to political subdivisions." The court instead found that "generally, Texas has not intentionally disregarded traditional districting criteria," and that only one pre-1991 congressional district in Texas was comparable in its irregularity and noncompactness to the three challenged districts. The court also noted that "compactness as measured by an 'eyeball' approach was much less important," in the 1991 plan, than in its predecessor, the 1980 Texas congressional districting plan, and that districts were especially irregular in shape in the Dallas and Harris County areas where the challenged districts are located.

These findings comport with the conclusions of an instructive study that attempted to determine the relative compactness of districts nationwide in objective, numerical terms. That study gave Texas' 1980 districting plan a roughly average score for the compactness and regularity of its district shapes, but ranked its 1991 plan among the worst in the Nation. See Pildes & Niemi, Expressive Harms, "Bizarre Districts," and Voting Rights: Evaluating Election-District Appearances After Shaw v. Reno, 92 Mich. L. Rev. 483, 571-573, table 6 (1993). The same study ranked Districts 18, 29, and 30 among the 28 least regular congressional districts nationwide. . . .

The District Court also found substantial direct evidence of the legislature's racial motivations. . . .

The means that Texas used to make its redistricting decisions provides further evidence of the importance of race. The primary tool used in drawing district lines was a computer program called "REDAPPL." REDAPPL permitted redistricters to manipulate district lines on computer maps, on which racial and other socioeconomic data were superimposed. At each change in configuration of the district lines being drafted, REDAPPL displayed updated racial composition statistics for the district as drawn. REDAPPL contained racial data at the block-by-block level, whereas other data, such as party registration and past voting statistics, were only available at the level of voter tabulation districts (which approximate election precincts). The availability and use of block-by-block racial data was unprecedented; before the 1990 census, data were not broken down beyond the census tract level. By providing uniquely detailed racial data, REDAPPL enabled districters to make more intricate refinements on the basis of race than on the basis of other demographic information. . . .

These findings — that the State substantially neglected traditional districting criteria such as compactness, that it was committed from the outset to creating majority-minority districts, and that it manipulated district lines to exploit unprecedentedly detailed racial data — together weigh in favor of the application of strict scrutiny. We do not hold that any one of these factors is independently sufficient to require strict scrutiny. The Constitution does not mandate regularity of district shape, and the neglect of traditional districting criteria is merely necessary, not sufficient. For strict scrutiny to apply, traditional districting criteria must be subordinated to race. Nor, as we have emphasized, is the decision to create a majority-minority district objectionable in and of itself. . . .

Several factors other than race were at work in the drawing of the districts. Traditional districting criteria were not entirely neglected. [The] District Court found that incumbency protection influenced the redistricting plan to an unprecedented extent. . . .

Strict scrutiny would not be appropriate if race-neutral, traditional districting considerations predominated over racial ones. We have not subjected political gerrymandering to strict scrutiny. [Because] it is clear that race was not the only factor that motivated the legislature to draw irregular district lines, we must scrutinize each challenged district to determine whether the District Court's conclusion that race predominated over legitimate districting considerations, including incumbency, can be sustained.

A . . .

Appellants do not deny that District 30 shows substantial disregard for the traditional districting principles of compactness and regularity, or that the redistricters pursued unwaveringly the objective of creating a majority-African-American district. But they argue that its bizarre shape is explained by efforts to unite communities of interest in a single district and, especially, to protect incumbents. . . .

Here, the District Court had ample bases on which to conclude both that racially motivated gerrymandering had a qualitatively greater influence on the drawing of district lines than politically motivated gerrymandering, and that political gerrymandering was accomplished in large part by the use of race as a proxy. . . .

[Most] significantly, the objective evidence provided by the district plans and demographic maps suggests strongly the predominance of race. Given that the districting software used by the State provided only racial data at the block-by-block level, the fact that District 30, unlike Johnson's original proposal, splits voter tabulation districts and even individual streets in many places, suggests that racial criteria predominated over other districting criteria in determining the district's boundaries. And, despite the strong correlation between race and political affiliation, the maps reveal that political considerations were subordinated to racial classification in the drawing of many of the most extreme and bizarre district lines.

B . . .

District 18's population is 51% African-American and 15% Hispanic. It "has some of the most irregular boundaries of any congressional district in the country[,] . . . boundaries that squiggle north toward Intercontinental Airport and northwest out radial highways, then spurt south on one side toward the port and on the other toward the Astrodome. Its "many narrow corridors, wings, or fingers . . . reach out to enclose black voters, while excluding nearby Hispanic residents."

District 29 has a 61% Hispanic and 10% African-American population. It resembles

a sacred Mayan bird, with its body running eastward along the Ship Channel from downtown Houston until the tail terminates in Baytown. Spindly legs reach south to Hobby Airport, while the plumed head rises northward almost to Intercontinental. In the western extremity of the district, an open beak appears to be searching for worms in Spring Branch. Here and there, ruffled feathers jut out at odd angles.

Not only are the shapes of the districts bizarre; they also exhibit utter disregard of city limits, local election precincts, and voter tabulation district lines. . . .

As with District 30, appellants adduced evidence that incumbency protection played a role in determining the bizarre district lines. The District Court found that one constraint on the shape of District 29 was the rival ambitions of its two "functional incumbents," who distorted its boundaries in an effort to include larger areas of their existing state legislative constituencies. But the District Court's findings amply demonstrate that such influences were overwhelmed in the determination of the districts' bizarre shapes by the State's efforts to maximize racial divisions. . . .

III

Having concluded that strict scrutiny applies, we must determine whether the racial classifications embodied in any of the three districts are narrowly tailored to further a compelling state interest. Appellants point to three compelling interests: the interest in avoiding liability under the "results" test of VRA §2(b), the interest in remedying past and present racial discrimination, and the "nonretrogression" principle of VRA §5 (for District 18 only). . . .

A

Section 2(a) of the VRA prohibits the imposition of any electoral practice or procedure that "results in a denial or abridgement of the right of any citizen . . . to vote on account of race or color." In 1982, Congress amended the VRA by changing the language of §2(a) and adding §2(b), which provides a "results" test for violation of §2(a). A violation exists if,

> based on the totality of circumstances, it is shown that the political processes leading to nomination or election in the State or political subdivision are not equally open to participation by members of a class of citizens protected by subsection (a) of this section in that its members have less opportunity than other members of the electorate to participate in the political process and to elect representatives of their choice. 42 U.S.C. §1973(b).

Appellants contend that creation of each of the three majority-minority districts at issue was justified by Texas' compelling state interest in complying with this results test.

213

As we have done in each of our previous cases in which this argument has been raised as a defense to charges of racial gerrymandering, we assume without deciding that compliance with the results test [can] be a compelling state interest. We also reaffirm that the "narrow tailoring" requirement of strict scrutiny allows the States a limited degree of leeway in furthering such interests. If the State has a "strong basis in evidence," for concluding that creation of a majority-minority district is reasonably necessary to comply with §2, and the districting that is based on race "substantially addresses the §2 violation," it satisfies strict scrutiny. We thus reject, as impossibly stringent, the District Court's view of the narrow tailoring requirement, that "a district must have the least possible amount of irregularity in shape, making allowances for traditional districting criteria.". . .

We assume, without deciding, that the State had a "strong basis in evidence" for finding the second and third threshold conditions for §2 liability to be present. We have, however, already found that all three districts are bizarrely shaped and far from compact, and that those characteristics are predominantly attributable to gerrymandering that was racially motivated and/or achieved by the use of race as a proxy. . . .

These characteristics defeat any claim that the districts are narrowly tailored to serve the State's interest in avoiding liability under §2, because §2 does not require a State to create, on predominantly racial lines, a district that is not "reasonably compact." . . .

B

The United States and the State next contend that the district lines at issue are justified by the State's compelling interest in "ameliorating the effects of racially polarized voting attributable to past and present racial discrimination." In support of that contention, they cite Texas' long history of discrimination against minorities in electoral processes, stretching from the Reconstruction to modern times, including violations of the Constitution and of the VRA. Appellants attempt to link that history to evidence that in recent elections in majority-minority districts, "Anglos usually bloc voted against" Hispanic and African-American candidates.

A State's interest in remedying discrimination is compelling when two conditions are satisfied. First, the discrimination that the State seeks to remedy must be specific, "identified discrimination"; second, the State "must have had a 'strong basis in evidence' to conclude that remedial action was necessary, 'before it embarks on an affirmative action program.'" Here, the only current problem that appellants cite as in need of remediation is alleged vote dilution as a consequence of racial bloc voting, the same concern that underlies their VRA §2 compliance defense, which we have assumed to be valid for purposes of this opinion. We have indicated that such problems will not justify race-based districting unless "the State employs sound districting principles, and . . . the affected racial group's residential patterns afford the opportunity of creating districts in which they will be in the majority." Once that standard is applied, our agreement with the District Court's finding that these districts are not narrowly tailored to comply with §2 forecloses this line of defense.

C

The final contention offered by the State and private appellants is that creation of District 18 (only) was justified by a compelling state interest in complying with VRA §5. We have made clear that §5 has a limited substantive goal: "'to insure that no voting-procedure changes would be made that would lead to a retrogression in the position of racial minorities with respect to their effective exercise of the electoral franchise.'" Appellants contend that this "nonretrogression" principle is implicated because Harris County had, for two decades, contained a congressional district in which African-American voters had succeeded in selecting representatives of their choice, all of whom were African-Americans.

The problem with the State's argument is that it seeks to justify not maintenance, but substantial augmentation, of the African-American population percentage in District 18. . . .

IV . . .

This Court has now rendered decisions after plenary consideration in five cases applying the *Shaw I* doctrine (*Shaw I, Miller, Hays, Shaw II,* and this case). The dissenters would have us abandon those precedents, suggesting that fundamental concerns relating to the judicial role are at stake. While we agree that those concerns are implicated here, we believe they point the other way. Our legitimacy requires, above all, that we adhere to stare decisis, especially in such sensitive political contexts as the present, where partisan controversy abounds. Legislators and district courts nationwide have modified their practices — or, rather, reembraced the traditional districting practices that were almost universally followed before the 1990 census — in response to Shaw I. Those practices and our precedents, which acknowledge voters as more than mere racial statistics, play an important role in defining the political identity of the American voter. Our Fourteenth Amendment jurisprudence evinces a commitment to eliminate unnecessary and excessive governmental use and reinforcement of racial stereotypes. We decline to retreat from that commitment today.

The judgment of the District Court is
Affirmed.

JUSTICE O'CONNOR, concurring.

I write separately to express my view on two points. First, compliance with
the results test of §2 of the Voting Rights Act (VRA) is a compelling state interest. Second, that test can co-exist in principle and in practice with Shaw v. Reno
and its progeny, as elaborated in today's opinions. . . .

JUSTICE KENNEDY, concurring.

I join the plurality opinion, but the statements in Part II of the opinion that
strict scrutiny would not apply to all cases of intentional creation of majority-
minority districts require comment. Those statements are unnecessary to our
decision, for strict scrutiny applies here. I do not consider these dicta to commit
me to any position on the question whether race is predominant whenever a
State, in redistricting, foreordains that one race be the majority in a certain number of districts or in a certain part of the State. In my view, we would no doubt
apply strict scrutiny if a State decreed that certain districts had to be at least 50
percent white, and our analysis should be no different if the State so favors minority races. . . .

JUSTICE THOMAS, with whom JUSTICE SCALIA joins, concurring in the judgment.

In my view, application of strict scrutiny in this case was never a close question. I cannot agree with Justice O'Connor's assertion that strict scrutiny is not
invoked by the intentional creation of majority-minority districts. . . .

Strict scrutiny applies to all governmental classifications based on race, and
we have expressly held that there is no exception for race-based redistricting. . . .

I am willing to assume without deciding that the State has asserted a compelling state interest. Given that assumption, I agree that the State's redistricting
attempts were not narrowly tailored to achieve its asserted interest. I concur in
the judgment.

JUSTICE STEVENS, with whom JUSTICE GINSBURG and JUSTICE BREYER join,
dissenting.

The 1990 census revealed that Texas' population had grown, over the past
decade, almost twice as fast as the population of the country as a whole. As a
result, Texas was entitled to elect three additional Representatives to the United
States Congress, enlarging its delegation from 27 to 30. Because Texas' growth
was concentrated in South Texas and the cities of Dallas and Houston, the state
legislature concluded that the new congressional districts should be carved out
of existing districts in those areas. The consequences of the political battle that

produced the new map are some of the most oddly shaped congressional districts in the United States.

Today, the Court strikes down three of Texas' majority- minority districts, concluding, inter alia, that their odd shapes reveal that the State impermissibly relied on predominantly racial reasons when it drew the districts as it did. For two reasons, I believe that the Court errs in striking down those districts.

First, I believe that the Court has misapplied its own tests for racial gerrymandering, both by applying strict scrutiny to all three of these districts, and then by concluding that none can meet that scrutiny. In asking whether strict scrutiny should apply, the Court improperly ignores the "complex interplay" of political and geographical considerations that went into the creation of Texas' new congressional districts, and focuses exclusively on the role that race played in the State's decisions to adjust the shape of its districts. A quick comparison of the unconstitutional majority-minority districts with three equally bizarre majority-Anglo districts demonstrates that race was not necessarily the predominant factor contorting the district lines. I would follow the fair implications of the District Court's findings and conclude that Texas' entire map is a political, not a racial, gerrymander. . . .

Even if strict scrutiny applies, I would find these districts constitutional, for each considers race only to the extent necessary to comply with the State's responsibilities under the Voting Rights Act while achieving other race-neutral political and geographical requirements. The plurality's finding to the contrary unnecessarily restricts the ability of States to conform their behavior to the Voting Rights Act while simultaneously complying with other race-neutral goals.

Second, even if I concluded that these districts failed an appropriate application of this still-developing law to appropriately read facts, I would not uphold the District Court decision. The decisions issued today serve merely to reinforce my conviction that the Court has, with its "analytically distinct" jurisprudence of racial gerrymandering, struck out into a jurisprudential wilderness that lacks a definable constitutional core and threatens to create harms more significant than any suffered by the individual plaintiffs challenging these districts. . . .

II . . .

The conclusion that race-conscious districting should not always be subject to strict scrutiny merely recognizes that our equal protection jurisprudence can sometimes mislead us with its rigid characterization of suspect classes and levels of scrutiny. As I have previously noted, all equal protection jurisprudence might be described as a form of rational basis scrutiny; we apply "strict scrutiny" more to describe the likelihood of success than the character of the test to be applied. Because race has rarely been a legitimate basis for state classifications, and more typically an irrational and invidious ground for discrimination, a "virtually automatic invalidation of racial classifications" has been the natural result of the application of our equal protection jurisprudence. In certain circumstances, however, when the state action (i) has neither the intent nor effect of harming any particular group, (ii) is not designed to give effect to irrational prejudices held by its citizens but to break them down, and (iii) uses race as a classification because race is "relevant" to the benign goal of the classification, we need not view the action with the typically fatal skepticism that we have used to strike down the most pernicious forms of state behavior. [While] any racial classification may risk some stereotyping, the risk of true "discrimination" in this case is extremely tenuous in light of the remedial purpose the classification is intended to achieve and the long history of resistance to giving minorities a full voice in the political process. Given the balancing of subtle harms and strong remedies—a balancing best left to the political process, not to our own well-developed but rigid jurisprudence—the plurality reasonably concludes that race-conscious redistricting is not always a form of "discrimination" to which we should direct our most skeptical eye.

III

While the Court has agreed that race can, to a point, govern the drawing of district lines, it nonetheless suggests that at a certain point, when the State uses race "too much," illegitimate racial stereotypes threaten to overrun and contaminate an otherwise legitimate redistricting process. . . .

IV . . .

The political, rather than the racial, nature of District 30's gerrymander is even more starkly highlighted by comparing it with the districts struck down in *Shaw II* and *Miller*. District 30's black population is, for instance, far more concentrated than the minority population in North Carolina's District 12. And in *Miller*, the Court made it clear that the odd shape of Georgia's Eleventh District was the result of a conscious effort to increase its proportion of minority populations: It was, the Court found, "'exceedingly obvious' from the shape of the Eleventh District, together with the racial demographics, that the drawing of narrow land bridges to incorporate within the District outlying appendages containing nearly 80% of the district's total black population was a deliberate attempt to bring black populations into the district."

District 30 is the precise demographic converse of the district struck down in Miller. District 30, for example, has a compact core in South Dallas which contains 50% of the district population and nearly 70% of the district's total black population. Unlike the appendages to Georgia's District 11, the tentacles stretching north and west from District 30 add progressively less in the way of population, and, more important for purposes of this inquiry, they actually reduce the proportional share of minorities in the district. . . .

In sum, a fair analysis of the shape of District 30, like the equally bizarre shape of District 6, belies the notion that its shape was determined by racial considerations. . . .

Perhaps conscious that noncompact congressional districts are the rule rather than the exception in Texas, the plurality suggests, that the real key is the direct evidence, particularly in the form of Texas' §5 Voting Rights Act submissions and the person of then-State Senator Johnson, that the State expressed an intent to create these districts with a given "minimum percentage of the favored minority." Even if it were appropriate to rest this test of dominance on an examination of the subjective motivation of individual legislators, or on testimony given in a legal proceeding designed to prove a conflicting conclusion, this information does little more than confirm that the State believed it necessary to comply with the Voting Rights Act. . . .

In an effort to provide a definitive explanation for the odd shape of the district, the State emphasized two factors: The presence of communities of interest tying together the populations of the district, and the role of incumbency protection. The District Court and the plurality improperly dismissed these considerations as ultimately irrelevant to the shape of the districts.

[The] appellants presented testimony that the districts were drawn to align with certain communities of interest, such as land use, family demographics, and transportation corridors. . . .

Nonracial Factors: Incumbency
The plurality admits that the appellants "present a . . . substantial case for their claim that incumbency protection rivalled race in determining the district's shape.". . .

Race as a Proxy
Faced with all this evidence that politics, not race, was the predominant factor shaping the district lines, the plurality ultimately makes little effort to contradict appellants' assertions that incumbency protection was far more important in the placement of District 30's lines than race. . . .

I note that in most contexts racial classifications are invidious because they are irrational. For example, it is irrational to assume that a person is not qualified to vote or to serve as a juror simply because she has brown hair or brown skin. It is neither irrational, nor invidious, however, to assume that a black resident of a particular community is a Democrat if reliable statistical evidence discloses that 97% of the blacks in that community vote in Democratic primary elections. For that reason, the fact that the architects of the Texas plan sometimes appear to have used racial data as a proxy for making political judgments seems to me to be no more "unjustified," and to have no more constitutional significance, than an assumption that wealthy suburbanites, whether black or white, are more likely to be Republicans than communists. Requiring the State to ignore the association between race and party affiliation would be no more logical, and potentially as harmful, as it would be to prohibit the Public Health Service from targeting African-American communities in an effort to increase awareness regarding sickle-cell anemia.

Despite all the efforts by the plurality and the District Court, then, the evidence demonstrates that race was not, in all likelihood, the "predominant" goal leading to the creation of District 30. The most reasonable interpretation of the record evidence instead demonstrates that political considerations were. In accord with the presumption against interference with a legislature's consideration of complex and competing factors, I would conclude that the configuration of District 30 does not require strict scrutiny.

VI

I cannot profess to know how the Court's developing jurisprudence of racial gerrymandering will alter the political and racial landscape in this Nation—although it certainly will alter that landscape. As the Court's law in this area has developed, it has become ever more apparent to me that the Court's approach to these cases creates certain perverse incentives and (I presume) unanticipated effects that serve to highlight the essentially unknown territory into which it strides. Because I believe that the social and political risks created by the Court's decisions are not required by the Constitution, my first choice would be to avoid the preceding analysis altogether, and leave these considerations to the political branches of our Government.

The first unintended outcome of the legal reasoning in *Shaw II* and Bush is the very result that those decisions seek to avoid: The predominance of race in the districting process, over all other principles of importance. Given the Court's unwillingness to recognize the role that race-neutral districting principles played in the creation of the bizarrely shaped districts in both this case and Shaw II, it now seems clear that the only way that a State can both create a majority-minority district and avoid a racial gerrymander is by drawing, "without much conscious thought," and within the "limited degree of leeway" granted by the Court, the precise compact district that a court would impose in a successful §2 challenge. After the Court's decisions today, therefore, minority voters can make up a majority only in compact districts, whether intentionally or accidentally drawn, while white voters can be placed into districts as bizarre as the State desires.

The great irony, of course, is that by requiring the State to place the majority-minority district in a particular place and with a particular shape, the district may stand out as a stark, placid island in a sea of oddly shaped majority-white neighbors. . . .

Regardless of the route taken by the States, the Court has guaranteed that federal courts will have a hand—and perhaps the only hand—in the "abrasive task of drawing district lines." Given the uniquely political nature of the redistricting process, I fear the impact this new role will have on the public's perception of the impartiality of the federal judiciary. . . .

JUSTICE SOUTER, with whom JUSTICE GINSBURG and JUSTICE BREYER join, dissenting.

When the Court devises a new cause of action to enforce a constitutional provision, it ought to identify an injury distinguishable from the consequences of concededly constitutional conduct, and it should describe the elements necessary and sufficient to make out such a claim. Nothing less can give notice to those whose conduct may give rise to liability or provide standards for courts charged with enforcing the Constitution. . . .

Today's opinions do little to solve *Shaw*'s puzzles or return districting responsibility to the States. To say this is not to denigrate the importance of Justice O'Connor's position in her separate opinion that compliance with §2 of the Voting Rights Act is a compelling state interest; her statement takes a very significant step toward alleviating apprehension that *Shaw* is at odds with the Voting Rights Act. It is still true, however, that the combined plurality, minority, and Court opinions do not ultimately leave the law dealing with a Shaw claim appreciably clearer or more manageable than *Shaw I* itself did. And to the extent that some clarity follows from the knowledge that race may be considered when reasonably necessary to conform to the Voting Rights Act, today's opinions raise the specter that this ostensible progress may come with a heavy constitutional price. The price of *Shaw I*, indeed, may turn out to be the practical elimination of a State's discretion to apply traditional districting principles, widely accepted in States without racial districting issues as well as in States confronting them.

As the flaws of *Shaw I* persist, and as the burdens placed on the States and the courts by *Shaw* litigation loom larger with the approach of a new census and a new round of redistricting, the Court has to recognize that *Shaw*'s problems result from a basic misconception about the relation between race and districting principles, a mistake that no amount of case-by-case tinkering can eliminate. There is, therefore, no reason for confidence that the Court will eventually bring much order out of the confusion created by *Shaw I*, and because it has not, in any case, done so yet, I respectfully dissent. . . .

Shaw v. Hunt
517 U.S. 899 (1996)

CHIEF JUSTICE REHNQUIST delivered the opinion of the Court. . . .

[Racial] classifications are antithetical to the Fourteenth Amendment, whose "central purpose" was "to eliminate racial discrimination emanating from official sources in the States." While appreciating that a racial classification causes "fundamental injury" to the "individual rights of a person," we have recognized that, under certain circumstances, drawing racial distinctions is permissible where a governmental body is pursuing a "compelling state interest." A State, however, is constrained in how it may pursue that end: "The means chosen to accomplish the State's asserted purpose must be specifically and narrowly framed to accomplish that purpose." North Carolina, therefore, must show not only that its redistricting plan was in pursuit of a compelling state interest, but also that "its districting legislation is narrowly tailored to achieve [that] compelling interest.

Appellees point to three separate compelling interests to sustain District 12: to eradicate the effects of past and present discrimination; to comply with §5 of the Voting Rights Act; and to comply with §2 of that Act. We address each in turn.

A State's interest in remedying the effects of past or present racial discrimination may in the proper case justify a government's use of racial distinctions. For that interest to rise to the level of a compelling state interest, it must satisfy two conditions. First, the discrimination must be "'identified discrimination.'" "While the States and their subdivisions may take remedial action when they possess evidence" of past or present discrimination, "they must identify that discrimination, public or private, with some specificity before they may use race-conscious relief." A generalized assertion of past discrimination in a particular industry or region is not adequate because it "provides no guidance for a legislative body to determine the precise scope of the injury it seeks to remedy." Accordingly, an effort to alleviate the effects of societal discrimination is not a compelling interest. Second, the institution that makes the racial distinction must have had a "strong basis in evidence" to conclude that remedial action was necessary, "before it embarks on an affirmative-action program."

In this case, the District Court found that an interest in ameliorating past discrimination did not actually precipitate the use of race in the redistricting plan. While some legislators invoked the State's history of discrimination as an argument for creating a second majority-black district, the court found that these members did not have enough voting power to have caused the creation of the second district on that basis alone.

[And] there is little to suggest that the legislature considered the historical events and social-science data that the reports recount, beyond what individual members may have recalled from personal experience. We certainly cannot say on the basis of these reports that the District Court's findings on this point were clearly erroneous.

Appellees devote most of their efforts to arguing that the race-based redistricting was constitutionally justified by the State's duty to comply with the Voting Rights Act. [In] Miller, we expressly left open the question whether under the proper circumstances compliance with the Voting Rights Act, on its own, could be a compelling interest. Here once again we do not reach that question because we find that creating an additional majority-black district was not required under a correct reading of § 5 and that District 12, as drawn, is not a remedy narrowly tailored to the State's professed interest in avoiding § 2 liability. . . .

For the foregoing reasons, the judgment of the District Court is
Reversed.

JUSTICE STEVENS, with whom JUSTICE GINSBURG and JUSTICE BREYER join as to Parts II-V, dissenting. . . .

II

[*Shaw I*] is entirely consistent with our holdings that race-based districting which respects traditional districting principles does not give rise to constitutional suspicion. As the District Court noted, Shaw I expressly reserved the question whether "'the intentional creation of majority-minority districts, without more,' always gives rise to an equal protection claim." Shaw I held only that an equal protection claim could lie as a result of allegations suggesting that the State's districting was "so extremely irregular on its face that it rationally can be viewed only as an effort to segregate the races for purposes of voting, without regard for traditional districting principles[.]"

Moreover, *Miller* belies the conclusion that strict scrutiny must apply to all deliberate attempts to draw majority-minority districts if the Equal Protection Clause is to provide any practical limitation on a State's power to engage in race-based districting. Although Georgia argued that it had complied with traditional districting principles, the *Miller* majority had little difficulty concluding that the State's race-neutral explanations were implausible. Thus, *Miller* demonstrates that although States may avoid strict scrutiny by complying with traditional districting principles, they may not do so by proffering pretextual, race-neutral explanations for their maps.

The notion that conscientious federal judges will be able to distinguish race-neutral explanations from pretextual ones is hardly foreign to our race discrimination jurisprudence. In a variety of contexts, from employment to juror selection, we have required plaintiffs to demonstrate not only that a defendant's action could be understood as impermissibly race-based, but also that the defendant's assertedly race-neutral explanation for that action was in fact a pretext for racial discrimination. . . .

North Carolina's admission reveals that it intended to create a second majority-minority district. That says nothing about whether it subordinated traditional districting principles in drawing District 12. States which conclude that federal law requires majority-minority districts have little choice but to give "overriding" weight to that concern. . . .

District 12's noncompact appearance also fails to show that North Carolina engaged in suspect race-based districting. There is no federal statutory or constitutional requirement that state electoral boundaries conform to any particular ideal of geographic compactness. . . .

There is a more fundamental flaw in the majority's conclusion that racial concerns predominantly explain the creation of District 12. The evidence of shape and intent relied on by the majority cannot overcome the basic fact that North Carolina did not have to draw Districts 1 and 12 in order to comply with the Justice Department's finding that federal law required the creation of two majority-minority districts. That goal could have been more straightforwardly accomplished by simply adopting the Attorney General's recommendation to draw a geographically compact district in the southeastern portion of the State in addition to the majority-minority district that had already been drawn in the northeastern and Piedmont regions.

That the legislature chose to draw Districts 1 and 12 instead surely suggests that something more than the desire to create a majority-minority district took precedence. For that reason, this case would seem to present a version of the very hypothetical that the principal opinion in Bush suggests should pose no constitutional problem—"an otherwise compact majority-minority district that is misshapen by nonracial, political manipulation." . . .

A deliberate effort to consolidate urban voters in one district and rural voters in another also explains District 12's highly irregular shape. Before District 12 had been drawn, members of the public as well as legislators had urged that "the observance of distinctive urban and rural communities of interest should be a prime consideration in the general redistricting process. As a result, the legislature was naturally attracted to a plan that, although less than aesthetically pleasing, included both District 12, which links the State's major urban centers, and District 1, which has a population that predominantly lives in cities with populations of less than 20,000.

Moreover, the record reveals that District 12's lines were drawn in order to unite an African-American community whose political tradition was quite distinct from the one that defines African-American voters in the Coastal Plain, which District 1 surrounds. Ibid. Indeed, two other majority-minority-district plans with less torturous boundaries were thought unsatisfactory precisely because they did not unite communities of interest. . . .

III

As the foregoing discussion illustrates, legislative decisions are often the product of compromise and mixed motives. For that reason, I have always been skeptical about the value of motivational analysis as a basis for constitutional adjudication. I am particularly skeptical of such an inquiry in a case of this type, as mixed motivations would seem to be endemic to the endeavor of political districting.

The majority's analysis of the "compelling interest" issue nicely demonstrates the problem with parsing legislative motive in this context. The majority posits that the legislature's compelling interest in drawing District 12 was its desire to avoid liability under §2 of the Voting Rights Act. Yet it addresses the question whether North Carolina had a compelling interest only because it first concludes that a racial purpose dominated the State's districting effort.

It seems to me that if the State's true purpose were to serve its compelling interest in staving off costly litigation by complying with federal law, then it cannot be correct to say that a racially discriminatory purpose controlled its line-drawing. A more accurate conclusion would be that the State took race into account only to the extent necessary to meet the requirements of a carefully thought out federal statute. The majority's implicit equation of the intentional consideration of race in order to comply with the Voting Rights Act with intentional racial discrimination reveals the inadequacy of the framework it adopts for considering the constitutionality of race-based districting.

However, even if I were to assume that strict scrutiny applies, and thus that it makes sense to consider the question, I would not share the majority's hesitancy in concluding that North Carolina had a "compelling interest" in drawing District 12. . . .

First, some legislators felt that the sorry history of race relations in North Carolina in past decades was a sufficient reason for making it easier for more black leaders to participate in the legislative process and to represent the State in the Congress of the United States. Even if that history does not provide the kind of precise guidance that will justify certain specific affirmative action programs in particular industries, it surely provides an adequate basis for a decision to facilitate the election of representatives of the previously disadvantaged minority. . . .

Second, regardless of whether §5 of the Act was actually violated, I believe the State's interest in avoiding the litigation that would have been necessary to overcome the Attorney General's objection to the original plan provides an acceptable reason for creating a second majority-minority district. . . .

IV . . .

In my judgment, if a State's new plan successfully avoids the potential litigation entirely, there is no reason why it must also take the form of a "remedy" for an unproven violation. Thus, the fact that no §2 violation has been proven in the territory that comprises District 12 does not show that the district fails to serve a compelling state interest. It shows only that a federal court, which is constrained by Article III, would not have had the power to require North Carolina to draw that district. It is axiomatic that a State should have more authority to institute a districting plan than would a federal court. . . .

V . . .

Because I have no hesitation in concluding that North Carolina's decision to adopt a plan in which white voters were in the majority in only 10 of the State's 12 districts did not violate the Equal Protection Clause, I respectfully dissent.

JUSTICE SOUTER, with whom JUSTICE GINSBURG and JUSTICE BREYER join, dissenting.

My views on this case are substantially expressed in my dissent to Bush v. Vera.

The North Carolina Twelfth Congressional District came before the Court for a third time in Hunt v. Cromartie, 119 S. Ct. 1545 (1999). There the Court reversed a lower court grant of summary judgment against the defendants; the Court held that there were triable issues on whether the legislature had acted with an impermissible motivation. The Court acknowledged that the circumstantial evidence "tends to support an inference that the State drew its district lines with an impermissible racial motive." This evidence included maps showing a lack of continuity; expert testimony involving departures from traditional measures of compactness; apparent disrespect for political subdivisions and communities of interest; and statistical and demographic evidence. But the motivation of the legislature is "a factual question," and to rebut the evidence, the state urged that the lines were drawn to make District 12 "a strong Democratic district." It also provided evidence to that effect, which meant that summary judgment was inappropriate. "Our prior decisions have made clear that a jurisdiction may engage in constitutional political gerrymandering, even if it so happens that the most loyal Democrats happen to be black democrats and even if the State were conscious of that fact." Thus the case was remanded for trial.

Page 906. At the end of the Note, add the following:

7. Consider also M.L.B. v. S.L.J., 119 S. Ct. 555 (1996), striking down a state law providing that a termination of parental rights may be appealed only

upon the payment of record preparation fees (in this case amounting to $2,352.36). The Court invoked both due process and equal protection principles. The Court, per Justice Ginsburg, said that a person may not be "forever branded unfit for affiliation with her children" on the basis of a procedure that made appeal available "but for her inability to advance required costs." The Court emphasized the constitutional status of a parent's interest in continued connection with the child.

Page 918.   Before "4. Welfare," add the following:

In Saenz v. Roe, 119 S. Ct. 1518 (1999), the Court reaffirmed Shapiro v. Thompson and invalidated a California law imposing durational residence requirements by limiting welfare benefits during the recipient's first year of residence. More particularly, California amended its welfare program by limiting new residents to the benefits they would have received in the state of their prior residence — a change approved by the Secretary of Health and Human Services and subsequently by Congress. The Court held that the change violated the privileges or immunities clause of the Fourteenth Amendment.

The Court began by distinguishing three components of the right to travel: (1) the right to enter and leave another state, an inference from the federal structure without explicit textual support; (2) the right to be treated as "a welcome visitor rather than an unfriendly alien when temporarily present" in a second state, a right rooted in Art. IV, section 2; and (3) "for those travallers who elect to become permanent residents, the right to be treated like other citizens of that state. It was the third component of the right that was at issue in *Saenz,* and the Court squarely rooted that right on the Fourteenth Amendment ban on "any law which shall abridge the privileges or immunities of citizens of the Unites States." The discrimination at issue here, against those "who have completed their interstate travel," was clearly a "penalty" on the exercise of the right to travel.

Adhering to *Shapiro,* the Court said that it was illegitimate to defend the classifications "by a purpose to deter welfare applicants from migrating to California"; this was an impermissible purpose. Nor was the prospect of saving $10.9 million annually sufficient. The question is "whether the state may accomplish that end by the discriminatory means it has chosen." The Citizenship Clause of the Fourteenth Amendment "does not tolerate a hierarchy of 45 subclasses of similarly situated citizens based on the location of their prior residence." Nor was federal approval sufficient to save the law, since "Congress may not authorize the States to violate the Fourteenth Amendment," and since "the protection afforded to the citizen by the Citizenship Clause of that Amendment is a limitation on the powers of the National Government as well as the States."

Chief Justice Rehnquist, joined by Justice Thomas, dissented. He urged that here the right to travel was not implicated, for anyone who has finished his journal is "no longer 'travelling.'" He also objected to what he saw as a new reading of the privileges or immunities clause, contending that the California provision was a reasonable and "bona fide residence requirement," akin to durational residence requirements for college eligibility and for divorce. Thus this was a legitimate effort to ensure that services provided for state residents are enjoyed only by state residents. Justice Thomas, joined by Justice Rehnquist, urged the Court to investigate the original meaning of the privileges or immunities clause, which, he said, was quite limited. Thus the "privileges or immunities of citizens" were understood as "fundamental rights, rather than every public benefit established by positive law."

F. Modern Substantive Due Process: Privacy, Personhood, and Family

Page 1015.   Before the Note, add the following:

Stenberg v. Carhart
— US — (2000)

JUSTICE BREYER delivered the opinion of the Court.

Three established principles determine the issue before us. We shall set them forth in the language of the joint opinion in Casey. First, before "viability . . . the woman has a right to choose to terminate her pregnancy." 505 U.S. at 870 (joint opinion of O'CONNOR, KENNEDY, and SOUTER, JJ.).

Second, "a law designed to further the State's interest in fetal life which imposes an undue burden on the woman's decision before fetal viability" is unconstitutional. An "undue burden is . . . shorthand for the conclusion that a state regulation has the purpose or effect of placing a substantial obstacle in the path of a woman seeking an abortion of a nonviable fetus."

Third, "'subsequent to viability, the State in promoting its interest in the potentiality of human life may, if it chooses, regulate, and even proscribe, abortion except where it is necessary, in appropriate medical judgment, for the preservation of the life or health of the mother.'" 505 U.S. at 879 (quoting Roe v. Wade, 410 U.S. at 164-165).

We apply these principles to a Nebraska law banning "partial birth abortion." The statute reads as follows:

"No partial birth abortion shall be performed in this state, unless such procedure is necessary to save the life of the mother whose life is endangered by a physical disorder, physical illness, or physical injury, including a life-endangering physical condition caused by or arising from the pregnancy itself."

The statute defines "partial birth abortion" as:

> an abortion procedure in which the person performing the abortion partially delivers vaginally a living unborn child before killing the unborn child and completing the delivery.

It further defines "partially delivers vaginally a living unborn child before killing the unborn child" to mean

> deliberately and intentionally delivering into the vagina a living unborn child, or a substantial portion thereof, for the purpose of performing a procedure that the person performing such procedure knows will kill the unborn child and does kill the unborn child. Ibid.

The law classifies violation of the statute as a "Class III felony" carrying a prison term of up to 20 years, and a fine of up to $ 25,000. It also provides for the automatic revocation of a doctor's license to practice medicine in Nebraska.

We hold that this statute violates the Constitution.

I

[Because] Nebraska law seeks to ban one method of aborting a pregnancy, we must describe and then discuss several different abortion procedures. Considering the fact that those procedures seek to terminate a potential human life, our discussion may seem clinically cold or callous to some, perhaps horrifying to others. There is no alternative way, however, to acquaint the reader with the technical distinctions among different abortion methods and related factual matters, upon which the outcome of this case depends.

The evidence before the trial court, as supported or supplemented in the literature, indicates the following:

[1. About] 90% of all abortions performed in the United States take place during the first trimester of pregnancy, before 12 weeks of gestational age. Centers for Disease Control and Prevention, Abortion Surveillance — United States, 1996, p. 41 (July 30, 1999) (hereinafter Abortion Surveillance). During the first trimester, the predominant abortion method is "vacuum aspiration," which involves insertion of a vacuum tube (cannula) into the uterus to evacuate the contents. Such an abortion is typically performed on an outpatient basis under local anesthesia. 11 F. Supp. 2d at 1102; Obstetrics: Normal & Problem Pregnancies

1253-1254 (S. Gabbe, J. Niebyl, & J. Simpson eds. 3d ed. 1996). Vacuum aspiration is considered particularly safe. The procedure's mortality rates for first trimester abortion are, for example, 5 to 10 times lower than those associated with carrying the fetus to term. Complication rates are also low. Id. at 1251; Lawson et al., Abortion Mortality, United States, 1972 through 1987, 171 Am. J. Obstet. Gynecol. 1365, 1368 (1994); M. Paul, et al., [*19] A Clinicians Guide to Medical and Surgical Abortion 108-109 (1999) (hereinafter Medical and Surgical Abortion). As the fetus grows in size, however, the vacuum aspiration method becomes increasingly difficult to use.

2. Approximately 10% of all abortions are performed during the second trimester of pregnancy (12 to 24 weeks). [The] most commonly used procedure is called "dilation and evacuation" (D&E). That procedure (together with a modified form of vacuum aspiration used in the early second trimester) accounts for about 95% of all abortions performed from 12 to 20 weeks of gestational age. Abortion Surveillance 41.

3. D&E "refers generically to transcervical procedures performed at 13 weeks gestation or later." American Medical Association, Report of Board of Trustees on Late-Term Abortion, App. 490 (hereinafter AMA Report). The AMA Report, adopted by the District Court, describes the process as follows.

Between 13 and 15 weeks of gestation:

> D&E is similar to vacuum aspiration except that the cervix must be dilated more widely because surgical instruments are used to remove larger pieces of tissue. Osmotic dilators are usually used. Intravenous fluids and an analgesic or sedative may be administered. A local anesthetic such as a paracervical block may be administered, dilating agents, if used, are removed and instruments are inserted through the cervix into the uterus to removal fetal and placental tissue. Because fetal tissue is friable and easily broken, the fetus may not be removed intact. The walls of the uterus are scraped with a curette to ensure that no tissue remains. Id. at 490-491.

After 15 weeks:

> Because the fetus is larger at this stage of gestation (particularly the head), and because bones are more rigid, dismemberment or other destructive procedures are more likely to be required than at earlier gestational ages to remove [*21] fetal and placental tissue. Id. at 491.

After 20 weeks:

> Some physicians use intrafetal potassium chloride or digoxin to induce fetal demise prior to a late D&E (after 20 weeks), to facilitate evacuation. Id. at 491-492.

There are variations in D&E operative strategy; compare ibid. with W. Hern, Abortion Practice 146-156 (1984), and Medical and Surgical Abortion 133-135. However, the common points are that D&E involves (1) dilation of the cervix; (2) removal of at least some fetal tissue using nonvacuum instruments; and (3) (after the 15th week) the potential need for instrumental disarticulation or dismemberment of the fetus or the collapse of fetal parts to facilitate evacuation from the uterus.

4. When instrumental disarticulation incident to D&E is necessary, it typically occurs as the doctor pulls a portion of the fetus through the cervix into the birth canal. Dr. Carhart testified at trial as follows:

"Dr. Carhart: . . . 'The dismemberment occurs between the traction of . . . my instrument and the counter-traction of the internal os of the cervix . . . .

"Counsel: 'So the dismemberment occurs after you pulled a part of the fetus through the cervix, is that correct?

"Dr. Carhart: 'Exactly. Because you're using—The cervix has two strictures or two rings, the internal os and the external os . . . that's what's actually doing the dismembering . . . .

"Counsel: 'When we talked before or talked before about a D&E, that is not—where there is not intention to do it intact, do you, in that situation, dismember the fetus in utero first, then remove portions?

"Dr. Carhart: 'I don't think so. . . . I don't know of any way that one could go in and intentionally dismember the fetus in the uterus. . . . It takes something that restricts the motion of the fetus against what you're doing before you're going to get dismemberment.'" 11 F. Supp. 2d at 1104.

[5. The] D&E procedure carries certain risks. The use of instruments within the uterus creates a danger of accidental perforation and damage to neighboring organs. Sharp fetal bone fragments create similar dangers. And fetal tissue accidentally left behind can cause infection and various other complications. Nonetheless studies show that the risks of mortality and complication that accompany the D&E procedure between the 12th and 20th weeks of gestation are significantly lower than those accompanying induced labor procedures (the next safest midsecond trimester procedures).

6. At trial, Dr. Carhart and Dr. Stubblefield described a variation of the D&E procedure, which they referred to as an "intact D&E." See 11 F. Supp. 2d at 1105, 1111. Like other versions of the D&E technique, it begins with induced dilation of the cervix. The procedure then involves removing the fetus from the uterus through the cervix "intact," i.e., in one pass, rather than in several passes. Ibid. It is used after 16 weeks at the earliest, as vacuum aspiration becomes ineffective and the fetal skull becomes too large to pass through the cervix. 11 F. Supp. 2d at 1105. The intact D&E proceeds in one of two ways, depending on the presentation of the fetus. If the fetus presents head first (a vertex presenta-

tion), the doctor collapses the skull; and the doctor then extracts the entire fetus through the cervix. If the fetus presents feet first (a breech presentation), the doctor pulls the fetal body through the cervix, collapses the skull, and extracts the fetus through the cervix. Ibid. The breech extraction version of the intact D&E is also known commonly as "dilation and extraction," or D&X. 11 F. Supp. 2d at 1112. In the late second trimester, vertex, breech, and traverse/compound (sideways) presentations occur in roughly similar proportions. Medical and Surgical Abortion 135; 11 F. Supp. 2d at 1108.

7. The intact D&E procedure can also be found described in certain obstetric and abortion clinical textbooks, where two variations are recognized. The first, as just described, calls for the physician to adapt his method for extracting the intact fetus depending on fetal presentation. A slightly different version of the intact D&E procedure, associated with Dr. Martin Haskell, calls for conversion to a breech presentation in all cases.

8. The American College of Obstetricians and Gynecologists describes the D&X procedure in a manner corresponding to a breech-conversion intact D&E, including the following steps:

"1. deliberate dilatation of the cervix, usually over a sequence of days;

"2. instrumental conversion of the fetus to a footling breech;

"3. breech extraction of the body excepting the head; and

"4. partial evacuation of the intracranial contents of a living fetus to effect vaginal delivery of a dead but otherwise intact fetus." American College of Obstetricians and Gynecologists Executive Board, Statement on Intact [*26] Dilation and Extraction (Jan. 12, 1997) (hereinafter ACOG Statement), App. 599-560.

Despite the technical differences we have just described, intact D&E and D&X are sufficiently similar for us to use the terms interchangeably.

10. [The] materials presented at trial referred to the potential benefits of the D&X procedure in circumstances involving nonviable fetuses, such as fetuses with abnormal fluid accumulation in the brain (hydrocephaly). Others have emphasized its potential for women with prior uterine scars, or for women for whom induction of labor would be particularly dangerous.

11. There are no reliable data on the number of D&X abortions performed annually.

II

The question before us is whether Nebraska's statute, making criminal the performance of a "partial birth abortion," violates the Federal Constitution, as interpreted in Planned Parenthood of Southeastern Pa. v. Casey, and Roe v. Wade, We conclude that it does for at least two independent reasons. First, the law lacks any exception "'for the preservation of the . . . health of the mother.'" Casey, 505 U.S. at 879 (joint opinion of O'CONNOR, KENNEDY, and SOUTER, JJ.). Second, it "imposes an undue burden on a woman's ability" to choose a D&E abortion, thereby unduly burdening the right to choose abortion itself. We shall discuss each of these reasons in turn.

A

[The] fact that Nebraska's law applies both pre- and postviability aggravates the constitutional problem presented. The State's interest in regulating abortion previability is considerably weaker than postviability. See Casey, supra, at 870. Since the law requires a health exception in order to validate even a postviability abortion regulation, it at a minimum requires the same in respect to previability regulation. [The] Nebraska law, of course, does not directly further an interest "in the potentiality of human life" by saving the fetus in question from destruction, as it regulates only a method of performing abortion. Nebraska describes its interests differently. It says the law "'shows concern for the life of the unborn,'" "prevents cruelty to partially born children," and "preserves the integrity of the medical profession." Brief for Petitioners 48. But we cannot see how the interest-related differences could make any difference to the question at hand, namely, the application of the "health" requirement.

Consequently, the governing standard requires an exception "where it is necessary, in appropriate medical judgment for the preservation of the life or health of the mother," Casey, supra, at 879, for this Court has made clear that a State may promote but not endanger a woman's health when it regulates the methods of abortion.

JUSTICE THOMAS says that the cases just cited limit this principle to situations where the pregnancy itself creates a threat to health. He is wrong. The cited cases, reaffirmed in Casey, recognize that a State cannot subject women's health to significant risks both in that context, AND ALSO where state regulations force women to use riskier methods of abortion. Our cases have repeatedly invalidated statutes that in the process of regulating the methods of abortion, imposed significant health risks. They make clear that a risk to a women's health is the same whether it happens to arise from regulating a particular method of abortion, or from barring abortion entirely.

[Nebraska] responds that the law does not require a health exception unless there is a need for such an exception. And here there is no such need, it says. It argues that "safe alternatives remain available" and "a ban on partial-birth abortion/D&X would create no risk to the health of women." Brief for Petitioners 29, 40. The problem for Nebraska is that the parties strongly contested this factual question in the trial court below; and the findings and evidence support Dr. Carhart. The State fails to demonstrate that banning D&X without a health exception may not create significant health risks for women, because the record shows that significant medical authority supports the proposition that in some circumstances, D&X would be the safest procedure.

The upshot is a District Court finding that D&X significantly obviates health risks in certain circumstances, a highly plausible record-based explanation of why that might be so, a division of opinion among some medical experts over whether D&X is generally safer, and an absence of controlled medical studies that would help answer these medical questions. Given these medically related evidentiary circumstances, we believe the law requires a health exception.

[The] Eighth Circuit found the Nebraska statute unconstitutional because, in Casey's words, it has the "effect of placing a substantial obstacle in the path of a woman seeking an abortion of a nonviable fetus." 505 U.S. at 877. It thereby places an "undue burden" upon a woman's right to terminate her pregnancy before viability. Nebraska does not deny that the statute imposes an "undue burden" if it applies to the more commonly used D&E procedure as well as to D&X. And we agree with the Eighth Circuit that it does so apply.

Our earlier discussion of the D&E procedure shows that it falls within the statutory prohibition. The statute forbids "deliberately and intentionally delivering into the vagina a living unborn child, or a substantial portion thereof, for the purpose of performing a procedure that the person performing such procedure knows will kill the unborn child. We do not understand how one could distinguish, using this language, between D&E (where a foot or arm is drawn through the cervix) and D&X (where the body up to the head is drawn through the cervix).

[Even] if the statute's basic aim is to ban D&X, its language makes clear that it also covers a much broader category of procedures. The language does not track the medical differences between D&E and D&X — though it would have been a simple matter, for example, to provide an exception for the performance of D&E and other abortion procedures. Nor does the statute anywhere suggest that its application turns on whether a portion of the fetus' body is drawn into the vagina as part of a process to extract an intact fetus after collapsing the head as opposed to a process that would dismember the fetus. Thus, the dissenters' argument that the law was generally intended to bar D&X can be both correct and irrelevant. The relevant question is not whether the legislature wanted to ban D&X; it is whether the law was intended to apply only to D&X. The plain language covers both procedures.

[The] Nebraska State Attorney General argues that the statute does differentiate between the two procedures. He says that the statutory words "substantial portion" mean "the child up to the head." He consequently denies the statute's application where the physician introduces into the birth canal a fetal arm or leg or anything less than the entire fetal body.

[We] cannot accept the Attorney General's narrowing interpretation of the

Nebraska statute. This Court's case law makes clear that we are not to give the Attorney General's interpretative views controlling weight. [Even] were we to grant the Attorney General's views "substantial weight," we still have to reject his interpretation, for it conflicts with the statutory language.

[We] are aware that adopting the Attorney General's interpretation might avoid the constitutional problem discussed in this section. But we are "without power to adopt a narrowing construction of a state statute unless such a construction is reasonable and readily apparent.

In sum, using this law some present prosecutors and future Attorneys General may choose to pursue physicians who use D&E procedures, the most commonly used method for performing previability second trimester abortions. All those who perform abortion procedures using that method must fear prosecution, conviction, and imprisonment. The result is an undue burden upon a woman's right to make an abortion decision. We must consequently find the statute unconstitutional.

The judgment of the Court of Appeals is

Affirmed.

JUSTICE STEVENS, with whom JUSTICE GINSBURG joins, concurring.

Although much ink is spilled today describing the gruesome nature of late-term abortion procedures, that rhetoric does not provide me a reason to believe that the procedure Nebraska here claims it seeks to ban is more brutal, more gruesome, or less respectful of "potential life" than the equally gruesome procedure Nebraska claims it still allows. [The] notion that either of these two equally gruesome procedures performed at this late stage of gestation is more akin to infanticide than the other, or that the State furthers any legitimate interest by banning one but not the other, is simply irrational.

JUSTICE O'CONNOR, concurring.

[First,] the Nebraska statute is inconsistent with Casey because it lacks an exception for those instances when the banned procedure is necessary to preserve the health of the mother. [Second,] Nebraska's statute is unconstitutional on the alternative and independent ground that it imposes an undue burden on a woman's right to choose to terminate her pregnancy before viability. Nebraska's ban covers not just the dilation and extraction (D&X) procedure, but also the dilation and evacuation (D&E) procedure, "the most commonly used method for performing previability second trimester abortions." [It] is important to note that, unlike Nebraska, some other States have enacted statutes more narrowly tailored to proscribing the D&X procedure alone. [If] Nebraska's statute limited its application to the D&X procedure and included an exception for the life and health of the mother, the question presented would be quite different than the one we face today. . . .

JUSTICE GINSBURG, with whom JUSTICE STEVENS joins, concurring.

[A] state regulation that "has the purpose or effect of placing a substantial obstacle in the path of a woman seeking an abortion of a nonviable fetus" violates the Constitution. Such an obstacle exists if the State stops a woman from choosing the procedure her doctor "reasonably believes will best protect the woman in [the] exercise of [her] constitutional liberty." [As] stated by Chief Judge Posner, "if a statute burdens constitutional rights and all that can be said on its behalf is that it is the vehicle that legislators have chosen for expressing their hostility to those rights, the burden is undue."

CHIEF JUSTICE REHNQUIST, dissenting.

[I] believe JUSTICE KENNEDY and JUSTICE THOMAS have correctly applied Casey's principles and join their dissenting opinions.

JUSTICE SCALIA, dissenting.

I am optimistic enough to believe that, one day, Stenberg v. Carhart will be assigned its rightful place in the history of this Court's jurisprudence beside Korematsu and Dred Scott.

[I] never put much stock in Casey's explication of the inexplicable. In the last analysis, my judgment that Casey does not support today's tragic result can be traced to the fact that what I consider to be an "undue burden" is different from what the majority considers to be an "undue burden" -- a conclusion that can not be demonstrated true or false by factual inquiry or legal reasoning. It is a value judgment, dependent upon how much one respects (or believes society ought to respect) the life of a partially delivered fetus, and how much one respects (or believes society ought to respect) the freedom of the woman who gave it life to kill it. Evidently, the five Justices in today's majority value the former less, or the latter more, (or both), than the four of us in dissent. Case closed. There is no cause for anyone who believes in Casey to feel betrayed by this outcome. It has been arrived at by precisely the process Casey promised — a democratic vote by nine lawyers, not on the question whether the text of the Constitution has anything to say about this subject (it obviously does not); nor even on the question (also appropriate for lawyers) whether the legal traditions of the American people would have sustained such a limitation upon abortion (they obviously would); but upon the pure policy question whether this limitation upon abortion is "undue" — i.e., goes too far.

[I] must recall my bemusement, in Casey, at the joint opinion's expressed belief that Roe v. Wade had "called the contending sides of a national controversy to end their national division by accepting a common mandate rooted in the Constitution," and that the decision in Casey would ratify that happy truce. [If] only for the sake of its own preservation, the Court should return this matter to the people — where the Constitution, by its silence on the subject, left it —

and let them decide, State by State, whether this practice should be allowed. Casey must be overruled.

JUSTICE KENNEDY, with whom THE CHIEF JUSTICE joins, dissenting.

[The] Court's failure to accord any weight to Nebraska's interest in prohibiting partial-birth abortion is erroneous and undermines its discussion and holding. The Court's approach in this regard is revealed by its description of the abortion methods at issue, which the Court is correct to describe as "clinically cold or callous." The majority views the procedures from the perspective of the abortionist, rather than from the perspective of a society shocked when confronted with a new method of ending human life. Words invoked by the majority, such as "transcervical procedures," "osmotic dilators," "instrumental disarticulation," and "paracervical block," may be accurate and are to some extent necessary, but for citizens who seek to know why laws on this subject have been enacted across the Nation, the words are insufficient. Repeated references to sources understandable only to a trained physician may obscure matters for persons not trained in medical terminology. Thus it seems necessary at the outset to set forth what may happen during an abortion.

[As] described by Dr. Carhart, the D&E procedure requires the abortionist to use instruments to grasp a portion (such as a foot or hand) of a developed and living fetus and drag the grasped portion out of the uterus into the vagina. Dr. Carhart uses the traction created by the opening between the uterus and vagina to dismember the fetus, tearing the grasped portion away from the remainder of the body. The traction between the uterus and vagina is essential to the procedure because attempting to abort a fetus without using that traction is described by Dr. Carhart as "pulling the cat's tail" or "dragging a string across the floor, you'll just keep dragging it. It's not until something grabs the other end that you are going to develop traction." The fetus, in many cases, dies just as a human adult or child would: It bleeds to death as it is torn from limb from limb. The fetus can be alive at the beginning of the dismemberment process and can survive for a time while its limbs are being torn off. Dr. Carhart agreed that "when you pull out a piece of the fetus, let's say, an arm or a leg and remove that, at the time just prior to removal of the portion of the fetus, . . . the fetus [is] alive." Dr. Carhart has observed fetal heartbeat via ultrasound with "extensive parts of the fetus removed," and testified that mere dismemberment of a limb does not always cause death because he knows of a physician who removed the arm of a fetus only to have the fetus go on to be born "as a living child with one arm." At the conclusion of a D&E abortion no intact fetus remains. In Dr. Carhart's words, the abortionist is left with "a tray full of pieces."

The other procedure implicated today is called "partial-birth abortion" or the D&X. The D&X can be used, as a general matter, after 19 weeks gestation because the fetus has become so developed that it may survive intact partial delivery from the uterus into the vagina. In the D&X, the abortionist initiates the woman's natural delivery process by causing the cervix of the woman to be dilated, sometimes over a sequence of days. The fetus' arms and legs are delivered outside the uterus while the fetus is alive; witnesses to the procedure report seeing the body of the fetus moving outside the woman's body. At this point, the abortion procedure has the appearance of a live birth. As stated by one group of physicians, "as the physician manually performs breech extraction of the body of a live fetus, excepting the head, she continues in the apparent role of an obstetrician delivering a child." Brief for Association of American Physicians and Surgeons et al. as Amici Curiae 27. With only the head of the fetus remaining in utero, the abortionist tears open the skull. According to Dr. Martin Haskell, a leading proponent of the procedure, the appropriate instrument to be used at this stage of the abortion is a pair of scissors. M. Haskell, Dilation and Extraction for Late Second Trimester Abortion (1992), in 139 Cong. Rec. 8605 (1993). Witnesses report observing the portion of the fetus outside the woman react to the skull penetration. Brief for Petitioners 4. The abortionist then inserts a suction tube and vacuums out the developing brain and other matter found within the skull. The process of making the size of the fetus' head smaller is given the clinically neutral term "reduction procedure." 11 F. Supp. 2d 1099, 1106 (Neb. 1998). Brain death does not occur until after the skull invasion, and, according to Dr. Carhart, the heart of the fetus may continue to beat for minutes after the contents of the skull are vacuumed out. The abortionist next completes the delivery of a dead fetus, intact except for the damage to the head and the missing contents of the skull.

Of the two described procedures, Nebraska seeks only to ban the D&X. In light of the description of the D&X procedure, it should go without saying that Nebraska's ban on partial-birth abortion furthers purposes States are entitled to pursue.

[States have] an interest in forbidding medical procedures which, in the State's reasonable determination, might cause the medical profession or society as a whole to become insensitive, even disdainful, to life, including life in the human fetus. [It] is argued, however, that a ban on the D&X does not further these interests. This is because, the reasoning continues, the D&E method, which Nebraska claims to be beyond its intent to regulate, can still be used to abort a fetus and is no less dehumanizing than the D&X method. While not adopting the argument in express terms, the Court indicates tacit approval of it by refusing to reject it in a forthright manner. Rendering express what is only implicit in the majority opinion, JUSTICE STEVENS and JUSTICE GINSBURG are forthright in declaring that the two procedures are indistinguishable and that Nebraska has acted both irrationally and without a proper purpose in enacting the law. The issue is not whether members of the judiciary can see a difference between the two procedures. It is whether Nebraska can. The Court's refusal to recognize Nebraska's right to declare a moral difference between the procedure is a dispiriting disclosure of the illogic and illegitimacy of the Court's approach to the entire case.

Nebraska was entitled to find the existence of a consequential moral difference between the procedures. We are referred to substantial medical authority that D&X perverts the natural birth process to a greater degree than D&E, commandeering the live birth process until the skull is pierced. American Medical Association (AMA) publications describe the D&X abortion method as "ethically wrong." AMA Board of Trustees Factsheet on HR 1122 (June 1997), in App. to Brief for Association of American Physicians and Surgeons et al. as Amici Curiae 1 (AMA Factsheet). The D&X differs from the D&E because in the D&X the fetus is "killed outside of the womb" where the fetus has "an autonomy which separates it from the right of the woman to choose treatments for her own body." Ibid. Witnesses to the procedure relate that the fingers and feet of the fetus are moving prior to the piercing of the skull; when the scissors are inserted in the back of the head, the fetus' body, wholly outside the woman's body and alive, reacts as though startled and goes limp. D&X's stronger resemblance to infanticide means Nebraska could conclude the procedure presents a greater risk of disrespect for life and a consequent greater risk to the profession and society, which depend for their sustenance upon reciprocal recognition of dignity and respect. The Court is without authority to second-guess this conclusion.

[Demonstrating] a further and basic misunderstanding of Casey, the Court holds the ban on the D&X procedure fails because it does not include an exception permitting an abortionist to perform a D&X whenever he believes it will best preserve the health of the woman. Casting aside the views of distinguished physicians and the statements of leading medical organizations, the Court awards each physician a veto power over the State's judgment that the procedures should not be performed. Dr. Carhart has made the medical judgment to use the D&X procedure in every case, regardless of indications, after 15 weeks gestation. Requiring Nebraska to defer to Dr. Carhart's judgment is no different than forbidding Nebraska from enacting a ban at all; for it is now Dr. Leroy Carhart who sets abortion policy for the State of Nebraska, not the legislature or the people. Casey does not give precedence to the views of a single physician or a group of physicians regarding the relative safety of a particular procedure.

[Substantial] evidence supports Nebraska's conclusion that its law denies no woman a safe abortion. The most to be said for the D&X is it may present an unquantified lower risk of complication for a particular patient but that other proven safe procedures remain available even for this patient. Under these circumstances, the Court is wrong to limit its inquiry to the relative physical safety of the two procedures, with the slightest potential difference requiring the invalidation of the law. [It] is also important to recognize that the D&X is effective only when the fetus is close to viable or, in fact, viable; thus the State is regulating the process at the point where its interest in life is nearing its peak.

Courts are ill-equipped to evaluate the relative worth of particular surgical procedures. The legislatures of the several States have superior factfinding capabilities in this regard.

[The] Court's next holding is that Nebraska's ban forbids both the D&X procedure and the more common D&E procedure. In so ruling the Court misapplies settled doctrines of statutory construction and contradicts Casey's premise that the States have a vital constitutional position in the abortion debate. [Like] the ruling requiring a physician veto, requiring a State to meet unattainable standards of statutory draftsmanship in order to have its voice heard on this grave and difficult subject is no different from foreclosing state participation altogether. [In] light of the statutory text, the commonsense understanding must be that the statute covers only the D&X.

[Ignoring] substantial medical and ethical opinion, the Court substitutes its own judgment for the judgment of Nebraska and some 30 other States and sweeps the law away. [From] the decision, the reasoning, and the judgment, I dissent.

JUSTICE THOMAS, with whom THE CHIEF JUSTICE and JUSTICE SCALIA join, dissenting.

[The] standard set forth in the Casey joint opinion has no historical or doctrinal pedigree. The standard is a product of its authors' own philosophical views about abortion, and it should go without saying that it has no origins in or relationship to the Constitution and is, consequently, as illegitimate as the standard it purported to replace. Even assuming, however, as I will for the remainder of this dissent, that Casey's fabricated undue-burden standard merits adherence (which it does not), today's decision is extraordinary. Today, the Court inexplicably holds that the States cannot constitutionally prohibit a method of abortion that millions find hard to distinguish from infanticide and that the Court hesitates even to describe.

[To] reach its decision, the majority must take a series of indefensible steps. The majority must first disregard the principles that this Court follows in every context but abortion: We interpret statutes according to their plain meaning and we do not strike down statutes susceptible of a narrowing construction. The majority also must disregard the very constitutional standard it purports to employ, and then displace the considered judgment of the people of Nebraska and 29 other States. The majority's decision is lamentable, because of the result the majority reaches, the illogical steps the majority takes to reach it, and because it portends a return to an era I had thought we had at last abandoned.

[Starting] with the statutory definition of "partial birth abortion," I think it highly doubtful that the statute could be applied to ordinary D&E. [Having] resolved that Nebraska's partial birth abortion statute permits doctors to perform D&E abortions, the question remains whether a State can constitutionally prohibit the partial birth abortion procedure without a health exception. Although the majority and JUSTICE O'CONNOR purport to rely on the standard articulated in the Casey joint opinion in concluding that a State may not, they in fact disregard it entirely.

[There] is no question that the State of Nebraska has a valid interest—one not designed to strike at the right itself—in prohibiting partial birth abortion. Casey itself noted that States may "express profound respect for the life of the unborn." Ibid. States may, without a doubt, express this profound respect by prohibiting a procedure that approaches infanticide, and thereby dehumanizes the fetus and trivializes human life. The AMA has recognized that this procedure is "ethically different from other destructive abortion techniques because the fetus, normally twenty weeks or longer in gestation, is killed outside the womb. The 'partial birth' gives the fetus an autonomy which separates it from the right of the woman to choose treatments for her own body." Thirty States have concurred with this view.

[The] testimony of one nurse who observed a partial birth abortion procedure makes the point even more vividly:

"The baby's little fingers were clasping and unclasping, and his little feet were kicking. Then the doctor stuck the scissors in the back of his head, and the baby's arms jerked out, like a startle reaction, like a flinch, like a baby does when he thinks he is going to fall.

"The doctor opened up the scissors, stuck a high-powered suction tube into the opening, and sucked the baby's brains out. Now the baby went completely limp." H. R. 1833 Hearing 18 (statement of Brenda Pratt Shafer).

The question whether States have a legitimate interest in banning the procedure does not require additional authority.

[The] next question, therefore, is whether the Nebraska statute is unconstitutional because it does not contain an exception that would allow use of the procedure whenever "necessary in appropriate medical judgment, for the preservation of the . . . health of the mother." According to the majority, such a health exception is required here because there is a "division of opinion among some medical experts over whether D&X is generally safer [than D&E], and an absence of controlled medical studies that would help answer these medical questions." In other words, unless a State can conclusively establish that an abortion procedure is no safer than other procedures, the State cannot regulate that procedure without including a health exception

It is clear that the Court's understanding of when a health exception is required is not mandated by our prior cases. [The] majority assiduously avoids addressing the actual standard articulated in Casey—whether prohibiting partial birth abortion without a health exception poses a substantial obstacle to obtaining an abortion. And for good reason: Such an obstacle does not exist. There are two essential reasons why the Court cannot identify a substantial obstacle. First, the Court cannot identify any real, much less substantial, barrier to any woman's ability to obtain an abortion. And second, the Court cannot demonstrate that any such obstacle would affect a sufficient number of women to justify invalidating the statute on its face. [Like] the Casey 24-hour waiting period, and in contrast to the situation in Danforth, any increased health risk to women imposed by the partial birth abortion ban is minimal at most. Of the 5.5% of abortions that occur after 15 weeks (the time after which a partial birth abortion would be possible), the vast majority are performed with a D&E or induction procedure. And, for any woman with a vertex presentation fetus, the vertex presentation form of intact D&E, which presumably shares some of the health benefits of the partial birth abortion procedure but is not covered by the Nebraska statute, is available. Of the remaining women—that is, those women for whom a partial birth abortion procedure would be considered and who have a breech presentation fetus—there is no showing that any one faces a significant health risk from the partial birth abortion ban. [In] fact, there was evidence before the Nebraska Legislature that partial birth abortion increases health risks relative to other procedures.

[The] majority justifies its result by asserting that a "significant body of medical opinion" supports the view that partial birth abortion may be a safer abortion procedure. I find this assertion puzzling. If there is a "significant body of medical opinion" supporting this procedure, no one in the majority has identified it. [Moreover,] even if I were to assume credible evidence on both sides of the debate, that fact should resolve the undue-burden question in favor of allowing Nebraska to legislate. Where no one knows whether a regulation of abortion poses any burden at all, the burden surely does not amount to a "substantial obstacle."

[Even] if I were willing to assume that the partial birth method of abortion is safer for some small set of women, such a conclusion would not require invalidating the Act, because this case comes to us on a facial challenge.

[We] were reassured repeatedly in Casey that not all regulations of abortion are unwarranted and that the States may express profound respect for fetal life. Under Casey, the regulation before us today should easily pass constitutional muster. But the Court's abortion jurisprudence is a particularly virulent strain of constitutional exegesis. And so today we are told that 30 States are prohibited from banning one rarely used form of abortion that they believe to border on infanticide. It is clear that the Constitution does not compel this result.

I respectfully dissent.

Page 1016. At the end of section 3 of the Note, add the following:

See Frances Myrna Kamm, Abortion and Creation 98 (1992):

(1) It may be wrong if it suggests that abortion would be morally impermissible if its permissibility were not necessary to achieve social equality (that is, if women were socially dominant to men, [would] abortion be impermissible?). (2) It may be wrong if it claims that one may kill someone simply because this is necessary for social equality. [One] cannot kill infants [if] their existence led to social inequality for women because women but not men could not resist taking care of them.

Page 1016. At the end of section 5 of the Note, add the following:

For general discussion of what burdens should be deemed incidental, and of why and when it matters, see Dorf, Incidental Burdens on Fundamental Rights, 109 Harv. L. Rev. 1175 (1996).

Page 1027. Before section 6 of the Note, add the following:

5a. In the context of family relations, substantive due process received a firm endorsement in Troxel v. Granville, — S Ct. — (2000). The case involved a Washington statute that allowed any person to petition a court for visitation rights "at any time," and authorized the court to grant visitation rights whenever "visitation may serve the best interest of the child." The Troxels had petitioned a court for the right to visit their grandchildren; the mother, a single parent, sought a limitation on visitation rights, which the court overrode, ordering significantly more visitation than the mother wanted. The Supreme Court held that the statute was unconstitutional as applied. The Court reaffirmed *Meyer* and *Pierce*, suggesting that the Due Process Clause has a substantive component encompassing "the fundamental right of parents to make decisions concerning the care, custody, and control of their children." The law at issue here infringed on this right, partly because it "is breathtakingly broad." There is "no requirement that a court accord a parent's decision that visitation would not be in the child's best interest a presumption of validity or any weight whatever." The decision to reject the mother's judgment here "was based on precisely the type of mere disagreement we have just described and nothing more." There was no finding that the parent was unfit, and thus the court's framework "directly contravened the traditional presumption that a fit parent will act in the best interest of his or her child." The Constitution required "at least some special weight to the parent's own determination." Nor did the mother ever seek "to cut off visitation entirely." Justice Thomas concurred on the ground that neither party had argued "that our substantive due process cases were wrongly decided and that the original understanding of the Due Process Clause precludes judicial enforcement of unenumerated rights under that constitutional provision." Justice Stevens dissented on the ground that the statute was constitutional on its face. He emphasized that "there may be circumstances in which a child has a stronger interest at stake than mere protection from serious harm caused by the termination of visitation by a 'person' other than a parent." Justice Scalia dissented on the ground that the Constitution does not protect the "unenumerated right" at issue in the case. Justice Kennedy also dissented, objecting to the Court's "concept that the conventional nuclear family ought to establish the visitation standard for every domestic relations case."

Page 1039. Before "4. The Right to Die," add the following:

10. *Civil confinement.* An unusual substantive due process case is Kansas v. Hendricks, 117 S. Ct. 2072 (1997). The relevant statute established procedures for civil commitment of people who, because of a "mental abnormality" or a "personality disorder," are likely to engage in "predatory acts of sexual violence." Hendricks was civilly committed after a long history of sexually molesting children. The Court upheld the statute on the ground that the state had a sufficient ground to overcome the interest in avoiding physical restraint. According to the Court, the required finding of dangerousness to self or others, in the form of evidence of past sexually violent behavior and a present mental condition making future such conduct likely, was an adequate ground for civil confinement. On the substantive due process issue, the Court was unanimous.

Page 1045. After the first full paragraph on the page, ending with "the particular medical treatment is specified," add:

Justice Stevens, dissenting.

Page 1046. At the end of section 1 of the Note, add the following:

For a defense of a general right to die on grounds of autonomy, see Dworkin et al., Assisted Suicide: The Philosophers' Brief, N.Y. Rev. of Books, Mar. 27,

1997, at 41; for a contrary view, emphasizing institutional limitations of the courts and empirical questions about whether a right to die would actually promote autonomy, see R. Posner, Aging and Old Age 235-61 (1995); Sunstein, The Right to Die, 106 Yale L.J. 1123 (1997).

Washington v. Glucksberg
117 S. Ct. 2258 (1997)

CHIEF JUSTICE REHNQUIST delivered the opinion of the Court.

The question presented in this case is whether Washington's prohibition against "caus[ing]" or "aid[ing]" a suicide offends the Fourteenth Amendment to the United States Constitution. We hold that it does not.

It has always been a crime to assist a suicide in the State of Washington. In 1854, Washington's first Territorial Legislature outlawed "assisting another in the commission of self-murder." Today, Washington law provides: "A person is guilty of promoting a suicide attempt when he knowingly causes or aids another person to attempt suicide." Wash. Rev. Code 9A.36.060(1) (1994). "Promoting a suicide attempt" is a felony, punishable by up to five years' imprisonment and up to a $10,000 fine. At the same time, Washington's Natural Death Act, enacted in 1979, states that the "withholding or withdrawal of life-sustaining treatment" at a patient's direction "shall not, for any purpose, constitute a suicide."

Petitioners in this case are the State of Washington and its Attorney General. Respondents Harold Glucksberg, M. D., Abigail Halperin, M. D., Thomas A. Preston, M. D., and Peter Shalit, M. D., are physicians who practice in Washington. These doctors occasionally treat terminally ill, suffering patients, and declare that they would assist these patients in ending their lives if not for Washington's assisted-suicide ban. In January 1994, respondents, along with three gravely ill, pseudonymous plaintiffs who have since died and Compassion in Dying, a nonprofit organization that counsels people considering physician-assisted suicide, sued in the United States District Court, seeking a declaration that Wash Rev. Code 9A.36.060(1) (1994) is, on its face, unconstitutional. . . .

I

We begin, as we do in all due-process cases, by examining our Nation's history, legal traditions, and practices. In almost every State — indeed, in almost every western democracy — it is a crime to assist a suicide. The States' assisted-suicide bans are not innovations. Rather, they are longstanding expressions of the States' commitment to the protection and preservation of all human life. [Indeed], opposition to and condemnation of suicide — and, therefore, of assisting suicide—are consistent and enduring themes of our philosophical, legal, and cultural heritages. . . .

More specifically, for over 700 years, the Anglo-American common-law tradition has punished or otherwise disapproved of both suicide and assisting suicide. . . . In the 13th century, Henry de Bracton, one of the first legal-treatise writers, observed that "[j]ust as a man may commit felony by slaying another so may he do so by slaying himself." 2 Bracton on Laws and Customs of England 423 (f.150) (G. Woodbine ed., S. Thorne transl., 1968). The real and personal property of one who killed himself to avoid conviction and punishment for a crime were forfeit to the king; however, thought Bracton, "if a man slays himself in weariness of life or because he is unwilling to endure further bodily pain . . . [only] his movable goods [were] confiscated." Id., at 423-424 (f.150). Thus, "[t]he principle that suicide of a sane person, for whatever reason, was a punishable felony was . . . introduced into English common law." Centuries later, Sir William Blackstone, whose Commentaries on the Laws of England not only provided a definitive summary of the common law but was also a primary legal authority for 18th and 19th century American lawyers, referred to suicide as "self-murder" and "the pretended heroism, but real cowardice, of the Stoic philosophers, who destroyed themselves to avoid those ills which they had not the fortitude to endure. . . ." 4 W. Blackstone, Commentaries *189. Blackstone emphasized that "the law has . . . ranked [suicide] among the highest crimes," ibid, although, anticipating later developments, he conceded that the harsh and shameful punishments imposed for suicide "borde[r] a little upon severity." Id., at *190.

For the most part, the early American colonies adopted the common-law approach. [Over] time, however, the American colonies abolished these harsh common-law penalties. [The] movement away from the common law's harsh sanctions did not represent an acceptance of suicide; rather, as Chief Justice Swift observed, this change reflected the growing consensus that it was unfair to punish the suicide's family for his wrongdoing. [That] suicide remained a grievous, though nonfelonious, wrong is confirmed by the fact that colonial and early state legislatures and courts did not retreat from prohibiting assisting suicide. . . .

Though deeply rooted, the States' assisted-suicide bans have in recent years been reexamined and, generally, reaffirmed. Because of advances in medicine and technology, Americans today are increasingly likely to die in institutions, from chronic illnesses. President's Comm'n for the Study of Ethical Problems in Medicine and Biomedical and Behavioral Research, Deciding to Forego Life-Sustaining Treatment 16-18 (1983). Public concern and democratic action are therefore sharply focused on how best to protect dignity and independence at the end of life, with the result that there have been many significant changes in state laws and in the attitudes these laws reflect. Many States, for example, now permit "living wills," surrogate health-care decisionmaking, and the withdrawal or refusal of life-sustaining medical treatment. [At] the same time, however, voters and legislators continue for the most part to reaffirm their States' prohibitions on assisting suicide. . . .

California voters rejected an assisted-suicide initiative similar to Washington's in 1993. On the other hand, in 1994, voters in Oregon enacted, also through ballot initiative, that State's "Death With Dignity Act," which legalized physician-assisted suicide for competent, terminally ill adults. Since the Oregon vote, many proposals to legalize assisted-suicide have been and continue to be introduced in the States' legislatures, but none has been enacted. [And just last year, Iowa and Rhode Island joined the overwhelming majority of States explicitly prohibiting assisted suicide. [Also], on April 30, 1997, President Clinton signed the Federal Assisted Suicide Funding Restriction Act of 1997, which prohibits the use of federal funds in support of physician-assisted suicide.

Thus, the States are currently engaged in serious, thoughtful examinations of physician-assisted suicide and other similar issues. . . . Attitudes toward suicide itself have changed since Bracton, but our laws have consistently condemned, and continue to prohibit, assisting suicide. Despite changes in medical technology and notwithstanding an increased emphasis on the importance of end-of-life decisionmaking, we have not retreated from this prohibition. Against this backdrop of history, tradition, and practice, we now turn to respondents' constitutional claim.

II

The Due Process Clause guarantees more than fair process, and the "liberty" it protects includes more than the absence of physical restraint. [But] we "ha[ve] always been reluctant to expand the concept of substantive due process because guideposts for responsible decisionmaking in this unchartered area are scarce and open-ended." Collins [v. Harker Heights], 503 U.S., at 125. By extending constitutional protection to an asserted right or liberty interest, we, to a great extent, place the matter outside the arena of public debate and legislative action. We must therefore "exercise the utmost care whenever we are asked to break new ground in this field," ibid, lest the liberty protected by the Due Process Clause be subtly transformed into the policy preferences of the members of this Court, [Moore v. East Cleveland, casebook p. 1017].

Our established method of substantive-due-process analysis has two primary features: First, we have regularly observed that the Due Process Clause specially protects those fundamental rights and liberties which are, objectively, "deeply rooted in this Nation's history and tradition," id., at 503 (plurality opinion); Snyder v. Massachusetts, 291 U.S. 97, 105 (1934) ("so rooted in the traditions and conscience of our people as to be ranked as fundamental"), and "implicit in the concept of ordered liberty," such that "neither liberty nor justice would exist if they were sacrificed," Palko v. Connecticut, 302 U.S. 319, 325, 326 (1937). Second, we have required in substantive-due-process cases a "careful description" of the asserted fundamental liberty interest. [Reno v.] Flores [casebook p. 1027]; *Collins*; *Cruzan* [casebook p. 1039]. Our Nation's history, legal traditions, and practices thus provide the crucial "guideposts for responsible decisionmaking," *Collins*, that direct and restrain our exposition of the Due Process Clause. As we stated recently in *Flores*, the Fourteenth Amendment "forbids the government to infringe . . . 'fundamental' liberty interests at all, no matter what process is provided, unless the infringement is narrowly tailored to serve a compelling state interest." 507 U. S., at 302.

Justice Souter, relying on Justice Harlan's dissenting opinion in Poe v. Ullman, would largely abandon this restrained methodology, and instead ask "whether [Washington's] statute sets up one of those 'arbitrary impositions' or 'purposeless restraints' at odds with the Due Process Clause of the Fourteenth Amendment." In our view, however, the development of this Court's substantive-due-process jurisprudence, has been a process whereby the outlines of the "liberty" specially protected by the Fourteenth Amendment—never fully clarified, to be sure, and perhaps not capable of being fully clarified—have at least been carefully refined by concrete examples involving fundamental rights found to be deeply rooted in our legal tradition. This approach tends to rein in the subjective elements that are necessarily present in due-process judicial review. In addition, by establishing a threshold requirement — that a challenged state action implicate a fundamental right — before requiring more than a reasonable relation to a legitimate state interest to justify the action, it avoids the need for complex balancing of competing interests in every case.

[We] now inquire whether this asserted right has any place in our Nation's traditions. Here, as discussed above, we are confronted with a consistent and almost universal tradition that has long rejected the asserted right, and continues explicitly to reject it today, even for terminally ill, mentally competent adults. To hold for respondents, we would have to reverse centuries of legal doctrine and practice, and strike down the considered policy choice of almost every State. [Respondents] contend, however, that the liberty interest they assert is consistent with this Court's substantive-due-process line of cases, if not with this Nation's history and practice. Pointing to *Casey* and *Cruzan*, respondents read our jurisprudence in this area as reflecting a general tradition of "self-sovereignty," and as teaching that the "liberty" protected by the Due Process Clause includes "basic and intimate exercises of personal autonomy." According to respondents, our liberty jurisprudence, and the broad, individualistic principles it reflects, protects the "liberty of competent, terminally ill adults to make end-of-life decisions free of undue government interference." The question presented in this case, however, is whether the protections of the Due Process Clause include a right to commit suicide with another's assistance. With this "careful description" of respondents' claim in mind, we turn to *Casey* and *Cruzan*.

[The] right assumed in *Cruzan* [was] not simply deduced from abstract concepts of personal autonomy. Given the common-law rule that forced medication was a battery, and the long legal tradition protecting the decision to refuse unwanted medical treatment, our assumption was entirely consistent with this Nation's history and constitutional traditions. The decision to commit suicide with the assistance of another may be just as personal and profound as the decision to refuse unwanted medical treatment, but it has never enjoyed similar legal protection. Indeed, the two acts are widely and reasonably regarded as quite distinct.

[Respondents] also rely on *Casey*. [The] opinion moved from the recognition that liberty necessarily includes freedom of conscience and belief about ultimate considerations to the observation that "though the abortion decision may originate within the zone of conscience and belief, it is more than a philosophic exercise. That many of the rights and liberties protected by the Due Process Clause sound in personal autonomy does not warrant the sweeping conclusion that any and all important, intimate, and personal decisions are so protected, San Antonio Independent School Dist. v. Rodriguez, 411 U.S. 1 33-35 (1973), and *Casey* did not suggest otherwise.

The history of the law's treatment of assisted suicide in this country has been and continues to be one of the rejection of nearly all efforts to permit it. That being the case, our decisions lead us to conclude that the asserted "right" to assistance in committing suicide is not a fundamental liberty interest protected by the Due Process Clause. The Constitution also requires, however, that Washington's assisted-suicide ban be rationally related to legitimate government interests. See Heller v. Doe, 509 U.S. 312, 319-320 (1993); Flores, 507 U.S. at 305. This requirement is unquestionably met here.

[First,] Washington has an "unqualified interest in the preservation of human life." [*Cruzan*]. The State's prohibition on assisted suicide, like all homicide laws, both reflects and advances its commitment to this interest. [This] interest is symbolic and aspirational as well as practical: "While suicide is no longer prohibited or penalized, the ban against assisted suicide and euthanasia shores up the notion of limits in human relationships. It reflects the gravity with which we view the decision to take one's own life or the life of another, and our reluctance to encourage or promote these decisions." New York Task Force 131-132.

[Relatedly,] all admit that suicide is a serious public-health problem, especially among persons in otherwise vulnerable groups. [Those] who attempt suicide — terminally ill or not — often suffer from depression or other mental disorders. [Research] indicates, however, that many people who request physician-assisted suicide withdraw that request if their depression and pain are treated.

[The] State also has an interest in protecting the integrity and ethics of the medical profession. [And] physician-assisted suicide could, it is argued, undermine the trust that is essential to the doctor-patient relationship by blurring the time-honored line between healing and harming.

[Next,] the State has an interest in protecting vulnerable groups — including the poor, the elderly, and disabled persons — from abuse, neglect, and mistakes. The Court of Appeals dismissed the State's concern that disadvantaged persons might be pressured into physician-assisted suicide as "ludicrous on its face." We have recognized, however, the real risk of subtle coercion and undue influence in end-of-life situations. [*Cruzan*]. Similarly, the New York Task Force warned that "[l]egalizing physician-assisted suicide would pose profound risks to many individuals who are ill and vulnerable. . . . The risk of harm is greatest for the many individuals in our society whose autonomy and well-being are already compromised by poverty, lack of access to good medical care, advanced age, or membership in a stigmatized social group." New York Task Force 120; see Compassion in Dying, 49 F.3d at 593 ("[A]n insidious bias against the handicapped — again coupled with a cost-saving mentality — makes them especially in need of Washington's statutory protection"). If physician-assisted suicide were permitted, many might resort to it to spare their families the substantial financial burden of end-of-life health-care costs.

The State's interest here goes beyond protecting the vulnerable from coercion; it extends to protecting disabled and terminally ill people from prejudice, negative and inaccurate stereotypes, and "societal indifference." 49 F. 3d, at 592. The State's assisted-suicide ban reflects and reinforces its policy that the lives of terminally ill, disabled, and elderly people must be no less valued than the lives of the young and healthy, and that a seriously disabled person's suicidal impulses should be interpreted and treated the same way as anyone else's. See New York Task Force 101-102; Physician-Assisted Suicide and Euthanasia in the Netherlands: A Report of Chairman Charles T. Canady, at 9, 20 (discussing prejudice toward the disabled and the negative messages euthanasia and assisted suicide send to handicapped patients).

Finally, the State may fear that permitting assisted suicide will start it down the path to voluntary and perhaps even involuntary euthanasia. [This] concern is further supported by evidence about the practice of euthanasia in the Netherlands. The Dutch government's own study revealed that in 1990, there were 2,300 cases of voluntary euthanasia (defined as "the deliberate termination of another's life at his request"), 400 cases of assisted suicide, and more than 1,000 cases of euthanasia without an explicit request. In addition to these latter 1,000 cases, the study found an additional 4,941 cases where physicians administered lethal morphine overdoses without the patients' explicit consent. Physician-Assisted Suicide and Euthanasia in the Netherlands: A Report of Chairman Charles T. Canady, at 12-13 (citing Dutch study). This study suggests that, despite the existence of various reporting procedures, euthanasia in the Netherlands has not been limited to competent, terminally ill adults who are enduring physical suffering, and that regulation of the practice may not have prevented abuses in cases involving vulnerable persons, including severely disabled neonates and elderly persons suffering from dementia.

[We] need not weigh exactingly the relative strengths of these various interests. They are unquestionably important and legitimate, and Washington's ban on assisted suicide is at least reasonably related to their promotion and protection. We therefore hold that Wash. Rev. Code § 9A.36.060(1) (1994) does not violate the Fourteenth Amendment, either on its face or "as applied to competent, terminally ill adults who wish to hasten their deaths by obtaining medication prescribed by their doctors." 79 F.3d at 838.

* * *

Throughout the Nation, Americans are engaged in an earnest and profound debate about the morality, legality, and practicality of physician-assisted suicide. Our holding permits this debate to continue, as it should in a democratic society. The decision of the en banc Court of Appeals is reversed, and the case is remanded for further proceedings consistent with this opinion.

JUSTICE O'CONNOR, concurring.

[The] Court frames the issue in this case as whether the Due Process Clause of the Constitution protects a "right to commit suicide which itself includes a right to assistance in doing so," and concludes that our Nation's history, legal traditions, and practices do not support the existence of such a right. I join the Court's opinions because I agree that there is no generalized right to "commit suicide." But respondents urge us to address the narrower question whether a mentally competent person who is experiencing great suffering has a constitutionally cognizable interest in controlling the circumstances of his or her imminent death. I see no need to reach that question in the context of the facial challenges to the New York and Washington laws at issue here. [The] parties and amici agree that in these States a patient who is suffering from a terminal illness and who is experiencing great pain has no legal barriers to obtaining medication, from qualified physicians, to alleviate that suffering, even to the point of causing unconsciousness and hastening death. In this light, even assuming that we would recognize such an interest, I agree that the State's interests in protecting those who are not truly competent or facing imminent death, or those whose decisions to hasten death would not truly be voluntary, are sufficiently weighty to justify a prohibition against physician-assisted suicide.

[In] sum, there is no need to address the question whether suffering patients have a constitutionally cognizable interest in obtaining relief from the suffering that they may experience in the last days of their lives. There is no dispute that dying patients in Washington and New York can obtain palliative care, even when doing so would hasten their deaths. The difficulty in defining terminal illness and the risk that a dying patient's request for assistance in ending his or her life might not be truly voluntary justifies the prohibitions on assisted suicide we uphold here.

JUSTICE STEVENS, concurring in the judgments.

[Today], the Court decides that Washington's statute prohibiting assisted suicide is not invalid "on its face," that is to say, in all or most cases in which it might be applied. That holding, however, does not foreclose the possibility that some applications of the statute might well be invalid.

As originally filed, this case presented a challenge to the Washington statute on its face and as it applied to three terminally ill, mentally competent patients and to four physicians who treat terminally ill patients. After the District Court issued its opinion holding that the statute placed an undue burden on the right to commit physician-assisted suicide, the three patients died. Although the Court of Appeals considered the constitutionality of the statute "as applied to the pre-scription of life-ending medication for use by terminally ill, competent adult patients who wish to hasten their deaths," the court did not have before it any individual plaintiff seeking to hasten her death or any doctor who was threatened with prosecution for assisting in the suicide of a particular patient; its analysis and eventual holding that the statute was unconstitutional was not limited to a particular set of plaintiffs before it.

[History] and tradition provide ample support for refusing to recognize an open-ended constitutional right to commit suicide. Much more than the State's paternalistic interest in protecting the individual from the irrevocable conse-quences of an ill-advised decision motivated by temporary concerns is at stake. [The] State has an interest in preserving and fostering the benefits that every human being may provide to the community—a community that thrives on the exchange of ideas, expressions of affection, shared memories and humorous incidents as well as on the material contributions that its members create and support. The value to others of a person's life is far too precious to allow the individual to claim a constitutional entitlement to complete autonomy in making a decision to end that life.

[The] state interests supporting a general rule banning the practice of physi-cian-assisted suicide do not have the same force in all cases. First and foremost of these interests is the "'unqualified interest in the preservation of human life," which is equated with "'the sanctity of life.'" That interest not only justifies— it commands—maximum protection of every individual's interest in remaining alive, which in turn commands the same protection for decisions about whether to commence or to terminate life-support systems or to administer pain medica-tion that may hasten death. Properly viewed, however, this interest is not a col-lective interest that should always outweigh the interests of a person who be-cause of pain, incapacity, or sedation finds her life intolerable, but rather, an aspect of individual freedom.

252

Many terminally ill people find their lives meaningful even if filled with pain or dependence on others. Some find value in living through suffering; some have an abiding desire to witness particular events in their families' lives; many believe it a sin to hasten death. Individuals of different religious faiths make different judgments and choices about whether to live on under such circumstances. There are those who will want to continue aggressive treatment; those who would prefer terminal sedation; and those who will seek withdrawal from life-support systems and death by gradual starvation and dehydration. Although as a general matter the State's interest in the contributions each person may make to society outweighs the person's interest in ending her life, this interest does not have the same force for a terminally ill patient faced not with the choice of whether to live, only of how to die. Allowing the individual, rather than the State, to make judgments "'about the "quality" of life that a particular individual may enjoy.'" does not mean that the lives of terminally-ill, disabled people have less value than the lives of those who are healthy. Rather, it gives proper recognition to the individual's interest in choosing a final chapter that accords with her life story, rather than one that demeans her values and poisons memories of her.

[Similarly,] the State's legitimate interests in preventing suicide, protecting the vulnerable from coercion and abuse, and preventing euthanasia are less significant in this context. I agree that the State has a compelling interest in preventing persons from committing suicide because of depression, or coercion by third parties. But the State's legitimate interest in preventing abuse does not apply to an individual who is not victimized by abuse, who is not suffering from depression, and who makes a rational and voluntary decision to seek assistance in dying.

[There] remains room for vigorous debate about the outcome of particular cases that are not necessarily resolved by the opinions announced today. How such cases may be decided will depend on their specific facts. In my judgment, however, it is clear that the so-called "unqualified interest in the preservation of human life," [*Cruzan*], is not itself sufficient to outweigh the interest in liberty that may justify the only possible means of preserving a dying patient's dignity and alleviating her intolerable suffering.

JUSTICE SOUTER, concurring in the judgment.

[My] understanding of unenumerated rights in the wake of the *Poe* dissent and subsequent cases avoids the absolutist failing of many older cases without embracing the opposite pole of equating reasonableness with past practice described at a very specific level. [This] approach calls for a court to assess the relative "weights" or dignities of the contending interests, and to this extent the judicial method is familiar to the common law.

[Just] as results in substantive due process cases are tied to the selections of statements of the competing interests, the acceptability of the results is a function of the good reasons for the selections made. It is here that the value of common-law method becomes apparent, for the usual thinking of the common law is suspicious of the all-or-nothing analysis that tends to produce legal petrification instead of an evolving boundary between the domains of old principles. Common-law method tends to pay respect instead to detail, seeking to understand old principles afresh by new examples and new counterexamples. The "tradition is a living thing," *Poe*, 367 U.S. at 542 (Harlan, J., dissenting), albeit one that moves by moderate steps carefully taken. "The decision of an apparently novel claim must depend on grounds which follow closely on well-accepted principles and criteria. The new decision must take its place in relation to what went before and further [cut] a channel for what is to come." Id., at 544 (Harlan, J., dissenting) (internal quotation marks omitted). Exact analysis and characterization of any due process claim is critical to the method and to the result.

[The] liberty interest in bodily integrity was phrased in a general way by then-Judge Cardozo when he said, "[e]very human being of adult years and sound mind has a right to determine what shall be done with his own body" in relation to his medical needs. Schloendorff v. Society of New York Hospital, 211 N.Y. 125, 129, 105 N.E. 92, 93 (1914). The familiar examples of this right derive from the common law of battery and include the right to be free from medical invasions into the body [*Cruzan*], as well as a right generally to resist enforced medication, see Washington v. Harper, 494 U.S. 210, 221-222, 229 (1990). Thus "[i]t is settled now . . . that the Constitution places limits on a State's right to interfere with a person's most basic decisions about . . . bodily integrity." [*Casey*]; see also [*Cruzan*]; [Washington v. Harper]; Winston v. Lee, 470 U.S. 753, 761-762 (1985); Rochin v. California, 342 U.S. at 172. Constitutional recognition of the right to bodily integrity underlies the assumed right, good against the State, to require physicians to terminate artificial life support, [*Cruzan*] ("we assume that the United States Constitution would grant a competent person a constitutionally protected right to refuse lifesaving hydration and nutrition"), and the affirmative right to obtain medical intervention to cause abortion, see [*Casey*]; cf. Roe v. Wade, 410 U.S. at 153.

It is, indeed, in the abortion cases that the most telling recognitions of the importance of bodily integrity and the concomitant tradition of medical assistance have occurred. In Roe v. Wade, the plaintiff contended that the Texas statute making it criminal for any person to "procure an abortion," for a pregnant woman was unconstitutional insofar as it prevented her from "terminat[ing] her pregnancy by an abortion 'performed by a competent, licensed physician, under safe, clinical conditions,'" and in striking down the statute we stressed the importance of the relationship between patient and physician.

The analogies between the abortion cases and this one are several. Even though the State has a legitimate interest in discouraging abortion, see [*Casey*], [*Roe*], the Court recognized a woman's right to a physician's counsel and care. Like the decision to commit suicide, the decision to abort potential life can be made irresponsibly and under the influence of others, and yet the Court has held in the abortion cases that physicians are fit assistants. Without physician assistance in abortion, the woman's right would have too often amounted to nothing more than a right to self-mutilation, and without a physician to assist in the suicide of the dying, the patient's right will often be confined to crude methods of causing death, most shocking and painful to the decedent's survivors.

There is, finally, one more reason for claiming that a physician's assistance here would fall within the accepted tradition of medical care in our society, and the abortion cases are only the most obvious illustration of the further point. While the Court has held that the performance of abortion procedures can be restricted to physicians, the Court's opinion in *Roe* recognized the doctors' role in yet another way. For, in the course of holding that the decision to perform an abortion called for a physician's assistance, the Court recognized that the good physician is not just a mechanic of the human body. [This] idea of the physician as serving the whole person is a source of the high value traditionally placed on the medical relationship.

[The] argument supporting respondents' position thus progresses through three steps of increasing forcefulness. First, it emphasizes the decriminalization of suicide. Reliance on this fact is sanctioned under the standard that looks not only to the tradition retained, but to society's occasional choices to reject traditions of the legal past. See Poe v. Ullman, 367 U.S. at 542 (Harlan, J., dissenting). While the common law prohibited both suicide and aiding a suicide, with the prohibition on aiding largely justified by the primary prohibition on self-inflicted death itself, see, e.g., American Law Institute, Model Penal Code § 210.5, Comment 1, pp. 92-93, and n. 7 (1980), the State's rejection of the traditional treatment of the one leaves the criminality of the other open to questioning that previously would not have been appropriate. The second step in the argument is to emphasize that the State's own act of decriminalization gives a freedom of choice much like the individual's option in recognized instances of bodily autonomy. One of these, abortion, is a legal right to choose in spite of the interest a State may legitimately invoke in discouraging the practice, just as suicide is now subject to choice, despite a state interest in discouraging it. The third step is to emphasize that respondents claim a right to assistance not on the basis of some broad principle that would be subject to exceptions if that continuing interest of the State's in discouraging suicide were to be recognized at all. Respondents base their claim on the traditional right to medical care and counsel, subject to the limiting conditions of informed, responsible choice when death is imminent, conditions that support a strong analogy to rights of care in other situations in which medical counsel and assistance have been available as a matter of course. There can be no stronger claim to a physician's assistance than at the time when death is imminent, a moral judgment implied by the State's own recognition of the legitimacy of medical procedures necessarily hastening the moment of impending death.

In my judgment, the importance of the individual interest here, as within that class of "certain interests" demanding careful scrutiny of the State's contrary claim, see [*Poe*], cannot be gainsaid. Whether that interest might in some circumstances, or at some time, be seen as "fundamental" to the degree entitled to prevail is not, however, a conclusion that I need draw here, for I am satisfied that the State's interests described in the following section are sufficiently serious to defeat the present claim that its law is arbitrary or purposeless.

The State has put forward several interests to justify the Washington law as applied to physicians treating terminally ill patients, even those competent to make responsible choices: protecting life generally, discouraging suicide even if knowing and voluntary, and protecting terminally ill patients from involuntary suicide and euthanasia, both voluntary and nonvoluntary.

It is not necessary to discuss the exact strengths of the first two claims of justification in the present circumstances, for the third is dispositive for me. That third justification is different from the first two, for it addresses specific features of respondents' claim, and it opposes that claim not with a moral judgment contrary to respondents', but with a recognized state interest in the protection of nonresponsible individuals and those who do not stand in relation either to death or to their physicians as do the patients whom respondents describe. The State claims interests in protecting patients from mistakenly and involuntarily deciding to end their lives, and in guarding against both voluntary and involuntary euthanasia. Leaving aside any difficulties in coming to a clear concept of imminent death, mistaken decisions may result from inadequate palliative care or a terminal prognosis that turns out to be error; coercion and abuse may stem from the large medical bills that family members cannot bear or unreimbursed hospitals decline to shoulder. Voluntary and involuntary euthanasia may result once doctors are authorized to prescribe lethal medication in the first instance, for they might find it pointless to distinguish between patients who administer their own fatal drugs and those who wish not to, and their compassion for those who suffer may obscure the distinction between those who ask for death and those who may be unable to request it. The argument is that a progression would occur, obscuring the line between the ill and the dying, and between the responsible and the unduly influenced, until ultimately doctors and perhaps others would abuse a limited freedom to aid suicides by yielding to the impulse to end another's suffering under conditions going beyond the narrow limits the respondents propose. The State thus argues, essentially, that respondents' claim is not as narrow as it sounds, simply because no recognition of the interest they assert could be limited to vindicating those interess and affecting no others. The State says that the claim, in practical effect, would entail consequences that the State could, without doubt, legitimately act to prevent.

The mere assertion that the terminally sick might be pressured into suicide decisions by close friends and family members would not alone be very telling. Of course that is possible, not only because the costs of care might be more than family members could bear but simply because they might naturally wish to see an end of suffering for someone they love. But one of the points of restricting any right of assistance to physicians, would be to condition the right on an exercise of judgment by someone qualified to assess the patient's responsible capacity and detect the influence of those outside the medical relationship.

The State, however, goes further, to argue that dependence on the vigilance of physicians will not be enough. First, the lines proposed here (particularly the requirement of a knowing and voluntary decision by the patient) would be more difficult to draw than the lines that have limited other recently recognized due process rights. Limiting a state from prosecuting use of artificial contraceptives by married couples posed no practical threat to the State's capacity to regulate contraceptives in other ways that were assumed at the time of Poe to be legitimate; the trimester measurements of Roe and the viability determination of Casey were easy to make with a real degree of certainty. But the knowing and responsible mind is harder to assess. Second, this difficulty could become the greater by combining with another fact within the realm of plausibility, that physicians simply would not be assiduous to preserve the line. They have compassion, and those who would be willing to assist in suicide at all might be the most susceptible to the wishes of a patient, whether the patient were technically quite responsible or not. Physicians, and their hospitals, have their own financial incentives, too, in this new age of managed care. Whether acting from compassion or under some other influence, a physician who would provide a drug for a patient to administer might well go the further step of administering the drug himself; so, the barrier between assisted suicide and euthanasia could become porous, and the line between voluntary and involuntary euthanasia as well. The case for the slippery slope is fairly made out here, not because recognizing one due process right would leave a court with no principled basis to avoid recognizing another, but because there is a plausible case that the right claimed would not be readily containable by reference to facts about the mind that are matters of difficult judgment, or by gatekeepers who are subject to temptation, noble or not.

Respondents propose an answer to all this, the answer of state regulation with teeth. Legislation proposed in several States, for example, would authorize physician-assisted suicide but require two qualified physicians to confirm the patient's diagnosis, prognosis, and competence; and would mandate that the patient make repeated requests witnessed by at least two others over a specified time span; and would impose reporting requirements and criminal penalties for various acts of coercion.

But at least at this moment there are reasons for caution in predicting the effectiveness of the teeth proposed. Respondents' proposals, as it turns out, sound much like the guidelines now in place in the Netherlands, the only place where experience with physician-assisted suicide and euthanasia has yielded empirical evidence about how such regulations might affect actual practice. Dutch physicians must engage in consultation before proceeding, and must decide whether the patient's decision is voluntary, well considered, and stable, whether the request to die is enduring and made more than once, and whether the patient's future will involve unacceptable suffering. See C. Gomez, Regulating Death 40-43 (1991). There is, however, a substantial dispute today about what the Dutch experience shows. Some commentators marshall evidence that the Dutch guidelines have in practice failed to protect patients from involuntary euthanasia and have been violated with impunity. See, e.g., H. Hendin, Seduced By Death 75-84 (1997) (noting many cases in which decisions intended to end the life of a fully competent patient were made without a request from the patient and without consulting the patient); Keown, Euthanasia in the Netherlands: Sliding Down the Slippery Slope?, in Euthanasia Examined 261, 289 (J. Keown ed. 1995) (guidelines have "proved signally ineffectual; non-voluntary euthanasia is now widely practised and increasingly condoned in the Netherlands"); Gomez, supra, at 104-113. This evidence is contested. See, e.g., R. Epstein, Mortal Peril 322 (1997) ("Dutch physicians are not euthanasia enthusiasts and they are slow to practice it in individual cases"); R. Posner, Aging and Old Age 242, and n. 23 (1995) (noting fear of "doctors' rushing patients to their death" in the Netherlands "has not been substantiated and does not appear realistic"); Van der Wal, Van Eijk, Leenen, & Spreeuwenberg, Euthanasia and Assisted Suicide, 2, Do Dutch Family Doctors Act Prudently?, 9 Family Practice 135 (1992) (finding no serious abuse in Dutch practice). The day may come when we can say with some assurance which side is right, but for now it is the substantiality of the factual disagreement, and the alternatives for resolving it, that matter. They are, for me, dispositive of the due process claim at this time.

[The] experimentation that should be out of the question in constitutional adjudication displacing legislative judgments is entirely proper, as well as highly desirable, when the legislative power addresses an emerging issue like assisted suicide. The Court should accordingly stay its hand to allow reasonable legislative consideration. While I do not decide for all time that respondents' claim should not be recognized, I acknowledge the legislative institutional competence as the better one to deal with that claim at this time.

JUSTICE GINSBURG, concurring in the judgments.

I concur in the Court's judgments in these cases substantially for the reasons stated by Justice O'Connor in her concurring opinion.

JUSTICE BREYER, concurring in the judgments.

I believe that Justice O'Connor's views, which I share, have greater legal significance than the Court's opinion suggests. I join her separate opinion, except insofar as it joins the majority. And I concur in the judgments. I shall briefly explain how I differ from the Court.

[I] would not reject the respondents' claim without considering a different formulation, for which our legal tradition may provide greater support. That formulation would use words roughly like a "right to die with dignity." But irrespective of the exact words used, at its core would lie personal control over the manner of death, professional medical assistance, and the avoidance of unnecessary and severe physical suffering- combined.

[I] do not believe, however, that this Court need or now should decide whether or a not such a right is "fundamental." That is because, in my view, the avoidance of severe physical pain (connected with death) would have to comprise an essential part of any successful claim and because, as Justice O'Connor points out, the laws before us do not force a dying person to undergo that kind of pain. Rather, the laws of New York and of Washington do not prohibit doctors from providing patients with drugs sufficient to control pain despite the risk that those drugs themselves will kill. Cf. New York State Task Force on Life and the Law, When Death Is Sought: Assisted Suicide and Euthanasia in the Medical Context 163, n. 29 (May 1994). And under these circumstances the laws of New York and Washington would overcome any remaining significant interests and would be justified, regardless.

[Were] the legal circumstances different—for example, were state law to prevent the provision of palliative care, including the administration of drugs as needed to avoid pain at the end of life—then the law's impact upon serious and otherwise unavoidable physical pain (accompanying death) would be more directly at issue. And as Justice O'Connor suggests, the Court might have to revisit its conclusions in these cases.

Note: Assisted Suicide

1. What is the precise holding of *Glucksberg*? Note that Justice O'Connor joins the majority opinion (indeed, her vote is necessary to make it a majority opinion) but also writes separately. Does her opinion suggest that there may be a right to physician-assisted suicide in cases involving both intense pain and im-

minent death? Do five justices so suggest? If so, what is the status of the majority opinion?

2. Probably the major theoretical dispute is between the majority, stressing the need to anchor substantive due process in history, and Justice Souter, emphasizing Justice Harlan's belief that the tradition of liberty grows over time. Is this a repeat of the debate between two wings of the Court in *Casey*? Has the plurality opinion in *Casey* been rejected by a majority of the Court?

3. Is *Glucksberg* a return to the majority opinion in Bowers v. Hardwick? What room, if any, remains for substantive due process?

Page 1048. Before "G. Procedural Due Process," add the following:

Note: Punitive Damages and Substantive Due Process

Can an award of punitive damages be so excessive as to violate the due process clause in its substantive dimension? A majority of the Court concluded that it can in BMW of North America v. Gore, 517 U.S. 559 (1996). Dr. Gore had sought punitive damages because his new BMW had actually been repainted, and he was not informed of this fact. The jury granted an award of punitive damages that was very large in comparison to the compensatory damages awarded in the case. There was a $4000 compensatory award and a $4 million punitive award.

Presented by this disparity, the Court ruled for the first time that an award of punitive damages violates the due process clause. (In a set of past cases the Court had left the issue open.) But there was an important internal division. The opinion for the Court spoke in terms of a form of substantive due process. Justice Breyer's concurring opinion did not reject this characterization, but it was procedurally oriented.

In finding the award grossly excessive, the Court referred to three points: the degree of reprehensibility, the ratio of punitive to compensatory damages, and the available penalties for comparable misconduct.

First, the Court said that nothing was especially horrible about BMW's behavior. There was no effect on performance or safety of the car, no indifference to or reckless disregard for health and safety. The failure to disclose the relevant material was very plausibly a wrong, but not a matter of egregious affirmative misconduct. (Thus the judgment about reprehensibility seemed to focus on both harm and state of mind.) Second, the ratio of punitive damages to compensatory damages was especially bad.

Third, the civil and criminal penalties that could be imposed for comparable misconduct were far more limited, involving, for example, a maximum civil penalty for deceptive trade practices of $2000. The Court also emphasized the state's lack of power to enact policies for the entire nation, or to impose its own policies on other states. Economic penalties must therefore be supported by the state's interest in protecting its own consumers and economy, rather than those of other states. The award therefore had to be analyzed in light of conduct within Alabama, and could not include conduct elsewhere.

Justice Breyer pressed some different points. He suggested that the most serious problem was not sheer excessiveness but the absence of legal standards that could reduce decisionmaker caprice. Here the relevant standards "are vague and open-ended to the point where they risk arbitrary results." The jury operated under no statute with standards distinguishing among permissible punitive damage awards. In Alabama, the seven factors used to constrain punitive damages awards have not been applied in a way that makes up for actual constraint. Nor have the state courts made any effort to discipline those factors in such a way as to generate a legally constraining standard. The excessiveness of the penalty combined with the absence of procedural safeguards to justify a judgment that the due process clause had been violated.

Justice Scalia wrote a dissenting opinion, joined by Justice Thomas, suggesting that this was a form of substantive due process that was entirely illegitimate. In Justice Scalia's view, punitive damage judgments should be left to the states. Justice Ginsburg also dissented, in an opinion joined by Justice Rehnquist, suggesting that states were actively considering the issue and coming close to the Scalia-Thomas position.

After *BMW*, it is clear that a majority of the Court is willing to hold that an award of punitive damages may be excessive and therefore inconsistent with substantive due process. How does this line of analysis compare with other cases in which the Court has used substantive due process to invalidate legislation? Is it more or less legitimate?

See also Bennis v. Michigan, 116 S. Ct. 994 (1996). There the Court upheld, against procedural due process challenge, a forfeiture scheme operating against an admittedly innocent property owner. Bennis was a joint owner, with her husband, of a car that had been forfeited as a public nuisance because her husband was found engaged in the automobile in illegal sexual activity with a prostitute. Bennis lacked knowledge of the activity and claimed that it was unconstitutional not to allow an "innocent owner" defense. The Court concluded that past cases had said the Constitution did not recognize the defense and that in any case the absence of such a defense prevented evasion by dispensing with the need for a judicial inquiry into possible collusion. Justice Stevens dissented, in an opinion joined by Justices Souter and Breyer.

G. Procedural Due Process

Page 1059. At the end of section 2 of the Note, add the following:

See also Young v. Harper, 117 S. Ct. 1148 (1997), holding that a "pre-parole" program, which allowed prisoners to be released from prison before expiration of their sentences, was very close to a parole program; thus a person placed in a preparole program is entitled under the due process clause to procedural protections before being removed from the program.

7
FREEDOM OF EXPRESSION

A. Introduction

Page 1078. **Before the citation to R. Nye in section 6 of the Note, add the following:**

Curtis, The 1837 Killing of Elijah Lovejoy by an Anti-Abolition Mob: Free Speech, Mobs, Republican Government, and the Privileges of American Citizens, 44 U.C.L.A. L. Rev. 1109 (1997).

Page 1080. **Before section 2 of the Note, add the following:**

e. Marshall, In Defense of the Search for Truth as a First Amendment Justification, 30 Ga. L. Rev. 1, 2-5 (1995):

> In the contemporary postmodern world, the notion that there is positive value in the search for truth would strike some as a quaint anachronism. [To] the contemporary mind, objective or transcendent truth is seen as nonsensical. . . . The Enlightenment claim that the powers of reason could lead humanity to a knowledge of truth has been savaged. [Although] objective truth may [be] non-existent, [this] attack misfires when it suggests that the First Amendment value inherent in the search for truth exists only in [the] actual finding of truth. The value that is to be realized is not in the possible attainment of truth, but rather, in the existential value of the search itself.

But "can there be First Amendment value in pursuing what is considered likely to be unattainable [and] unintelligible?" Marshall, supra, at 8.

Page 1085. **Before section 4 of the Note, add the following:**

e. Wells, Reinvigorating Autonomy: Freedom and Responsibility in the Supreme Court's First Amendment Jurisprudence, 32 Harv. C.R..-C.L. L. Rev. 159, 163-168 (1997):

Autonomy [is generally understood to mean] individual freedom from government interference. [Once] conceived of as a negative liberty, autonomy [conjures] up images of atomistic individuals saying whatever they wish with little regard for the needs of others. [A] richer and more complex notion of autonomy [would focus] not only on freedom from government interference but also on private citizens' relationships with each other. This conception of autonomy is far removed from atomistic individualism. Instead, it recognizes that we are social beings with rights and responsibilities. [This conception] derives primarily from Immanuel Kant, [who] believed that the State could bring its coercive power to bear against its citizens and thereby limit their freedom, in one, and only one, circumstance — when some citizens' actions infringe upon the freedom of others, and coercion is necessary to preserve the others' autonomy. Such coercive action preserves the dignity of its citizens by ensuring that individuals act in a manner that respects the freedom of others. Thus, the capacity for autonomy creates a moral entitlement that imposes an obligation, enforceable by the State, to respect the autonomy of other persons.

Page 1086.   Before section 5 of the Note, add the following:

d. *Speech as a property right.* For the view that "the function of the First Amendment is not to promote the collective interest in self-governance, [but] to prohibit regulation of an important property right peculiarly threatened by the government," see McGinnis, The Once and Future Property-Based Vision of the First Amendment, 63 U. Chi. L. Rev. 49, 57 (1996).

B.   Content-Based Restrictions: Dangerous Ideas and Information

Page 1093.   At the end of section 1 of the Note, add the following:

1a. *The facts of* Masses. The following is one of the poems in the August 1917 issue of *The Masses* magazine that led to the postmaster's action:

"A Tribute"
Josephine Bell

Emma Goldman and Alexander Berkman
Are in prison,
Although the night is tremblingly beautiful
And the sound of water climbs down the rocks
And the breath of the night air moves through multitudes and
  multitudes of leaves
That love to waste themselves for the sake of the summer.

Emma Goldman and Alexander Berkman
Are in prison tonight,
But they have made themselves elemental forces,
Like the water that climbs down the rocks:
Like the wind in the leaves:
Like the gentle night that holds us:
They are working on our destinies:
They are forging the love of the nations:
. . . .
Tonight they lie in prison.

Page 1102.   At the end of section 6 of the Note, add the following:

(d) The state should not "punish a speaker as a culpable actor unless the speaker . . . exerted a power over the listener so profound that the listener herself could not be held morally accountable for her actions." Dow, The Moral Failure of the Clear and Present Danger Test, 6 Wm. & Mary Bill of Rts. J. 733, 751-752 (1998).

Page 1114.   At the end of section 4 of the Note, add the following:

Consider White, The First Amendment Comes of Age: The Emergence of Free Speech in Twentieth Century America, 95 Mich. L. Rev. 299, 301, 303-305, 308-309 (1996):

... [T]he most complete and satisfactory account of the [emergence] of the First Amendment [connects] the elevation of speech to special status with the emergence, in the early years of the twentieth century, of a "modernist" consciousness, [which] assumed that the cognitive capabilities of humans would be a source of [enlightened] policymaking [and] rested on the assumption [that] "conflicts thought to be endemic to modern society could be rationally controlled, [justly], equitably, and democratically. [To guard against the danger] of tyrannical or arbitrary governance, [the modernist view embraced] a central distinction between laws [that] were arbitrary and those that were rational. A rational decision [was defined as] one that was [defensible] by appeal to something other than the power [of] those making it. . . .

As First Amendment jurisprudence became more progressively speech-protective, [the] capitalist model of economics, in its idealized late nineteenth-century version of a laissez-faire economic marketplace characterized by the absence of governmental regulation, receded in influence. [This led to] a double standard of constitutional review in which judges would defer to legislative regulation of the economy but scrutinize legislative regulation of [speech] rights. [The] basis for that heightened scrutiny was the close connection between [speech] rights and democratic theory. The basis for judicial deference to legislative regulation of economic rights was similar. [Such deference was premised on] the perceived truth that unregulated economic activity [infringed] on the freedom of a significant number of actors in the economic marketplace. . . ."

Page 1129.   At the end of section 8 of the Note, add the following:

Suppose a publisher distributes a book, entitled *Hit Man*, that extols the lifestyle of contract murderers and offers detailed instructions on how to commit a contract murder. The book explains, for example, how to make a silencer, how to break into a home, how to shoot a victim to ensure he is dead, and how to dispose of the weapon. Following these instructions precisely, X kills V in a contract murder. Thereafter, V's survivors sue the publisher of *Hit Man* for damages. Should *Brandenburg* govern this situation? Can the publisher be held liable? See Rice v. The Paladin Enterprises, 128 F.3d 233 (4th Cir. 1997), in which the court held that *Brandenburg* does not control this situation and that the publisher could be held liable where the publisher "intended and had knowledge that the publication would be used by criminals to execute the crime of murder for hire."

Page 1133.   At the end of section 3 of the Note, add the following:

Suppose defendant X establishes a Web site (called the "Nuremberg Files") that says abortion providers are "guilty of crimes against humanity," compares abortion to "war crimes," lists the names and addresses of abortion providers and their families, includes photographs of some abortion providers in Old West-style "Wanted" posters, and crosses out the names of abortion providers who have been murdered. Can X's speech be restricted on the ground that it constitutes incitement? On the ground that it constitutes a threat? See Planned Parenthood v. ACLA, 23 F. Supp. 2d 1182 (D. Ore. 1998). For an interesting analysis of this problem see Rothchild, Menacing Speech and the First Amendment: A Function Approach to Incitement that Threatens, 8 Tex. J. Women & L. 207 (1999).

Is a threat "outside the scope of First Amendment protection because it operates more like a physical action than [a] communication of ideas or emotions"? If so, in what circumstances may a threat be prohibited? Do you agree that all "three elements of *Brandenburg*—intent, immediate danger, and [objective] language"—must be present in order for the government to punish a public threat? Gey, *The Nuremberg Files* and the First Amendment Value of Threats, 78 Tex. L. Rev. 541, 591-593 (2000). What does "danger" mean in this context? Is it the danger that the threat actually will be carried out or is it the harm caused by the very fact of the threat itself? See also E. Baker, Human Liberty and Freedom of Speech 59-60 (1989) (the first amendment does not protect "speech designed to disrespect and distort the integrity of another's mental processes or autonomy"); K. Greenawalt, Speech, Crime and the Uses of Language 94 (1989) (the first amendment does not protect speech that "involves the creation of prospective harmful consequences in order toachieve one's objective"

How do these concepts apply to the *Nuremberg Files* case? To *Watts*? To *Bridges*? To *Claiborne Hardware*? Should there be a difference between publicly communicated threats and privately communicated threats? Consider the following: (a) "Unless you pay me $100 I will tell the voters about your affair with your aide." (b) "If you don't end your affair with your aide, I will disclose it to the voters."

Page 1139.   At the end of the first paragraph on the page, after the cite to Stone, add the following:

Kagan, Private Speech, Public Purpose: The Role of Governmental Motive in First Amendment Doctrine, 63 U. Chi. L. Rev. 415, 431-432 (1996) ("the government may not limit speech because other citizens deem the ideas offered to be wrong or offensive [because] the First Amendment protects no less against majority oppression than against runaway government").

Page 1154.   At the end of the first paragraph on the page, add the following:

Consider Heyman, Righting the Balance: An Inquiry into the Foundations and Limits of Freedom of Expression, 78 B.U. L. Rev. 1275, 1378-1379 (1998):

Suppose that the Ku Klux Klan burns a cross in front of the home of an African-American family that has recently moved into a white neighborhood, in order to terrorize the family and induce them to move. It is difficult to imagine a more serious invasion of personal security. [It might] be argued that the Klansmen's conduct should be privileged because it is intended, at least in part, to express a political view. Even if cross-burning is entitled to protection as political speech, however, [it] does not follow that this protection should apply to acts directed against particular persons. The Klan could communicate its political message just as effectively burning a cross elsewhere, without inflicting serious injuries to specific individuals. Or, if this is not true, then the increased effectiveness arises solely from the wrongful aspect of the conduct, the terror and degradation it inflicts on the family. For these reasons, cross-burning directed toward particular persons should not be protected as free expression.

Consider also Douglas-Scott, The Hatefulness of Protected Speech: A Comparison of the American and European Approaches, 7 Wm. & Mary Bill of Rts. J. 305, 309, 317, 343-345 (1999):

[C]ontrols on free speech long have been permitted in many European countries to curb incitement to race hatred. [For] example, in the United Kingdom, Part III of the Public Order Act of 1986 prohibits behavior intended to or likely to have the result of stirring up racial hatred. [The European approach to free speech emphasizes] particular values—dignity, protection of personal identity, and equality. [This] approach recognizes a different sort of harm caused by the abuse of freedom than the danger of imminent lawless action required under American law. The *Brandenburg* requirement that violence be imminent before hateful speech may be proscribed is objectionable. Different listeners respond in different ways to so-called fighting words. Not all react by violence. . . .

European case law looks not only to the harm caused by such expression, but also proceeds from a particular conception of individual personality and psychology. [European] case law rejects a conception of individuals as beings who merely should be left to their own devices to make up their own minds about the value of expression in the public domain, to be free to ignore it, or to counter it with more speech. Such an approach isolates human beings by forcing them to take the consequences of painful conduct and ignores the particular susceptibility of certain groups to injury, especially when the offense of the speech seems to be targeted at such groups because of their identity. [Surely] it is not enough for societies that claim to be committed to the ideals of social and political equality and respect for individual dignity to remain neutral and passive when threats to these value exist. Sometimes the state must act to show its solidarity with vulnerable minority groups and its commitment to equality.

Page 1168.   At the end of the paragraph before the first full paragraph on the page, add the following:

For such an argument, see Volokh, Freedom of Speech, Permissible Tailoring and Transcending Strict Scrutiny, 144 U. Pa. L. Rev. 2417, 2425-2431 (1996).

C. Overbreadth, Vagueness, and Prior Restraint

Page 1180.   Before section 6 of the Note, add the following:

d. In National Endowment for the Arts v. Finley, — S.Ct. — (1998), section E2 infra this Supplement, the Court upheld a federal statute that directs the NEA, in establishing procedures to judge the artistic merit of grant applications, to "tak[e] into consideration general standards of decency and respect for the diverse beliefs and values of the American public." Noting that "facial invalidation" is "generally disfavored," the Court held that because there were constitutionally permissible applications of the "decency" and "respect" criteria, it would "not now pass upon the constitutionality of [the provision] by envisioning the most extreme applications conceivable, but will deal with those problems if and when they arise."

Page 1180.   At the end of section 6 of the Note, add the following:

See also Reno v. American Civil Liberties Union, 117 S. Ct. 2329 (1997) (applying *Brockett* to hold that, in "considering a facial challenge, [the] Court may impose a limiting construction on a statute only if it is 'readily susceptible' to such a construction").

7. *Additional limitations on the overbreadth doctrine.* In Los Angeles Police Department v. United Reporting Publishing Corp., — U.S. — (1999), the respondent, a private publishing company which sells the names and addresses of recently arrested individuals to attorneys, insurance companies and drug counselors, challenged the constitutionality of a California statute authorizing public access to information about the addresses of arrestees for "scholarly, journalistic, political or governmental" purposes, but prohibiting such access for commercial purposes. The Court held that the respondent could not invoke the overbreadth doctrine to challenge this statute because "this is not a case in which the government is prohibiting a speaker from conveying information that the speaker already possesses." Rather, "what we have before us is nothing more than a governmental denial of access to information in its possession. California could decide not to give out arrestee information at all without violating the First Amendment." "To the extent that [plaintiff's] 'facial challenge' seeks to rely on the effect of the statute on parties not before the Court, [its] claim does not fit within the case law allowing courts to entertain facial challenges. No threat of prosecution [or] cutoff of funds [hangs] over their heads. They may seek access under the statute on their own [without] incurring any burden other than the prospect that their request will be denied. Resort to a facial challenge here is not warranted because there 'is no possibility that protected speech will be muted.'"

Page 1182. After section 4 of the Note, add the following:

5. *Vagueness and the standards for government subsidies.* In National Endowment for the Arts v. Finley, — S. Ct. — (1998), section E2 infra this Supplement, the Court held that a federal statute directing the NEA, in establishing procedures to judge the artistic merit of grant applications, to "tak[e] into consideration general standards of decency and respect for the diverse beliefs and values of the American public" was not unconstitutionally vague. The Court explained: "The terms of the provision are undeniably opaque, and if they appeared in a criminal statute [they] could raise substantial vagueness concerns. It is unlikely, however, that speakers will be compelled to steer too far clear of any 'forbidden area' in the context of grants of this nature. [Thus,] when the Government is acting as patron rather than as sovereign, the consequences of imprecision are not constitutionally severe. [Moreover, in] the context of selective subsidies, it is not always feasible for Congress to legislate with clarity. Indeed, if this statute is unconstitutionally vague, then so too are all government programs awarding scholarships and grants on the basis of subjective criteria such as 'excellence.'"

Page 1185.   At the end of the third line, add the following:

See Kagan, Private Speech, Public Purpose: The Role of Governmental Motive in First Amendment Doctrine, 63 U. Chi. L. Rev. 415, 459-463 (1996) ("the rule against standardless licensing [serves the] function of flushing out bad motive by establishing a safeguard against administrative action based on the content of expression").

Page 1187.   At the end of section 4 of the Note, add the following:

For a discussion of the history of the licensing of speech, see Schiller, Free Speech and Expertise: Administrative Censorship and the Birth of the Modern First Amendment, 86 Va. L. Rev. 1 (2000).

D. Content-Based Restrictions: "Low" Value Speech

Page 1243.   At the end of section 2 of the Note, add the following:

2a. *"The greater includes the lesser."* Is there an effective answer to Chief Justice Rehnquist's argument in *Posadas* that it would "be a strange constitutional doctrine which would concede to the legislature the authority to totally ban a product or activity, but deny to the legislature the authority to forbid the stimulation of demand for the product or activity through advertising"? Consider Redish, Tobacco Advertising and the First Amendment, 81 Iowa L. Rev. 589, 600-601 (1996):

> . . . [This logic] stands the Constitution on its head, by reducing the level of constitutional protection afforded expression to that afforded [conduct.] The fallacy of [the Court's argument] can be demonstrated by examining [its] application in the noncommercial speech context. Government clearly has the power to prohibit attempts at violent overthrow; [the Court] has nevertheless extended substantial First Amendment protection to the *advocacy* of violent overthrow.
>
> . . . [T]here are important reasons [why] government's power to regulate conduct is greater than its power to regulate expression. Initially, the Constitution's choice to provide greater protection to expression reflects the special value placed on the human capacities for thought and verbal communication. Because thought is so highly valued as a uniquely human activity, interfer-

ences with the operations of the mind are deemed to constitute greater impairments of human dignity than are restrictions on most forms of conduct. Secondly, to allow government to halt a particular activity, not by direct regulatory means but rather indirectly by suppressing advocacy and dissemination of information about that activity, effectively enables government to subvert the traditional democratic value of accountability. Instead of exposing attainment of its goal to the normal pressures and debates of the democratic process, government is authorized to employ furtiveness and stealth to achieve its desired social ends.

Page 1244.   Before the Note, add the following:

44 LIQUORMART, INC. V. RHODE ISLAND, 517 U.S. 484 (1996): In a divided set of opinions, the Court invalidated a Rhode Island statute prohibiting "advertising in any manner whatsoever" of the price of any alcoholic beverage offered for sale in the State, except for price tags or signs displayed within licensed premises and not visible from the street.

Justice Stevens delivered a plurality opinion joined by Justices Kennedy and Ginsburg, and joined in different parts by Justices Souter and Thomas: "As [a] review of our case law reveals, [not] all commercial speech regulations are subject to a similar form of constitutional [review]. When a State regulates commercial messages to protect consumers from misleading, deceptive, or aggressive sales practices, or requires the disclosure of beneficial consumer information, the purpose of its regulation is consistent with the reasons for according constitutional protection to commercial speech and therefore justifies less than strict review.

"However, when a State entirely prohibits the dissemination of truthful, nonmisleading commercial messages for reasons unrelated to the preservation of a fair bargaining process, there is far less reason to depart from the rigorous review that the First Amendment generally demands. [Citing *Linmark*; *Virginia Pharmacy*; and *Went For It.*] The special dangers that attend complete bans on truthful, nonmisleading commercial speech cannot be explained away by appeals to the 'commonsense distinctions' that exist between commercial and noncommercial speech. [Neither] the 'greater objectivity' nor the 'greater hardiness' of truthful, nonmisleading commercial speech justifies reviewing its complete suppression with added deference. [Bans] against truthful, nonmisleadng commercial speech [usually] rest solely on the offensive assumption that the public will respond 'irrationally' to the truth. The First Amendment directs us to be especially skeptical of regulations that seek to keep people in the dark for what the government perceives to be their own good. That teaching applies equally to state attempts to deprive consumers of accurate information about their chosen products. . . .

"The State argues that the price advertising prohibition should [be] upheld because it directly advances the State's substantial interest in promoting tolerance, and because it is no more extensive than necessary. [We] can agree that common sense supports the conclusion that a prohibition against price advertising [will] tend to [maintain] prices at a higher level than would prevail in a completely free market [and that] consumption [is likely to be] somewhat lower whenever a higher, noncompetitive price level prevails. However, without any [evidentiary] support [we] cannot agree with the assertion that the price advertising ban will significantly advance the State's interest. . . . [Speculation about such matters] does not suffice when the State takes aim at accurate commercial information for paternalistic ends. . . .

"The State also cannot satisfy the requirement that its restriction on speech be no more extensive than necessary. It is perfectly obvious that alternative forms of regulation that would not involve any restriction on speech would be more likely to achieve the State's goal of promoting temperance. [Higher] prices can be maintained either by direct regulation or by increased taxation. Per capita purchases could be limited as is the case with prescription drugs. Even educational campaigns focused on the problems [of] drinking might prove to be more effective. As a result, even under the less than strict standard that generally applies in commercial speech cases, the State has failed to establish a 'reasonable fit' between its abridgment of speech and its temperance goal. [It] necessarily follows that the price advertising ban cannot survive the more stringent constitutional review that *Central Hudson* itself concluded was appropriate for the complete suppression of truthful, nonmisleading commercial speech. . . .

"Relying on *Posadas* and *Edge Broadcasting*, Rhode Island [argues] that, because expert opinions as to the effectiveness of the price advertising ban 'go both ways' [the legislation should be upheld as] a 'reasonable choice' by the legislature. The State next contends that *Posadas* requires us to give particular deference to that legislative choice because the State could, if it chose, ban the sale of alcoholic beverages outright. Finally, the State argues that deference is appropriate because alcoholic beverages are so-called 'vice' products. We consider each of these arguments in turn.

"The State's first argument fails [because the State] errs in concluding that *Edge* and *Posadas* establish the degree of deference that [is appropriate in this case.] In *Edge*, [the] statute [regulated] advertising about an activity that [was] illegal in the jurisdiction in which the broadcaster was located. Here, by contrast, the commercial speech ban targets information about entirely lawful behavior. *Posadas* is more directly relevant. [But] we are now persuaded that [*Posadas*] clearly erred in concluding that it was 'up to the legislature' to choose suppression over a less speech-restrictive policy. [In] keeping with [our pre-*Posadas*] holdings, we conclude that a state legislature does not [have] broad discretion to suppress truthful, nonmisleading information for paternalistic purposes. . . .

"We also cannot accept the State's second contention, which is premised [on] the 'greater-includes-the-lesser' reasoning endorsed [in] *Posadas*. [This reasoning] is inconsistent with both logic and well-settled doctrine. [Contrary] to the assumption made in *Posadas*, [the] Constitution presumes that attempts to regulate speech are more dangerous than attempts to regulate conduct. [As] the entire Court apparently now agrees, the statements in [*Posadas*] on which Rhode Island relies are no longer persuasive.

"Finally, we [reject] the State's contention that [the] price advertising ban should be upheld because it targets commercial speech that pertains to a 'vice' activity. [The] scope of any 'vice' exception to the protection afforded by the First Amendment would be difficult, if not impossible, to define. . . .

"Because Rhode Island has failed to carry its heavy burden of justifying its complete ban on price advertising, we conclude that [the challenged legislation is unconstitutional]."

Justice Scalia concurred in the judgment. Scalia observed that, "where the core offense of suppressing particular political ideas is not at issue," the Court should interpret the first amendment in light of "the long accepted practices of the American people," with particular reference to "the state legislative practices prevalent at the time" the first and fourteenth amendments were adopted. Because the parties in this case provided "no evidence on these points," however, Scalia concluded that the legislation was invalid under the Court's "existing jurisprudence."

Justice Thomas also filed a concurring opinion: "In cases such as this, in which the government's asserted interest is to keep legal users of a product or service ignorant in order to manipulate their choices in the marketplace, the balancing test adopted in *Central Hudson* should not be applied. [Such] an 'interest' is per se illegitimate and can no more justify regulation of 'commercial' speech than it can justify regulation of 'noncommercial' speech. [Both] Justice Stevens and Justice O'Connor appear to adopt a stricter [interpretation] of *Central Hudson* than that suggested in some of our other opinions, one that could [go] a long way toward the position I take. [But] rather than 'applying' [*Central Hudson*] to reach the inevitable result [in this case], I would [hold that] all attempts to dissuade legal choices by citizens by keeping them ignorant are impermissible."

Justice O'Connor, joined by Chief Justice Rehnquist and Justices Souter and Breyer, all filed an opinion concurring in the judgment: "[This legislation] fails the final prong [of *Central Hudson*]; that is, its ban is more extensive than necessary to serve the State's interest. [The] fit between Rhode Island's method and

[its] goal is not reasonable. [As demonstrated by Justice Stevens, the] State has other methods at its disposal—methods that would more directly accomplish [its] goal without intruding on sellers' ability to provide truthful, nonmisleading information to customers. [The State points] for support to *Posadas*. Since *Posadas*, however, this Court has examined more searchingly the State's professed goal, and the speech restriction put into place to further it, before accepting a State's claim that the speech restriction satisfies First Amendment scrutiny. [Citing, e.g., *Went for It* and *Coors Brewing*]. [Because the challenged legislation] fails even [the] standard set out in *Central Hudson*, nothing here requires the adoption of a new analysis for the evaluation of commercial speech regulation."

Consider Sullivan, Cheap Spirits, Cigarettes, and Free Speech: The Implications of *44 Liquormart*, 1996 Sup. Ct. Rev. 123, 126-128, 148-149, 152,157:

> Since *Virginia Pharmacy,* the Court has treated commercial speech as protected speech, but not as fully protected speech. The principal differences are (1) that regulation of false and misleading commercial speech is subject to no First Amendment scrutiny, (2) that advertisements of illegal transactions may be banned even if they fall short of proscribable incitement, and (3) that all [other] commercial speech regulations are subject to a form of intermediate rather than strict scrutiny. . . .
>
> After *Liquormart*, it [would] appear [that the Court now views] suppressing commercial speech by reason of [its] communicative impact as suspicious, [and will test such regulations by the same standards it uses to test similar regulations of noncommercial speech.] [Having gone this far,] why does the Court not simply dissolve the category of commercial speech and assimilate advertising to the general run of First Amendment law?
>
> . . . What are the possible downsides, or perceived bad consequences, of assimilating commercial speech to the Court's existing approaches to fully protected speech? There are three areas of current law [that might be especially affected by such a change: "advertisement of an illegal product or transaction"; "false or misleading commercial speech"; and content-based commercial speech regulations that, unlike the regulation at issue in *Liquormart*, are not "motivated by paternalistic concern that the listener will act wrongly on true factual information," such as "regulations designed to prevent advertisers from conveying particular images that they seek to associate with their product or service," (e.g., Joe Camel).]

How would assimilating these three types of commercial advertising "to the Court's existing approaches to fully protected speech" affect the extent to which they can be regulated? Would these changes, if any, be "bad consequences"? See Sullivan, supra.

GREATER NEW ORLEANS BROADCASTING ASS'N, INC. v. UNITED STATES, ___ U.S. ___ (1999): Applying *Central Hudson*, the Court unanimously invalidated 18 U.S.C. section 1304, which prohibited radio and television broadcasters from carrying advertisements about privately operated commercial casino gambling, as applied to broadcast stations located in states where such gambling is legal. In an opinion by Justice Stevens, the Court concluded that, even if the federal government has "substantial" interests in "reducing the social costs associated with 'gambling'" and in "assisting States that 'restrict gambling' . . . within their own borders," the challenged legislation was nonetheless unconstitutional because it did not "directly and materially advance the asserted government interest" and it was "more extensive than necessary to serve the interests that [assertedly] support it." Citing *Rubin*, the Court noted that, because the federal legislation exempted advertising for legal tribal casino gambling and state-operated lotteries and parimutuel gambling, it was "so pierced by exemptions and inconsistencies that the Government cannot hope to exonerate it." Thus, the Court concluded that, "even under the degree of scrutiny that we have applied in commercial speech cases, decisions that select among speakers conveying virtually identical messages are in serious tension with the principles underlying the First Amendment."

Chief Justice Rehnquist and Justice Thomas each concurred separately in the result.

Page 1246.   At the end of section 6 of the Note, add the following:

6a. *Compelled commercial speech.* The Agricultural Marketing Agreement Act of 1937, which is designed to maintain orderly agricultural markets, authorizes collective action by groups of agricultural producers on such matters as uniform prices, product standards, and generic advertising. The cost of such collective action, which must be approved by two-thirds of the affected producers, is covered by compulsory assessments on the producers. In Glickman v. Wileman Brothers & Elliott, Inc., 117 S. Ct. 2130 (1997), the Court held that marketing orders promulgated by the Secretary of Agriculture pursuant to the Act, which assessed respondent producers for the cost of generic advertising of California nectarines, plums, and peaches, did not violate respondents' First Amendment rights, even though respondents objected to the requirement that they pay for such advertising. The Court explained:

> Three characteristics of the regulatory scheme at issue distinguish it from laws that we have found to abridge [the] First Amendment. First, the marketing orders impose no restraint on the freedom of any producer to communi-

cate any message to any audience. Second, they do not compel any person to engage in any actual or symbolic speech. Third, they do not compel the producers to endorse or to finance any political or ideological views. Indeed, since all of the respondents are engaged in the business of marketing California nectarines, plums, and peaches, it is fair to presume that they agree with the central message of the speech that is generated by the generic program. . . .

None of the advertising in this record promotes any particular message other than encouraging consumers to buy California tree fruit. Neither the fact that respondents may prefer to foster that message independently in order to promote and distinguish their own products, nor the fact that they think more or less money should be spent fostering it, makes this case comparable to those in which an objection rested on political or ideological disagreement with the content of the message. The mere fact that the objectors believe their money is not being well spent 'does not mean [that] they have a First Amendment complaint.'

In such circumstances, the Court held *Central Hudson* inapplicable, and concluded that the wisdom of the overall program "is simply a question of economic policy for Congress and the Executive to resolve."

Justice Souter, joined by Chief Justice Rehnquist and Justices Scalia and Thomas, dissented. Justice Souter argued that the Court was wrong in suggesting that "the First Amendment places no limits on government's power to force one individual to pay for another's speech, except when the speech in question [is] ideological or political in character." In Justice Souter's view, "forced payment for commercial speech should be subject to the same level of judicial scrutiny as any [other] restriction on [commercial speech]," whether or not it is "ideological or political in character." Applying such scrutiny, he concluded that the challenged program violated the First Amendment. For more on the problem of compelled expression, see infra section F-3.

Page 1252. Before section 2 of the Note, add the following:

Consider also Hamilton, Art Speech, 49 Vand. L. Rev. 73, 77-78 (1996):

[A]rt cannot receive its due as long as attempts to justify its place in the pantheon of first amendment freedoms are focused only upon the protection of ideas or information. Art can carry ideas and information, but it also goes beyond logical, rational, and discursive communication. [A] strong analogy can be drawn between the protection of art and the protection of religion. . . . Art and religion form a prism through which the First Amendment is transformed from a haven for ideas to a means of protecting vital spheres of personal freedom. [Art] construct[s] paths out of repression [and helps to preserve] the constitutional balance between the governed and the governing. [Art serves an] integral function in a successful representative democracy, [for it] provides the opportunity to experience alternative worlds and therefore to gain distance and perspective on the prevailing status quo.

Page 1253. At the end of section d of the Note, add the following:

On the other hand, might it be said that the very concept of "obscenity" embodies a forbidden "viewpoint based restriction" because "it is justified by moral objections to the ideas or messages that sexual speech is said to convey"? Heins, Viewpoint Discrimination, 24 Hast. Const. L.Q. 99, 103 (1996).

Page 1281. At the end of section b of the Note, add the following:

Consider Balkin, Media Filters, the V-Chip, and the Foundations of Broadcast Regulation, 45 Duke L.J. 1131, 1139, 1142, 1148, 1150, 1157, 1165, 1168, 1173 (1996):

Most parents [want] the government to assist them in controlling their children in ways they think appropriate. [Thus, the real issue in the V-chip controversy is] the issue of parental control. [Print] media lend themselves easily to filtering [because] print media are easy to exclude. If I want to avoid the information contained in a newspaper, I can simply avoid buying it. If I go into a bookstore, I can buy the book I want without buying other books. I can take the books I want home and then lock them up so that my children cannot see them. [Broadcast media, on the other hand, are different because] they offer limited practical means of filtering. Parents may want to keep their children from certain kinds of television programs. But their ability to do so is limited. [If] children insist on watching television when their parents are not at home or cannot supervise them, parents have no choice other than to remove the television entirely. [The] V-chip and similar technologies promise to change the nature of broadcast media because they offer the possibility of new types of filtering mechanisms. . . .

[But the] development of a ratings system poses a [significant] constitutional problem. [The] regulatory apparatus surrounding the V-chip will work an enormous new delegation of information filtering to a centralized bureaucracy, whether one operated by the federal government or [by] private industry. [While] overt expressions of homophobia are likely to remain un-coded, overt homosexual expressions of affection will probably be among the first to be coded as inappropriate for children, [and the] very assumption that exposure to racist messages is less harmful to our children [than] exposure to violence [or indecency] already carries considerable political freight. [And the] more the FCC becomes involved in the ratings system, the more heavily that system will become politicized. It is politics, after all, that has led to the new system, and politics will not soon depart once the system is in place. [Imagine, for example], a made-for-television movie that depicts a fictional cover-up by the church hierarchy of child abuse allegations made against Catholic priests, and a movie in which Freddy Krueger murders a hapless teenage couple having sex in the woods at midnight. It is not difficult to imagine different groups of parents disagreeing heatedly about the relative inappropriateness for children of these two examples.

Page 1290.   Before Young v. American Mini-Theatres, add the following:

Reno v. American Civil Liberties Union
117 S. Ct. 2329 (1997)

JUSTICE STEVENS delivered the opinion of the Court.

At issue is the constitutionality of two statutory provisions enacted to protect minors from "indecent" and "patently offensive" communications on the Internet. Notwithstanding the legitimacy and importance of the congressional goal of protecting children from harmful materials, we [conclude] that the statute abridges "the freedom of speech" protected by the First Amendment. . . .

[Section 223(a) of the Communications Decency Act of 1996 prohibits any person from making any communication over the Internet "which is obscene or indecent, knowing that the recipient of the communication is under 18 years of age." Section 223(d) prohibits any person from knowingly sending over the Internet any communication that will be available to a person under 18 years of age and "that, in context, depicts or describes, in terms patently offensive as measured by contemporary community standards, sexual or excretory activities or organs."] The breadth of these prohibitions is qualified by two affirmative defenses. [Section 223(e)(5)(A)] covers those who take "good faith, reasonable, effective, and appropriate actions" to restrict access by minors to the prohibited communications. [Section 223(e)(5)(B)] covers those who restrict access to covered material by requiring certain designated forms of age proof, such as a verified credit card or an adult identification number or code. . . .

[T]he Government contends that the CDA is plainly constitutional under Ginsberg v. New York [and] FCC v. Pacifica Foundation. A close look at these cases, however, raises—rather than relieves—doubts concerning the constitutionality of the CDA.

In *Ginsberg*, we upheld the constitutionality of a New York statute that prohibited selling to minors under 17 years of age material that was considered obscene as to them even if not obscene as to adults. [In several] important respects, the statute upheld in *Ginsberg* was narrower than the CDA. First, we noted in *Ginsberg* that "the prohibition against sales to minors does not bar parents who so desire from purchasing the magazines for their children." Under the CDA, by contrast, neither the parents' consent — nor even their participation — in the communication would avoid the application of the statute. Second, the New York statute applied only to commercial transactions, whereas the CDA contains no such limitation. Third, the New York statute cabined its definition of material that is harmful to minors with the requirement that it be "utterly without redeeming social importance for minors." The CDA fails to provide us with any definition of the term "indecent" [and], importantly, omits any requirement that the "patently offensive" material covered by §223(d) lack serious literary, artistic, political, or scientific value. . . .

[T]here are [also] significant differences between the order upheld in *Pacifica* and the CDA. First, the order in *Pacifica*, issued by an agency that had been regulating radio stations for decades, targeted a specific broadcast that represented a rather dramatic departure from traditional program content in order to designate when — rather than whether — it would be permissible to air such a program in that particular medium. The CDA's broad categorical prohibitions are not limited to particular times and are not dependent on any evaluation by an agency familiar with the unique characteristics of the Internet. Second, unlike the CDA, the Commission's declaratory order was not punitive; we expressly refused to decide whether the indecent broadcast "would justify a criminal prosecution." Finally, the Commission's order applied to a medium which as a matter of history had "received the most limited First Amendment protection," in large part because warnings could not adequately protect the listener from unexpected program content. The Internet, however, has no comparable history. Moreover, [the] risk of encountering indecent material [on the Internet] by accident is remote because a series of affirmative steps is required to access specific material. . . .

These precedents, then, surely do not require us to uphold the CDA and are fully consistent with the application of the most stringent review of its provisions.

[We have] observed that "[e]ach medium of expression . . . may present its own problems." Thus, some of our cases have recognized special justifications for regulation of the broadcast media that are not applicable to other speakers, [citing, e.g., *Pacifica*]. In these cases, the Court relied on the history of extensive government regulation of the broadcast medium, the scarcity of available frequencies at its inception, and its "invasive" nature.

Those factors are not present in cyberspace. Neither before nor after the enactment of the CDA have the vast democratic fora of the Internet been subject to the type of government supervision and regulation that has attended the broadcast industry. Moreover, the Internet is not as "invasive" as radio or television. The District Court specifically found that "[c]ommunications over the Internet do not 'invade' an individual's home or appear on one's computer screen unbidden. Users seldom encounter content 'by accident.'" [Finally], unlike the conditions that prevailed when Congress first authorized regulation of the broadcast spectrum, the Internet can hardly be considered a "scarce" expressive commodity. It provides relatively unlimited, low cost capacity for communication of all kinds. [Our] cases provide no basis for qualifying the level of First Amendment scrutiny that should be applied to this medium.

[T]he many ambiguities concerning the scope of [the Act's] coverage render it problematic for purposes of the First Amendment. For instance, each of the two parts of the CDA uses a different linguistic form. The first uses the word "indecent," while the second speaks of material that "in context, depicts or describes, in terms patently offensive as measured by contemporary community standards, sexual or excretory activities or organs." Given the absence of a definition of either term, this difference in language will provoke uncertainty among speakers about how the two standards relate to each other and just what they mean. Could a speaker confidently assume that a serious discussion about birth control practices, homosexuality, the First Amendment issues raised by the [text of the broadcast at issue in *Pacifica*], or the consequences of prison rape would not violate the CDA? This uncertainty undermines the likelihood that the CDA has been carefully tailored to the congressional goal of protecting minors from potentially harmful materials. [Moreover, the] vagueness of the CDA [raises] special First Amendment concerns because of its obvious chilling effect on free speech. [Given] the vague contours of [the] statute, it unquestionably silences some speakers whose messages would be entitled to constitutional protection. That danger provides further reason for insisting that the statute not be overly broad. The CDA's burden on protected speech cannot be justified if it could be avoided by a more carefully drafted statute.

We are persuaded that the CDA lacks the precision that the First Amendment requires when a statute regulates the content of speech. In order to deny minors access to potentially harmful speech, the CDA effectively suppresses a large amount of speech that adults have a constitutional right to receive and to address to one another. That burden on adult speech is unacceptable if less restrictive alternatives would be at least as effective in achieving the legitimate purpose that the statute was enacted to serve.

In evaluating the free speech rights of adults, we have made it perfectly clear that "[s]exual expression which is indecent but not obscene is protected by the First Amendment." [It] is true that we have repeatedly recognized the governmental interest in protecting children from harmful materials. [See *Ginsberg*; *Pacifica*]. But that interest does not justify an unnecessarily broad suppression of speech addressed to adults. As we have explained, the Government may not "reduc[e] the adult population [to] only what is fit for children." . . .

In arguing that the CDA does not so diminish adult communication, the Government relies on the incorrect factual premise that prohibiting a transmission whenever it is known that one of its recipients is a minor would not interfere with adult to adult communication. [Given] the size of the potential audience for most messages, in the absence of a viable age verification process, the sender must be charged with knowing that one or more minors will likely view it. Knowledge that, for instance, one or more members of a 100 person chat group will be minor — and therefore that it would be a crime to send the group an indecent message — would surely burden communication among adults.

The District Court found that at the time of trial existing technology did not include any effective method for a sender to prevent minors from obtaining access to its communications on the Internet without also denying access to adults. [By] contrast, the District Court found that "[d]espite its limitations, currently available user based software suggests that a reasonably effective method by which parents can prevent their children from accessing sexually explicit and other material which parents may believe is inappropriate for their children will soon be widely available."

The breadth of the CDA's coverage is wholly unprecedented. Unlike the regulations upheld in *Ginsberg* and *Pacifica*, the scope of the CDA is not limited to commercial speech or commercial entities. Its open ended prohibitions embrace all nonprofit entities and individuals posting indecent messages or displaying them on their own computers in the presence of minors. The general, undefined terms "indecent" and "patently offensive" cover large amounts of nonpornographic material with serious educational or other value. [The] breadth of this content based restriction of speech imposes an especially heavy burden on the Government to explain why a less restrictive provision would not be as effective as the CDA. It has not done so. The arguments in this Court have referred to possible alternatives such as requiring that indecent material be "tagged" in a way that facilitates parental control of material coming into their homes, making exceptions for messages with artistic or educational value, providing some tolerance for parental choice, and regulating some portions of the Internet—such as commercial web sites—differently than others, such as chat rooms. Particularly in the light of the absence of any detailed findings by the Congress, or even hearings addressing the special problems of the CDA, we are persuaded that the CDA is not narrowly tailored if that requirement has any meaning at all.

The Government's three remaining arguments focus on the defenses provided in §223(e)(5). First, relying on the "good faith, reasonable, effective, and appropriate actions" provision, the Government suggests that "tagging" provides a defense that saves the constitutionality of the Act. The suggestion assumes that transmitters may encode their indecent communications in a way that would indicate their contents, thus permitting recipients to block their reception with appropriate software. It is the requirement that the good faith action must be "effective" that makes this defense illusory. The Government recognizes that its proposed screening software does not currently exist. Even if it did, there is no way to know whether a potential recipient will actually block the encoded material. Without the impossible knowledge that every guardian in America is screening for the "tag," the transmitter could not reasonably rely on its action to be "effective."

For its second and third arguments concerning defenses — which we can consider together — the Government relies on the latter half of §223(e)(5), which applies when the transmitter has restricted access by requiring use of a verified credit card or adult identification. Such verification is not only technologically available but actually is used by commercial providers of sexually explicit material. These providers, therefore, would be protected by the defense. Under the findings of the District Court, however, it is not economically feasible for most noncommercial speakers to employ such verification. Accordingly, this defense would not significantly narrow the statute's burden on noncommercial speech. Even with respect to the commercial pornographers that would be protected by the defense, the Government failed to adduce any evidence that these verification techniques actually preclude minors from posing as adults. [The] Government thus failed to prove that the proffered defense would significantly reduce the heavy burden on adult speech produced by the prohibition on offensive displays. [The] CDA places an unacceptably heavy burden on protected speech, and thus the defenses do not constitute the sort of "narrow tailoring" that will save an otherwise patently invalid unconstitutional provision.

[Finally], the Government asserts that — in addition to its interest in protecting children — its "[e]qually significant" interest in fostering the growth of the Internet provides an independent basis for upholding the constitutionality of the CDA. The Government apparently assumes that the unregulated availability of "indecent" and "patently offensive" material on the Internet is driving countless citizens away from the medium because of the risk of exposing themselves or their children to harmful material.

We find this argument singularly unpersuasive. The dramatic expansion of this new marketplace of ideas contradicts the factual basis of this contention. The record demonstrates that the growth of the Internet has been and continues to be phenomenal. As a matter of constitutional tradition, in the absence of evidence to the contrary, we presume that governmental regulation of the content of speech is more likely to interfere with the free exchange of ideas than to encourage it. The interest in encouraging freedom of expression in a democratic society outweighs any theoretical but unproven benefit of censorship.

[Affirmed.]

JUSTICE O'CONNOR, with whom the CHIEF JUSTICE joins, concurring in the judgment in part and dissenting in part.

I write separately to explain why I view the Communications Decency Act of 1996 as little more than an attempt by Congress to create "adult zones" on the Internet. [The] creation of "adult zones" is by no means a novel concept. [The] Court has previously sustained such zoning laws, but only if (i) [the law] does not unduly restrict adult access to the material [and] (ii) minors have no right to read or view the banned material. [In *Ginsberg*], for example, the Court sustained a New York law that barred store owners from selling pornographic magazines to minors in part because adults could still buy those magazines.

[Before] today, [the Court had] only considered laws that operated in the physical world, a world with two characteristics that make it possible to create "adult zones": geography and identity. A minor can see an adult dance show only if he enters an establishment that provides such entertainment. And should he attempt to do so, the minor will not be able to conceal completely his identity (or, consequently, his age). Thus, the twin characteristics of geography and identity enable the establishment's proprietor to prevent children from entering the establishment, but to let adults inside.

The electronic world is fundamentally different. [Because cyberspace] allows speakers and listeners to mask their identities [it] is not currently possible to exclude persons from accessing certain messages on the basis of their identity. [But it is increasingly] possible to construct barriers in cyberspace and use them to screen for identity, making cyberspace more like the physical world and, consequently, more amenable to zoning laws. [For example, Internet] speakers [have] begun to zone cyberspace [through] the use of "gateway" technology. Such technology requires Internet users to enter information about themselves —perhaps an adult identification number or a credit card number—before they can access certain areas of cyberspace. [Although] the prospects for the eventual zoning of the Internet appear promising, I agree with the Court that we must evaluate the constitutionality of the CDA as it applies to the Internet as it exists today. Given the present state of cyberspace, [a] speaker cannot be reasonably assured that the speech he displays will reach only adults because it is impossible to confine speech to an "adult zone."

[Nonetheless, I believe the Act is constitutional at least] as applied to a conversation involving only an adult and one or more minors—e.g., when an adult speaker sends an e-mail knowing the addressee is a minor, or when an adult and minor converse by themselves or with other minors in a chat room. In this context, these provisions are no different from the law we sustained in *Ginsberg*. Restricting what the adult may say to the minors in no way restricts the adults' ability to communicate with other adults. . . .

The analogy to *Ginsberg* breaks down, however, when more than one adult is a party to the conversation. If a minor enters a chat room otherwise occupied by adults, the CDA [unconstitutionally] requires the adults in the room to stop using indecent speech. [But I would sustain the provisions] to the extent they apply to the transmission of Internet communications where the party initiating the communication knows that all of the recipients are minors.

Page 1297.   At the end of section 3 of the Note, add the following:

In 44 Liquormart, Inc. v. Rhode Island, 517 U.S. 484 (1996), the Court disavowed *LaRue*'s reliance on the twenty-first amendment, concluding that the twenty-first amendment does not qualify the first amendment's prohibition against laws abridging the freedom of speech.

Page 1297.   At the end of section 5 of the Note, add the following:

5A. *Indecency and subsidies for the arts.* In considering the constitutionality of government regulations of "indecent" expression, to what extent should it matter whether the government directly restricts such expression (as in *Reno*, *Pacifica* and *Sable*) or merely refuses to subsizie it in a government-sponsored grant program? See National Endowment for the Arts v. Finley, — S. Ct. — (1998), infra section E2 this Supplement, in which the Court upheld against both overbreadth and vagueness challenges a federal statute that directs the NEA, in establishing procedures to judge the artistic merit of grant applications, to "tak[e] into consideration general standards of decency and respect for the diverse beliefs and values of the American public."

Page 1298.   At the end of the Note, add the following:

7. Reno: *right result, wrong reason?* Consider Volokh, Freedom of Speech, Shielding Children, and Transcending Balancing, 1997 Sup. Ct. Rev. 141, 148-149, 156-157, 165-166, 169, 172, 185:

The CDA is invalid, the Court said, because it is possible to protect speech in this context without any sacrifice of shielding of children. [The Court reasoned that the Act was thus] "an *unnecessarily broad* suppression of speech addressed to adults." [But] the Court is wrong. None of the Court's proposed alternatives to the CDA [would] have been as effective [at shielding children from indecent material] as the CDA's more or less total ban.

[This] error is more than just a harmless misstatement, [for the] pregnant negative in the Court's reasoning is that, had there really been no equally effective alternatives, the CDA should have been upheld. [This is consistent with the notion that government] "may . . . regulate [indecent expression] in order to promote [its] compelling interest [in shielding children] if it chooses the least restrictive means."

[This view] is unsound. As Butler v. Michigan correctly holds, the government may not reduce adults to reading only what is fit for children. This is true even though letting adults access indecent material would necessarily sacrifice a great deal of shielding of children—even though a total ban would genuinely be the only means to effectively further the interest. [Thus, the correct approach would provide that if] the law imposes a substantial burden on generally protected speech, then it is per se impermissible, even if this means we must sacrifice a significant amount of shielding of children. [Under this approach, the] CDA would be unconstitutional because [banning these] communications substantially burdens speech to adults, [even if there are no less restrictive alternatives].

Page 1298.   Before Section 6, add the following:

DENVER AREA EDUCATIONAL TELECOMMUNICATIONS CONSORTIUM, INC. v. FCC, 116 S. Ct. 2374 (1996): In the Cable Act of 1984, Congress required cable operators to reserve approximately 15 percent of their channels for commercial lease to "unaffiliated persons." In addition, the Act authorized local governments to require cable operators to set aside a certain number of channels for "public, educational, or governmental use." The 1984 Act expressly prohibited cable operators from exercising any editorial control over the content of programs broadcast on either "leased access" or "public access" channels. In this case, the Court considered the constitutionality of three provisions of the Cable Television Consumer Protection and Competition Act of 1992, which altered this scheme with respect "indecent progamming," defined as programming that depicts or describes "sexual activities or organs in a patently offensive manner."

Section 10(a). This provision authorized cable operators to prohibit programming they "believe to be indecent," as defined above, on leased access channels. In defense of this provision, the FCC argued that a cable operator is analogous to a newspaper, which, as a private actor, can refuse to carry such material without violating the first amendment. The FCC maintained that section

10(a) does nothing more than to give a cable operator, also a private actor, the same authority as a newspaper. Petitioners (a consortium of leased access channel "unaffiliated" programmers) offered a different view of the matter. Noting that section 10(a) is an exception to the general prohibition against cable operators exercising editorial control over leased-access programming, petitioners argued that section 10(a) is an unconstitutional content-based restriction because it authorizes cable operators to exercise editorial control over only this form of expression. In a seven-to-two decision, the Court upheld this provision.

In a plurality opinion, Justice Breyer, joined by Justices Stevens, O'Connor, and Souter, concluded that section 10(a) does not violate the first amendment. Noting "the changes taking place in the law, the technology, and the industrial structure related to telecommunications," Breyer maintained that the Court should "decide this case . . . narrowly, by closely scrutinizing §10(a) to assure that it properly addresses an extremely important problem, without imposing [an] unnecessarily great restriction on speech."

Applying that approach, Breyer invoked several considerations to justify his conclusion. First, "the provision [serves] an extremely important justification— the need to protect children from exposure to patently offensive sex-related material." Second, "the provision arises in a very particular context—congressional permission to regulate programming that, but for a previous Act of Congress, would have [no access to such channels] free of an operator's control." Third, "the problem Congress addressed here is remarkably similar to the problem addressed [in] *Pacifica*." Fourth, "the permissive nature of §10(a) means that it likely restricts speech less than, not more than, the ban at issue in *Pacifica*," for cable operators need not exercise the authority granted them under the Act. In light of these considerations, Breyer concluded that "the permissive nature of the provision, coupled with its viewpoint-neutral application, [suggests that section 10(a) is] a constitutionally permissible way to protect [children], while accommodating both the First Amendment interests served by the access requirements and those served in restoring to cable operators a degree of the editorial control that Congress removed in 1984."

Justice Thomas, joined by Chief Justice Rehnquist and Justice Scalia, concurred in the result. Thomas took a very different approach, however. In Thomas's view, programmers have no first amendment "right to transmit over an operator's cable system." Thomas drew an "analogy to the print media" where, "for example, the author of a book [has] no right to have the book sold in a particular bookstore without the store owner's consent." Thus, "the proper question" posed by these regulations is not whether section 10(a) violates the "free speech rights" of programmers, but whether "the leased and public access requirements [are] improper restrictions on the operators' free speech rights." Returning to the print media analogy, Thomas observed that if "Congress passed a law forcing bookstores to sell books published on the subject of congressional politics, we would undoubtedly entertain a claim by bookstores that this law violated the First Amendment, [but] I doubt we would similarly find merit in a claim by publishers of gardening books that the law violated their First Amendment rights." Thomas concluded that, "if that is so, then the petitioners [cannot] reasonably assert that the Court should strictly scrutinize [section 10(a)] in a way that maximizes their ability to speak [and], by necessity, minimizes the operators' discretion."

Justice Kennedy, joined by Justice Ginsburg, dissented. At the outset, Kennedy sharply criticized the plurality for applying "no standard" and for losing "sight of existing First Amendment doctrine." Kennedy argued that, "when confronted with a threat to free speech in the context of an emerging technology, we ought to have the discipline to analyze the case by reference to existing elaborations of constant First Amendment principles," not "wander into uncharted areas of the law with no compass other than our own opinions about good policy." In Kennedy's view, the issue here is "straightforward" and provides "no reason to discard our existing First Amendment jurisprudence."

Kennedy emphasized that in section 10(a), "Congress singles out one sort of speech for vulnerability to private censorship in a context where [it does not otherwise permit] content-based discrimination." Specifically, section 10(a) expressly disadvantages "nonobscene, indecent programming, a protected category of expression, [citing *Sable*], on the basis of its content." In such circumstances, Kennedy observed, "strict scrutiny applies," and however "compelling Congress' interest in shielding children from indecent programming," section 10(a) "cannot survive this exacting review." This is so, Kennedy argued, because "to the extent cable operators prohibit indecent programming on access channels, not only children but adults will be deprived of it," and in light of the availability of other means of regulating such expression, such as blocking mechanisms available to individual subscribers, the government "has no legitimate interest in making access channels pristine."

Finally, Kennedy rejected the government's argument that, under *Pacifica*, a lower standard of review is appropriate for regulations of "indecent" speech. Echoing *Cohen*, Kennedy maintained that, in "artistic or political settings, indecency may have strong communicative content, protesting conventional norms or giving an edge to a work by conveying 'otherwise inexpressible emotions.'" Moreover, indecent speech "often is inseparable from the ideas and viewpoints conveyed, or separable only with the loss of truth or expressive power." Thus, such restrictions should be permitted only if they are "narrowly tailored to serve a compelling interest."

Section 10(c). This section is essentially identical to section 10(a), but regulates public access rather than leased-access channels. In a 5-4 decision, the Court invalidated section 10(c). In a plurality opinion, Justice Breyer, joined by Justices Stevens and Souter, identified "four important differences" that, in their view, distinguished section 10(c) from section 10(a). First, "cable operators have traditionally agreed to reserve channel capacity for public [access] channels as part of the consideration they give municipalities that award them cable franchises. [Thus], these are channels over which cable operators have not historically exercised editorial control. Unlike §10(a) therefore, §10(c) does not restore to cable operators editorial rights that they once had." Second, unlike leased access channels, where "the lessee has total control of programming during the leased time slot," public-access channels "are normally subject to complex supervisory systems [with] public and private elements." Third, because in the public-access context there is already in place "a locally accountable body capable of addressing the problem [of] patently offensive programming broadcast to children," there is less need for a "cable operator's veto" to "achieve the statute's objective." Fourth, there is no "factual basis" demonstrating that the existing mechanisms of control for public-access channels are not sufficient to address the statute's concern. "The upshot," Breyer concluded, is that "the Government cannot sustain its burden of showing that §10(c) is necessary to protect children or that it is appropriately tailored to secure that end."

Justice Kennedy, joined by Justice Ginsburg, concurred in the result. Although rejecting Justice Breyer's reasoning, Kennedy concluded that section 10(c) is unconstitutional for essentially the same reasons he thought section 10(a) is unconstitutional.

Justice O'Connor dissented because she was not "persuaded" that "the asserted 'important differences'" that Justice Breyer identified to distinguish section 10(a) from section 10(c) "are sufficient to justify striking down §10(c)." In her view, both provisions are constitutional.

Justice Thomas, joined by Chief Justice Rehnquist and Justice Scalia, dissented. In their view, section 10(c) is constitutional for the same reasons he thought section 10(a) is constitutional.

Section 10(b). This section of the Act, which applies only to leased-access channels, requires cable operators to segregate "indecent" programming on a single channel, to block that channel from viewer access, and to unblock it only on a subscriber's written request (and within thirty days of receiving the request). The Court, in a 6-3 decision, invalidated this provision. Justice Breyer delivered the opinion of the Court. At the outset, the Court noted that this provision "significantly differs" from sections 10(a) and 10(c) because "it does not simply permit, but rather requires cable operators to restrict [such] speech." The Court observed that this provision has "obvious restrictive effects" on the access of individuals to this sort of programming, including the potential chilling effect of the "written notice" requirement on subscribers who may "fear for their reputations should the operator, advertently or inadvertently, disclose the list of those who wish to watch the 'patently offensive' channel."

The Court found it unnecessary to "determine whether, or the extent to which, *Pacifica* does, or does not, impose some lesser standard of review where indecent speech is at issue." Although agreeing with the government that the "protection of children is a 'compelling interest,'" the Court concluded that the provision is nonetheless invalid because "it is not a 'least restrictive alternative,'" is "not 'narrowly tailored,'" and is "'more extensive than necessary.'" Thus, "it fails to satisfy this Court's formulations of the First Amendment's 'strictest,' as well as its somewhat less 'strict,' requirements." The most important consideration leading the Court to this conclusion was the availability of other, less speech-restrictive, means to achieve the objective of the provision. Other legislation, for example, governing channels other than leased-access channels, "requires cable operators to [scramble] such programming"; requires cable operators to "honor a subscriber's request to block any, or all, programs on any channel to which he or she does not wish to subscribe"; requires cable operators to provide subscribers, on request, with a "lockbox," which enables parents "to 'lock out' those programs or channels that they [do] not want their children to see"; and requires "manufacturers, in the future, [to] make television sets with a so-called 'V-chip' — a device that will be able automatically to identify and block sexually explicit or violent programs." Although not deciding "whether these [alternative] provisions are themselves unlawful," the Court emphasized that "they are significantly less restrictive than the provision here at issue." Although "conceding" that "no provision, [short] of an absolute ban, can offer certain protection against assault by a determined child," the Court emphasized that it has not "generally allowed this fact alone to justify 'reduc[ing] the adult population [to] only what is fit for children.'"

Justice Thomas, joined by Chief Justice Rehnquist and Justice Scalia, dissented. Although conceding that "§10(b) must be subjected to strict scrutiny and can be upheld only if it furthers a compelling governmental interest by the least restrictive means available," Thomas concluded that section 10(b) satisfies this standard. After asserting that "Congress has 'a compelling [interest in] shielding minors from the influence of [indecent speech] that is not obscene by adult standards,'" Thomas turned to his disagreement with the Court: "The Court strikes down §10(b) by pointing to alternatives, such as reverse-blocking and lockboxes, that it says are less restrictive than segregation and blocking. Though these methods attempt to place in parents' hands the ability to permit their children to watch as little, or as much, indecent programming as the parents think proper, they do not effectively support parents' authority to direct the moral upbringing of their children. [Because] indecent programming on leased access channels is 'especially likely to be shown randomly or intermittently between non-indecent programs, [parents] armed with only a lockbox must carefully monitor all leased-access programming and constantly reprogram the lockbox to keep out undesired programming. [This] characteristic of leased access channels makes lockboxes and reverse-blocking largely ineffective."

Thomas also dismissed the Court's concern that section 10(b) requires subscribers who want access to indecent programming to give written consent. Thomas argued that if a segregation and blocking scheme is otherwise permissible, then it can hardly be invalidated because subscribers must request access, for any "request for access to blocked programming—by whatever method—ultimately will make the subscriber's identity knowable. But this is hardly the kind of chilling effect that implicates the First Amendment."

UNITED STATES v. PLAYBOY ENTERTAINMENT GROUP, INC., ___ **U.S.** ___ **(2000):** Section 505 of the Telecommunications Act of 1996 requires cable operators who provide channels "primarily dedicated to sexually-oriented programming" either to "fully scramble" those channels or to limit their transmission to between 10 p.m. and 6 a.m. Even before the enactment of section 505, cable operators used scrambling to ensure that only paying customers had access to such programming, but the technology of scrambling is imperfect and the scrambled programs occasionally "bleed" through to the viewer. The purpose of section 505 was to shield children from exposure to sexually-oriented "signal bleed." Because the technology to "fully" eliminate signal bleed is very expensive, most cable operators conformed to the requirements of section 505 by limiting transmission to only the eight authorized hours.

In a five-to-four decision, the Court invalidated section 505. Justice Kennedy wrote the opinion of the Court: "[The statute] is content-based [because it] applies only to channels primarily dedicated to 'sexually explicit adult programming or other programming that is indecent.' [Moreover, the] overriding justification for the regulation is concern for the effect of the [content] on young viewers. . . .

"[The] only reasonable way for a substantial number of cable operators to comply with [section 505] is to time channel, which silences the protected speech for two-thirds of the day in every [home], regardless of the presence or [absence] of children or of the wishes of the viewers. According to the District Court, '30% to 50% of all adult programming is viewed by households prior to 10 p.m. [To] prohibit this much speech is a significant restriction of communication. [It] is of no moment that the statute does not impose a complete prohibition. The distinction between laws burdening and laws banning speech is but a matter of degree. The Government's content-based burdens must satisfy the same rigorous scrutiny as its content-based bans.

"Since section 505 is a content-based speech restriction, it can stand only if it [is] narrowly tailored to promote a compelling Government interest. If a less restrictive alternative would serve the Government's purpose, the legislature must use that alternative. [Citing Reno.] Where the designed benefit of a content-based speech restriction is to shield the sensibilities of listeners, the general rule is that the right of expression prevails. [Citing Cohen, Erznoznik, Bolger.] Our zoning cases [are] irrelevant to the question here. [Citing Renton and Young.] We have made clear that the lesser scrutiny afforded regulations targeting the secondary effects of crime or declining property values has no application to content-based regulations targeting the primary effects of protected speech. [Citing Reno.]

"There is, moreover, a key difference between cable television and the broadcasting media, which is the point on which this case turns: Cable systems have the capacity to block unwanted channels on a household-by-household basis. The option to block reduces the likelihood, so concerning to the Court in *Pacifica*, that traditional First Amendment scrutiny would deprive the Government of all authority to address this sort of problem. The corollary, of course, is that targeted blocking enables the Government to support parental authority without affecting the First Amendment interests of speakers and willing listeners. [Simply] put, targeted blocking is less restrictive than banning, and the Government cannot ban speech if targeted blocking is a feasible and effective means of furthering its compelling interests. . . .

"[In this case,] a less restrictive alternative is available: Section 504 [of the same Act,] requires cable operators to [fully] block undesired channels at individual households upon request, [with no limitation as to whether the programming is sexually oriented or indecent]. [This alternative approach] is narrowly tailored to the Government's goal of supporting parents who want those channels blocked. [When such] a plausible, less restrictive alternative is offered to a content-based restriction, it is the Government's obligation to prove that the alternative will be ineffective to achieve its goals. The Government has not met that burden here.

"In support of its position [that this is an ineffective alternative], the Government cites empirical evidence showing that section 504 [has] generated few requests for household-by-household blocking. [Indeed,] fewer that 0.5% of cable subscribers requested full blocking [during the more than a year in which the Government was enjoined from enforcing section 505]. [But] the Government has failed to prove that this was due to the ineffectiveness of this alternative, rather than to its failure adequately to inform people about this alternative or to the possibility that] the actual signal bleed problem might be far less of a concern than the Government at first had supposed. . . .

[Indeed, the] Government has failed [to] prove [that] section 504 with adequate notice [of its availability] would be an ineffective alternative to section 505. [There] is no evidence that a well-promoted voluntary blocking provision would not be capable at least of informing parents about signal bleed (if they are not yet aware of it) and about their rights to have the bleed blocked (if they consider it a problem and have not yet controlled it themselves). [It] is no response that voluntary blocking requires a consumer to take action, or may be inconvenient, or may not go perfectly every time. A court should not assume a plausible, less restrictive alternative would be ineffective; and a court should not presume parents, given full information, will fail to act. . . .

"[Finally,] the Government [argues] that society's independent interests will be unserved if parents fail to act [the availability of the section 504 alternative]. [But even] upon the assumption that the Government has an interest in substituting itself for informed and empowered parents, its interest is not sufficiently compelling to justify this widespread restriction on speech. The Government's argument stems from the idea that parents do not know their children are viewing the material on a scale or frequency to cause concern, or if so, that parents do not want to take affirmative steps to block it and their decisions are to be superceded. [The] Government has not [shown, however,] that [the section 504] alternative [would] be insufficient to secure its objective, or that any overriding harm justifies its intervention."

Justice Breyer, joined by Chief Justice Rehnquist and Justices O'Connor and Scalia, dissented: "The specific question is whether section 504's 'opt-out' [alternative] amounts to a 'less restrictive,' but *similarly* practical and *effective*, way to accomplish section 505's child-protecting objective. As *Reno* tell us, a 'less restrictive alternative' must be 'at least as effective in achieving the legitimate purpose that the statute was enacted to serve.' [Section 504] is not a similarly effective alternative. [Section 504] gives parents the power to tell cable operators to keep any channel out of their home. Section 505 does more. Unless parents explicitly consent, it inhibits the transmission of adult cable channels to children whose parents may be unaware of what they are watching, whose parents cannot easily supervise television viewing habits, whose parents do not know of the section 504 'opt-out' rights, or whose parents are simply unavailable at critical times. In this respect, section 505 serves the same interests as the laws that deny children access to adult cabarets or X-rated movies. These laws, and section 505, all act in the absence of direct parental supervision. [Section] 504's 'opt-out, even with [a] plan for 'better notice,' is *not* similarly effective in achieving the legitimate goals that the statute was enacted to serve.

"Section 505 raises the cost of adult channel broadcasting. In doing so, it restricts, but does not ban adult speech. Adults may continue to watch adult channels, though less conveniently, by watching at night [or by] recording programs with a VCR. [Citing *Renton*]. The Government's justification for imposing this restriction—limiting the access of children to channels that broadcast virtually 100% 'sexually explicit' material—is 'compelling.' The record shows no similarly effective, less restrictive alternative. Consequently section 505's restriction, viewed in the light of the proposed alternative, is proportionate to need. That is to say, it restrict speech no more than necessary to further that compelling need."

Page 1303.   At the end of sub-section d of the Note, add the following:

Consider also Powell, As Justice Requires/Permits: The Delimitation of Harmful Speech in a Democratic Society, 16 Law & Inequ. J. 97, 103, 147-149 (1998):

[T]he insights proffered by critical race and post-modern theorists [suggest] that the classic remedy for harmful speech — that is, more speech — will, in some instances, perpetuate disparities of power and destabilize our sense of self. The marketplace of ideas cannot self-regulate so long as objections to lack of participatory access are subsumed by claims that the liberty interest in expression is primary to the equality interest in participatory access. A self-regulating marketplace presupposes an equal starting line — an assumption that has never been a reality in American political life.

[A decision of the Canadian Supreme Court, Regina v. Keegstra, 2 W.W.R. 1 (1991) illustrates] an alternative way of using democratic principles to valorize liberty and equality. [In *Keegstra,* a Canadian high school teacher was convicted of "communicating statements [that] willfully promote hatred against any identifiable group" for making anti-Semitic statements to his students. The Canadian Supreme Court rejected Keegstra's claim that his conviction violated the Canadian Charter of Rights and Freedoms because his speech] was not expression that "serves individual and societal values in a free and democratic society." [This decision] follows a path within the bounds of a commitment to both liberty and equality, and mediates between these values by recourse to a collective concern for the underlying values and principles of the society, including social justice. [Commenting] that it is destructive of free expression values themselves, as well as other democratic values, "to treat all expression as equally crucial to those principles at the core" of free expression, the Court suggested that democratic principles recommend viewing free expression as a function of three underlying goals. These goals are truth attainment, ensuring self-fulfillment and the development of self-identity, and most importantly, [the] guarantee that the opportunity for *participation in the democratic process is open to all.* The Court simultaneously supports these rationales with the observations that hate speech can impede the search for truth, impinge on the autonomy necessary to individual development and subvert the democratic process. Cognizant that the regulation "muzzles the participation of a [few]," the Court remains certain that the loss of that voice is not substantial. [What] is most instructive about the decision is that the Court was willing to employ a democratic calculus.

Page 1304.   After section g of the Note, add the following:

gg. Adler, What's Left? Hate Speech, Pornography, and the Problem for Artistic Expression, 84 Cal. L. Rev. 1499, 1500-1506 (1996):

> ... [T]he feminist anti-pornography movement [and] the anti-"hate speech" [movement deliberately] disregard the measures of value—such as "public debate" or "artistic expression"—that traditionally have been the foundation of First Amendment law. [As a consequence, these censors are] on a collision course with a new kind of political speech that is developing in outsider communities. [In recent years,] race, gender and sexual orientation have become the subjects of art, and art has become a central medium to activists concerned with achieving equality in these realms. [Moreover, these] new artists want to use and exploit the very speech the censors would ban. [Advocates] of rights for women, gays, lesbians, blacks, and other outsiders have turned increasingly to a subversive style of political argument. Using this subtle and pervasive mode, "victims" adopt the language of "victimizers" to turn oppression on its head. [This] technique [may] function on multiple levels: to frame the horror and absurdity of the speech it appropriates, to erase its sting by taking it as its own, to borrow its effectiveness, or to destroy its power to hurt. [Ironically, then, the] accomplishments of the left in banning speech could be its greatest undoing, restricting the very activists who depend on subversion and reversal as their primary techniques of political criticism. In rushing to silence its opposition, the left may inadvertently silence itself."

Page 1315.   At the end of section 3 of the Note, add the following:

Consider also Brownstein, Rules of Engagement for Cultural Wars: Regulating Conduct, Unprotected Speech, and Protected Expression in Anti-Abortion Protests, 29 U.C. Davis L. Rev. 553, 586-588, 628 (1996):

> The critical dichotomy that justifies heightened review for certain regulations and more deferential review of others is not the distinction between speech and conduct, as Justice Scalia asserts in *R.A.V.* and the Court confirms in *Mitchell*. [Instead], it is the difference between content-neutral, content-discriminatory, and viewpoint-discriminatory regulations. . . .
> Content-neutral regulations of unprotected speech and conduct should be upheld as long as the law is minimally rational. Content-discriminatory regulations [of] unprotected speech and expressive conduct should [both] be

evaluated under a standard similar to the multi-factor balancing test used to evaluate content-neutral regulations of protected speech. [See infra section E.] [Courts] should review viewpoint-discriminatory regulations [of] unprotected speech [or] conduct under strict scrutiny.

Justice Scalia is surely correct in *R.A.V.* when he argues [that] a law prohibiting obscenity or fighting words derogating right-wing political ideas but not left-wing political ideas would be unconstitutional. But so would a law enhancing the penalty imposed on an aggressor who physically assaulted Democrats while providing a lesser sanction for those who perpetrated physical assaults on Republicans. [The] critical point is that a viewpoint-discriminatory law may seriously burden freedom of speech regardless of the nature of the activity that is being regulated. [Unlike laws that regulate protected expression, such laws do not "deprive society of any positive communications that deserve to be heard" or restrict legitimate media of expression. But they require strict scrutiny because they distort "the marketplace of ideas by empowering one side of an ideological conflict with dangerous weapons that are denied to its opponents."]

Conversely, a law prohibiting political fighting words and a law prohibiting physical assaults in which the victim is selected because of his political beliefs should be upheld under less than stringent review despite the fact that both laws involve content discrimination. It should make no difference that the former law regulates unprotected speech while the latter law regulates conduct. Both laws are viewpoint-neutral [and] can be defended as attempts to accomplish legitimate objectives in an even-handed way. Neither law intrinsically favors one side or the other on any contested public issue.

Page 1317.   At the end of the first paragraph on the page, add the following:

Consider also Estlund, Freedom of Expression in the Workplace and the Problem of Discriminatory Harassment, 75 Tex. L. Rev. 687, 693-695 (1997):

> ... [T]he workplace [is] a "satellite domain" of public discourse—a domain that lies outside of the core of public discourse but contributes to that discourse in unique and important ways. [It] is at work that citizens gain [much] of their experience with participation in governance. Speech about [the] internal governance of the workplace contributes to the richness of public discourse and the formation of citizens in a democratic society. [Moreover, the] workplace is a crucial intermediate institution in society—an institution in which [unrelated] individuals from diverse backgrounds interact and cooperate in support of shared instrumental ends. ... The workplace

functions ideally as a kind of laboratory of diversity in which the laws of democratic engagement can be learned and practiced. [In that context], unconstrained speech among coworkers who are forced into daily proximity could destroy the possibility of constructive engagement, and [reasonable] civility constraints on employee freedom of expression are [therefore] necessary to reinforce the norms of tolerance that hold together the workplace community. . . .

An understanding of the nature of the workplace thus offers grounds for a principled compromise between the conflicting imperatives of freedom and constraint—a compromise that recognizes the unique capacity of workplace discourse to contribute to public discourse within a democracy.

I propose a compromise in the form of certain constraints on the *manner* of expression in the workplace forum. [In particular, I] would leave unprotected, first, speech that is directed at a listener whom the speaker knows to be offended on the basis of race, sex, or religion, and, second, speech the manner of which is manifestly offensive on the basis of race, sex, or religion —independent of the viewpoint expressed—and that is uttered at a time and place that could not reasonably be avoided by listeners who are thus offended. Speech of this nature [could] be freely relied upon to establish harassment liability [under Title VII].

E. Content-Neutral Restrictions: Means of Communication

Page 1330. After the citation of Williams in the last paragraph of section 1 of the Note, add the following:

Brownstein, Rules of Engagement for Culture Wars: Regulating Conduct, Unprotected Speech, and Protected Expression in Anti-Abortion Protests, 29 U.C. Davis L. Rev. 553 (1996).

Page 1330. At the end of section 1 of the Note, add the following:

Kagan, Private Speech, Public Purpose: The Role of Governmental Motive in First Amendment Doctrine, 63 U. Chi. L. Rev. 415, 446-463 (1996) (arguing that the concern with improper government motivatation best explains the content-based/content-neutral distinction).

Page 1333.   At the end of section 2 of the Note, add the following:

For another application of the secondary effects doctrine, see City of Erie v. Pap's A. M., section E3, infra in this Supplement, in which the Court upheld an ordinance banning public nudity.

Page 1334.   At the end of section 5 of the Note, add the following:

6. *Content-neutrality: another look.* In Hill v. Colorado, — U.S. —(2000), the Court upheld as a "content-neutral" time, place or manner regulation a Colorado statute that makes it unlawful for any person within 100 feet of a health care facility to "knowingly approach" within eight feet of another person, without that person's consent, in order to pass "a leaflet or handbill to, [display] a sign to, or [engage] in oral protest, education, or counseling with, such other person." Is this law content-based or content-neutral?

Consider Justice Scalia's argument in dissent that the law is content-based: "A speaker wishing to approach another for the purpose of communicating *any* message except one of protest, education, or counseling may do so without first securing the other's consent. Whether a speaker must obtain permission before approaching within eight feet—and whether he will be sent to prison for failing to do so—depends entirely on *what he intends to say* when he gets there. [Moreover,] when applied, as it is here, at the entrance to medical facilities, [such a law is clearly] a means of impeding speech against abortion. The Court's confident assurance that the statute poses no special threat to First Amendment freedoms because it applies alike to 'used car salesmen, animal rights activists, fundraisers, environmentalists, and missionaries,'. . . is a wonderful replication (except for its lack of sarcasm) of Anatole France's observation that '[t]he law, in its majestic equality, forbids the rich as well as the poor to sleep under bridges . . . .'"

Consider the Court's response: "[The statute] seeks to protect those who enter a health care facility from the harassment, the nuisance [and] the implied threat of physical touching that can accompany an unwelcome approach within eight feet of a patient by a person wishing to argue vociferously face-to-face and perhaps thrust an undesired handbill upon her. The statutory phrases, 'oral protest, education, or counseling,' distinguish speech activities likely to have those consequences from speech activities [that] are most unlikely to have those consequences. The statute does not distinguish among speech instances that are similarly likely to raise the legitimate concerns to which it responds. Hence, the statute cannot be struck down for failure to maintain 'content neutrality.' [Similarly], the contention that a statute is 'viewpoint based' simply because its enactment was motivated by the conduct of the partisans on one side of a debate is without support. [The] statute is not limited to those who oppose abortion. It applies to all 'protest,' to all 'counseling,' and to all demonstrators whether or not the demonstration concerns abortion, and whether they oppose or support the woman who has made an abortion decision. That is the level of neutrality that the Constitution demands."

Page 1341. At the end of section 6 of the Note, add the following:

6a. *Demonstrating near an abortion clinic II.* In Schenck v. Pro-Choice Network of Western New York, 117 S. Ct. 855 (1997), several abortion clinics in upstate New York were subjected to a series of large-scale blockades in which anti-abortion protesters marched, stood, knelt, or lay in clinic parking lots and doorways, blocking cars from entering the lots and interfering with patients and clinic employees who attempted to enter the clinics. Smaller groups of protesters, called "sidewalk counselors," crowded, jostled, pushed, and yelled and spit at women entering the clinics. Police officers who attempted to control the protests often were harassed by the protesters both verbally and by mail. A federal district court issued an injunction against 50 individuals and three organizations (including Operation Rescue) which, among other things, (a) prohibited them from demonstrating within 15 feet of clinic doorways, parking lots and driveways ("fixed buffer zones"); (b) prohibited them from demonstrating within 15 feet of any person or vehicle seeking access to or leaving a clinic ("floating buffer zones"); and (c) permitted them to have two "sidewalk counselors" inside the buffer zones on the condition that they "cease and desist" their "counseling" if the person with whom they are speaking so requests.

Applying *Madsen*, the Court asked whether these provisions of the injunction "burden more speech than necessary to serve a significant governmental interest." In upholding the "fixed buffer zones" as appropriate means of ensuring "that people and vehicles trying to enter or exit the clinic property [can] do so," the Court rejected the claim that such zones were unnecessary in light of other provisions of the injunction prohibiting the protesters from "blocking, impeding or obstructing access to" the clinics. The Court explained that, in light of the prior conduct of the protesters, the district court "was entitled to conclude" that fixed buffer zones were necessary to prevent the protesters from doing "what they had done before: aggressively follow and crowd individuals right up to the clinic door and then refuse to move, or purposefully mill around parking lot entrances in an effort to impede or block the progress of cars." Moreover, because the petitioners' "harassment of police hampered [their] ability to respond quickly to a problem, a prophylactic measure was even more appropriate." Finally, although noting that "one might quibble about whether 15 feet is too great or too small a distance to ensure access," the Court deferred "to the district court's reasonable assessment."

On the other hand, the Court invalidated the "floating buffer zones." The Court was particularly concerned that, because sidewalks near the clinics are usually only 17 feet wide, protesters wishing to communicate with an individual entering or leaving a clinic would either have to walk in the street, walk 15 feet behind the individual, or walk backwards 15 feet in front of the individual. The Court concluded that this was "hazardous" and would effectively prevent protesters "from communicating a message from a normal conversational distance or handing leaflets to people entering or leaving the clinics [on] the public sidewalks." The Court concluded that, because "there may well be other ways" to "effect such separation" without burdening so much protected speech, "the floating buffer zones burden more speech than necessary to serve the relevant governmental interests."

Finally, the Court upheld the "cease and desist" provision which "limits the exception for sidewalk counselors in connection with the fixed buffer zone." At the outset, the Court cast doubt on the district court's explanation that this provision was designed "to protect the right of the people approaching and entering the facilities to be left alone," noting that "as a general matter, we have indicated that in public debate [our] citizens must tolerate insulting, and even outrageous, speech in order to provide adequate breathing space to the freedoms protected by the First Amendment." But the Court nonetheless upheld the "cease and desist" provision because "the entire exception for sidewalk counselors was an effort to enhance [the] speech rights" of the protesters.

Justice Scalia, joined by Justices Kennedy and Thomas, dissented from the upholding of the fixed buffer zones and the "cease and desist" provision. Justice Breyer dissented from the invalidation of the floating buffer zones.

6b. *Demonstrating near an abortion clinic III.* In Hill v. Colorado, — U.S. — (2000), the Court, in a six-to-three decision, upheld a Colorado statute that makes it unlawful for any person within 100 feet of a health care facility to "knowingly approach" within eight feet of another person, without that person's consent, in order to pass "a leaflet or handbill to, [display] a sign to, or [engage] in oral protest, education, or counseling with, such other person." Citing *Frisby*, the Court explained that although the right to free speech "includes the right to attempt to persuade others to change their views, and may not be curtailed simply because the speaker's message may be offensive to his audience," the "protection afforded to offensive messages does not always embrace offensive speech that is so intrusive that the unwilling audience cannot avoid it." Indeed, "no one has a right to press even 'good' ideas on an unwilling recipient," and "none of our decisions has minimized the enduring importance of 'the right to be free' from persistent 'importunity, following and dogging' after an offer to communicate has been declined. The Court thus concluded that the statute "is a valid time, place, and manner regulation [because it] serves governmental interests that are significant and legitimate and [is] 'narrowly tailored' to serve those interests and . . . leaves open ample alternative channels for communication."

Justice Scalia, joined by Justice Thomas dissented. Scalia argued that the "burdens this law imposes upon the right to speak are substantial," for "most of the 'counseling' and 'educating' likely to take place outside a health care facility cannot be done at a distance and at a high-decibel level," and "leafletting will be rendered utterly ineffectual by a requirement that the leafletter obtain from each subject permission to approach." Scalia maintained that "that simply is not how it is done," for "a leafletter, whether he is working on behalf of Operation Rescue [or] Bubba's Bar-B-Que, stakes out the best piece of real estate he can, and then walks a few steps toward individuals passing in his vicinity, extending his arm and making it *as easy as possible* for the passerby, whose natural inclination is generally not to seek out such distributions, to simply accept the offering. Few pedestrians are likely to give their 'consent' to the approach of a handbiller (indeed, by the time he requested it they would likely have passed by)." Justice Kennedy also dissented.

Page 1375.   Before section 5 of the Note, add the following:

In light of the Court's reasoning in *Lamb's Chapel* and *Rosenberger*, does it follow that the regulation of "obscenity" is also impermissibly viewpoint-based "because it is justified by moral objections to the ideas or messages that sexual speech is said to convey"? Heins, Viewpoint Discrimination, 24 Hast. Const. L.Q. 99, 103 (1996).

4a. *Cable television: public access channels.* In the Cable Act of 1984, Congress authorized local governments to require cable operators to set aside a certain number of channels for "public, educational, or governmental use." The 1984 Act expressly prohibited cable operators from exercising any editorial control over the content of programs broadcast on "public access" channels. In the Cable Television Consumer Protection and Competition Act of 1992, Congress amended this scheme to authorize cable operators to restrict "indecent" programming on public access channels. "Indecent" programming is defined as programming that the cable operator "reasonably believes depicts or describes sexual activities or organs in a patently offensive manner." In Denver Area Education Telecommunications Consortium, Inc. v. FCC, supra section VII-D-5, this Supplement, the Court invalidated this provision. Although the Court as a whole did not decide whether a public-access channel constitutes a "designated public forum," several of the Justices did debate the issue. Consider the following views:

a. Justice Kennedy, joined by Justice Ginsburg:

[P]ublic access channels [are] available at low or no cost to members of the public, often on a first-come, first-served basis. [They clearly] meet the definition of a [designated] public forum. [The] House Report for the 1984 Cable Act is consistent with this view. It characterizes public access channels as "the video equivalent of the speaker's soapbox or [the] printed leaflet." [We] need not decide here any broad issue of whether private property can be declared a public forum by simple governmental decree. That is not what happens in the creation of public access channels. Rather, in return for granting cable operators easements to use public rights-of-way for their cable lines, local governments have bargained for a right to use cable lines for public access channels. [It] seems to me clear that when a local government contracts to use private property for public expressive activity [in this manner], it creates a public forum.

b. Justice Stevens:

In my view, [Congress has not] established a public forum. [When] the federal government opens cable channels that would otherwise be left in private hands, it deserves more deference than a rigid application of the public forum doctrine would allow. At this early stage in the regulation of this developing industry, Congress should not be put to an all or nothing-at-all choice in deciding whether to open certain cable channels to programmers who would otherwise lack the resources to participate in the marketplace of ideas. [If] the Government had a reasonable basis for concluding that there were already enough classical musical programs or cartoons being telecast—or, perhaps, even enough political debate—I would find no First Amendment objection to an open access requirement that was extended on an impartial basis to all but those particular subjects. A contrary conclusion would ill-serve First Amendment values by dissuading the Government from creating access rights altogether.

c. Justice Thomas, joined by Chief Justice Rehnquist and Justice Scalia:

[P]ublic access channels are [not] public fora. [Cable] systems are not public property. Cable systems are privately owned and privately managed, and [there is] no case is which we have held that government may designate private property as a public forum. [It] may be true [that] title is not dispositive of the public forum analysis, but the nature of the regulatory restrictions placed on cable operators by local franchising authorities are not consistent with the kinds of governmental property interests we have said may be formally dedicated as public fora. Our public forum cases have involved property in which the government has held at least some formal easement or other property interest permitting the government to treat the property as its own in designating the property as a public forum. That is simply not true [here]. [Public] access requirements [are merely] a regulatory restriction on the exercise of cable operators' editorial discretion, not a transfer of a sufficient property interest in the channels to support a designation of that property as a public forum.

Page 1376.   After section 6 of the Note, add the following:

ARKANSAS EDUCATIONAL TELEVISION COMMISSION v. FORBES, — S.Ct. — (1998): The AETC is a state agency that owns and operates a network of five noncommercial television stations in Arkansas. In 1992, the AETC planned a series of debates between candidates for federal office. Given the time constraints of such debates, the AETC decided to limit participation "to the major party candidates or any other candidate who had strong popular support." Forbes, an independent candidate for Congress, had satisfied the Arkansas requirement that he obtain 2,000 signatures to qualify him to appear on the ballot, but the AETC nonetheless refused to include him in the debates because he "had not generated appreciable voter support" and "was not regarded as a serious candidate by the press." It was undisputed that the AETC did not exclude Forbes because of any "disagreement with his views." Forbes claimed that his exclusion violated the First Amendment.

The Court, in an opinion by Justice Kennedy, rejected this claim. At the outset, the Court concluded that, as a general matter, the public forum doctrine was inapplicable to the activities of a state-owned television station:

In the case of television broadcasting, [broad] rights of access for outside speakers would be antithetical, as a general rule, to the discretion that stations [must] exercise to fulfill their journalistic purpose. [As] a general rule, the nature of editorial discretion counsels against subjecting broadcasters to claims of viewpoint discrimination. Programming decisions would be particularly vulnerable to claims of this type because even principled exclusions, rooted in sound journalistic judgment, can often be characterized as viewpoint-based. [Much] like a university selecting a commencement speaker, [or] a public school prescribing its curriculum, a broadcaster by its nature will facilitate the expression of some viewpoints instead of others.

Thus, "as a general matter," a state-owned television station is not a nonpublic forum, but "not a forum at all," and the ordinary requirement of viewpoint-neutrality, which governs nonpublic fora, does not apply.

Although concluding that "public broadcasting as a general matter does not lend itself to scrutiny under the forum doctrine," the Court nonetheless found that "candidate debates" are subject to the doctrine:

> For two reasons, a candidate debate [is] different from other programming. First, [the] debate was by design a forum for political speech by the candidates. Consistent with the long tradition of candidate debates, the implicit representation of the broadcaster was that the views expressed were those of the candidates, not its own. The very purpose of the debate was to allow the candidates to express their views with minimal intrusion by the broadcaster. In this respect the debate differed even from a political talk show, whose host can express partisan views and then limit the discussion to those views. Second, in our tradition, candidate debates are of exceptional significance in the electoral process. [Thus, although] in many cases it is not feasible for the broadcaster to allow unlimited access to a candidate debate, [the] requirement of neutrality remains, [and] a broadcaster cannot grant or deny access [on] the basis of whether it agrees with a candidate's views. [The] special characteristics of candidate debates support the conclusion that the AETC debate was a forum of some type.

The Court next turned to the question whether the debate was a designated public forum or a nonpublic forum:

> To create a [designated public forum], the government must intend to make the property "generally available" to a class of speakers. [A] designated public forum is not created when the government allows selective access for individual speakers rather than general access for a class of speakers. [Citing *Perry* and *Cornelius*.] These cases illustrate the distinction between "general access," which indicates the property is a designated public forum, and "selective access," which indicates the property is a nonpublic forum. On the one hand, the government creates a designated public forum when it makes its property generally available to a certain class of speakers, as the university made its facilities generally available to student groups in *Widmar*. On the other hand, the government does not create a designated public forum when it does no more than reserve eligibility for access to the forum to a particular class of speakers, whose members must then, as individuals, "obtain permission" to use it. For instance, the [government] did not create a designated public forum in *Cornelius* when it reserved eligibility for participation in the CFC drive to charitable agencies, and then made individual, non-ministerial judgments as to which of the eligible agencies would participate. [This] distinction [furthers] First Amendment interests. By recognizing the distinction, we encourage the government to open its property to some

expressive activity in cases where, if faced with an all-or-nothing choice, it might not open the property at all.

Applying this analysis, the Court held that the "AETC debate was not a designated public forum":

> Here, the debate did not have an open-microphone format. [The] AETC did not make its debate generally available to candidates for [this congressional] seat. Instead, just as the [government] in *Cornelius* reserved eligibility for participation in the CFC program to certain classes of voluntary agencies, AETC reserved eligibility for participation in the debate to candidates for [this congressional] seat (as opposed to some other seat). At that point, just as the government in *Cornelius* made agency-by-agency determinations as to which of the eligible agencies would participate in the CFC, AETC made candidate-by-candidate determinations as to which of the eligible candidates would participate in the debate. "Such selective access, unsupported by evidence of a purposeful designation for public use, does not create a public forum." Thus the debate was a nonpublic forum.

To bolster this conclusion, the Court observed that a contrary holding "would result in less speech, not more [because] a public television editor might, with reason, decide that the inclusion of all ballot-qualified candidates [in the debates] would 'actually undermine the educational value and quality of debates'" and therefore cancel the debates altogether.

Finally, applying the standard for exclusions from a nonpublic forum, the Court concluded that the decision to exclude Forbes "because he had generated no appreciable public support" was constitutionally permissible because it was not "based on the speaker's viewpoint" and was "reasonable in light of the purpose of the property."

Justice Stevens, joined by Justices Souter and Ginsburg, dissented. Although agreeing with the general analysis of the Court, Justice Stevens objected that the broad "flexibility of AETC's purported standard" for excluding individual candidates gave it "nearly limitless discretion to exclude Forbes from the debate based on ad hoc justifications":

> [T]he First Amendment will not tolerate arbitrary definitions of the scope of the forum. [The] dispositive issue in this case, then, is not whether AETC created a designated public forum or a nonpublic forum, [but] whether AETC defined the contours of the debate forum with sufficient specificity to justify the exclusion of a ballot-qualified candidate. [The] importance of avoiding arbitrary or viewpoint-based exclusions from political debates militates strongly in favor of requiring the controlling state agency to use (and

adhere to) pre-established, objective criteria to determine who among qualified candidates may participate.

Page 1385.   At the end of section 1 of the Note, add the following:

Consider the argument that *Rust* can be understood as a misapplication of the principle underlying *Posadas*: "Under the *Posadas* rationale, viewpoint-based suppression of speech simply was not an issue because the Court viewed casino advertising as an activity and not as speech. [The] *Rust* Court's reasoning was similar; because abortion counseling was merely an activity within the Title X project, it was not subject to traditional strictures of the First Amendment. Thus, as casino gambling was to gambling, abortion counseling was to abortion." Wells, Abortion Counseling as Vice Activity: The Free Speech Implications of *Rust v. Sullivan* and *Planned Parenthood v. Casey*, 95 Colum. L. Rev. 1724, 1749 (1995).

Page 1385.   At the end of section 2 of the Note, add the following:

Suppose a school district authorizes the student body to elect a student to speak for two or three minutes at the beginning of each home football game on a subject of her or his choice. Does this create a public forum? Suppose the students consistently elect very conservative students. Does that pose a problem? Consider Santa Fe Independent School District v. Doe, — U.S. — (2000): "'To the extent the referendum substitutes majority determinations for viewpoint neutrality it would undermine the constitutional protection the program requires. The whole theory of viewpoint-neutrality is that minority views are treated with the same respect as are majority views. Access to a public forum, for instance, does not depend upon majoritarian consent.'" [Quoting Board of Regents of University of Wisconsin v. Southworth, — U.S. — (2000), infra this Supplement]. *In Santa Fe Independent School District*, the Court invalidated under the Establishment Clause a school district policy that authorized the student body to elect a student to speak before each football game where the implicit purpose of the program was to facilitate prayer. In reaching this result, the Court rejected the argument that this policy created a public forum, or that the speaker's expression was truly "private" speech, because the school's "policy, by its terms, invites and encourages religious messages."

2A. *What's wrong with* Rust? Consider Redish and Kessler, Government Subsidies and Free Expression, 80 Minn. L. Rev. 543, 576-577 (1996):

> The problem with the [Court's analysis in *Rust*] is that it allows the government to define its subsidization programs in a wholly unchecked, self-referential manner. [The] fallacy of [this approach] becomes clear if one visualizes the subsidization of private expression exclusively in favor of such ideas as a free-market economic philosophy, or the political theories of Mao Zedong or Rush Limbaugh. [Government] may appropriately choose neutrally to fund works on family planning, on the viability of free-market economic philosophy, or on the wisdom of Mao Zedong's or Rush Limbaugh's political thought. Each of these subsidies would foster First Amendment values by adding to the public's knowledge. [But] government may not foster public acceptance of its own viewpoints on these issues by manipulating private expression [in a viewpoint-based manner].

Consider also Post, Subsidized Speech, 106 Yale L. J. 151, 152, 155, 157, 164, 169-170, 173-174 (1996):

> . . . Subsidized speech [forces] us to determine whether subsidies should be characterized as government regulations imposed on persons or instead as a form of government participation in the marketplace of ideas. [The] Court's point [in *Rosenberger*] is that when the state itself speaks it may adopt a determinate content and viewpoint, even "when it enlists private entities to convey its own message." But when the state attempts to restrict the independent contributions of citizens to public discourse, even if those contributions are subsidized, First Amendment rules prohibiting content and viewpoint discrimination will apply. The reasoning of *Rosenberger* thus rests on two premises. First, speech may be subsidized and yet remain within public discourse; the mere fact of subsidization is not sufficient to justify classifying speech as within or outside public discourse. Second, substantive First Amendment analysis will depend on whether the citizen who speaks is characterized as a public functionary or as an independent participant in public discourse.
>
> . . . The public forum cases provide the most obvious illustration of how persons can receive government benefits and nevertheless remain within public discourse. [Publications] that receive the "subsidy" extended by the United States to second-class mail provide another example of subsidized speech that receives significant First Amendment protection. . . .
>
> Public discourse must be distinguished from domains that I have [called] "managerial." Within managerial domains, the state organizes its resources so as to achieve specified ends. [Managerial] domains are necessary so that a

democratic state can actually achieve objectives that have been democratically agreed upon. Yet managerial domains are organized along lines that contradict the premises of democratic self-governance. For this reason, First Amendment doctrine within managerial domains differs fundamentally from First Amendment doctrine within public discourse. [Thus] the state can regulate speech within public educational institutions so as to achieve the purposes of education; it can regulate speech within the judicial system so as to attain the ends of justice; it can regulate speech within the military so as to preserve the national defense; it can regulate the speech of public employees so as to promote the efficiency of the public services [the government] performs through its employees. . . . [For analysis of the regulation of speech is these contexts, see infra sections F-1 and F-2.]

As a result of this instrumental orientation, viewpoint discrimination occurs frequently within managerial domains. To give but a few obvious examples: the president may fire cabinet officials who publicly challenge rather than support administration policies; the military may discipline officers who publicly attack rather than uphold the principle of civilian control over the armed forces; [and] public defenders who prosecute instead of defend their clients may be sanctioned. . . . Viewpoint discrimination occurs within managerial domains whenever the attainment of legitimate managerial objectives requires it.

[In *Rust*, it is at least] superficially plausible to locate [the speech of the Title X clinics and their employees] within a managerial domain established by Title X. [The argument] would be that Congress enacted Title X to accomplish certain purposes, that these purposes are legitimate, and that the HHS regulations function within this managerial domain to regulate speech so as to achieve these purposes. [By] upholding the HHS regulations, [the] Court in *Rust* in effect stated that [even "viewpoint discriminatory"] regulations within managerial domains would not be deemed [unconstitutional] so long as they were necessary to accomplish legitimate managerial ends.

In the end, however, Professor Post concludes that "the Court in *Rust* lacked justification for its implicit decision to allocate medical counseling to the managerial domain" because if the government "were to control the independent judgment" of the physician, the government's control "might conflict with the [physician's] primary and unequivocal duty [as a professional] to exercise his or her independent judgment." Because "neither the role of physician nor that of patient warrants any inference of acceptance of such a purely instrumental orientation," the "viewpoint discrimination inherent in the HHS regulations cannot be justified by reference to managerial authority."

Page 1386.   After the Note, add the following:

NATIONAL ENDOWMENT FOR THE ARTS v. FINLEY, — S.Ct. — (1998): Since its creation by Congress in 1965, the NEA has made more than 100,000 grants, totaling some three billion dollars, to promote "public knowledge, education, understanding and appreciation of the arts." In 1989, two provocative works that were supported by NEA grants—a series of homoerotic photographs by Robert Mapplethorpe and a photograph by Andres Serrano that depicted a crucifix immersed in urine ("Piss Christ")—prompted a public controversy that led to a congressional reevaluation of the NEA's funding priorities and procedures. Thus, in 1990 Congress enacted §954(d)(1), which directs the NEA, in establishing procedures to judge the artistic merit of grant applications, to "tak[e] into consideration general standards of decency and respect for the diverse beliefs and values of the American public." In implementing this provision, the NEA concluded that it was not required to do anything more than ensure that its peer review panels were constituted in such a way as to represent geographic, ethnic and aesthetic diversity.

The Court, in an opinion by Justice O'Connor, held that §954(d)(1) is not unconstitutional "on its face": "Respondents argue that the provision is a paradigmatic example of viewpoint discrimination. [But the challenged provision merely] adds 'considerations' to the grant-making process; it does not preclude awards to projects that might be deemed 'indecent' or 'disrespectful,' [or] even specify that those factors be given any particular weight in reviewing an application. . . .

"[Moreover], the considerations that the provision introduces [do] not engender the kind of directed viewpoint discrimination that would prompt this Court to invalidate a statute on its face. [The considerations enumerated in §954(d)(1) are] susceptible to multiple interpretations, [and particularly because the NEA considers grant applications through the decisions of many diverse review panels], the provision does not introduce considerations that, in practice, would effectively preclude or punish the expression of particular views."

Although acknowledging that the provision could conceivably be applied in ways that could violate the first amendment, the Court was "reluctant . . . to invalidate legislation 'on the basis of its hypothetical application to situations not before the Court,'" particularly where, as here, there are numerous "constitutional applications" for both the "decency" and "respect" criteria. For example, "educational programs are central to the NEA's mission," and "it is well-established that 'decency' is a permissible factor where 'educational suitability' motivates its consideration. [Citing *Pico*.]" And "permissible applications of the mandate to consider 'respect for the diverse beliefs and values of the American public' are also apparent, [for the] agency expressly takes diversity into account, giving special consideration to 'projects and productions . . . that reach, or reflect the culture of, a minority, inner city, rural, or tribal community.'"

The Court was unpersuaded that "the language of §954(d)(1) itself will give rise to the suppression of protected expression": "Any content-based considerations that may be taken into account in the grant-making process are a consequence of the nature of arts funding. The NEA has limited resources and it must deny the majority of the grant applications that it receives, including many that propose 'artistically excellent' projects. The agency may decide to fund particular projects for a wide variety of reasons, 'such as the technical proficiency of the artist, the creativity of the work, the anticipated public interest in or appreciation of the work, the work's contemporary relevance, its educational value, its suitability for or appeal to special audiences (such as children or the disabled), its service to a rural or isolated community, or even simply that the work could increase public knowledge of an art form.' [The] very 'assumption' of the NEA is [that] absolute neutrality is simply 'inconceivable.'"

The Court therefore distinguished its decision in *Rosenberger* on the ground that, in "the context of arts funding, in contrast to many other subsidies, the Government does not indiscriminately 'encourage a diversity of views from private speakers.' The NEA's mandate is to make aesthetic judgments, and the inherently content-based 'excellence' threshold for NEA support sets it apart from the subsidy issue in *Rosenberger*— which was available to all student organizations that were 'related to the educational purpose of the University' — and from comparably objective decisions on allocating public benefits, such as access to a school auditorium or a municipal theater, [citing *Lamb's Chapel* and *Southeastern Promotions*]."

The Court emphasized that "we have no occasion here to address an as-applied challenge in a situation where the denial of a grant may be shown to be the product of invidious viewpoint discrimination. If the NEA were to leverage its power to award subsidies on the basis of subjective criteria into a penalty on disfavored viewpoints, then we would confront a different case. [Even] in the provision of subsidies, the Government may not 'ai[m] at the suppression of dangerous ideas,' and if a subsidy were 'manipulated' to have a 'coercive effect,' then relief could be appropriate. In addition, as the NEA itself concedes, a more pressing constitutional question would arise if government funding resulted in the imposition of a disproportionate burden calculated to drive 'certain ideas or viewpoints from the marketplace.'". . .

"Finally, although the First Amendment certainly has application in the subsidy context, we note that the Government may allocate competitive funding according to criteria that would be impermissible were direct regulation of speech or a criminal penalty at stake. So long as legislation does not infringe on other constitutionally protected rights, Congress has wide latitude to set spending priorities. [Citing *Regan*.] [In 1990,] Congress modified the declaration of purpose in the NEA's enabling act to provide that arts funding should 'contribute to public support and confidence in the use of taxpayer funds,' and that '[p]ublic funds . . . must ultimately serve public purposes the Congress defines.' And as we held in *Rust*, Congress may 'selectively fund a program to encourage certain activities it believes to be in the public interest, without at the same time funding an alternative program which seeks to deal with the problem in another way.' In doing so, 'the Government has not discriminated on the basis of viewpoint; it has merely chosen to fund one activity to the exclusion of the other.'"

Justice Scalia, joined by Justice Thomas, concurred in the result: "[Under the challenged provision, to] the extent a particular applicant exhibits disrespect for the diverse beliefs and values of the American public or fails to comport with general standards of decency, the likelihood that he will receive a grant diminishes. [This] unquestionably constitutes viewpoint discrimination. That conclusion is not altered by the fact that the statute does not 'compel' the denial of funding, any more than a provision imposing a five-point handicap on all black applicants for civil service jobs is saved from being race discrimination by the fact that it does not compel the rejection of black applicants. [And] the conclusion of viewpoint discrimination is not affected by the fact that what constitutes 'decency' or 'the diverse beliefs and values of the American people' is difficult to pin down, any more than a civil-service preference in favor of those who display 'Republican-party values' would be rendered nondiscriminatory by the fact that there is plenty of room for argument as to what 'Republican-party values' might be. [I] turn, then, to whether such viewpoint discrimination violates the Constitution. . . .

"[The challenged provision does] not *abridge* the speech of those who disdain the beliefs and values of the American public, nor [does] it *abridge* indecent speech. Those who wish to create indecent and disrespectful art are as unconstrained now as they were before the enactment of this statute. [They] are merely deprived of the [satisfaction] of having the [public] taxed to pay for it. It is preposterous to equate the denial of taxpayer subsidy with measures 'aimed at the *suppression* of dangerous ideas.' 'The reason that denial of participation in a tax exemption or other subsidy scheme does not necessarily "infringe" a fundamental right is that—unlike direct restriction or prohibition—such a denial does not, as a general rule, have any significant coercive effect.' One might contend, I suppose, that a threat of rejection by the only available source of free money would constitute coercion and hence 'abridgment' within the meaning of the First Amendment. [But] even if one accepts the contention, it would have no application here. The NEA is far from the sole source of funding for art—even indecent, disrespectful, or just plain bad art. Accordingly, the Government may earmark NEA funds for projects it deems to be in the public interest without thereby abridging speech. [Citing *Regan* and *Rust*.]

311

"Respondents, relying on [*Rosenberger*], argue that viewpoint-based discrimination is impermissible unless the government is the speaker or the government is 'disburs[ing] public funds to private entities to convey a governmental message.' It is impossible to imagine why that should be so; one would think that directly involving the government itself in the viewpoint discrimination [would] make the situation even worse. [But it] is the very business of government to favor and disfavor points of view, [and] it makes not a bit of difference, insofar as either common sense or the Constitution is concerned, whether these officials further their (and in a democracy, our) favored point of view by achieving it directly (having government-employed artists paint pictures); or by advocating it officially (establishing an Office of Art Appreciation); or by giving money to others who achieve or advocate it (funding private art classes). None of this has anything to do with abridging anyone's speech. [*Rosenberger*] found the viewpoint discrimination unconstitutional, not because funding of 'private' speech was involved, but because the government had established a limited public forum—to which the NEA's granting of highly selective [awards] bears no resemblance. The nub of the difference between me and the Court is that I regard the distinction between 'abridging' speech and funding it as a fundamental divide, on this side of which the First Amendment is inapplicable."

Justice Souter dissented: "The decency and respect proviso mandates viewpoint based decisions in the disbursement of government subsidies, and the Government has wholly failed to explain why the statute should be afforded an exemption from the fundamental rule of the First Amendment that viewpoint discrimination in the exercise of public authority over expressive activity is unconstitutional. '[If] there is a bedrock principle underlying the First Amendment, it is that the government may not prohibit the expression of an idea simply because society finds the idea itself offensive or disagreeable.' [Because] this principle applies not only to affirmative suppression of speech, but also to disqualification for government favors, Congress is generally not permitted to pivot discrimination against otherwise protected speech on the offensiveness or unacceptability of the views it expresses. [Citing *Rosenberger* and *Lamb's Chapel*.] One need do nothing more than read the text of [this] statute to conclude that Congress's purpose in imposing the decency and respect criteria was to prevent the funding of art that conveys an offensive message; the [provision] on its face is quintessentially viewpoint-based, [for] it penalizes [art] that disrespects the ideology, opinions, or convictions of a significant segment of the American [public, but not] art that reinforces those values. . . .

"[Moreover, that §954(d)(1)] does not preclude awards to projects that might be deemed 'indecent' or 'disrespectful' [should] make no difference at all on the question of constitutionality. What if the statute required a panel to apply [criteria] 'taking into consideration whether the artist is a communist [or] the superiority of the white race'? Would the Court hold these considerations facially constitutional, merely because the statute had no requirement to give [them] controlling, weight? I assume not. In such instances, the Court would hold that the First Amendment bars the government from considering viewpoint when it decides whether to subsidize private speech. . . .

"[Another] basic strand in the Court's [analysis], and the heart of Justice Scalia's, in effect assumes that whether or not the statute mandates viewpoint discrimination, [government] art subsidies fall within a zone of activity free from First Amendment restraints. [This argument] calls attention to the roles of government-as-speaker and government-as-buyer, in which the government is of course entitled to engage in viewpoint discrimination: if the Food and Drug Administration launches an advertising campaign on the subject of smoking, it may condemn the habit without also having to show a cowboy taking a puff on the opposite page; and if the Secretary of Defense wishes to buy a portrait to decorate the Pentagon, he is free to prefer George Washington over George the Third.

"[But the government] neither speaks through the expression subsidized by the NEA, nor buys anything itself with NEA grants. On the contrary, [in this context] the government acts as a patron, financially underwriting the production of art by private artists [for] independent consumption. [And] outside of the contexts of government-as-buyer and government-as-speaker, we have held time and again that Congress may not 'discriminate invidiously in its subsidies in such a way as to aim at the suppression of ideas.' [As we held in *Rosenberger*, when] the government acts as patron, subsidizing the expression of others, it may not prefer one lawfully stated view over another. [The Court attempts] to distinguish *Rosenberger* on the ground that the student activities funds in that case were generally available to most applicants, whereas NEA funds are disbursed selectively and competitively to a choice few. But the Court in *Rosenberger* [specifically] rejected just this distinction when it held [that] '[t]he government cannot justify viewpoint discrimination among private speakers on the economic fact of scarcity.' Scarce money demands choices, of course, but choices 'on some acceptable [viewpoint] neutral principle,' like artistic excellence; 'nothing in our decision[s] indicates that scarcity would give the State the right to exercise viewpoint discrimination that is otherwise impermissible.'"

Page 1395.   At the end of section 6 of the Note, add the following:

Kagan, Private Speech, Public Purpose: The Role of Governmental Motive in First Amendment Doctrine, 63 U. Chi. L. Rev. 415, 494-508 (1996) (arguing that the distinction between direct and incidental restrictions in first amendment analysis can be explained largely in terms of the concern with avoiding possible improper governmental motivation).

Dorf, Incidental Burdens on Fundamental Rights, 109 Harv. L. Rev. 1175 (1996) (arguing that although "sound reasons can be advanced for taking direct burdens more seriously than incidental burdens," this does not mean "that incidental burdens should never count as constitutional infringements," but concluding that only "*substantial* incidental burdens" raise "a bona fide constitutional problem"). When is an incidental burden "substantial"? Consider Stone, supra, at 114: "The general presumption is that incidental restrictions do not raise a question of first amendment review. The presumption is waived, however, whenever an incidental restriction either has a highly disproportionate impact on free expression [or] significantly limits the opportunities for free expression."

For an example of a (relatively rare) decision in which the Court has invalidated an incidental restriction on expression, see NAACP v. Alabama, infra page 1473 of the main text, in which the Court held that an Alabama statute requiring that all out-of-state corporations doing business in the State must disclose the names and addresses of all Alabama "members" was invalid as applied to the NAACP because "on past occasions revelation of the identity of [the NAACP's] rank-and-file members has exposed these members to economic reprisal, loss of employment, threat of physical coercion, and other manifestations of public hostility." The Court concluded that, "under these circumstances, [compelled] disclosure of [the NAACP's] Alabama membership is likely to adversely affect the ability of [the NAACP] and its members to pursue their [constitutional rights]."

Page 1404.   At the end of *Barnes*, add the following:

For the argument that "the outcome in *Barnes* would have been different" had Indiana attempted to apply its "statute to accepted media for the communication of ideas, as for example by attempting to prohibit nudity in movies or in the theater," see Post, Recuperating First Amendment Doctrine, 47 Stan. L. Rev. 1249, 1255-1259 (1995) (arguing that "[c]rucial to the result in *Barnes* [is] the distinction between what the Court is prepared to accept as a medium for the communication of ideas and its implicit understanding of nude dancing in nightclubs").

CITY OF ERIE v. PAP'S A.M. ___ U.S. ___ (2000): Erie, Pennsylvania, enacted an ordinance banning public nudity. The preamble stated that the "purpose" of the ordinance was to respond to "a recent increase in nude live entertainment within the City, which activity adversely impacts . . . the public health, safety and welfare by providing an atmosphere conducive to violence, sexual harassment, public intoxication, prostitution, the spread of sexually transmitted diseases and other deleterious effects." The ordinance was challenged by the owner of Kandyland, a nude dancing establishment. Does the existence of this preamble distinguish this case from *Barnes*? The Court, in a six-to-three decision, upheld the ordinance.

Justice O'Connor delivered a plurality opinion, joined by Chief Justice Rehnquist, Justice Kennedy and Justice Breyer: "The ordinance here, like the statute in Barnes, is on its face a general prohibition on public nudity. [It] bans all public nudity, regardless of whether than nudity is accompanied by expressive activity. [Moreover, the] State's interest in preventing harmful secondary effects is not related to the suppression of expression. In trying to control the secondary effects of nude dancing, the ordinance seeks to deter crime and the other deleterious effects caused by the presence of such an establishment in the neighborhood. [Citing *Renton*.]

"[E]ven if Erie's public nudity ban has some minimal effect on the erotic message by muting that portion of the expression that occurs when the last stitch is dropped, [erotic dancers] are free to perform wearing pasties and G-strings. Any effect on the overall expression is *de minimis*. . . .

"[This] case is, in fact, similar to [*O'Brien*]. The justification for the government regulation in each case prevents harmful 'secondary' effects that are unrelated to the suppression of expression. [While] the doctrinal theories behind 'incidental burdens' and 'secondary effects' are, of course, not identical, there is nothing objectionable about a city passing a general ordinance to ban public nudity (even though such a ban may place incidental burdens on some protected speech) and at the same time recognizing that one specific occurrence of public nudity – nude erotic dancing – is particularly problematic because it produces harmful secondary effects. . . .

"We conclude that Erie's asserted interest in combating the negative secondary effects associated with adult entertainment establishments [is] unrelated to the suppression of the erotic message conveyed by nude dancing. The ordinance [is] therefore valid if it satisfies the four-factor test from *O'Brien* for evaluating restrictions on symbolic speech." Justice O'Connor then went on to find that the ordinance did, indeed, satisfy the *O'Brien* test.

Justice Scalia, joined by Justice Thomas, concurred in the judgment, reaffirming his position in *Barnes* that because the public nudity ordinance is "a general law regulating conduct and not specifically directed at expression, it is not subject to First Amendment scrutiny at all." Justice Scalia argued further that the existence of the preamble is irrelevant to the constitutionality of the ordinance because it neither "make[s] the law any less general in its reach nor demonstrate[s] that what the municipal authorities *really* find objectionable is expression rather than public nakedness."

Justice Stevens, joined by Justice Ginsburg, dissented: "The Court relies on the so-called 'secondary effects' test to defend the ordinance. [But] never before have we approved the use of that doctrine to justify a total ban on protected First Amendment expression. [The ordinances upheld in *Young* and *Renton* did] not ban adult theaters altogether, but merely 'circumscribe[d] their choice as to location.' [The] reason we have limited our secondary effects cases to zoning and declined to extend their reasoning to total bans is [that a] dispersal [is] a minimal imposition whereas a total ban is the most exacting of restrictions. The State's interest in fighting presumed secondary effects is sufficiently strong to justify the former, but far too weak to support the latter, more severe burden. . . .

'The Court is also quite mistaken in equating our secondary effects cases with the 'incidental burdens' doctrine applied in cases such as *O'Brien*; and it aggravates the error by invoking the latter line of cases to support its assertion that Erie's ordinance is unrelated to speech. [Either] Erie's ordinance was not aimed at speech and the Court may attempt to justify the regulation under the incidental burdens test, or Erie has aimed its law at the secondary effects of speech, and the Court can try to justify the law under that doctrine. But it cannot conflate the two. . . .

"The censorial purpose of Erie's ordinance precludes reliance on [*Barnes*]. As its preamble forthrightly admits, the ordinance's 'purpose' is to 'limit' a protected form of speech. [Moreover,] Erie's ordinance differs from the statute in *Barnes* in another respect, [for in] an earlier proceeding in this case, [the city stipulated that it had] permitted a production of [the play] Equus to proceed without prosecution [even though it included public nudity]. [Thus, unlike the statute in *Barnes*, the Erie] ordinance is deliberately targeted at Kandyland's type of nude dancing (to the exclusion of plays like Equus). [And this] narrow aim is confirmed by the expressed views of the Erie City Councilmembers who voted for this ordinance, [each of whom stated] that the ordinance was aimed specifically at nude adult establishments, and not at more mainstream forms of entertainment that include total nudity, nor even at nudity in general. [Given] that the Court has not even tried to defend the ordinance's total ban on the ground that its censorship of protected speech might be justified by an overriding state interest, it should conclude that the ordinance is patently invalid."

In her plurality opinion, Justice O'Connor offered the following response to Justice Stevens's argument about the purpose of the ordinance: "The argument that the ordinance is 'aimed' at suppressing expression through a ban on nude dancing—an argument [supported] by pointing to statements [that] the public nudity ban was not intended to apply to 'legitimate' theater productions—is really an argument that the city council [had] an illicit motive in enacting the ordinance. [But] this Court will not strike down an otherwise constitutional statute on the basis of an alleged illicit motive. [Citing *O'Brien*.]"

Justice Souter also dissented, arguing that the appropriate level of scrutiny in this case requires the "government to make some demonstration of an evidentiary basis for the harm it claims to flow from the expressive activity, and for the alleviation expected from the restriction imposed." Justice Souter maintained that "the record before us today is deficient in its failure to reveal any evidence on which Erie may have relied, either for the seriousness of the threatened harm or for the efficacy of its chosen remedy." Finally, Justice Souter confessed that his "dissent rests on a demand for an evidentiary basis that I failed to make when I concurred in *Barnes*," explaining that "I have come to believe that a government must toe the mark more carefully than I first insisted."

In response to this argument, Justice O'Conner noted that cases like *Barnes, Renton* and *O'Brien* did not require such specific evidentiary proof, and that in this situation Erie could reasonably rely upon information "generated by other cities" and "the experience of the local government."

Page 1419.   After the quotation from BeVier, add the following:

Consider Kagan, Private Speech, Public Purpose: The Role of Governmental Motive in First Amendment Doctrine, 63 U. Chi. L. Rev. 415, 467-475 (1996):

> In what has become one of the most castigated passages in modern First Amendment case law, the Court pronounced in *Buckley v. Valeo* that "the concept that government may restrict the speech of some elements of our society in order to enhance the relative voice of others is wholly foreign to the First Amendment. . . ." [The] *Buckley* principle emerges not from the view that redistribution of speech opportunities is itself an illegitimate end, but from the view that governmental actions justified as redistributive devices often (though not always) stem partly from hostility or sympathy toward ideas—or, even more commonly, from self-interest. [The] nature of [such] regulations, as compared with other content-neutral regulations, creates [a special problem]: that governmental officials (here, legislators) more often will take account of improper factors. [This] increased probability of taint arises [from] the very design of laws directed at equalizing the realm of public expression. Unlike most content-neutral regulations, these laws not only have, but are supposed to have, content-based effects. . . . In considering such a law, a legislator's own views of the ideas (or speakers) that the equalization effort means to suppress or promote may well intrude, consciously or not, on her decision making process. [Thus,] there may be good reason to distrust the motives of politicians when they apply themselves to reconstructing the realm of expression.

Page 1420.   Before section 2 of the Note, add the following:

Consider also the following views:

a. Blasi, How Campaign Spending Limits Can Be Reconciled with the First
Amendment, 7 The Responsive Community 1, 5-8 (1996-97):

> *Buckley* was a defensible decision when it was rendered in 1976. Enter
> next the law of unintended consequences. The combination of strict limits on
> the size of direct financial contributions to candidates (upheld in *Buckley*)
> and no limits on candidate spending (the result of *Buckley's* invalidation of
> spending limits) left standing an incoherent patchwork regime of campaign
> finance regulation. Then came breakthroughs in expensive but effective elec-
> toral techniques such as focus group research, tracking polls, Madison Ave-
> nue-style advertising, and demographically targeted direct mail. Today can-
> didates need a great deal of money if they are to compete, but they cannot
> raise it in the traditional, relatively efficient way, i.e., from a small number
> of large donors. So instead challengers and incumbents alike must beat the
> bushes—day after day, week after week, year after year—to accumulate
> dizzying numbers of small contributions.
>
> This is a terrible way for representatives and would-be representatives to
> be spending their time. [Opponents] of spending limits no doubt will argue
> that the government has no more business deciding how large a role fund-
> raising should play in the electoral process than it has prescribing a "bal-
> anced" public discourse. . . . As a matter of First Amendment principle,
> however, the two objectives are very different. Any effort to balance public
> debate or protect voters from too much campaign speech places government
> in the role of saving listeners from their own cognitive susceptibilities. Such
> paternalism in the realm of ideas is [constitutionally disfavored]. When cam-
> paign spending is regulated in order to reduce candidate fundraising chores
> rather than protect audiences, the traditional First Amendment antipaternal-
> ism principle is not implicated. [What] makes the fundraising-control ration-
> ale for spending limits constitutionally legitimate is that the harm sought to
> be remedied is a product not of the communicative impact of speech but of
> the practices that generate the speech. Legislatures have far more leeway to
> regulate such practices than to attempt to forestall or alter communicative ef-
> fects.

b. Baker, Campaign Expenditures and Free Speech, 33 Harv. C.R.-C.L. L.
Rev. 1, 21-25, 46 (1998):

> Within institutions of democratic governance, acceptable regulation of
> speech, including content regulation, is ubiquitous. Restrictions occur, for

example, [in] Congress and before its committees. [Similarly, in a court-room], a combination of court rules and the judge's discretion [determines] who speaks and whether particular content is barred. . . . [The] electoral process [should] be viewed as a special governmental institution [designed] to further the governing process. [Thus], the determinative issue in a First Amendment challenge to a restriction on campaign speech should be the restriction's effect on the openness and fairness of the electoral process. [Under this approach], candidates enter campaigns the way trial participants enter a courtroom, officials enter a legislative hall, or witnesses appear before an agency hearing. Their speech can be legally restricted [by] rules that further the proper functioning of the particular institution. [This] approach does not abandon constitutional protection for speech in the campaign context, [but it significantly] changes the First Amendment analysis [from that employed in *Buckley*].

c. Sullivan, Political Money and Freedom of Speech, 30 U.C. Davis L. Rev. 663, 664, 667-673 (1997):

[T]he view that political money should be limited has become mainstream orthodoxy. [Arguments] for greater limits on political contributions and expenditures typically suggest that any claims for individual liberty to spend political money ought yield to an overriding interest in a well-functioning democracy. But what is meant by democracy here? [For example, one] argument for campaign finance limits is that they further individual rights to political equality among voters in an election. [Reformers] often proceed from the premise of equal suffrage in elections to the conclusion that equalization of speaking power in electoral campaigns is similarly justifiable in furtherance of democracy. [The extreme version of this principle] would be one person, one vote, one dollar. [But there] is an alternative possibility: that political finance more resembles political speech than voting. That is the analogy drawn by the *Buckley* Court, [and] the choice of analogy is crucial. In the formal realm of voting — like other formal governmental settings, such as legislative committee hearings and trials in court — speech may be constrained in the interest of the governmental function in question. [By] contrast, in the informal realm of political speech — the kind that goes on continuously between elections as well as during them — conventional First Amendment principles generally preclude a norm of equality of influence.

d. Smith, Money Talks: Speech, Corruption, Equality and Campaign Finance, 86 Geo. L.J. 45, 71 (1997):

When we look at the literature of campaign finance reform and the public policy decisions that upset those in favor of greater regulation to "enhance" free speech, it seems doubtful that any reform measure would pass a content neutrality test. Indeed, those who argue that campaign finance regulation is constitutional if it is content neutral fail to understand the point of the entire exercise. Regulations are proposed precisely because certain "experts" believe that some views — which they do not like — are heard too much, and other views — which they prefer — are heard too little.

Page 1425. Before section 1 of the Note, add the following:

1a. *Corporate speakers.* To what extent, if any, should corporations enjoy the freedom of speech? In Pacific Gas & Electric Co. v. Public Utilities Commission of California, section F3, infra, page 1468 of the main volume, Chief Justice Rehnquist observed in a separate opinion that "[e]xtension of [first amendment protection to corporations based on] individual freedom of conscience [strains] the rationale [of the first amendment beyond] the breaking point. To ascribe to such artificial entities an 'intellect' or 'mind' [is] to confuse metaphor with reality." Consider also Bezanson, Institutional Speech, 80 Iowa L. Rev. 735, 755, 761, 739 (1995):

[S]peech is fundamentally a human act, [and] for purposes of the First Amendment, protected speech is primarily a product of the human act of speaking. [Under] the First Amendment, meaning and intention, speech and authorship, are inextricably tied together, and therefore it is critically important that protected speech originate in a human agent acting in a willful communicative way to express his or her ideas. . . .

[T]he First Amendment contains within it two theoretical elements: one concerning individual liberty and freedom of thought, and the other concerning the value of free information and opinion in a democratic and free society. [The] First Amendment should be understood as principally [a] protection for individual speech, or speech that reflects an individual's liberty to engage in the voluntary and intentional act of expressing his or her own beliefs. [Institutional] speech, in contrast, is abstracted from the individual. [It] has nothing to do with liberty and no necessary relationship to freedom, a term that is meaningless outside the context of individuals. [Institutional speech] can lay no legitimate claim to protection under the heading of individual liberty, and thus must be assessed only in terms of the second element relating to the functional value of speech in a democratic and free society. [Institutional] speech, therefore, should be protected by a separate and distinct framework [and] should be judged not by standards of freedom, but by broader and more forgiving criteria that relate to the information needed by the members of a free and self-governing society. Such criteria would permit not only an assessment of institutional speech's value, but also its manner of presentation (accuracy, for example) and the medium of its distribution (fairness, access, and market conditions).

## Page 1425.	Before section 2 of the Note, add the following:

1a. *Regulating political parties*. After *Buckley*, can the government constitutionally limit the amount a political party can spend in support of its own candidates? Are such expenditures "contributions" or "expenditures" within the meaning of *Buckley*? In Colorado Republican Federal Campaign Committee v. Federal Election Commission, 116 S. Ct.2309(1996), the Court considered the constitutionality of a provision of the Federal Election Campaign Act that imposes dollar limits on political party "expenditures in connection with the general election campaign of a [congressional] candidate." In a plurality opinion, Justice Breyer, joined by Justices O'Connor and Souter, held that, under *Buckley*, the first amendment prohibits the application of this provision to expenditures that the political party makes "independently, without coordination with a candidate," but found it unnecessary to decide whether the provision would be unconstitutional as applied to coordinated expenditures.

In a separate opinion, Justice Kennedy, joined by Chief Justice Rehnquist and Justice Scalia, went further and concluded that the first amendment prohibits the application of this provision even to expenditures that a political party makes "in cooperation, consultation, or concert [with] a candidate." Although the Act characterizes such expenditures as "contributions," which ordinarily would be regulable under *Buckley*, Justice Kennedy argued that "political party spending" in this manner "does not fit within our description of 'contributions' in *Buckley*":

> It makes no sense [to] ask [whether] a party's spending is made "in cooperation, consultation, or concert with" its candidate. [It] would be impractical and imprudent [for] a party to support its own candidates without some form of "cooperation" or "consultation." The party's speech, legitimate on its own behalf, cannot be separated from speech on the candidate's behalf without constraining the party in advocating its most essential positions and pursuing its most basic goals. [Party] spending "in cooperation, consultation, or concert with" a candidate [is] indistinguishable in substance from expenditures by the candidate. . . . We held in *Buckley* that the First Amendment does not permit regulations of the latter, and it should not permit this regulation of the former.

In another separate opinion, Justice Thomas, joined by Chief Justice Rehnquist and Justice Scalia, agreed with Justice Kennedy:

As applied in the specific context of campaign funding by political parties, the anti-corruption rationale [relied on by the Court in *Buckley* to uphold contribution limitations] loses its force. What could it mean for a party to "corrupt" its candidate or to exercise "coercive" influence over him? The very aim of a political party is to influence its candidate's stance on issues and, if the candidate takes [office], his votes. When [a Party] spends large sums of money in support of a candidate who wins, takes office, and then implements the Party's platform, that is not corruption; that is successful advocacy of ideas in the political marketplace and representative government in a party system.

Justice Stevens, joined by Justice Ginsburg, dissented on the ground that "all money spent by a political party to secure the election of its candidate [should] be considered a [regulable] 'contribution,'" whether or not the expenditure is made "in cooperation, consultation, or concert" with the candidate's campaign. Justice Stevens argued that "such limits serve the interest in avoiding both the appearance and the reality of a corrupt political process," they are necessary to "supplement other spending limitations [which] are likewise designed to prevent corruption," and they serve the government's "important interest in leveling the playing field by constraining the cost of federal campaigns."

Page 1425.   At the end of section 2 of the Note, add the following:

See also Buckley v. American Constitutional Law Foundation, ___ U.S. ___ (1999), in which the Court, relying upon *Meyer*, invalidated a state law providing that (a) only registered voters may circulate ballot-initiative petitions; (b) petition circulators must wear a badge identifying them by name; and (c) ballot-initiative proponents must file a report listing each petition circulator by name and stating the amount paid to each circulator.

Page 1426.   After the cite to Burdick v. Takushi in section 4 of the Note, add the following:

Timmons v. Twin Cities Area New Party, 117 S. Ct. 1364 (1997) (upholding a ban on multi-party, or "fusion," candidacies); California Democratic Party v. Jones, ___ U.S. ___ (2000) (invalidating a state law permitting individuals who are not members of a political party to vote in that party's primary).

Page 1426.   At the end of the Note, add the following:

5. *State contribution limits and the future of* Buckley. In Nixon v. Shrink Missouri Government PAC, ___ U.S. ___ (2000), the Court upheld a Missouri statute imposing limits ranging from $275 to $1,075 on contributions to candidates for state offices (different limits were applicable to different offices). In an opinion by Justice Souter, the Court held that *Buckley* "is authority for state limits on contributions to state political candidates" and that it authorizes "comparable state regulation, which need not be pegged to *Buckley's* dollars." The Court rejected the argument that "Buckley set a minimum constitutional threshold for contribution limits, which in dollars adjusted for loss of purchasing power are now well above the lines drawn by Missouri." Rather, in *"Buckley,* we specifically rejected the contention that $1,000, or any other amount, was a constitutional minimum below which legislatures could not regulate. [W]e referred instead to the outer limits of contribution regulation by asking whether there was any showing that the limits were so low as to impede the ability of candidates to 'amas[s] the resources necessary for effective advocacy.'" The Court found no such showing in this case.

Justice Kennedy dissented: "[T]he compromise the Court invented in *Buckley* set the stage for a new kind of speech to enter the political system. It is covert speech. The Court has forced a substantial amount of political speech underground, as contributors and candidates devise ever more elaborate methods of avoiding contribution limits, limits which take no account of rising campaign costs. The preferred method has been to conceal the real purpose of the speech. Soft money may be contributed to political parties in unlimited amounts [citing *Colorado Republican Federal Campaign Comm.*], and is often used to fund so-called issue advocacy, advertisements that promote or attack a candidate's positions without specifically urging his or her election or defeat. Issue advocacy, like soft money, is unrestricted [citing *Buckley*], while straightforward speech in the form of financial contributions paid to a candidate, speech subject to full disclosure and prompt evaluation by the public, is not. [This] mocks the First Amendment. [I] would overrule *Buckley.* . . . ."

Justice Thomas, joined by Justice Scalia, also dissented: "[O]ur decision in *Buckley* was in error, and I would overrule it. I would subject campaign contribution limitations to strict scrutiny, under which Missouri's contribution limits are patently unconstitutional. ['P]reventing corruption or the appearance of corruption are [legitimate] and compelling interests, [but] the State's contribution limits are not narrowly tailored to that harm. The limits directly suppress the political speech of both contributors and candidates, and only clumsily further the governmental interests that they allegedly serve. They are crudely tailored because they are massively overinclusive, prohibiting all donors who wish to contribute in excess of the cap from doing so and restricting donations without regard to whether the donors pose any real corruption risk. [Moreover], the government has less restrictive means of addressing its interest in curtailing corruption. Bribery laws bar precisely the *quid pro quo* arrangements that are targeted here. And disclosure laws "'deter actual corruption and avoid the appearance of corruption by exposing large contributions and expenditures to the light of publicity.'" [In] the end, contribution limits find support only in the proposition that other means will not be as effective at rooting out corruption. But when it comes to a significant infringement on our fundamental liberties, that some undesirable conduct may or may not be deterred is an insufficient justification to sweep in vast amounts of protected political speech. [Citing Martin v. Struthers; Schenider v. State.]"

Page 1432.   After the first sentence of the second paragraph of section 1 of the Note, add the following:

See California Democratic Party v. Jones, — U.S. — (2000) (invalidating a state law permitting individuals who are not members of a political party to vote in that party's primary).

Page 1433.   After the Note on Association and the First Amendment, add the following:

BOY SCOUTS OF AMERICA v. DALE. ___ U.S. ___ (2000): Dale's position as an adult scoutmaster in the Boy Scouts was revoked when the Boy Scouts learned that he is an "avowed homosexual" and a gay rights activist. New Jersey's public accommodations law, which prohibits discrimination on the basis of sexual orientation, was interpreted by the New Jersey courts to prohibit the Boy Scouts from revoking Dale's position. The Court, in a five-to-four decision, held that this application of the New Jersey public accommodations law violates the Boy Scouts' First Amendment right of expressive association.

Chief Justice Rehnquist delivered the opinion of the Court: In *Roberts,* we observed that 'implicit in the right to engage in activities protected by the First Amendment' is 'a corresponding right to associate with others in pursuit of a wide variety of political, social, economic, educational, religious, and cultural ends.' This right is crucial in preventing the majority from imposing its views on groups that would rather express other, perhaps unpopular, ideas. [Government] actions that may unconstitutionally burden this freedom may take many forms, one of which is [a] 'regulation that forces the group to accept members it does not desire.' . . .

"The forced inclusion of an unwanted person in a group infringes the group's freedom of expressive association if the presence of that person affects in a significant way the group's ability to advocate public or private viewpoints. [But] the freedom of expressive association, like many freedoms, is not absolute. We have held that the freedom could be overridden 'by regulations adopted to serve compelling state interests, unrelated to the suppression of ideas, that cannot be achieved through means significantly less restrictive of associational freedoms.' [*Roberts*].

"To determine whether a group is protected by the First Amendment's expressive associational right, we must determine whether the group engages in 'expressive association.' The First Amendment's protection of expressive association is not reserved for advocacy groups. But to come within its ambit, a group must engage in some form of expression, whether it be public or private. . . .

"The Boy Scouts is a private, nonprofit organization. According to its 'mission statement,' [the] general mission of the Boy Scouts is '[t]o instill values in young people.' The Boy Scouts seeks to instill these values by having its adult leaders spend time with the youth members, instructing and engaging them in activities like camping, archery, and fishing. During the time spent with the youth members, the scoutmasters and assistant scoutmasters inculcate them with the Boy Scouts' values -- both expressly and by example. It seems indisputable that an association that seeks to transmit such a system of values engages in expressive activity. . . .

"Given that the Boy Scouts engages in expressive activity, we must determine whether the forced inclusion of Dale as an assistant scoutmaster would significantly affect the Boy Scouts' ability to advocate public or private viewpoints. This inquiry necessarily requires us first to explore, to a limited extent, the nature of the Boy Scouts' view of homosexuality. [Although the] Boy Scout Oath and Law do not expressly mention sexuality or sexual orientation, [the] Boy Scouts asserts that it 'teach[es] that homosexual conduct is not morally straight' [and] that it does 'not want to promote homosexual conduct as a legitimate form of behavior.' [We] accept the Boy Scouts' assertion. . . .

"We must then determine whether Dale's presence as an assistant scoutmaster would significantly burden the Boy Scouts' desire to not 'promote homosexual conduct as a legitimate form of behavior.' As we give deference to an association's assertions regarding the nature of its expression, we must also give deference to an association's view of what would impair its expression. [That] is not to say that an expressive association can erect a shield against antidiscrimination laws simply by asserting that mere acceptance of a member from a particular group would impair its message. But here Dale, by his own admission, is one of a group of gay Scouts who have 'become leaders in their community and are open and honest about their sexual orientation.' Dale was the co-president of a gay and lesbian organization at college and remains a gay rights activist. Dale's presence in the Boy Scouts would, at the very least, force the organization to send a message, both to the youth members and the world, that the Boy Scouts accepts homosexual conduct as a legitimate form of behavior.

"The New Jersey Supreme Court determined that the Boy Scouts' ability to disseminate its message was not significantly affected by the forced inclusion of Dale as an assistant scoutmaster because 'Boy Scout members do not associate for the purpose of disseminating the belief that homosexuality is immoral.' [We] disagree with the New Jersey Supreme Court's [reasoning]. First, associations do not have to associate for the 'purpose' of disseminating a certain message in order to be entitled to the protections of the First Amendment. An association must merely engage in expressive activity that could be impaired in order to be entitled to protection. Second, [the] First Amendment simply does not require that every member of a group agree on every issue in order for the group's policy to be 'expressive association.' The Boy Scouts takes an official position with respect to homosexual conduct, and that is sufficient for First Amendment purposes. . . .

"Having determined that the Boy Scouts is an expressive association and that the forced inclusion of Dale would significantly affect its expression, we inquire whether the application of New Jersey's public accommodations law to require that the Boy Scouts accept Dale as an assistant scoutmaster runs afoul of the Scouts' freedom of expressive association. We conclude that it does. . . .

"We recognized in cases such as *Roberts* and *Duarte* that States have a compelling interest in eliminating discrimination against women in public accommodations. But in each of these cases we went on to conclude that the enforcement of these statutes would not materially interfere with the ideas that the organization sought to express. In *Roberts,* we said '[i]ndeed, the Jaycees has failed to demonstrate . . . any serious burden on the male members' freedom of expressive association.' We thereupon concluded in each of these cases that the organizations' First Amendment rights were not violated by the application of the States' public accommodations laws.

". . . We have already concluded that a state requirement that the Boy Scouts retain Dale as an assistant scoutmaster would significantly burden the organization's right to oppose or disfavor homosexual conduct. The state interests embodied in New Jersey's public accommodations law do not justify such a severe intrusion on the Boy Scouts' rights to freedom of expressive association. That being the case, we hold that the First Amendment prohibits the State from imposing such a requirement through the application of its public accommodations law."

Justice Stevens, joined by Justices Souter, Ginsburg and Breyer, dissented: "[Until] today, we have never once found a claimed right to associate in the selection of members to prevail in the face of a State's antidiscrimination law. To the contrary, we have squarely held that a State's antidiscrimination law does not violate a group's right to associate simply because the law conflicts with that group's exclusionary membership policy. [Citing *Roberts; Duarte.*]

"Surely there are instances in which an organization that truly aims to foster a belief at odds with the purposes of a State's antidiscrimination laws will have a First Amendment right to association that precludes forced compliance with those laws. But that right is not a freedom to discriminate at will, nor is it a right to maintain an exclusionary membership policy simply out of fear of what the public reaction would be if the group's membership were opened up. It is an implicit right designed to protect the enumerated rights of the First Amendment, not a license to act on any discriminatory impulse. To prevail in asserting a right of expressive association as a defense to a charge of violating an anti-discrimination law, the organization must at least show it has adopted and advocated an unequivocal position inconsistent with a position advocated or epitomized by the person whom the organization seeks to exclude. . . .

"Dale's inclusion in the Boy Scouts [sends] no cognizable message to the Scouts or to the world. [If] there is any kind of message being sent, then, it is by the mere act of joining the Boy Scouts. Such an act does not constitute an instance of symbolic speech under the First Amendment. [The] only apparent explanation for the majority's holding, then, is that homosexuals are simply so different from the rest of society that their presence alone—unlike any other individual's—should be singled out for special First Amendment treatment. Under the majority's reasoning, an openly gay male is irreversibly affixed with the label 'homosexual.' [Reliance] on such a justification is tantamount to a constitutionally prescribed symbol of inferiority. . . .

"Furthermore, it is not likely that BSA would be understood to send any message, either to Scouts or to the world, simply by admitting someone as a member. Over the years, BSA has generously welcomed over 87 million young Americans into its ranks. In 1992 over one million adults were active BSA members. [The] notion that an organization of that size and enormous prestige implicitly endorses the views that each of those adults may express in a non-Scouting context is simply mind boggling. Indeed, in this case there is no evidence that the young Scouts in Dale's troop, or members of their families, were even aware of his sexual [orientation]. It is equally farfetched to assert that Dale's open declaration of his homosexuality, reported in a local newspaper, will effectively force BSA to send a message to anyone simply because it allows Dale to be an Assistant Scoutmaster."

Page 1434.   At the end of the first full paragraph on the page, add the following:

Consider also Bhagwat, Purpose Scrutiny in Constitutional Analysis, 85 Calif. L. Rev. 297, 362 (1997):

> [T]he Court should abandon its current distinction between content-based and content-neutral regulations. The Court appears to employ this analysis mainly to identify improperly motivated regulations, but "content" is a poorly-suited tool for such a task. To be sure, content-based regulations are often motivated by hostility to targeted speech, which is certainly an impermissible purpose. Equally clearly, however, that is not always the case. [This] suggests that the relationship between content and purpose could be captured more accurately by a rebuttable presumption than by the current inflexible, categorical analysis. Rather than using content as a proxy for bad motive, the Court would be better served simply to conduct a direct inquiry into purpose, guided by whatever presumptions it cares to establish.

F. Additional Problems

Page 1452.   At the end of section 3 of the Note, add the following:

On the public/private speech distinction, see Gray, Public and Private Speech: Toward a Practice of Pluralistic Convergence in Free-Speech Values, 1 Tex. Wesleyan L. Rev. 1 (1994).

Page 1453.   At the end of section 4 of the Note, add the following:

5. *Independent contractors.* Wabaunsee County, Kansas, contracted with respondent for him to be the exclusive hauler of trash for cities in the county. By its terms, the contract between the county and respondent was automatically renewed annually unless either party terminated it by giving at least sixty days' notice. Respondent was an outspoken critic of the County Board of Commissioners. According to the allegations of respondent's complaint, the Board decided not to renew his contract because of his political opposition to its policies. In Board of County Commissioners, Wabaunsee County, Kansas v. Umbehr, 116 S. Ct. 2342 (1996), the Court

held that, like public employees, independent contractors are protected by the first amendment against discharge in retaliation for their speech and that "the *Pickering* balancing test, adjusted to weigh the government's interests as contractor rather than as employer, determines the extent of their protection." See also O'Hare Truck Service, Inc. v. City of Northlake, 116 S. Ct. 2353 (1996) (same result with respect to patronage).

Page 1456.   At the end of the paragraph at the bottom of the page discussing Rutan v. Republican Party of Illinois, add the following:

Do *Elrod* and *Branti* apply to independent contractors? O'Hare Truck Service, Inc. v. City of Northlake, 116 S. Ct. 2353 (1996), involved a situation in which the city coordinates towing services and maintains a rotation list of available towing companies. When petitioner refused to make a political contribution to the Mayor's reelection campaign, he was removed from the rotation list. The Court held that, in such circumstances, the protections of *Elrod* and *Branti* govern. See also Board of County Commissioners, Wabaunsee County, Kansas v. Umbehr, 116 S. Ct. 2342 (1996) (same result with respect to political expression critical of the government).

Page 1466.   At the end of *Barnette*, add the following:

Is *Barnette* wrong because reasonable observers would understand that the speech was compelled? Consider Greene, The Pledge of Allegiance Problem, 64 Fordham L. Rev. 451, 473, 482 (1995):

> For an act to be considered expressive, and thus worthy of prima facie protection under the Free Speech Clause, that act must involve (or appear to a reasonable observer to involve) the communication of the speaker's internal mental state, such as her beliefs, attitudes or convictions. [Neither] a law compelling the utterance of the pledge of allegiance nor a law compelling a left turn signal requires the agent to reveal the contents of her mind.... [Because] a reasonable observer [would] understand the teacher-led pledge of allegiance, with no opt-out provision, as compelled and thus as not reflective of the beliefs of the [students, there is no violation of the free speech clause].

Page 1470.   Before Elrod v. Burns, add the following:

On the constitutionality of applying antidiscrimination laws to groups like the Jaycees and the Boy Scouts, see Roberts v. Jaycees, 468 U.S. 609 (1984) (a law prohibiting the Jaycees from excluding women does not violate the first amendment right of expressive association), and Boy Scouts of America v. Dale, — U.S. — (2000) (a law prohibiting the Boy Scouts from excluding gays does violate the first amendment right of expression association), supra section E-5.

Page 1471. At the end of the last full paragraph on the page, add the following:

Consider also Glickman v. Wileman Brothers & Elliott, Inc., 117 S. Ct. 2130 (1997): The Agricultural Marketing Agreement Act of 1937, which is designed to maintain orderly agricultural markets, authorizes collective action by groups of agricultural producers on such matters as uniform prices, product standards, and generic advertising. The cost of such collective action, which must be approved by two-thirds of the affected producers, is covered by compulsory assessments on the producers. In *Glickman*, the Court held that marketing orders promulgated by the Secretary of Agriculture pursuant to the Act, which assessed respondent producers for the cost of generic advertising of California nectarines, plums, and peaches, did not violate respondents' First Amendment rights, even though respondents objected to the requirement that they pay for such advertising. Distinguishing *Abood*, the Court explained:

> Three characteristics of the regulatory scheme at issue distinguish it from laws that we have found to abridge [the] First Amendment. First, the marketing orders impose no restraint on the freedom of any producer to communicate any message to any audience. Second, they do not compel any person to engage in any actual or symbolic speech. Third, they do not compel the producers to endorse or to finance any political or ideological views. Indeed, since all of the respondents are engaged in the business of marketing California nectarines, plums, and peaches, it is fair to presume that they agree with the central message of the speech that is generated by the generic program. . . .
>
> None of the advertising in this record promotes any particular message other than encouraging consumers to buy California tree fruit. Neither the fact that respondents may prefer to foster that message independently in order to promote and distinguish their own products, nor the fact that they think more or less money should be spent fostering it, makes this case comparable to those in which an objection rested on political or ideological disagreement with the content of the message. The mere fact that the objectors believe their money is not being well spent 'does not mean [that] they have a First Amendment complaint.'

In such circumstances, the Court held that the challenged program did not raise "a First Amendment issue for us to resolve," but "a question of economic policy for Congress and the Executive to resolve."

Justice Souter, joined by Chief Justice Rehnquist and Justices Scalia and Thomas, dissented. Justice Souter argued that the Court had misread *Abood* as standing "for the proposition that the First Amendment places no limits on government's power to force one individual to pay for another's speech, except when the speech in question [is] ideological or political in character." In Justice's Souter's view, "forced payment for commercial speech should be subject to the same level of judicial scrutiny as any [other] restriction on [commercial speech]," whether or not it is "ideological or political in character."

Page 1472.   Before the Note, add the following:

May a state permit individuals who are not members of a political party to vote in that party's primary? In California Democratic Party v. Jones, ___ U.S. ___ (2000), the Court invalidated such a law on the ground that the challenged law "forces political parties to associate with—to have their nominees and hence their positions, determined by—those who, at best, have refused to affiliate with the party, and, at worst, have expressly affiliated with a rival." The Court explained that "freedom of association would prove an empty guarantee if associations could not limit control over their decisions to those who share the interests and persuasions that underlie the association's being."

Page 1472.   Before the Note, add the following:

BOARD OF REGENTS OF THE UNIVERSITY OF WISCONSIN SYSTEM v. SOUTHWORTH, — U.S. — (2000): The University of Wisconsin requires all full-time students to pay an annual activities fee, part of which is allocated by the student government to support registered student organizations, which engage in a broad range of expressive and other activities. Examples of the more than 600 registered students organizations at the University of Wisconsin are the College Democrats, the College Republicans, the International Socialist Organization and the Future Financial Gurus of America. Citing *Abood*, respondents challenged the constitutionality of this program on the grounds that by compelling them financially to support political and ideological expression with which they disagree the challenged program violates their first amendment right "not to speak."

In a unanimous decision, the Court rejected this challenge. Justice Kennedy authored the opinion of the Court: "In *Abood* [the] constitutional rule took the form of limiting the required subsidy to speech germane to the purposes of the [union]. The standard of germane speech as applied to student speech at a university is [unworkable]. The speech the University seeks to encourage in the program before us is distinguished not by discernable limits but by its vast, unexplored bounds. To insist upon asking what speech is germane would be contrary to the very goal the University seeks to pursue. It is not for the Court to say what is or is not germane to the ideas to be pursued in an institution of higher learning. . . .

"It is all but inevitable that the fees will result in subsidies to speech which some students find objectionable and offensive to their personal beliefs. If the standard of germane speech is inapplicable, then, it might be argued the remedy is to allow each student to list those causes which he or she will or will not support. If a university decided that its students' First Amendment interests were better protected by some type of optional or refund system it would be free to do so. We decline to impose a system of that sort as a constitutional requirement, however. The restriction would be so disruptive and expensive that the program to support extracurricular speech would be ineffective.

"The University may determine that its mission is well served if students have the means to engage in dynamic discussion of philosophical, religious, social and political subjects in their extracurricular campus life outside the lecture hall. If the University reaches this conclusion, it is entitled to impose a mandatory fee to sustain an open dialogue to these ends.

"The University must provide some protection to its students' First Amendment interests, however. The proper measure, and the principal standard of protection for objecting students, we conclude, is the requirement of viewpoint neutrality in the allocation of funding support. [Citing *Rosenberger.*] When a university requires its students to pay fees to support the extracurricular speech of other students, all in the interest of open discussion, it may not prefer some viewpoints to others. [We] conclude that the University of Wisconsin may sustain the extracurricular dimensions of its program by using mandatory student fees with viewpoint neutrality as the operational principle. [Because the] parties have stipulated that the program the University has developed to stimulate extracurricular student expression respects the principle of viewpoint neutrality, [the] program in its basic structure must be found consistent with the First Amendment."

There was one aspect of the University's program that the Court found more problematic, however. In addition to authorizing the student government to make funding decisions (subject to a University-imposed requirement of viewpoint-neutrality), funding decisions could also be made through student referenda: "[It] appears that by majority vote of the student body a given [registered student organization] may be funded or defunded. It is unclear to us what protection, if any, there is for viewpoint neutrality in this part of the process. To

the extent the referendum substitutes majority determinations for viewpoint neutrality it would undermine the constitutional protection the program requires.
The whole theory of viewpoint neutrality is that minority views are treated with
the same respect as are majority views. Access to a public forum, for instance,
does not depend upon majoritarian consent. That principle is controlling here. A
remand is necessary [to] resolve this point. . . ."

Justice Souter, joined by Justices Stevens and Breyer, filed a concurring
opinion, noting that "a cast-iron viewpoint neutrality requirement" may not be
appropriate in this setting because the very nature of universities may make such
a requirement inappropriate.

Page 1472. In section 1, after the citation to Turner Broadcasting System, Inc. v. FCC, add the following:

Denver Area Education Telecommunications Consortium, Inc. v. FCC, 116
S. Ct. 2374 (1996) (considering the constitutionality of several provisions of the
Cable Television Consumer Protection and Competition Act of 1992 concerning
the broadcasting of "indecent" programming on public access and leased access
channels);

Page 1472. After section 1 of the Note, add the following:

1A. *A coherent doctrine?* Consider Jacobs, Pledges, Parades and Mandatory
Payments, 52 Rutgers L. Rev. 123, 183-184 (1999):

> There is currently no coherent doctrine apparent in the Court's compelled
> expression cases. It is possible, however, to pick among the mass of labels
> and distinctions those considerations that should, consistent with underlying
> free speech values, guide decision of these cases. . . .
> . . . Most fundamentally, compelled expression analysis should look to
> whether the government's purpose is to manipulate the marketplace of ideas
> or whether its purpose is not related to expression. Where the government
> acts to manipulate the marketplace of ideas [*e.g., Barnette, Tornillo, PG&E,
> Wooley*], strict scrutiny applies. . . . Where the government acts for a non-
> speech purpose but incidentally compels expression or compels contribu-
> tions, some of which are used to fund expression [*e.g., Turner, Hurley
> Abood*], the government's nonspeech purpose invokes mid-level balancing
> review.

Page 1477.   At the bottom of the page, add the following:

See also Buckley v. American Constitutional Law Foundation, ___ U.S. ___ (1999), in which the Court invalidated a state law requiring petition circulators to wear a badge identifying them by name and requiring ballot-initiative proponents to file a report listing each petition circulator by name and stating the amount paid to each circulator. The Court explained that, in light of the state law requirement that ballot-initiative *sponsors* disclose how much they have spent in support of the initiative, it was unnecessary also to require disclosure of the names of the petition circulators and the amounts each was paid.

Page 1492.   At the end of section 1 of the Note, add the following:

Consider also Bezanson, Means and Ends and Food Lion: The Tension Between Exemption and Independence in Newsgathering by the Press, 47 Emory L.J. 895, 924 (1998):

> A rule that takes as its starting point [that] the press should be subject to generally applicable law respects the press's constitutional interest in independence from government. . . . Such a rule does not, however, demand an unyielding application of any form of generally applicable law. . . . Instead, it sets up a presumption, but can admit exceptions. It justifies placing the burden of persuasion and proof for an exception to the general legal rule on the press in a manner similar to the operation of the common law necessity defense. The necessity defense is a defense of common law origin that operates to excuse or justify criminal violations on a case-by-case basis. To succeed in making out the defense the defendant must show that the illegal act was taken "to avoid imminent harm; . . . that no reasonable legal alternatives existed; . . . that the harm of [the] act was not disproportional to the harm avoided; and . . . that there was a direct causal relationship between [the] act and the harm avoided."

Page 1495.   At the end of section 4 of the Note, add the following:

Should the Court hold that "plaintiffs claiming injury resulting from a tort committed during the course of gathering news" must prove "outrageous conduct" on "the part of the defendant, where the plaintiff is a public official or public figure, or where the defendant is covering government operations, or where the plaintiff seeks to recover punitive damages"? Easton, Two Wrongs

Mock a Right: Overcoming the Cohen Maledicta That Bar First Amendment Protection for Newsgathering, 58 Ohio St. L.J. 1135, 1215 (1997).

Page 1495.   After the citation to Patterson in section 5 of the Note, add the following:

Volokh & McDonnell, Freedom of Speech and Independent Judgment Review in Copyright Cases, 107 Yale L.J. 2431 (1998).

Page 1517.   At the end of section d of the Note, add the following:

e. Logan, Getting Beyond Scarcity: A New Paradigm for Assessing the Constitutionality of Broadcast Regulation, 85 Cal. L. Rev. 1687, 1709-1714 (1997):

> If the Supreme Court were to reject the scarcity rationale, the public forum doctrine could provide an alternative basis for upholding broadcast content regulation. [The] central premise of this argument is that broadcasters have been granted the exclusive use of a valuable resource — the electromagnetic specrum — which Congress has deemed to be public property. [Because] access to the spectrum [has traditionally been] limited to those broadcasters who have received a license to use the airwaves, and they [have traditionally been allowed to] program their channels as they see fit as long as they abide by their public interest obligations, [the] broadcast spectrum is best characterized as a limited designated public forum, [in which the] government may impose content-based restrictions [provided] they are "reasonable in light of the purpose served by the forum" and do not "discriminate against speech on the basis of its viewpoint."

Page 1518.   At the end of section d of the Note, add the following:

Consider the following proposal made by Reed Hundt, the Chairman of the FCC, in Hundt, The Public's Airwaves: What Does the Public Interest Require of Television Broadcasters?, 45 Duke L.J. 1089, 1099-1100, 1105-1106 (1996):

> In the aggregate, political candidates at all levels spent [$500 million in 1996] on media advertising. [The] cost of television advertising makes fundraising an enormous entry barrier for candidates seeking public office, an oppressive burden for incumbents seeking reelection, a continuous threat to the integrity of our political institutions, and a principal cause of the erosion

of public respect for public service. [To address this problem,] broadcasters should be required, [as] a condition of their licenses, to provide free airtime for political candidates. . . . [This could be accomplished by requiring] broadcasters [to] donate [$500-million worth of] airtime to [a time] bank and [authorizing] candidates [to] draw airtime from the bank during their campaigns. [How] would we divide the time contributed to a time bank? One approach would be to grant each eligible candidate a right to a specific dollar amount of free time. Candidates would then negotiate with broadcasters for advertising time, just as they currently do, but would pay with time bank credits rather than actual dollars. Why would broadcasters accept credits? Because they would be required to provide free time worth, say, 2 percent of their annual advertising revenues as a condition of using the public airwaves for free. Indeed, it would be important for broadcasters to provide time to candidates lest they lose their licenses.

Page 1525. At the end of section 1 of the Note, add the following:

Is the Court's content-based/content-neutral analysis unhelpful in cases like *Turner*? Consider Bhagwat, Of Markets and Media: The First Amendment, the New Mass Media, and the Political Components of Culture, 74 N. Car. L. Rev. 141, 176 (1995):

[T]he Court's basic [content-based/content-neutral] analysis [has] performed relatively well in defending individual speakers — generally dissidents with unpopular views — from direct censorship by the government. [That analysis assumes] an atomistic marketplace of speech, speakers, and listeners; and when those assumptions hold, the categories are generally workable. With respect to regulation of the modern mass media, however, where those assumptions assuredly do not hold, the Court's categories tend to collapse, and its [analysis] fails. What is needed [is] a rethinking [of] the underlying doctrine, based on a more realistic model of mass media markets. [S]uch a reappraisal must take into account [both] the role of the mass media in today's society, including its power to shape preferences and discourse through a process of socialization, [and] the danger that the government will seek, through regulation of the media, to take control of that process itself. . . .

Page 1525. After section 1 of the Note, add the following:

1a. Turner II. In Turner Broadcasting System, Inc. v. FCC, 117 S. Ct. 1174 (1997), the Court, in a 5-to-4 decision, upheld under "intermediate scrutiny" the constitutionality of the must-carry provisions at issue in *Turner I*, affirming the district court's decision that the expanded record presented to it on remand from *Turner I* contained substantial evidence supporting Congress' predictive judgment that the must-carry provisions further important governmental interests in preserving cable carriage of local broadcast stations, and that the provisions are narrowly tailed to promote those interests.

In reaching this conclusion, the Court, in an opinion by Justice Kennedy, emphasized that "we owe Congress' findings deference [because Congress] 'is far better equipped than the judiciary to "amass and evaluate the vast amounts of data" bearing upon' legislative questions." Moreover, the Court observed, "this principle has special significance in cases, like this one, involving congressional judgments concerning regulatory schemes of inherent complexity and assessments about the likely interaction of industries undergoing rapid economic and technological change." Thus, the Court concluded, "the issue before us is whether, given conflicting views of the probable development of the television industry, Congress had substantial evidence for making the judgment that it did. We need not put our imprimatur on Congress' economic theory in order to validate the reasonableness of its judgment," nor should we "re-weigh the evidence de novo" or "replace Congress' factual predictions with our own."

In a concurring opinion, Justice Stevens emphasized that "if this statute regulated the content of speech, rather than the structure of the market, our task would be quite different." In a separate concurring opinion, Justice Breyer noted that, unlike the plurality, which concluded that the must-carry provisions were justified in terms of each of three "important" government interests — " preserving the benefits of free, over-the-air local broadcast television; promoting the widespread dissemination of information from a multiplicity of sources; and promoting fair competition in the market for television programming" — he rested his conclusion only on the first two of these interests.

Justice O'Connor, joined by Justices Scalia, Thomas, and Ginsburg, dissented. Justice O'Connor argued that "the Court errs in two crucial respects." First, by failing to understand that the must-carry rules are content-based, "the Court adopted the wrong analytic framework" in *Turner I*. "Second, the Court misapplies the 'intermediate scrutiny' framework it adopts." With respect to her second objection, Justice O'Connor argued that, although "Congress' reasonable conclusions are entitled to deference, [in] the course of our independent review we cannot ignore sharp conflicts in the record that call into question the reasonableness of Congress' findings." And, in this case, "the record on remand does not permit the conclusion [that] Congress could reasonably have predicted serious harm to a significant number of stations in the absence of must-carry." In Justice O'Connor's view, "the principal opinion" fails "to closely scrutinize the logic of the regulatory scheme," and exhibits "an extraordinary and unwarranted deference for congressional judgments, a profound fear of delving into complex economic matters, and a willingness to substitute untested assumptions for evidence." As a consequence, the principal opinion "trivializes the First Amendment issue at stake in this case."

Page 1526.   Before section 5 of the Note, add the following:

4a. *Regulation of cable: another look.* In Denver Area Educational Telecommunications Consortium, Inc. v. FCC, supra section VII-D-5, this Supplement, the Court considered the constitutionality of several provisions of the Cable Television Consumer Protection and Competition Act of 1992 regulating public access and leased access chanels. In a plurality opinion, Justice Breyer, joined by Justices Stevens, O'Connor, and Souter, maintained that, in light of "the changes taking place in the law, the technology, and the industrial structure related to telecommunications," the Court should adopt a narrow, highly contextual, and fact-specific approach, rather than articulate hard-and-fast rules or import into this new and complex area doctrines developed in other areas of first amendment jurisprudence. Is this a wise approach? Consider the following views, expressed in separate opinions in this case:

a. Justice Souter:

All of the relevant characteristics of cable are presently in a state of technological and regulatory flux. [In such circumstances], we should be shy about saying the final word today about what will be accepted as reasonable tomorrow. [Not] every nuance of our old standards will necessarily do for the new technology. [Thus], the job of the courts [in this area will be to recognize] established First Amendment interests through a close analysis that constrains [government], without wholly incapacitating [it], maintaining the high value of open communication, measuring the costs of regulation by exact attention to fact, and compiling a pedigree of experience with the changing subject. These are familiar judicial responsibilities in times when we know too little to risk the finality of precision, and attention to them will probably take us through the communications revolution. Maybe the judicial obligation to shoulder these responsibilities can itself be captured by a much older rule, familiar to every doctor of medicine: "First, do no harm."

b. Justice Kennedy, joined by Justice Ginsburg:

The plurality opinion [is] adrift. The opinion [applies] no standard, and by this omission loses sight of existing First Amendment doctrine. When confronted with a threat to free speech in the context of an emerging technology, we ought to have the discipline to analyze the case by reference to existing elaborations of constant First Amendment principles. [Rather] than undertake this task, however, the plurality just declares that, all things considered, [the challenged provision] seems fine. [The] novelty and complexity of the case is a reason to look for help from other areas of our First Amendment jurisprudence, not a license to wander into uncharted areas of the law with no compass other than our own opinions about good policy. [Justice] Souter recommends to the Court the precept, "First, do no harm." The question, though, is whether the harm is in sustaining the law or striking it down. If the plurality is concerned about technology's direction, it ought to begin by allowing speech, not suppressing it.

c. Justice Thomas, joined by Chief Justice Rehnquist and Justice Scalia:

For many years, we have failed to articulate how and to what extent the First Amendment protects cable operators, programmers, and viewers from state and federal regulation. I think it is time we did so, and I cannot go along with the plurality's assiduous attempts to avoid addressing that issue openly. [Our] First Amendment distinctions between media, dubious from their infancy, placed cable in a doctrinal wasteland in which regulators and cable operators alike could not be sure whether cable was entitled to the substantial First Amendment protections afforded the print media or was subject to the more onerous obligations shouldered by the broadcast media. [In] *Turner*, by adopting much of the print paradigm, and by rejecting *Red Lion*, we adopted with it a considerable body of precedent that governs the respective First Amendment rights of competing speakers. In *Red Lion*, we [legitimized] consideration of the public interest and emphasized the rights of viewers, at least in the abstract. Under that view, "[i]t is the right of the viewers and listeners, not the right of broadcasters, which is paramount." After Turner, however, that view can no longer be given any credence in the cable context. It is the operator's right that is preeminent.

4b. *Cable Operators v. Cable Programmers.* In the Cable Act of 1984, Congress authorized local governments to require cable operators to set aside a certain number of channels for "public, educational, or governmental use." The 1984 Act expressly prohibited cable operators from exercising any editorial control over the content of programs broadcast on such "public-access" channels. In the Cable Television Consumer Protection and Competition Act of 1992, Congress altered this scheme and authorized cable operators to restrict on public-access channels programming that depicts or describes "sexual activities or organs in a patently offensive manner." In Denver Area Educational Telecommunications Consortium, Inc. v. FCC, supra section VII-D-5, this Supplement, the Court invalidated this provision. Consider the argument of Justice Thomas, joined by Chief Justice Rehnquist and Justice Scalia, in dissent:

[Programmers have no first amendment] right to transmit over an operator's cable system. [Accordingly], when there is a conflict, a programmer's asserted right to transmit over an operator's cable system must give way to the operator's editorial discretion. [Citing *Tornillo*]. Drawing an analogy to the print media, [the] author of a book [has] no right to have the book sold in a particular bookstore without the store owner's consent. [Thus], the proper question [posed by this regulation is not whether section 10(c) violates the] free speech rights [of programmers because it authorizes operators to restrict indecent expression, but whether the] public access requirements [are] improper restrictions on the operators' free speech rights. [This being so, the programmers cannot] reasonably assert that the Court should strictly scrutinize [section 10(c)] in a way that maximizes their ability to speak [and], by necessity, minimizes the operators' discretion.

Page 1528.   After example (c) on the first line of the page, add the following:

In Reno v. American Civil Liberties Union, 117 S. Ct. 2329 (1997), supra section D-5 in this Supplement, the Court invalidated provisions of the Communications Decency Act of 1996 that prohibited any person from sending over the Internet in a way that would be available to a person under 18 years of age any "indecent" material or any material that "depicts or describes, in terms patently offensive as measured by contemporary community standards, sexual or execratory activities or organs." In distinguishing the Internet from broadcasting, the Court explained:

[We have] observed that "[e]ach medium of expression . . . may present its own problems." Thus, some of our cases have recognized special justifications for regulation of the broadcast media that are not applicable to other speakers, [citing, e.g., *Red Lion; Pacifica*]. In these cases, the Court relied on the history of extensive government regulation of the broadcast medium, the scarcity of available frequencies at its inception, and its "invasive" nature.

Those factors are not present in cyberspace. Neither before nor after the enactment of the CDA have the vast democratic fora of the Internet been subject to the type of government supervision and regulation that has attended the broadcast industry. Moreover, the Internet is not as "invasive" as radio or television. The District Court specifically found that "[c]ommunications over the Internet do not 'invade' an individual's home or appear on one's computer screen unbidden. Users seldom encounter content 'by accident.'" [Finally], unlike the conditions that prevailed when Congress first authorized regulation of the broadcast spectrum, the Internet can hardly be considered a "scarce" expressive commodity. It provides relatively unlimited, low cost capacity for communication of all kinds. [Our] cases provide no basis for qualifying the level of First Amendment scrutiny that should be applied to this medium.

Page 1528.   At the end of section c. of the Note, add the following:

7. *The liability of cable and on-line carriers for the speech of users.* In what circumstances, if any, should cable or on-line carriers be liable for the libelous, obscene, or otherwise actionable speech they carry? Consider the liability of (a) a store that sells typewriters for the messages typed by purchasers; (b) a telephone company for the speech of callers; (c) a bookstore for the contents of the books it sells; (d) a news vendor for the contents of the newspapers it sells; (e) a newspaper or magazine for the statements made by guest columnists; (f) a cable operator for the programs it carries; and (g) a computer network, such as CompuServe, for the messages it transmits. Should the standards of liability differ across these different situations? Should it matter whether the defendant exercises "editorial" control? Should the defendants in all or some of these cases be liable only "if they have actual notice that the speech has previously been adjudicated illegal or unprotected"? Myerson, Authors, Editors, and Uncommon Carriers: Identifying the "Speaker" Within the New Media, 71 Notre Dame L. Rev. 79, 122 (1995).

Page 1529.   After the quote from Nagel, add the following:

Consider also Post, Recuperating First Amendment Doctrine, 47 Stan. L. Rev. 1249, 1249-50 (1995):

Contemporary First Amendment doctrine [is] striking chiefly for its superficiality, its internal incoherence, its distressing failure to facilitate constructive judicial engagement with significant contemporary social issues connected with freedom of speech. . . . [It] has become increasingly a doctrine of words merely, and not of things.

8

THE CONSTITUTION AND RELIGION

A. Introduction: Historical and Analytical Overview

Page 1539.   Add the following as Note 3a.

3a. *A revisionist defense of originalist approaches.* Consider this comment on Everson: "We survivors of this history, Black suggests, adopted the Establishment Clause to commemorate, rather than repeat, it. [Black] is arguing that liberal constitutionalism is a rationale for excluding the promotion of certain historically troubling goals from the public agenda on straightforward Lincolnian grounds — national unity and a commitment not to repeat the past." Meister, Sojourners and Survivors: Two Logics of Constitutional Protection, 9 Studies in American Pol. Development 229, 276 (1995). Might exclusion of those goals contribute to national disunity instead? To what extent do current controversies implicate a concern not to repeat the past? See Chief Justice Burger's observations in *Lynch v. Donnelly* and Justice Powell's, quoted in *Mueller v. Allen.*

Page 1541.   At the end of Note 2, add the following:

Daniel O. Conkle, The Path of American Religious Liberty: From the Original Theology to Formal Neutrality and an Uncertain Future, 75 Indiana L. J. 1 (2000), argues that formal neutrality "implies that religion is neither distinct nor distinctly important," and has adverse "consequences for religion and religious liberty." He suggests that "the general appeal of formal equality" — its similarity to other constitutional doctrines — coupled with "the ever-more-difficult problem of defining religion, and the increasing importance of judicial restraint and federalism," will lead the courts to continue to rely on formal neutrality in their decisions.

Page 1543.   At the end of the Note, add the following:

6A. *Baselines*. Douglas Laycock, The Underlying Unity of Separation and Neutrality, 46 Emory L.J. 49, 49, 69-71 (1997), discusses the "no aid" and "equal access" theories, similar to strict separation and nonpreferentialism.

> In the no-aid theory, the baseline is government inactivity, because doing nothing neither helps nor hurts religion. Any government aid to a religion is a departure from that baseline, and thus a departure from neutrality. In the nondiscrimination theory, the baseline is the government's treatment of analogous secular activities; a government that pays for medical care should pay equally whether the care is provided in a religious or a secular hospital.
>
> Laycock argues for a standard of "minimizing government influence," which "requires that we minimize government incentives to change religious behavior in either direction. [The] underlying criterion for choosing among baselines depends on the incentives that government creates. If government says that it will pay for your soup kitchen if and only if you secularize it, that is a powerful incentive to secularize. [In] this context, the baseline of analogous secular activity is substantively neutral: if government will pay both religious and secular providers, it creates no incentive for either to change. [In] the regulatory context, substantive neutrality generally requires the baseline of government inactivity. If government says it will send you to jail if you consume peyote in a worship service, that is a powerful disincentive to religious behavior. But an exemption for religious behavior rarely encourages people to join the exempted church. [When] the claim to religious exemption is not contaminated by secular self-interest, exemption minimizes government influence on religion. [If] government were free to praise or condemn religion, celebrate religious holidays, or lead prayers or worship services, government could potentially have enormous influence on religious belief and liturgy. Government is large and highly visible; for better or worse, it would model one form of religious speech or observance as compared to others.

7. *Why protect religion?:* Is the constitutional text alone sufficient to justify giving religion special protection? Must we also have reasons for thinking that religion ought to be specially protected? Consider these observations: (a) Laycock, Religious Liberty as Liberty, 7 J. of Contemp. Legal Issues 313, 317 (1996): "First, in history that was recent to the American founders, government attempts to suppress disapproved religious views had caused vast human suffering. [Second], beliefs about religion are often of extraordinary importance to the

individual — important enough to die for, to suffer for, to rebel for, to emigrate for, to fight to control the government for. [Third], beliefs at the heart of religion [are] of little importance to the civil government." Are the first and second reasons distinctive to religion? Is the third reason true? (b) Garvey, An Anti-Liberal Argument for Religious Freedom, 7 J. of Contemp. Legal Issues 275 (1996): "We protect it because religion is important."

Page 1546. At the end of section 2 of the Note, add the following:

For an argument that protection should be extended to claims based on conscience as well as religion, see Smith, Converting the Religious Equality Amendment into a Statute with a Little "Conscience," 1996 BYU L. Rev. 645.

B. The Establishment Clause

Page 1557. At the end of Note 1, add the following:

Consider this perspective on *Lee*:

[The] harm inflicted by government-sponsored religious exercises is twofold. First, civic religious exercises force religious minorities to sever civil communion to avoid spiritual pollution. [The] second harm is that civic religious exercises wound the civil community by compelling the severance of religious minorities and thus fracturing community. [In] contrast with Justice Scalia's proposed inoculation against bigotry, [a] very different view of toleration [does] not necessarily engender affection among believers of different stripes, but simply civil cooperation. [Roger Williams] and the Separatists [remind] us that we must deny to ecumenical impulses any right to a smug place of preeminence in the history of religious freedom in America. Separatists have frequently been on what we would now designate the side of the angels in important disputes, and the more ecumenically spirited have championed causes that now smack of intolerance.

Timothy L. Hall, Separating Church and State: Roger Williams and Religious Liberty 158, 159-160 (1998).

Page 1558. At the end of section 2 of the Note, add the following:

Is coercion inevitable, at least in the public schools? Consider the argument of Stephen L. Carter, Parents, Religion, and Schools: Reflections on *Pierce,* 70 Years Later, 27 Seton Hall L. Rev. 1194, 1214, 1214 (1997):

> [If] beginning the school day with a prayer is unconstitutional because it prefers religion over nonreligion, then why is not a curriculum devoid of any religious observance unconstitutional because it prefers non-religion over religion? [By] compelling school attendance, [the] state as much as announces that what occurs in its schools is of vital importance. So if none of the material is religious, children will receive the message that the state deems religion unimportant. [The] ban on prayer must be intended to help individuals to make up their own minds [about] what religions to follow. But prayer and other formal religious instruction are hardly the only things that can do that. [If] our concern is for state interference with religious choice, we would surely want to take a hard look at the curriculum and rid it of other topics of instruction that make it difficult for individuals to make up their own minds about what religions to follow.

Page 1559. After section 3 of the Note, add the following:

4. Prayers at football games. Sante Fe Independent School Dist. v. Doe, 530 U.S. ___ (2000), held unconstitutional a district's policy that authorized students to vote, first, whether to allow "invocations" at high school football games, and then to chose a person to deliver them. Relying on Board of Regents v. Southworth [this Supplement, page 368], Justice Stevens, writing for six justices, concluded that the speech the selected student gave would not be private speech because of the policy authorizing an election in which a majority would determine whether to have invocations. The Court then held that an invocation at a high school football game violated the principle established in *Lee.* The Establishment Clause was designed "to remove debate over this kind of issue from governmental supervision or control." Some students, such as cheerleaders and team members, were compelled to attend the games, and other students would feel "immense social pressure" and "truly genuine desire" to attend the games. The delivery of a religious invocation would therefore coerce them in the way condemned in *Lee.* Chief Justice Rehnquist and Justices Scalia and Thomas dissented.

Page 1567.   At the end of Note 2, add the following:

Consider this defense of religious liberty founded on the principle of "equal regard": "[One's] status as a member of our political community ought not to depend in any way upon one's religious beliefs. [The] government is obliged to treat the deep religious commitments of members of minority religious faiths with the same regard as it treats the deep commitments of other members of the society. [Government] policy must be justified by public reason, by secular reasons recognizable by—and in principle, endorsable by—any person committed to living in a pluralist society governed by the precepts of equal regard. [Government] must not act so as to divide the community along lines of religious affiliation." Eisgruber & Sager, Unthinking Religious Freedom, 74 Tex. L. Rev. 577, 600-601 (1996). In response to the criticism that this "amounts to a 'secular establishment,'" Eisgruber and Sager reply, this "would overlook the distinction between a secular constitution and a secular faith. One can reject the idea that the civil government should presuppose the truth of some religious faith without thereby rejecting religion. Many religious views [are] consistent with the idea that constitutional principles should be justified on secular grounds." Id. at 604. Does this approach offer equal regard to religious views that are inconsistent with that idea?

Page 1569.   After the quotation from Howe, add the following:

For an argument that most aspects of "ceremonial deism" violate the Court's Establishment Clause doctrine, see Epstein, Rethinking the Constitutionality of Ceremonial Deism, 96 Colum. L. Rev. 2083 (1996).

Page 1570.   At the end of section 4 of the Note, add the following:

Consider the observation of Feldman, Principle, History, and Power: The Limits of the First Amendment Religion Clauses, 81 Iowa L. Rev. 833, 863 (1996): "In Lynch, the Court supported its conclusion by noting that [nobody] had complained about the crèche even though it had been publicly displayed for forty years. To the Court, this silence meant that the crèche had not generated dissension. [The] Court overlooked the possibility [that] Christian cultural imperialism had produced the silence of religious outgroup members. Silence often demonstrates domination, not consensus."

Page 1579.   At the end of the carry-over paragraph, add the following:

(Mitchell v. Helms, 530 U.S. — (2000), overruled the portions of Meek v. Pittenger and Wolman v. Walter described in this paragraph).

Page 1584.   Replace Aguilar v. Felton with the following:

AGOSTINI v. FELTON, 117 S. Ct. — (1997): Title I of the Elementary and Secondary Education Act of 1965 channels federal funds through the States to "local educational agencies" for remedial education, guidance, and job counseling to students who reside within the attendance boundaries of a public school located in a low-income area who are failing, or are at risk of failing, the State's student-performance standards. Title I services may be provided only to those private school students eligible for aid and cannot be used to provide services on a "school-wide" basis. The local agency must retain complete control over Title I funds; retain title to all materials used to provide Title I services; and provide those services through public employees or other persons independent of the private school and any religious institution. The Title I services themselves must be "secular, neutral, and nonideological" and must "supplement, and in no case supplant, the level of services" already provided by the private school. New York City's plan called for the provision of Title I services on private school premises during school hours. Only public employees could serve as Title I instructors and counselors. Assignments to private schools were made on a voluntary basis and without regard to the religious affiliation of the employee or the wishes of the private school, and a large majority of Title I teachers worked in nonpublic schools with religious affiliations different from their own. The vast majority of Title I teachers also moved among the private schools, spending fewer than five days a week at the same school. Before any public employee could provide Title I instruction at a private school, he or she would be given a detailed set of written and oral instructions emphasizing the secular purpose of Title I and setting out the rules to be followed to ensure that this purpose was not compromised. Specifically, employees would be told that (i) they were employees of the Board and accountable only to their public school supervisors; (ii) they had exclusive responsibility for selecting students for the Title I program and could teach only those children who met the eligibility criteria for Title I; (iii) their materials and equipment would be used only in the Title I program; (iv) they could not engage in team-teaching or other cooperative instructional activities with private school teachers; and (v) they could not introduce any religious matter into their teaching or become involved in any way with the religious activities of the private schools. All religious symbols were to be removed from classrooms used for Title I services. The rules acknowledged that it might be necessary for Title I teachers to consult with a student's regular classroom teacher to assess the student's particular needs and progress, but admonished instructors to limit those consultations to mutual professional concerns regarding the student's education. To ensure compliance with these rules, a publicly employed field supervisor was to attempt to make at least one unannounced visit to each teacher's classroom every month.

Justice O'Connor, writing for the Court, found New York's plan constitutional. Initially, the Court wrote, the questions were "whether the government acted with the purpose of advancing or inhibiting religion" and "whether the aid has the 'effect' of advancing religion." But the Court would not presume "that the placement of public employees on parochial school grounds inevitably results in the impermissible effect of state-sponsored indoctrination or constitutes a symbolic union between government and religion." [*Zobrest*, discussed at p. 1586.] Nor would the Court assume "that the presence of a public employee on private school property creates an impermissible 'symbolic link' between government and religion." In addition, the Court said, not "all government aid that directly aids the educational function of religious schools is invalid." [*Witters*, discussed at p. 1586.] "First, there is no reason to presume that, simply because she enters a parochial school classroom, a full-time public employee such as a Title I teacher will depart from her assigned duties and instructions and embark on religious indoctrination, any more than there was a reason in *Zobrest* to think an interpreter would inculcate religion by altering her translation of classroom lectures. Certainly, no evidence has ever shown that any New York City Title I instructor teaching on parochial school premises attempted to inculcate religion in students. Thus, both our precedent and our experience require us to reject respondents' remarkable argument that we must presume Title I instructors to be 'uncontrollable and sometimes very unprofessional.'

"*Zobrest* also repudiates [the] assumption that the presence of Title I teachers in parochial school classrooms will, without more, create the impression of a 'symbolic union' between church and state. Justice Souter maintains that [Title] I continues to foster a 'symbolic union' between the Board and sectarian schools because it mandates 'the involvement of public teachers in the instruction provided within sectarian schools,' and 'fuses public and private faculties.' Justice Souter does not disavow the notion [that] Title I services may be provided to sectarian school students in off-campus locations, even though that notion necessarily presupposes that the danger of 'symbolic union' evaporates once the services are provided off-campus. Taking this view, the only difference between a constitutional program and an unconstitutional one is the location of the classroom, since the degree of cooperation between Title I instructors and parochial school faculty is the same no matter where the services are provided. We do not see any perceptible (let alone dispositive) difference in the degree of symbolic union between a student receiving remedial instruction in a classroom on his sectarian school's campus and one receiving instruction in a van parked just at the school's curbside. To draw this line based solely on the location of the public employee is neither 'sensible' nor 'sound.' . . .

"What is most fatal to the argument that New York City's Title I program directly subsidizes religion is that it applies with equal force when those services are provided off-campus, and Aguilar implied that providing the services off-campus is entirely consistent with the Establishment Clause. Justice Souter resists the impulse to upset this implication, contending that it can be justified on the ground that Title I services are 'less likely to supplant some of what would otherwise go on inside [the sectarian schools] and to subsidize what remains' when those services are offered off-campus. But Justice Souter does not explain why a sectarian school would not have the same incentive to 'make patently significant cut-backs' in its curriculum no matter where Title I services are offered, since the school would ostensibly be excused from having to provide the Title I-type services itself. Because the incentive is the same either way, we find no logical basis upon which to conclude that Title I services are an impermissible subsidy of religion when offered on-campus, but not when offered off-campus."

The Court then addressed "the criteria by which an aid program identifies its beneficiaries. [The] criteria might themselves have the effect of advancing religion by creating a financial incentive to undertake religious indoctrination. This incentive is not present, however, where the aid is allocated on the basis of neutral, secular criteria that neither favor nor disfavor religion, and is made available to both religious and secular beneficiaries on a nondiscriminatory basis. Under such circumstances, the aid is less likely to have the effect of advancing religion. See Widmar v. Vincent, 454 U. S. 263, 274 (1981) ('The provision of benefits to so broad a spectrum of groups is an important index of secular effect'). [Title] I services are allocated on the basis of criteria that neither favor nor disfavor religion. The services are available to all children who meet the Act's eligibility requirements, no matter what their religious beliefs or where they go to school. The Board's program does not, therefore, give aid recipients any incentive to modify their religious beliefs or practices in order to obtain those services."

Finally, the Court addressed the argument "that New York City's Title I program resulted in an excessive entanglement between church and state. [The] factors we use to assess whether an entanglement is 'excessive' are similar to the factors we use to examine 'effect.' That is, to assess entanglement, we have looked to 'the character and purposes of the institutions that are benefited, the nature of the aid that the State provides, and the resulting relationship between the government and religious authority.' Similarly, we have assessed a law's 'effect' by examining the character of the institutions benefited (e.g., whether the religious institutions were 'predominantly religious') and the nature of the aid that the State provided (e.g., whether it was neutral and nonideological). [It] is simplest to recognize why entanglement is significant and treat it [as] an aspect of the inquiry into a statute's effect.

"Not all entanglements, of course, have the effect of advancing or inhibiting religion. Interaction between church and state is inevitable, and we have always tolerated some level of involvement between the two. Entanglement must be 'excessive' before it runs afoul of the Establishment Clause." Neither "administrative cooperation" nor the danger of political divisiveness created excessive entanglement, particularly in light of the fact that they would be present even if the Title I services were offered off campus. And, given the Court's refusal to assume that public school teachers working in parochial schools "would be tempted to inculcate religion," there was no need for "pervasive monitoring." The unannounced monthly visits were not excessive entanglement.

"To summarize, New York City's Title I program does not run afoul of any of three primary criteria we currently use to evaluate whether government aid has the effect of advancing religion: it does not result in governmental indoctrination; define its recipients by reference to religion; or create an excessive entanglement. We therefore hold that a federally funded program providing supplemental, remedial instruction to disadvantaged children on a neutral basis is not invalid under the Establishment Clause when such instruction is given on the premises of sectarian schools by government employees pursuant to a program containing safeguards such as those present here. The same considerations that justify this holding require us to conclude that this carefully constrained program also cannot reasonably be viewed as an endorsement of religion."

Justice Souter, joined by Justices Stevens and Ginsburg and in part by Justice Breyer, dissented. In the portion of the dissent that Justice Breyer did not join, Justice Souter said that the Court decision "authorize[d] direct state aid to religious institutions on an unparalleled scale, in violation of the Establishment Clause's central prohibition against religious subsidies by the government. [This] rule expresses the hard lesson learned over and over again in the American past and in the experiences of the countries from which we have come, that religions supported by governments are compromised just as surely as the religious freedom of dissenters is burdened when the government supports religion. [The] human tendency, of course, is to forget the hard lessons, and to overlook the history of governmental partnership with religion when a cause is worthy, and bureaucrats have programs. That tendency to forget is the reason for having the Establishment Clause (along with the Constitution's other structural and libertarian guarantees), in the hope of stopping the corrosion before it starts."

According to Justice Souter, the New York plan allowed the city's school system to "[assume] a teaching responsibility indistinguishable from the responsibility of the [private] schools themselves. The obligation of primary and secondary schools to teach reading necessarily extends to teaching those who are having a hard time at it, and the same is true of math. Calling some classes remedial does not distinguish their subjects from the schools' basic subjects, however inadequately the schools may have been addressing them. [There] is simply no line that can be drawn between the instruction paid for at taxpayers' expense and the instruction in any subject that is not identified as formally religious. While it would be an obvious sham, say, to channel cash to religious schools to be credited only against the expense of 'secular' instruction, the line between 'supplemental' and general education is likewise impossible to draw. If a State may constitutionally enter the schools to teach in the manner in question, it must in constitutional principle be free to assume, or assume payment for, the entire cost of instruction provided in any ostensibly secular subject in any religious school." Justice Souter suggested that the argument that off-campus and on-campus provision of remedial services might "prove too much," but said that "off-premises teaching is arguably less likely to open the door to relieving religious schools of their responsibilities for secular subjects simply because these schools are less likely [to] dispense with those subjects from their curriculums or to make patently significant cut-backs in basic teaching within the [schools]; if the aid is delivered outside of the schools, it is less likely to supplant some of what would otherwise go on inside [them]. On top of that, the difference in the degree of reasonably perceptible endorsement is substantial. Sharing the teaching responsibilities within a school having religious objectives is far more likely to telegraph approval of the school's mission than keeping the State's distance would do."

Justice Breyer joined the section of Justice Souter's dissent that argued that the Court had extended the holdings of *Zobrest* and *Witters*. That section also stated that "evenhandedness is a necessary but not a sufficient condition for an aid program to satisfy constitutional scrutiny. [If] a scheme of government aid results in support for religion in some substantial degree, or in endorsement of its value, the formal neutrality of the scheme does not render the Establishment Clause helpless. . . ."

Justice Ginsburg, joined by Justices Stevens, Souter, and Breyer, also dissented on procedural grounds.

Page 1586.   At the end of note 1, add the following:

Berg, *Religion Clause Anti-Theories*, 72 Notre Dame L. Rev. 693, 695, 703-04 (1997), defends a theory of neutrality against critics who assert "that no single principle [can] capture the constitutional commitment to religious freedom": "[Government] should, as much as possible, minimize the effect it has on the voluntary, indpendent religious decisions of the people of individuals and in voluntary groups. The baseline against which effects on religion should be compared is a situation in which religious beliefs and practices succeed or fail solely on their merits — as those merits are presented and judged by individuals and groups, not by government." Consider the assumptions implicit in the term "the merits" in this formulation.

For a discussion of the problem of identifying an appropriate baseline, see Frederick Mark Gedicks, The Rhetoric of Church and State: A Critical Analysis of Religion Clause Jurisprudence 57-58, 60 (1995): "How does one identify the baseline measure of religious neutrality? [In] the modern welfare state, [government] aid to both individuals and organizations is widespread and pervasive. Since in the United States most persons and entities are entitled to some kind of government aid, religious neutrality would generally seem to require that this aid not be denied to otherwise qualified recipients simply because they are religious. Indeed, to deny aid to such persons and entities constitutes a tax on religious exercise which skews private choice *away* from religion. [If] one were to imagine a world of minimalist government in which secular public schools did not exist, then government action mandating religious instruction [would] violate neutrality. If [all] children were wards of the state, with government providing for literally all of their needs, then the neutrality principle would require that opportunities for participation in religious worship and instruction be provided by the government for those who request it. [While] children [are] hardly in the situation of wards of the state, [the] state's control over children through secular public education and social welfare bureaucracies is still substantial. [For] example, it is not difficult to construct a plausible neutrality baseline that permits a religious values approach to sex education in public schools, so long as secular approaches are available as well, and students are permitted to choose between them."

Berg discusses some implications of Gedicks's position, at 743: "[If] a system of subsidized secular public schools does, in fact, discourage religiously informed education, why can't government include religious teaching in the public school curriculum? [Any] statement the government makes is bound to favor one faith over another. [It] may be [possible] for government to speak in favor of a variety of faiths over time—[to] give instruction in many faiths [over] the course of a school year. But the practical problems in working out such arrangements are likely to be great, and there are real dangers that such a series will end up favoring either the majority's faith or some watered down civil religion." Does this criticism support judicial invalidation of such programs? Does it take sufficiently into account Gedicks's argument that refraining from adopting such a program favors secularism?

Page 1588.   Before subsection 3 of the Note, add the following:

2a. *Neutrality revisited.* Justice Thomas, writing for a plurality in Mitchell v. Helms, 530 U.S. — (2000), proposed that statutes providing aid to "religious, irreligious, and areligious" institutions should generally be constitutional, because "no one would conclude that any indoctrination that any particular recipient conducts has been done at the behest of the government. [If] the government is offering assistance to recipients who provide [a] broad range of indoctrination, the government itself is not thought responsible for any particular indoctrination." *Mitchell* upheld a statute that provided funds for state education agencies to lend computers, including software, and library books, to non-public schools. The amount available to each school was determined by each school's enrollment. Justice Thomas's opinion rejected as "arbitrary" the distinction between direct and indirect aid to the religious missions of religious schools. It also found irrelevant the possibility that some forms of aid might be diverted to religious uses: "So long as the governmental aid is not itself 'unsuitable for use in the public schools because of religious content,' [*Allen*], and eligibility for aid is determined in a constitutionally permissible manner, any use of that aid to indoctrinate cannot be attributed to the government, and is thus not of constitutional concern. [A] concern for divertibility, as opposed to improper content, is misplaced [because] it is boundless [and] thus has only the most attenuated [link] to any realistic concern for preventing an 'establishment of religion.'"

Justice O'Connor, joined by Justice Breyer, concurred in the judgment. She criticized the plurality's "near-absolute position with respect to neutrality." She also believed "significant" the "distinction between a per-capita school-aid program and a true private-choice program. [In] terms of public perception, a government program of direct aid to religious schools based on the number of students attending each school differs meaningfully from the government distributing aid directly to individual students who, in turn, decide to use the aid at the same religious schools. In the former example, if the religious school uses the aid to inculcate religion in its students, it is reasonable to say that the government has communicated a message of endorsement." She found the program in *Mitchell* constitutional because it provided sufficient guarantees that the aid would not be diverted to religious uses and because the evidence of actual diversion was *de minimis*. Justices Souter, Stevens, and Ginsburg dissented.

What implications does *Mitchell* have for voucher programs, in which governments provide funds to parents, who can use the funds to pay all or part of the tuition charged by private schools, included religiously affiliated school? Justice Thomas's opinion noted that prior cases had found "'special Establishment Clause dangers' when *money* is given to religious schools or entities directly rather than [indirectly]. But [we] refuse to allow a 'special' case to create a rule for all cases." Justice O'Connor wrote, "If [a] per-capita-aid program is identical in relevant constitutional respects to a true private-choice program, then there is no reason that [the] government should be precluded from providing direct money payments to religious organizations [based] on the number of persons belonging to each organization. And, because actual diversion is permissible under the plurality's holding, the participating religious organizations (including churches) could use that aid to support religious indoctrination." If the distinction between direct and indirect aid is "arbitrary" when non-monetary resources are involved, is it less arbitrary when money is involved?

Page 1589. At the end of section 4 of the Note, add the following:

Justice Thomas's plurality opinion in Mitchell v. Helms, 530 U.S. — (2000), concluded that the doctrine barring pervasively sectarian institutions from receiving aid that was otherwise permissible should be rejected. "The pervasively sectarian recipient has not received any special favor, and it is most bizarre that the Court would [reserve] special hostility for those who take their religion seriously, who think that their religion should affect the whole of their lives, or who make the mistake of being effective in transmitting their views to children,." In addition, "the inquiry into the recipient's religious views [is offensive.]" Finally, "hostility to aid to pervasively sectarian schools has a shameful pedigree that we do not hesitate to disavow." That pedigree involved hostility to Catholic parochial schools. Justice O'Connor's opinion concurring in the judgment did not address the doctrine; the dissent treated the question of the degree of an institution's sectarianism as relevant to constitutional analysis.

Page 1590. At the end of the introductory paragraph of Part C, add the following:

Consider Garret Epps, What We Talk About When We Talk About Free Exercise, 30 Ariz. St. L.J. 563, 576, 577-78 (1998): The Free Exercise clause protects *"specifically religious ritual*—that is, religious ritual behavior. [Any] restriction on ritual behavior that consists *entirely of speech* will be invalid as a violation of the Speech Clause. [If] it requires or bans non-verbal behavior [intended] to send a message, it will almost certainly be protected as 'symbolic speech.'" According to Epps, distinctive free exercise issues arise only in connection with "rituals that are of a concededly religious nature with symbolic content but for which there is an empirical basis to believe that [the] ritual action may also have permanent consequences in the physical world."

Page 1591.   After the citation of Hamburger, add the following:

Justices Scalia and O'Connor examined the historical materials in their separate opinions in City of Boerne v. Flores, 117 S. Ct. 2157 (1997), with the latter concluding that the historical materials showed that the free exercise clause placed limits on government's ability to adopt neutral laws that adversely affected religious practices, and the former disagreeing.

C. The Free Exercise Clause: Required Accommodations

Page 1607.   At the end of section 1 of the Note, add the following:

Frederick Mark Gedicks, The Normalized Free Exercise Clause, 75 Ind. L.J. 77 (2000), argues that *Smith* adopts a "rational basis" standard of review and thereby "contradicts the Court's Speech Clause doctrine governing [incidental] burdens on speech occurring as the result of otherwise legitimate government regulations of conduct or the time, place, or manner of expression," which requires that such regulations satisfy an intermediate standard of review. Is Gedicks' description of free speech doctrine accurate. See Chapter 7 (E).

Page 1609.   After the quotation from Williams & Williams, add the following:

Note that, on some views, neither religious belief in general nor commitment to Christianity in particular results from volitional choices. See Garvey, An Anti-Liberal Argument for Religious Freedom, 7 J. of Contemp. Legal Issues 275, 278 (1996): "The individual does not have complete control over choosing the religious option. It is God who makes the choice."

Page 1610.   After the first sentence of note 4, add the following:

The Act was held unconstitutional as beyond Congress's power under §5 of the Fourteenth Amendment in *City of Boerne v. Flores,* ch. 2, section E of this Supplement.

D. *Permissible Accommodation*

Page 1623.   At the end of the first full paragraph, add the following:

For a discussion of balancing interests in religious liberty against harms to third parties, see Jonathan C. Lipson, On Balance: Religious Liberty and Third-Party Harms, 84 Minn. L.Rev. 589 (2000).

Page 1623.   At the end of section 2 of the Note, add the following:

Does *Kiryas Joel* raise serious questions about state laws protecting the practice of labeling certain foods *kosher* (that is, satisfying certain religious requirements), by making it a fraudulent practice to label a food as kosher when it has not received the approval of a specific religious institution? For a discussion, see Kent Greenawalt, Religious Law and Civil Law: Using Secular Law to Assure Observance of Practices With Religious Significance, 71 S. Cal. L. Rev. 781, 793-96 (1998).

Page 1626.   At the bottom of the page, add the following:

Consider the application of the "interest-convergence" thesis (Casebook, p. 528) by Feldman, Principle, History, and Power: The Limits of the First Amendment Religion Clauses, 81 Iowa L. Rev. 833, 871-72 (1996): "[Outgroup] religions benefit only when their interests happen to converge [with] the interests of Christians. The benefits to outgroups [are] merely *incidental*, while the *primary* benefits of separation of church and state flow [to] Christianity. [While] the accrual of primary benefits to Christianity occasionally entails incidental benefits for outgroup religions, it also [imposes] certain costs on those [religions]. [The] principle of separation of church and state [benefits] Christianity and harms minority religions by furnishing a facade of governmental neutrality and religious freedom that hides and legitimates [Christian] cultural imperialism."

10
THE CONSTITUTION, BASELINES, AND THE PROBLEM OF PRIVATE POWER

A. State Action, Federalism, and Individual Autonomy

Page 1699.   At the conclusion of section 3 of the Note, add the following:

The Supreme Court reaffirmed *The Civil Rights Cases* in United States v. Morrison, __ U.S. __ (2000). In a 5-4 decision, the Court, per Chief Justice Rehnquist, struck down portions of the Violence against Women Act, a federal statute that provided for a federal civil remedy for victims of gender-motivated violence. When it enacted the statute, Congress relied in part on its authority under section 5 of the fourteenth amendment, but the Court held that this reliance ran afoul of the "time-honored principle that [the amendment prohibits] only state action." The Court rejected petitioners' argument that "unlike the situation in the *Civil Rights Cases*, here there has been gender-based disparate treatment by state authorities, whereas in those cases there was no indication of such state action."

> There is abundant evidence [to] show that the Congresses that enacted the Civil Rights Acts of 1871 and 1875 had a purpose similar to that of Congress in enacting [The Violence against Women Act]: There were state laws on the books bespeaking equality of treatment, but in the administration of these laws there was discrimination against newly freed slaves. . . .
>
> But even if that distinction were valid, we do not believe it would save [the Act's] civil remedy. For the remedy is simply not "corrective in its character, adapted to counteract and redress the operation of such prohibited [state laws or proceedings of [state] officers." [citing *The Civil Rights*

Cases]. [The Act] is directed not at any State or state actor, but at individuals who have committed criminal acts motivated by gender bias.

In a portion of his dissenting opinion joined by justice Stevens, Justice Breyer quarreled with the majority's state action analysis:

The Court points out that in [the *Civil Rights Cases*] the Court held that § 5 does not authorize Congress to use the Fourteenth Amendment as a source of power to remedy the conduct of *private persons.* That is certainly so. The Federal Government's argument, however is that Congress used § 5 to remedy the actions of *state actors*, namely those States which, through discriminatory design or discriminatory conduct of their officials, failed to provide adequate (or any) state remedies for women injured by gender-motivated [violence].

D. *Constitutionally Required Departures from Neutrality? The Public Function Doctrine*

Page 1756.   Before section 2 of the Note, add the following:

g. What implications does *Jackson* hold for the treatment of political parties as state actors? The Court debated this issue in Morse v. Republican Party of Virginia, 517 U.S. 186 (1996). The case presented the court with a question of statutory construction—whether the Virginia Republican Party was obligated under the 1965 Voting Rights Act to obtain preclearance before changing the qualifications for participation in a state nominating convention. In the course of answering this question (in the affirmative), the Court had occasion to distinguish its prior state action precedent:

In [*Jackson*] and [*Flagg Brothers*] this Court concluded that the defendants were not acting under authority explicitly or implicitly delegated by the State when they carried out the challenged actions. In this case, however, . . . the Party acted under the authority conferred by the Virginia election code. It was the Commonwealth of Virginia—indeed *only* Virginia—that had exclusive power to reserve one of the two special ballot provisions for the Party.

Compare Justice Thomas's dissent:

> The Party's selection of a candidate at a convention does not satisfy [the exclusive public function] test. [We] have carefully distinguished the "conduct" of an election by the State from the exercise of private political rights within that State-created framework. Providing an orderly and fair process for the selection of public officers is a classic exclusive state function. . . .
>
> [By] contrast, convening the members of a political association in order to select the person who can best represent and advance the group's goals is not, and historically has never been, the province of the State—much less its exclusive province.

To be sure, the Party takes advantage of favorable State law when it certifies its candidate for automatic placement on the ballot. Nevertheless, according to our state action cases, that is no basis for treating the Party as the State. The State's conferral of benefits upon an entity—even so great a benefit as monopoly status—is insufficient to convent the entity into a State actor. See [*Jackson*].